Truth, Language, and

Other volumes of collected essays by Donald Davidson

Essays on Actions and Events
Inquiries into Truth and Interpretation
Subjective, Intersubjective, Objective
Problems of Rationality

Truth, Language, and History

DONALD DAVIDSON

CLARENDON PRESS · OXFORD

OXFORD
UNIVERSITY PRESS

Great Clarendon Street, Oxford OX2 6DP

Oxford University Press is a department of the University of Oxford.
It furthers the University's objective of excellence in research, scholarship,
and education by publishing worldwide in

Oxford New York

Auckland Cape Town Dar es Salaam Hong Kong Karachi
Kuala Lumpur Madrid Melbourne Mexico City Nairobi
New Delhi Shanghai Taipei Toronto

With offices in

Argentina Austria Brazil Chile Czech Republic France Greece
Guatemala Hungary Italy Japan South Korea Poland Portugal
Singapore Switzerland Thailand Turkey Ukraine Vietnam

Oxford is a registered trade mark of Oxford University Press
in the UK and in certain other countries

Published in the United States
by Oxford University Press Inc., New York

British Library Cataloguing in Publication Data

Data available

Library of Congress Cataloging in Publication Data

Data available

ISBN 0-19-823756-1
ISBN 0-19-823757-X (pbk.)

10 9 8 7 6 5 4 3 2 1

Typeset by Newgen Imaging Systems (P) Ltd., Chennai, India
Printed in Great Britain
on acid-free paper by Biddles Ltd, King's Lynn, Norfolk

To our Grandchildren—
  Max and Natalie Boyer
  Alex and Elizabeth Batkin

Contents

Provenance of the Essays and Acknowledgments   ix

Introduction   xii
Marcia Cavell

Truth   1

  1. Truth Rehabilitated (1997)   3
  2. The Folly of Trying to Define Truth (1996)   19
  3. Method and Metaphysics (1993)   39
  4. Meaning, Truth, and Evidence (1990)   47
  5. Pursuit of the Concept of Truth (1995)   63
  6. What is Quine's View of Truth? (1994)   81

Language   87

  7. A Nice Derangement of Epitaphs (1986)   89
  8. The Social Aspect of Language (1994)   109
  9. Seeing Through Language (1997)   127
 10. James Joyce and Humpty Dumpty (1989)   143
 11. The Third Man (1992)   159
 12. Locating Literary Language (1993)   167

Anomalous Monism   183

 13. Thinking Causes (1993)   185
 14. Laws and Cause (1995)   201

Historical Thoughts   221

 15. Plato's Philosopher (1985)   223
 16. The Socratic Concept of Truth (1992)   241
 17. Dialectic and Dialogue (1994)   251

18. Gadamer and Plato's *Philebus* (1997)   261
19. Aristotle's Action (2001)   277
20. Spinoza's Causal Theory of the Affects (1993)   295

Appendix: Replies to Rorty, Stroud, McDowell,   315
and Pereda (1998)

Contents List of Volumes of Essays by Donald Davidson   329

Bibliographical References   335

Index   343

Provenance of the Essays and Acknowledgments

Essay 1, 'Truth Rehabilitated', was delivered in October 1997 while Davidson was the Hill Visiting Professor at the University of Minnesota in Minneapolis. It was later published (perhaps in a revised version) in *Rorty and his Critics*, edited by R. B. Brandom (Oxford: Blackwell, 2000).

Essay 2, 'The Folly of Trying to Define Truth', was presented to the Academy of Science in Warsaw on 7 October 1995. It was then published in *Dialogue and Universalism*, 6 (1996), 39–53, in the special issue on 'Truth after Tarski,' edited by M. Hempoliski (1996); *Journal of Philosophy*, 94 (1997), 263–78; *Truth*, edited by S. Blackburn and K. Simmons (Oxford University Press, 1999); and *The Nature of Truth*, edited by M. P. Lynch (Cambridge, Mass.: MIT Press, 2001).

Essay 3, 'Method and Metaphysics', was published in *Deucalion*, 11 (1993), 239–48.

Essay 4, 'Meaning, Truth and Evidence', was delivered in April 1988 at a Quine conference in St Louis. It was then published in *Perspectives on Quine*, edited by R. Barrett and R. Gibson (Oxford: Blackwell, 1990).

Essay 5, 'Pursuit of the Concept of Truth', was published in *On Quine*, edited by P. Leonardi and M. Santambrogio (Cambridge University Press, 1995).

Essay 6, 'What is Quine's View of Truth?', was published in *Inquiry*, 37 (1994), 437–40, edited by D. Føllesdal and A. Hannay.

Essay 7, 'A Nice Derangement of Epitaphs', was delivered to the philosophy department at Queen's College, Kingston, Ontario, in September 1984. It was later published in *Philosophical Grounds of Rationality*, edited by R. Grandy and R. Warner (Oxford University Press, 1986).

Essay 8, 'The Social Aspect of Language', was presented as part of a celebration for Michael Dummett, held in Sicily 19–23 September 1991. It was later published in *The Philosophy of Michael Dummett*, edited by B. McGuinness and G. Oliveri (Dordrecht: Kluwer Academic Publishers, 1994).

Essay 9, 'Seeing Through Language' was first delivered in September 1996 to the Royal Institute of Philosophy in Reading, England, and again in 1997 at the Davidson Conference at the University of Mexico in Mexico City. It was published in *Thought and Language*, edited by J. M. Preston (Cambridge University Press, 1997).

Essay 10, 'James Joyce and Humpty Dumpty', was delivered to the Norwegian Academy of Science and Letters on 10 March 1988. It was later published in *Proceedings of the Norwegian Academy of Science and Letters* (1989), 54–66.

Essay 11, 'The Third Man', was written for an exhibition entitled *Robert Morris: Blind Time Drawings with Davidson*, at The Frank Martin Gallery at Mühlenberg College in Allentown, Pennsylvania, in 1992. It was published in *Critical Inquiry* 19 (Summer 1993).

Essay 12, 'Locating Literary Language', was published in *Literary Theory after Davidson*, edited by R. W. Dasenbrock (University Park, Penn.: Pennsylvania State University Press, 1993).

Essay 13, 'Thinking Causes' was delivered on 5 February 1991 to the department of philosophy at Birkbeck College, London. It was published in *Mental Causation*, edited by J. Heil and A. Mele (Oxford University Press, 1993).

Essay 14, 'Laws and Cause', was delivered to the department of philosophy at Stanford University on 24 February 1995. It was published in *Dialectica*, 49 (1995), 263–79.

Essay 15, 'Plato's Philosopher', was given as the S. V. Keeling Memorial Lecture in Greek Philosophy at University College London in March 1985. It was published in *The London Review of Books* 7, no. 14 (1985), 15–17.

Essay 16, 'The Socratic Concept of Truth', was published in *The Philosophy of Socrates: Elenchus, Ethics and Truth*, ii, edited by K. J. Boudouris (Athens: The International Center for Greek Philosophy and Culture, 1992).

Essay 17, 'Dialectic and Dialogue', was given when receiving the Hegel prize of the City of Stuttgart, and was first published under the title *Dialektik und Dialog: Rede von Donald Davidson anlässlich der Verleihung des Hegel-Preises*, translated into German by J. Schulte (Frankfurt am Main: Suhrkamp Verlag, 1993). It was later published in English with the current title in *Language, Mind and Epistemology: On Donald Davidson's Philosophy*, edited by G. Preyer, F. Siebelt, and A. Ulfig (Dordrecht: Kluwer Academic Publishers, 1994).

Essay 18, 'Gadamer and Plato's *Philebus*', was published in *The Philosophy of Hans-Georg Gadamer*, edited by L. Hahn (Chicago: Open Court, 1997).

Essay 19, 'Aristotle's Action', was published in French in *Quelle Philosophie pour le XXIe Siècle* (Paris: Gallimard/Centre Pompidou, 2001). This is its first appearance in English.

Essay 20, 'Spinoza's Causal Theory of the Affects', was presented to the department of philosophy at the University of Jerusalem on 20 January 1993. It was later published in *Desire and Affect: Spinoza as Psychologist*, edited by Y. Yovel (New York: Libble Room Press, 1999).

The Appendix, 'Replies to Rorty, Stroud, McDowell, and Pereda', was published as 'Replies' in *Crítica* 30, no. 90 (1998), in response to articles by Barry Stroud, John McDowell, Richard Rorty, and Carlos Pereda in *Crítica*, 28, no. 88 (1998).

Introduction

When my husband died, very unexpectedly, on 30 August 2003, volume 4, *Problems of Rationality*, and the present volume 5, *Truth, Language, and History*, of his Collected Essays had been contracted for by Oxford University Press. Both volumes were virtually ready to go except for the Introductions. In producing them on his behalf I have followed his example in volumes 1–3, which was to write something brief by way of introducing the collection as a whole, then one or two paragraphs on each essay in turn. I may have made errors of emphasis, even of content; but I hope Donald would feel that I am not too far off the mark—near enough, at least, to be of some help to his readers. As for the essays themselves, they are, but for a few corrected typos, exactly as they appeared in the various publications that are cited.

In the four groups of essays that comprise this volume Davidson continues to explore the themes that occupied him for more than fifty years: the relations between language and the world, speaker intention and linguistic meaning, language and mind, mind and body, mind and world, mind and other minds. He asks: What is the role of the concept of truth in these explorations? And: Can a scientific world view make room for human thought without reducing it to something material and mechanistic?

Davidson's underlying picture, which can be seen in many of these essays, is that we are acquainted directly with the world, not indirectly via some intermediary such as sense-data, representations, or language itself; that thought emerges in the first place through interpersonal communication in a shared material world, and continues to develop as we engage each other in dialogue; and that language depends on communication, not vice versa. This is the triangulating situation—two creatures communicating about a common world—about which Davidson has written elsewhere. As for the mind–body relation, our ontology need posit nothing more than material objects and events; but as explainers we require two mutually irreducible vocabularies: mind and body. In the last six essays Davidson finds interconnections between his own views and those of some of the major philosophers of the past.

Essay 1, 'Truth Rehabilitated', examines the wide-ranging skepticism in the past century about the concept of truth. Davidson agrees with skeptics about truth that correspondence, coherence, pragmatic, and epistemic theories of truth are all failures. But it does not follow, he argues, that the concept of truth can be dismissed as a useless concept, as various 'deflationists' about truth claim. On the contrary: the concept of truth plays a key role in our understanding of the world and the minds of agents.

Essay 2, 'The Folly of Trying to Define Truth', argues that the concept of truth, along with such related subjects of philosophical inquiry as knowledge, belief, intention, and memory, cannot be reduced to more elementary concepts, since they are themselves among the most elementary that we have. Davidson then turns to a consideration of Tarski's truth theory. Finally, he proposes a radical alternative to the truth theories considered in Essay 1: to trace out the empirical connections between the concept of truth and observable human behavior. A methodological model for this project is Frank Ramsey's decision theory for constructing subjective probability.

Essay 3, 'Method and Metaphysics', argues that semantics provides a method for metaphysics. Davidson quotes Tarski, quoting Aristotle: "To say of what is that it is not, or of what is not that it is, is false, while to say of what is that it is, or of what is not that it is not, is true." Thus if we have the semantics of a language right, we can know that the objects we assign to the expressions exist. Davidson considers two apparent problems with this conclusion. The first is the inscrutability of reference, the fact to which Quine called attention, that there is an endless number of ways in which an interpreter can assign objects to the expressions of an interpretant's language, all of which will do equally well. But this does not really threaten the objectivity of our ontological conclusions, Davidson answers; for if we are to find a language intelligible, we must find it capable of talking about many of the same things we talk about. "The inscrutability of reference may lead to a strange assignment of objects to words; it cannot affect the overall ontology to which we find the language committed."

The second problem is that in describing the semantics and hence the ontology of a language we must appeal to the entities *we* think exist, which are just the entities that belong to the ontology of our language. So there seems to be no way that we can progress from our semantics to truths about an objective world. (This problem parallels that discussed in Essays 15 and 16: How can dialogue take us beyond making our beliefs more consistent, to a discovery of which of our beliefs are true, or to new beliefs entirely?) To this Davidson answers that there are two methodological principles at work in interpretation which, combined, show us the way out of the apparent impasse: (1) the interpreter must find a generally consistent pattern in the beliefs he attributes to an agent; and (2) the interpreter must respect the causal connections between mind and world that are apparent in the interpretant's communications, connections that link speaker, hearer, and shared object in the external world to which they are responding. Tarski finds that semantics has no need for entities corresponding to sentences as a whole, just entities over which the variables range. Davidson holds that an accurate semantics will correctly locate some of these entities, since "direct conditionings of words to objects must lie at the basis of correct interpretations". (This is what Davidson calls 'triangulation'.)

Essay 4, 'Meaning, Truth and Evidence', asks: Is it the proximal stimulus at the nerve endings that provides the key to meaning, as Quine held? Or is it rather the distal stimulus, object or event in the shared, public world, on which interpreter and interpreted triangulate? Only the latter view, Davidson argues, tells us how communication is possible, and supports Quine's own thesis that there can be no more to meaning than an adequately equipped person—the interpreter—can learn and observe.

Essays 5 and 6, 'Pursuit of the Concept of Truth', and 'What is Quine's View of Truth?', continue the exploration of Quine begun in Essay 4, now taking up the further questions: Is Quine's a deflationary view of truth? What are the implications of indeterminacy of meaning for a theory of truth? And: What does Quine mean in saying that truth is 'immanent'?

In *Essay 7*, 'A Nice Derangement of Epitaphs', Davidson argues that our ability to understand a speaker's intentions even when she is using words incorrectly or in a novel way requires us to abandon the common account of linguistic competence and communication in terms of shared rules and conventions. In *Essay 8*, 'The Social Aspect of Language', Davidson clarifies his claim in 'A Nice Derangement of Epitaphs' that "There is no such thing as a language, not if a language is anything like what many philosophers and linguists have supposed." The concept of language Davidson opposes is that verbal communication depends on speaker and hearer sharing a specifiable set of syntactic and semantic rules. Something like this is in fact usually shared, but it is neither necessary nor sufficient for linguistic communication. What is essential is shared general information and familiarity with non-linguistic institutions. ("We have erased the boundary between knowing a language and knowing our way around the world generally".

Davidson agrees with Dummett that a theory of meaning requires the Wittgensteinian distinction between using words correctly and merely thinking one is, between following a rule and believing one is following a rule; and that a grasp of this distinction requires social interaction. It requires that the speaker and hearer have the idea of a norm, of getting it right. Speaking in accord with socially accepted usage might be such a norm, but it is irrelevant to communication. Rather, communication is successful if the speaker is taken to mean what he wants to be taken to mean. At base what is needed is not a set of shared rules but that speaker and hearer be able to correlate the speaker's responses with the occurrence of a shared stimulus in their common world. "Meaning something requires that by and large one can be understood by others. But there is no reason why practices must be shared". Meaning depends on successful interpretation rather than the other way around.

Essay 9, 'Seeing Through Language', argues that while there is an important sense in which we see the world through language, certain common ways of understanding this metaphor are false: language is not a medium that accurately records what is out there, nor is it a veil cast upon the world which occludes it. Without language we would not think of things as we do; but it doesn't follow that every view of things is necessarily distorted.

On the contrary, we might think of language as like an organ of perception, something through, that is *by dint of*, which, we are literally able to see the world. Language is different from the sense organs in that it is essential to them if they are to yield *propositional* knowledge. This leads Davidson to a criticism of *mentalese*, the thesis that there is an inborn 'language of thought', and to a discussion of the conditions necessary for creatures to acquire concepts, thought, and language. The birth of meaning takes place through interpersonal communication about a shared, public world, and depends on the fact that human creatures have shared needs and interests. Concepts, language, and thought, come together.

Essay 10, 'James Joyce and Humpty Dumpty', continues the exploration in Essays 7 and 8, and taken up again in Essay 12, of the tension between the idea that what a speaker intends by his words determines what he means, and the idea that what a speaker means depends on what he can expect his hearer to understand. This is a false choice, Davidson argues: meaning is a function of what the speaker intends, but this intention includes what the speaker expects his hearer to understand. Thus Humpty Dumpty's theory of meaning, "When *I* use a word it means just what I choose it to mean," omits the crucial interpersonal element. But language use can be more or less creative. As Joyce himself thought, his daring use of words put him in a sense beyond his own language, society, and self. Davidson argues that it forces a similar creativity and distancing in his reader.

Essay 11, 'The Third Man', discusses the series of 'Blind-Time Davidson' drawings, inspired by Davidson's *Essays on Actions and Events*, which were made by the artist Robert Morris. Each of the drawings contains a fragment from an essay by Davidson and a description of the artist's intention in making the drawing (blindfolded). Davidson writes: "Morris has depicted...the essential element on which the concept of an autonomous object (and world) depends: an intersubjective measure of error and success, of truth and falsity. He has put us in a position to triangulate with him the location of his creative acts".

Essay 12, 'Locating Literary Language', asks what constraints there are on the interpretation of a literary text. Davidson begins with a general introduction of the ways in which a speaker's or a writer's intentions—always multiple—are the key to what he means.

The first of these intentions is to speak words that will be assigned a certain meaning by an interpreter, what Davidson calls 'first meaning' and is called 'literal meaning' by others. The possibility of language, thought, and interpretation depends on the triangular situation mentioned above, which relates speaker and hearer, and both to a shared object in the public world which they can observe together, and to which they can observe each other's responses. Does something like this triangular situation hold in literature? Yes. The role of shared public object is now replaced by a common background, which constrains what an author can intelligibly be said to have intended his words to mean. Of course interpretations of a text will vary, from person to person, culture to culture, century to century. But it does not follow from this truism that a text means whatever its readers take it to mean, since disagreements about the meaning of a text—like disagreements about other objects and situations in the world—are possible only against a shared basis of agreement.

In *Essay 13*, 'Thinking Causes', Davidson takes up a common criticism of his theory of Anomalous Monism: namely, that according to this theory the mental is causally inert. Davidson argues that the criticism results from a misunderstanding of his use of the concept of supervenience, which implies ontological monism, but not definitional or nomological reductionism. The criticism also often fails to appreciate that causal relations are extensional relations which hold between singular events no matter how they are described; that Davidson denies only *strict* psycho-physical laws; and that Anomalous Monism hangs on a distinction between causal relations, which hold between particular events, and causal explanations, which deal with laws, and so with types of events.

In an Abstract for *Essay 14*, 'Laws and Cause', Davidson wrote: "The argument for Anomalous Monism rests in part on the claim that every true singular causal statement relating two events is backed by a law that covers those events when those events are properly described. This paper attempts to clarify and defend this claim by tracing out some conceptual relations among the concepts of event, law, and object."

Essays 15–18 take up the question whether the task of philosophy is to clarify, reconcile, unearth, and criticize the beliefs and assumptions with which one begins one's investigation;

or whether it is to lead to a discovery of truths that were not in sight at the start. In Essays 15 and 16, 'Plato's Philosopher' and 'The Socratic Concept of Truth', Davidson turns for answer to an examination of the Socratic elenchus, the inconclusive dialectic of conversational give-and-take in which Socrates elicits a statement from his interlocutor, then sets about to show the statement's inconsistency with other things the interlocutor believes. Why, one may ask, should this be thought a route to knowledge, since there is no reason to believe that any proposition in a consistent set is true? In the dialogues from his middle period Plato himself shows doubts about the value of the elenchus, looking rather to a world of Forms to give us knowledge that transcends our starting point. But Plato embraces the elenchus in the *Philebus*, a late dialogue and the last in which Socrates appears as principal interlocutor. Plato apparently is now convinced that, as Davidson has argued elsewhere, "there are enough truths in each of us to make it plausible that . . . when our beliefs are consistent they will in most large matters be true". And as in his earlier Socratic dialogues, Plato now appeals to the idea that truths emerge only in the context of frank discussion and communication.

Essay 17, 'Dialectic and Dialogue', explores this last idea by calling attention to the chasm between an exchange in which the participants have clear concepts and an exchange in which concepts themselves come into focus, are refined, and developed. The latter happens more readily in an oral conversation, and is something like the way in which language and thought themselves develop. Thus Davidson call the elenchus "a microcosm of the ongoing process of language formation itself."

In *Essay 18*, 'Gadamer and Plato's *Philebus*', Davidson focuses on the major points of agreement between himself and Gadamer, both about Plato's *Philebus* and about the nature of understanding, truth, and language generally. They agree that conversation is the route to a shared understanding; that conversation presumes a shared world; that language has, as Gadamer puts it, "its true being only in conversation"; and that (again Gadamer) "language is not just one of man's possessions in the world, but on it depends the fact that man has a world at all". But against Gadamer, Davidson insists that conversation does not presuppose a common language, a point he argued in Essays 7–10.

Essay 19, 'Aristotle's Action', traces the concept of an action from Aristotle to the present, and suggests how certain routes of empirical investigation may affect our understanding of action in the future.

Essay 20, 'Spinoza's Causal Theory of the Affects', returns to Anomalous Monism via a discussion of the familiar difficulties in reconciling with each other Spinoza's ontological monism; his thesis that mind and body, extension and thought, are two different and mutually irreducible ways of describing the universe; his insistence on the reality of the mental; and his denial of mind–body interaction. In particular, if *a* causes *b* under the attribute of extension, and *b* is identical with *c* under the attribute of thought, how can we deny that *a* causes *c*?

As a solution, Davidson proposes attributing to Spinoza something like the theory of Anomalous Monism, together with the distinction between cause and law that Davidson elaborated in Essay 14. According to AM, each particular that can be identified in the mental vocabulary can also be identified in the physical vocabulary. But the purpose of a vocabulary is to sort particulars into classes; and from the fact that each *individual* in a set can be described in a given vocabulary it does not follow that the *set* can be defined in terms of that same vocabulary. Thus while a particular event described in one vocabulary may cause a particular event described in the other, we might say, as Spinoza does, that no *fully adequate explanation* of a mental event can be given in physical terms, and vice versa. It was the latter thesis that Spinoza had in mind, Davidson suggests, in denying mind–body interaction.

In the *Appendix* Davidson replies to Rorty, Stroud, McDowell, and Pereda, elucidating his stance on the following: whether there is a fact-of-the-matter about mental attitudes; the indeterminacy of translation; the normativity of the mental; the relations between perceptual experience and the justification of beliefs; and the usefulness of formal semantics to an understanding of truth and language.

Donald would have wanted to thank many people. I mention only four, who appear several times in these essays: Michael Dummett, John McDowell, W. V. O. Quine, and Richard Rorty. I want once again to thank Ernie Lepore, who came to visit us several years ago to help Donald organize the essays for Volumes 4 and 5, and who has continued to be of help to me at every step of the way. I am also deeply grateful to Donald himself: reading and, in most cases, rereading these essays has been a great pleasure. They have taught me much.

MARCIA CAVELL
Berkeley, 2004

TRUTH

1 *Truth Rehabilitated*

There is a long tradition according to which the concept of truth is one of the most important subjects for philosophical discussion, but in this century the tradition has come to be seriously questioned by a large number of philosophers, not to mention historians, literary theorists, art critics, anthropologists, political scientists, psychoanalysts, sociologists, and others. I think this is because of various tempting errors and confusions. Here I examine a few of the reasons truth has become tarnished, or at least diminished, in the minds of many, and then go on to say why the concept of truth should be restored to its key role in our understanding of the world and of the minds of agents.

Before it could come to seem worthwhile to debunk truth, it was necessary to represent truth as something grander than it is, or to endow it with powers it does not have. When there was no clear line between philosophy and science, it was natural for philosophers to claim to be purveyors of the closest thing to truth on offer. Concentration on epistemology, especially when epistemology seemed called on to provide ultimate grounds of justification for knowledge, encouraged the confused idea that philosophy was the place to look for the final and most basic truths on which all other truths, whether of science, morality, or common sense, must rest. Plato's conflation of abstract universals with entities of supreme value reinforced the confusion of truth with the most eminent truths; the confusion is apparent in the view (which Plato ultimately came to question) that the only perfect exemplar of a universal or Form is the Form itself. Thus only Circularity (the universal or concept) is perfectly circular, only the concept of a hand is a perfect hand, only truth itself is completely true.

Here we have a deep confusion, a category mistake, which was apparently doomed to flourish. Truth isn't an object, and so it can't be true; truth is a concept, and is intelligibly attributed to things like sentences, utterances, beliefs and propositions, entities which have a propositional content. It is an error to think that if someone seeks to understand the *concept of truth,* that person is necessarily trying to discover important general *truths* about justice or the foundations of physics. The mistake percolates down to the idea that a theory of truth must somehow tell us what, in general, is true, or at least how to discover truths.

No wonder there has been a reaction! Philosophy was promising far more than it, or any other discipline, could deliver. Nietzsche famously reacted; so, in a different way, did the American pragmatists. Dewey, for example, quite properly rejected the idea that philosophers were privy to some special or foundational species of truth without which science could not hope to advance. But he coupled this virtuous modesty with an absurd theory about the concept of truth; having derided pretensions to superior access to truths, he felt he must attack the classical concept itself. The attack, in the fashion of the times, took the form of a persuasive redefinition. Since the word "Truth" has an aura of being something valuable, the trick of persuasive definitions is to redefine it to be something of which you approve, something "good to steer by" in a phrase Rorty endorses on Dewey's behalf. So Dewey declared that a belief or theory is true if and only if it promotes human affairs.[1]

---

[1] Most of what I say here about pragmatists early and contemporary is inspired by a review of Alan Ryan's *John Dewey and the High Tide of American Liberalism,* New York: Nortons 1996 by Richard Rorty. Rorty writes:

To take the traditional notion of Truth seriously, you have to do more than agree that some beliefs are true and some false ... You must agree with Clough that 'It fortifies my soul to know / That, though I perish, Truth is so.' You must feel uneasy at William James's claim that 'ideas ... become true just in so far as they help us to get into satisfactory relations with other parts of our experience.' You must become indignant when Ryan (accurately paraphrasing Dewey) says that 'to call a statement "true" is no more than to say that it is good to steer our practice by.' (Richard Rorty, 'Something to Steer by', *London Review of Books,* June 20, 1996, p. 7)

Ryan doesn't buy the idea that what is useful is necessarily true, but this "puts my [Rorty's] pragmatist back up. As I said ... the whole point of pragmatism is to stop distinguishing between the usefulness of a way of talking and its truth."

It would be otiose to review the obvious objections to this view, for both its proponents and critics are familiar with them. Proponents glory in the conflicts with common sense;[2] critics swell with the silly pleasure of having spotted irresponsible rhetoric. It is more interesting to ask why Dewey, and the others Rorty includes in Dewey's camp, James, Nietzsche, Foucault and himself, put forward a thesis so clearly contrary to the ordinary, but philosophically interesting, concept of truth. I think of four related reasons.

According to Rorty, Dewey "agreed with Nietzsche that the traditional notion of Truth, as correspondence to the intrinsic nature of Reality, was a remnant of the idea of submission to the Will of God". Truth as correspondence with reality may be an idea we are better off without, especially when, as in this quotation, "truth" and "reality" are capitalized. The formulation is not so much wrong as empty, but it does have the merit of suggesting that something is not true simply because it is believed, even if believed by everyone. The trouble lies in the claim that the formula has explanatory power. The notion of correspondence would be a help if we were able say, in an *instructive* way, which fact or slice of reality it is that makes a particular sentence true. No one has succeeded in doing this. If we ask, for example, what makes the sentence "The moon is a quarter of a million miles away" true, the only answer we come up with is that it is the fact that the moon is a quarter of a million miles away. Worse still, if we try to provide a serious semantics for reference to facts, we discover that they melt into one; there is no telling them apart. The proof of this claim is given by Alonzo Church, who credits it to Frege. Church thinks this is the reason Frege held that all true sentences name the same thing, which he called The True. Kurt Gödel quite independently produced essentially the same proof, holding that it was awareness of this line of thinking that led Russell to invent the theory of descriptions.[3] Whatever the

---

[2] Thus Rorty, in final praise of the pragmatic attitude to truth, says that "noncompetitive, though perhaps irreconcilable, beliefs [may] reasonably [be] called 'true'" (Rorty, 'Something to Steer by', p. 8). Of course one can imagine circumstances under which it might be reasonable to *say* this (for example to prevent a fist-fight), but could it be reasonable, or even possible, to *think* irreconcilable beliefs are true?

[3] Stephen Neale, 'The Philosophical Significance of Gödel's Slingshot', *Mind*, 104 (1995): 761–825.

history of the relevant argument (which is now often called "The Slingshot"), we must, I think, accept the conclusion: there are no interesting and appropriate entities available which, by being somehow related to sentences, can explain why the true ones are true and the others not. There is good reason, then, to be skeptical about the importance of the correspondence theory of truth.

When "truth" is spelled with a capital "T", it is perhaps natural to think there is a unique way of describing things which gets at their essential nature, "an interpretation of the world which gets it right", as Rorty puts it, a description of "Reality As It Is In Itself". Of course there is no such unique "interpretation" or description, not even in the one or more languages each of us commands, not in any possible language. Or perhaps we should just say this is an ideal of which no one has made good sense. It hardly matters, for no sensible defender of the objectivity of attributions of truth to particular utterances or beliefs is stuck with this idea, and so there is no reason why, if we abstain from the search for The Perfect Description of Reality, we have to buy the thesis that there is no distinction, "even in principle", between beliefs which are true and beliefs which are "merely good to steer by".[4]

We come here to a far more powerful consideration in favor of a somewhat tamer, but clearly recognizable, version of the pragmatic theory of truth. Rorty brings it to the fore when he credits Dewey with the thought that the correspondence theory adds nothing to "ordinary, workaday, fallible ways of telling...the true from the false". What is clearly right is a point made long ago by Plato in the *Theaetetus*: truths do not come with a "mark", like the date in the corner of some photographs, which distinguishes them from falsehoods. The best we can do is test, experiment, compare, and keep an open mind. But no matter how long and well we and coming generations keep at it, we and they will be left with fallible beliefs. We know many things, and will learn more; what we will never know for certain is which of the things we believe are true. Since it is neither visible as a target, nor recognizable when achieved, there is no point in calling truth a goal. Truth is not a value, so the "pursuit of truth" is an empty enterprise unless it means only that it is often worthwhile to

---

[4] Rorty, 'Something to Steer by', p. 7.

increase our confidence in our beliefs, by collecting further evidence or checking our calculations. From the fact that we will never be able to tell for certain which of our beliefs are true, pragmatists conclude that we may as well identify our best researched, most successful, beliefs with the true ones, and give up the idea of objectivity. (Truth is objective if the truth of a belief or sentence is independent of whether it is justified by all our evidence, believed by our neighbors, or is good to steer by.) But here we have a choice. Instead of giving up the traditional view that truth is objective, we can give up the equally traditional view (to which the pragmatists adhere) that truth is a norm, something for which to strive. I agree with the pragmatists that we can't consistently take truth to be both objective and something to be pursued. But I think they would have done better to cleave to a view that counts truth as objective, but pointless as a goal.[5]

Some contemporary pragmatists have moved away from the hopeless idea that a belief is true if it helps us get on with life, or the less foolish, but still wrong, view that truth is no different from what is, perhaps at its practical best, epistemically available. But other philosophers who would not call themselves pragmatists are still rocking in the wake of the legitimate reaction against inflated or misguided theories of truth. The tendency they have joined is a broad one, one which is perhaps now the mainstream of philosophical thought about the concept of truth. The banner under which these debunkers march is *deflationism*. The idea common to the various brands of deflationism is that truth, though a legitimate concept, is essentially trivial, and certainly not worth the grand metaphysical attention it has received. This view receives its strength from two sources. One is wide, and largely justified, dissatisfaction with the standard attempts to define, or

---

[5] Curiously, Rorty sensibly argues that truth is not a norm *and* that there is no difference in principle between what is true and what is justified. "Pragmatists think that if something makes no difference to practice, it should make no difference to philosophy. This conviction makes them suspicious of the philosopher's emphasis on the difference between justification and truth" (Richard Rorty, 'Is Truth a Goal of Inquiry? Davidson *vs.* Wright', *Philosophical Quarterly*, 45/180 (1995), p. 281). If there is no difference, truth is identical with what is justified; but Rorty claims there is lots to say about justification, yet little to say about truth. If, as seems right, it *is* a legitimate norm to want to be justified, but not to seek the truth, then there must be a large difference between them.

otherwise explicate, the concept. Probably the most familiar definition, and the most immediately attractive, declares that an utterance or belief is true if and only if it corresponds to the facts, or reality, or the way things are. I have already said why I think correspondence theories are without explanatory content. Coherence definitions or "theories" have their attractions, but only as epistemic theories, not as accounting for truth. For while it is clear that only a consistent set of beliefs could contain all true beliefs, there is no reason to suppose every consistent set of beliefs contains only truths. Openly epistemic theories have their powerful supporters: I think particularly of Michael Dummett and Hilary Putnam, both of whom, with modifications, hold that truth is warranted assertability. I respect this idea for the same reason I respect closely related pragmatic theories, because it relates truth to human attitudes like belief, intention, and desire, and I believe any complete account of truth must do this. But theirs cannot be the right way to express the relation. For either the conditions of warranted assertability are made so strong that they include truth itself, in which case the account is circular, or circularity is avoided by making the conditions explicit, and it then becomes clear that a fully warranted assertion may be false.

What, then, is wrong with deflationism? Why shouldn't we accept the view that truth is as shallow as the correspondence theory seems to show it to be? Deflationism has taken a number of forms in recent years. Frank Ramsey, so prescient in many areas, was one of the first to try to make out that, as he says, "[T]here is really no separate problem of truth but merely a linguistic muddle."[6] His argument begins by noting that "It is true that Caesar was murdered" means no more than "Caesar was murdered": in such contexts, "It is true that" simply operates like double negation, a sentential connective that maps true sentences onto true and false onto false; aside from emphasis and verbosity, the phrase adds nothing to what we can say. Ramsey makes the same point about phrases like "It is a fact that". More perspicuous than others, though, Ramsey notices that we cannot eliminate the truth predicate in this way in sentences like "He is always right", that is, "Whatever he says is true". Here the truth predicate seems

[6] Frank Plumpton Ramsey, 'Facts and Propositions', in *Philosophical Papers*, ed. D. H. Mellor, Cambridge University Press, 1990, p. 38.

indispensable.[7] Ramsey makes a confused (and unworkable) proposal for the elimination of the truth predicate in such cases; we have to conclude that he did not prove his case that the problem of truth is merely a linguistic muddle. (Confusions of use and mention make it impossible to be sure what Ramsey had in mind, but one suspects that if he had pursued the subject he would have come out pretty much where Tarski did.)

Ramsey's deflationist attempt, unlike most such attempts, hinged on taking the primary bearers of truth to be propositions. Recently, however, Paul Horwich has revived what we may call propositional deflationism.[8] Horwich's thesis is not that the concept of truth is eliminable, but that it is trivial. He points out that a sentence like "The proposition that Caesar was murdered is true if and only if Caesar was murdered" is surely true, and that such sentences specify precisely the circumstances under which any expressible proposition is true. He then claims that the totality of such sentences provides an infinite axiomatization of the concept of truth (he excludes by fiat sentences that lead to contradiction). Horwich allows that this does not provide an explicit definition of the concept of truth, but it does, he maintains, exhaust the content of that concept. In particular, there is no need to employ the concept in order to explain the concepts of meaning and belief, since these can be explicated in other ways. As will presently be clear, I do not accept these last claims. But it does not matter, since I think we do not understand Horwich's axiom schema or the particular axioms that instance it. The problem concerns the semantic analysis of sentences like "The proposition that Caesar was murdered is true if and only if Caesar was murdered". The predicate "is true" requires a singular term as subject; the subject is therefore "the proposition that Caesar

---

[7] It is also indispensable when we want to explain the validity of logical rules: we need to be able to say why, if *any* sentences of a specified sort are true, others must be (Alfred Tarski, 'On The Concept of Logical Consequence', in *Logic, Semantics, Metamathematics*, ed. J. H. Woodger, Oxford University Press, 1956). Rorty wonders why we use the same word, "truth", also to "caution people" that their beliefs may not be justified (Rorty, 'Is Truth a Goal of Inquiry?', p. 286). I doubt we can explain this in a philosophically interesting way; words can be used in many ways without having to change their meaning—that, as I keep saying, is their merit. But it is easy to explain why we use the same word to express validity and to talk about what we have to know to understand a sentence: we prove a rule of inference is valid by appeal to the truth conditions of sentences. [8] Paul Horwich, *Truth*, Oxford: Blackwell, 1990.

was murdered". Presumably it names or refers to a proposition. But then, what is the role of the sentence "Caesar was murdered" in this singular term or description? The only plausible answer is that the words "the proposition that" are a functional expression that maps whatever the following sentence names onto a proposition. In that case, the sentence itself must be a referring term. If we are Fregeans, we will say it names a truth value. On this hypothesis, the axiom is a straightforward tautology, and explains nothing (since the words "the proposition that" simply map a truth value onto itself).[9] The alternative is that in its first occurrence, the sentence names some more interesting entity. But then we do not understand the axiom, since the sentence "Caesar was murdered" is used once as a name of some interesting entity, and once as an ordinary sentence, and we have no idea how to accommodate this ambiguity in a serious semantics.

Horwich claims both Quine and Tarski as fellow deflationists. But are they? Quine can apparently be quoted in support of the claim. He has repeatedly spoken of what he calls the disquotational aspect of truth, applied, of course, to sentences, not propositions. The truth predicate, applied to sentences, is disquotational in this sense: a sentence like " 'Snow is white' is true" is always equivalent to the result of disquoting the contained sentence and removing the truth predicate; equivalent, then, in this case, to "Snow is white". Here we see clearly how we can eliminate the truth predicate under favorable circumstances. Quine knows, of course, that there are contexts in which this maneuver will not remove the truth predicate. Nevertheless, the totality of sentences like " 'Snow is white' is true if and only if snow is white" exhaust the extension of the truth predicate for a particular language, as Tarski emphasized, and each such sentence does tell us exactly under what conditions the quoted sentence is true.

Disquotation cannot, however, pretend to give a complete account of the concept of truth, since it works only in the special case where the metalanguage contains the object language. But neither object language nor metalanguage can contain its own truth predicate. In other words, the very concept we want to explain is explicitly excluded from expression in any consistent

---

[9] I owe this suggestion to Burt Dreben.

language for which disquotation works. To put this another way: if we want to know under what conditions a sentence containing a truth predicate is true, we cannot use that predicate in the disquotational mode. Disquotation does not give the entire content of the concept of truth.

At best, then, disquotation gives the extension of a truth predicate for a single language; if we ask what all such predicates have in common, disquotation cannot answer. Something analogous must be said about Tarski's truth definitions. Tarski showed how to give explicit definitions of truth for languages satisfying certain conditions, but at the same time he proved (given some natural assumptions) that no general definition was possible; the general concept escaped him. He did go far beyond anything implicit in disquotation, however, for he was able to give proper definitions of truth—relative to specific languages, it goes without saying, which disquotation cannot do. Tarski's truth definitions are not trivial, and they reveal something deep about languages of any serious expressive power. As long as a language has the equivalent of a first order quantificational structure and no decision method, there is no way to define truth for it except by introducing a sophisticated version of reference, what Tarski called satisfaction. Tarski's satisfiers are infinite sequences which pair the variables of a language with the entities in its ontology. The interesting work of the concept of satisfaction comes in characterizing the semantic properties of open sentences, but it turns out in the end that a closed sentence is true if and only if it is satisfied by some sequence. This may suggest that we have here the makings of a correspondence theory, but it would be a Fregean theory, since every sequence satisfies every true sentence. You could say that though this was not his intention, Tarski here indirectly vindicates Frege's slingshot argument.

We must conclude that Tarski's work gives no comfort to those who would like to revive the correspondence theory, nor does it support a deflationary attitude. Given how unsatisfactory the alternatives seem to be, should we nevertheless rest content with the genuine insight Tarski has given us into the nature of truth? I think not, for we have to wonder how we know that it is some single concept which Tarski indicates how to define for each of a number of well-behaved languages. Tarski does not, of course, attempt to define such a concept, though the title of his famous essay is *"The* Concept of Truth in Formalized Languages" ("Der Wahrheitsbegriff... "). Various remarks in this work and elsewhere also make clear that Tarski assumes there is one concept, even if it can't be defined. This comes out not only in his stated conviction that his work is directly relevant to the "classical" concept of truth with which philosophers have always been concerned, but also in his criterion for success in the project of defining truth for particular languages. This (informal) criterion requires that the definition entail as theorems all sentences of the form

   s is true-in-*L* iff *p*

where *s* is a description of any sentence of *L* and *p* is a translation of that sentence into the language of the defined predicate "true-in-*L*". Clearly, we cannot recognize that such a predicate is a truth predicate unless we already grasp the (undefined) general concept of truth. It is also significant that Tarski connects the concept of truth with translation: this is essential, since the language for which truth is being defined cannot be the language which contains the defined truth predicate.

   This brings me to my positive theme: if all the definitions of the general concept fail, and none of the short paraphrases seem to come close to capturing what is important or interesting about the concept, why do some of us persist in thinking it is interesting and important? One of the reasons is its connection with meaning. This is the connection of which Tarski makes use, for translation succeeds only if it preserves truth, and the traditional aim of translation is to preserve meaning. But to what extent does meaning depend on truth?

   Almost everyone agrees that some sentences, at least, have the value true or false, and that for such sentences, we may speak of truth conditions. But deflationists and others tend to doubt whether this fact has much to do with what sentences mean. Meaning, it is frequently said, has to do rather with the conditions under which it is justified or proper to use a sentence to make an assertion; in general, meaning has to do with how sentences are used rather than with their truth conditions. Here I sense two confusions. The first is that truth-conditional and use accounts of meaning are somehow in competition. One can legitimately dispute the claim that a Tarski-type truth definition can serve as a theory of meaning. I think it can so serve, when properly understood, but that is not my thesis here. What is clear is that someone who knows under what conditions a sentence would be true understands that sentence, and if the sentence has a truth value (true, false or perhaps neither), then someone who does not know under what conditions it would be true doesn't understand it. This simple claim doesn't rule out an account of meaning which holds that sentences mean what they do because of how they are used; it may be that they are used as they are because of their truth conditions, and they have the truth conditions they do because of how they are used.

The second confusion is the thought that there is a simple, direct, non-question-begging way to employ "uses" to provide a theory of meaning. There is not. It is empty to say meaning is use unless we specify what use we have in mind, and when we do specify, in a way that helps with meaning, we find ourselves going in a circle. Nevertheless, it is only by registering how a language is used that we can make it our own. How do we do it? Before we have an idea of truth or error, before the advent of concepts or propositional thought, there is a rudiment of communication in the simple discovery that sounds produce results. Crying is the first step toward language when crying is found to procure one or another form of relief or satisfaction. More specific sounds, imitated or not, are rapidly associated with more specific pleasures. Here use would be meaning, if anything like intention and meaning were in the picture. A large further step has been taken when the child notices that others also make distinctive sounds at the same time the child is having the experiences that provoke its own volunteered sounds. For the adult, these sounds have a meaning, perhaps as one word sentences. The adult sees herself as doing a little ostensive teaching: "Eat", "Red", "Ball", "Mama", "Milk", "No". There is now room for what the adult views as error: the child says "Block" when it is a slab. This move fails to be rewarded, and the conditioning becomes more complex. This is still pretty simple stuff, for nothing more is necessarily involved than verbal responses increasingly conditioned to what the teacher thinks of as appropriate circumstances, and the child finds satisfying, often enough. There is little point in trying to spot, in this process, the moment at which the child is talking and thinking. The interaction between adult and child in the ostensive learning situation I have described provides the necessary conditions for the emergence of language and propositional thought, by creating a space in which there can be success and failure. What is clear is that we can say the child *thinks* something is red, or a ball, only if it appreciates the distinction between the judgment and the truth for itself: the child thinks something is red or a ball only if it is in some sense aware that a mistake is possible. The child is classifying things, and it knows it may have put something in the wrong slot.

It is difficult to exaggerate the magnitude of the step from native or learned disposition to respond to stimuli of a certain sort, to employing a concept with the awareness of the chance of error. It is the step from reacting to proximal stimuli to the thought of distal objects and events, the step from mere conditioned response to what Wittgenstein called "following a rule". This is where the concept of truth enters, for there is no sense in saying a disposition is in error—one cannot fail to act in accord with a disposition, but one can fail to follow a rule.

Here we must ask: how can we reconcile the fact that a general appeal to how language is used cannot be parlayed into a theory of meaning with the present claim that ostensive learning is the entering wedge into language, for surely the ostending teacher is making a use of one-word sentences that the learner picks up? The answer lies in the transition just mentioned. At the start the learner does not register anything more than an association between object or situation and sound or gesture. The value of the association is supplied by the teacher or the environment in the form of reward. In the beginning there is not a word but a sound being given a use. The teacher sees the learner as picking up a bit of language with a meaning already there; the learner has no idea of prior meaning or use: for the learner, what was meaningless before now takes on significance. In the early stage of ostensive learning, error has no point for the learner, for there is nothing for him to be wrong about, and where error has no point, there is not a concept or thought. Once trial and error (from the teacher's point of view) is replaced with thought and belief (from the learner's point of view), the concept of truth has application.

During the learning process, the pragmatist's claim that there is nothing to be gained by distinguishing between success (as measured by the teacher's approval or getting what one wants) and truth is clearly right. This is a distinction that depends on further developments. These are not hard to imagine in rough outline. Ostensive learning works first and best with whole sentences, in practice often represented by what for the experienced speaker are single names, common nouns, verbs, adjectives, and adverbs ("Mama", "Man", "Come", "Good", "Careful"). The child who has no more is still a pragmatist. Once some grammar is in hand, however, separately learned parts can be assembled in new ways, and truth separates from the merely useful or approved. The references of names, the extensions of predicates, the combinatorial devices themselves, are in the hands of teachers and society; truth is not.

Sentences mean what they do because of the semantic properties of the words and the combinatorial devices they contain. You would not understand a sentence if you did not know that the names and other singular terms in it purported to refer, or if you were unaware of the extension of its predicates. But to know this is to know that the materials are present which make for truth and falsity. This is so even when we know that a term fails of reference or a predicate has an empty extension. Our understanding of truth conditions is central to our understanding of every sentence. This may escape our notice for many reasons. The first, and most general, reason is that in the normal course of conversation we do not care whether or not a sentence is true; it is a fairly rare occasion when we make an assertion by saying what we literally believe to be true. Our ordinary talk is studded with metaphor, ellipsis, easily recognized irony, and hyperbole, not to mention slips of the tongue, jokes, and malapropisms. But we understand a metaphor only because we know the usual meanings of the words, and know under what conditions the sentence containing the metaphor would be true. There are cases where we may decide a metaphorical sentence is neither true nor false, for example "The sound of the trumpet is scarlet". Our decision that this sentence has no truth value (if that is our decision, for we may choose to count it false) is based on our understanding of the sorts of things of which the predicate "scarlet" is true or false, and our decision that the sound of a trumpet is not one of them. Interrogatives may not themselves be true or false, but they have answers that are. Indeed, it is clear that one does not understand a yes–no interrogative if one does not know there are two (or perhaps three) possible answers, one of which is true and one of which is false. Imperatives, if taken to express an order or command, are understood only if one knows what would be true if they were obeyed. Sentences with non-referring names ("Pegasus is a winged horse") may or may not, according to one's semantic theory, have a truth value, but one comprehends such sentences only if one knows what it would be for the name "Pegasus" to name a horse with wings.

Sentences are understood on condition that one has the concept of objective truth. This goes also for the various propositional attitudes sentences are used to express. It is possible to have a belief only if one knows that beliefs may be true or false. I can believe it is now raining, but this is because I know that whether or not it is raining does not depend on whether I believe it, or everyone believes it, or it is useful to believe it; it is up to nature, not to me or my society or the entire history of the human race. What is up to us is what we mean by our words, but that is a different matter. Truth enters into the other attitudes in other ways. We desire that a certain state of affairs be true, we fear, hope or doubt that things are one way or another. We intend by our actions to make it true that we have a good sleep. We are proud or depressed that it is the case that we have won the second prize. Since all these, and many more attitudes, have a propositional content—the sort of content that can be expressed by a sentence—to have any of these attitudes is necessarily to know what it would be for the corresponding sentence, provided it is in our language, to be true. Without a grasp of the concept of truth, not only language, but thought itself, is impossible.

Truth is important, then, not because it is especially valuable or useful, though of course it may be on occasion, but because without the idea of truth we would not be thinking creatures, nor would we understand what it is for someone else to be a thinking creature. It is one thing to try to define the concept of truth, or capture its essence in a pithy summary phrase; it is another to trace its connections with other concepts. If we think of the various attempted characterizations as attempting no more than the latter, their merits become evident. Correspondence, while it is empty as a definition, does capture the thought that truth depends on how the world is, and this should be enough to discredit most epistemic and pragmatic theories. Epistemic and pragmatic theories, on the other hand, have the merit of relating the concept of truth to human concerns, like language, belief, thought and intentional action, and it is these connections which make truth the key to how mind apprehends the world.

Rorty doesn't much mind my saying that truth is one concept among a number of other related concepts which we use in describing, explaining, and predicting human behavior. But why, he asks, say truth is any more important than such concepts as intention, belief, desire, and so on?[10] Importance is a hard thing to argue about. *All* these concepts (and more) are essential to thought, and cannot be reduced to anything simpler or more fundamental. Why be niggardly in awarding prizes? I'm happy to hand out golden apples all round.

---

[10] Rorty, 'Is Truth a Goal of Inquiry?', p. 286.

2 The Folly of Trying to Define Truth

In the *Euthyphro* Socrates asks what holiness is, what "makes" holy things holy. It is clear that he seeks a *definition*, a definition with special properties. He spurns the mere provision of examples or lists, asking in each case what makes the examples *examples*, or puts an item on the list. He rejects merely coextensive concepts ("something is holy if and only if it is dear to the gods": what makes something dear to the gods is that it is holy, but not vice versa). The dialogue ends when Socrates begs Euthyphro to enlighten him by coming up with a satisfactory answer; Euthyphro decides he has another appointment.

The pattern of attempted definition, counterexample, amended definition, further counterexample, ending with a whimper of failure, is repeated with variations throughout the Socratic and middle Platonic dialogues. Beauty, courage, virtue, friendship, love, temperance are put under the microscope, but no convincing definitions emerge. The only definitions Plato seems happy with are tendentious characterizations of what it is to be a sophist. He also gives a few trivial samples of correct definitions: of a triangle; of mud (earth and water).

In the *Theaetetus* Plato attempts to define empirical knowledge. Like many philosophers since, he takes knowledge to be true belief plus something more—an account which justifies or warrants the belief. It is the last feature which stumps him (again foreshadowing the subsequent history of the subject). It seems no more to occur to Plato than it has to most others that the combination of causal and rational elements which must enter into an analysis of justified belief (as it must into accounts of memory, perception, and intentional action) may in the nature of the case not be amenable to sharp formulation in a clearer, more basic, vocabulary.

What is important in the present context, however, is the fact that in attempting to define knowledge, it is only with the concept of warrant that Plato concedes defeat. He does not worry much about the equal involvement of knowledge with truth and belief.

Again, though, Plato was simply blazing a trail which other philosophers over the ages have followed: you follow his lead if you worry about the concept of truth when it is the focus of your attention, but you pretend you understand it when trying to cope with knowledge (or belief, memory, perception, etc.). We come across the same puzzling strategy in Hume and others, who forget their skepticism about the external world when they formulate their doubts concerning knowledge of other minds. When a philosopher is troubled by the idea of an intentional action, he would be happy if he could analyze it correctly in terms of the concepts of belief, desire, and causality, and he does not for the moment worry too much about those (at least equally difficult) concepts. If memory is up for analysis, the connections with belief, truth, causality, and perhaps perception, constitute the problem, but these further concepts are pro tem taken to be clear enough to be used to clarify memory, if only the connections could be got right. It's okay to assume you have an adequate handle on intention and convention if your target is meaning. I could easily go on.

There is a lesson to be learned from these familiar, though odd, shifts in the focus of philosophical puzzlement. The lesson I take to heart is this: however feeble or faulty our attempts to relate these various basic concepts to each other, these attempts fare better, and teach us more, than our efforts to produce correct and revealing definitions of basic concepts in terms of clearer or even more fundamental concepts.

This is, after all, what we should expect. For the most part, the concepts philosophers single out for attention, like truth, knowledge, belief, action, cause, the good and the right, are the most elementary concepts we have, concepts without which (I am inclined to say) we would have no concepts at all. Why then should we expect to be able to reduce these concepts definitionally to other concepts that are simpler, clearer, and more basic? We should accept the fact that what makes these concepts so important must also foreclose on the possibility of finding a foundation for them that reaches deeper into bedrock.

We should apply this obvious observation to the concept of truth: we cannot hope to underpin it with something more transparent or easier to grasp. Truth is, as G. E. Moore, Bertrand Russell and Frege maintained, and Tarski proved, an indefinable concept. This does not mean we can say nothing revealing about it: we can, by relating it to other concepts like belief, desire, cause and action. Nor does the indefinability of truth imply that the concept is mysterious, ambiguous, or untrustworthy.

Even if we are persuaded that the concept of truth cannot be defined, the intuition or hope remains that we can characterize truth using some fairly simple formulae. What distinguishes much of the contemporary philosophical discussion of truth is that though there are many such formulae on the market, none of them seems to keep clear of fairly obvious counterexamples. One result has been the increasing popularity of minimalist or deflationary theories of truth—theories that hold that truth is a relatively trivial concept with no "important connections with other concepts such as meaning and reality".[1]

I sympathize with the deflationists; the attempts to pump more content into the concept of truth are not, for the most part, appealing. But I think the deflationists are wrong in their conclusion, even if mostly right in what they reject. I will not pause here to give my reasons for refusing to accept correspondence theories, coherence theories, pragmatic theories, theories that limit truth to what could be ascertained under ideal conditions or justifiably asserted, etc.[2] But since I am with the deflationists in being dissatisfied with all such characterizations of truth, I will say why deflationism seems to me equally unacceptable.

Semantics, as I conceive it, is primarily concerned with truth, which is a property of some sentences, or of certain closely related entities, such as utterances, judgments, beliefs or propositions. According to the Aristotelian conception,

> (1) *To say of what is that it is not, or of what is not that it is, is false, while to say of what is that it is, or of what is not that it is not, is true.*

[1] These words are quoted from Michael Dummett's jacket blurb for Paul Horwich's *Truth*, MIT Press, 1991.

[2] I spell out my reasons for rejecting such views in "The Structure and Content of Truth", *The Journal of Philosophy*, **87**, (1990), pp. 279–328.

When Tarski mentions this formulation in 1944,[3] he complains
that it is "not sufficiently precise and clear", though he prefers it to
two others:

> (2)   *The truth of a sentence consists in its agreement with
> (or correspondence to) reality.*
>
> (3)   *A sentence is true if it designates an existing state of
> affairs.*[4]

In 1969 Tarski again quotes (1), and adds,

[T]he formulation leaves much to be desired from the point of view of
precision and formal correctness. For one thing, it is not general enough;
it refers only to sentences that "say" about something "that it is" or "that
it is not"; in most cases it would hardly be possible to cast a sentence in
this mold without slanting the sense of the sentence and forcing the spirit
of the language.[5]

He adds that this may be the reason for such "modern substitutes"
for Aristotle's formulations as (2) and (3).

In the *Wahrheitsbegriff*, however, Tarski prefers the following
informal statement:

> (4)   *A true sentence is one which says that the state of
> affairs is so and so, and the state of affairs indeed is so and so.*[6]

It seems to me that Aristotle's formulation is clearly superior
to (2), (3) and (4); it is more in accord with Tarski's own work
on truth; and Tarski's comment that (1) is "not general enough"
is strangely out of keeping with the spirit of his own truth
definitions.

(1) is superior to (2)–(4) for three reasons. First, (3) and (4)
mention states of affairs, thus suggesting that postulating entities
to correspond to sentences might be a useful way of characterizing
truth. ("A true sentence is one that corresponds to the facts", or
"If a sentence is true, there is a state of affairs to which it corresponds.") But facts or states of affairs have never been shown to
play a useful role in semantics, and one of the strongest arguments

---

[3] "The Semantic Conception of Truth", *Philosophy and Phenomenological
Research*, **4** (1944), pp. 342–60.   [4] Ibid., p. 343.

[5] "Truth and Proof", *The Scientific American*, **220** (1969), p. 63.

[6] "The Concept of Truth in Formalized Languages", in *Logic, Semantics, Metamathematics*, Oxford University Press, 1956, p. 155 (originally published in German
in 1936).

for Tarski's definitions is that in them *nothing* plays the role of facts or states of affairs. This is not surprising, since there is a persuasive argument, usually traced to Frege (in one form) or Gödel (in another), to the effect that there can be at most one fact or state of affairs. (This is why Frege said all true sentences name the True.) Tarski's truth definitions make no use of the idea that a sentence "corresponds" to anything at all. We should not take seriously the mention of "states of affairs" in such remarks of Tarski's as this: "[S]emantical concepts express certain relations between objects (and states of affairs) referred to in the language discussed and expressions of the language referring to those objects."[7]

A second reason for preferring Aristotle's characterization of truth is that it avoids the awkward blanks marked by the words "so and so" in Tarski's version (4); one is hard pressed to see how the blanks are to be filled in. Aristotle's formula, on the other hand, sounds much like a generalization of Tarski's convention T.

The third reason for preferring Aristotle's characterization is that it makes clear, what the other formulations do not, that the truth of a sentence depends on the inner structure of the sentence, i.e., on the semantic features of the parts. In this it is once again closer to Tarski's approach to the concept of truth.

Tarski's convention T, which he understandably substitutes for the rough formulas I have been discussing, stipulates that a satisfactory definition of a truth predicate "is true" for a language *L* must be such as to entail as theorems all sentences of the form

    s is true if and only if *p*

where "*s*" is replaced by the description of a sentence, and "*p*" is replaced by that sentence, or a translation of the sentence into the metalanguage. Since it is assumed that there is an infinity of sentences in *L*, it is obvious that if the definition of the truth predicate is to be finite (Tarski insisted on this), the definition must take advantage of the fact that sentences, though potentially infinite in number, are constructed from a finite vocabulary. For the languages Tarski considered, and for which he showed how to define truth, all sentences can be put into the form of an existential

---

[7] "The Establishment of Scientific Semantics", in *Logic, Semantics, Metamathematics*, Oxford University Press, 1956, p. 403.

quantification, or the negation of an existential quantification, or a truth-functional compound of such sentences. So how "incomplete", from Tarski's point of view, is Aristotle's formulation (1)? It deals with four cases. There are the sentences that "say of what is that it is not": in modern terms it is a false sentence that begins "It is not the case that there exists an x such that . . .". An example might be, "There does not exist an x such that $x = 4$". Then there are sentences that "say of what is not that it is"; example: "There exists an x such that $x = 4$ & $x = 5$". There are sentences that "say of what is that it is"; example: "There exists an x such that $x = 4$". And, finally, there are sentences that "say of what is not that it is not", for example, "It is not the case that there exists an x such that $x^1 x$". According to the classical formulation, sentences of the first two kinds are false and of the second two kinds are true. Tarski is so far in agreement. What would Tarski add? Just the truth-functional compounds (beyond those involving negation) of the types of sentences already mentioned; these are true or false on the basis of the truth or falsity of the kinds of sentences already provided for. Of course, Tarski also showed in detail how the truth or falsity of the first four types of sentences depended in turn on their structure.

Thus the classical formulation regarded as an informal characterization is "incomplete" in only a minimal way compared to Tarski's own work, and is better than Tarski's informal attempts to state the intuitive idea. Needless to say, someone might question the extent to which natural languages can be adequately characterized using such limited resources; but this is a comment equally applicable to Tarski.[8]

It may be objected that not all sentences are in the form of an existential quantification or the negation of an existential generalization (or a truth-functional compound of such), for there are sentences that begin with a proper name. But there is a simple device, proposed by Quine in *Word and Object*, which gets around this. Thus "Socrates is a man" becomes "There exists an x such that x is identical with Socrates and x is a man".[9]

---

[8] The last few pages are taken, slightly modified, from my "Method and Metaphysics", *Deukalion*, **11** (1993) [Ch. 3 below].

[9] W. V. Quine, *Word and Object*, MIT press, 1960, §37.

Despite his nod in the direction of a correspondence theory, in which sentences are said to correspond to facts, Tarski ought not to be considered as giving comfort to serious partisans of correspondence theories, nor should Aristotle. For neither Aristotle's formula nor Tarski's truth definitions introduce entities like facts or states of affairs for sentences to correspond to. Tarski does define truth on the basis of the concept of satisfaction, which relates expressions to objects, but the sequences which satisfy sentences are nothing like the "facts" or "states of affairs" of correspondence theorists, since if one of Tarski's sequences satisfies a closed sentence, thus making it true, then that same sequence also satisfies every other true sentence, and thus also makes it true, and if any sequence satisfies a closed sentence, every sequence does.[10]

If Tarski isn't a correspondence theorist (and he certainly doesn't hold a coherence theory or a pragmatic theory or a theory that bases truth on warranted assertability), is he a deflationist? Here opinions differ widely: Quine thinks he is, and so does Scott Soames. Etchemendy thinks Tarski simply says nothing about truth as a semantic concept, and Putnam, though for somewhat different reasons, agrees.[11]

If Tarski has said "all there is to say" about truth, as Stephen Leeds, Paul Horwich, and Scott Soames all contend, and Quine has strongly hinted, then a sort of deflationary attitude is justified; this is not quite the same as the "redundancy" view, but close to it. The redundancy view, taken literally, is the same as the disquotational view taken literally: we can always substitute without loss a sentence for that same sentence quoted, and followed by the words "is true". What Tarski added, as Michael Williams and others have pointed out, is a way of predicating truth of whole classes of sentences, or of sentences to which we do not know how to refer; you may think of this as an elaboration of the redundancy theory in that it allows the elimination of the truth predicate when

[10] At one time I suggested calling Tarski's concept of truth a correspondence theory on the strength of the role of sequences in satisfying closed sentences, but I subsequently withdrew the suggestion as misleading. For the suggestion, see "True to the Facts", in *Inquiries into Truth and Interpretation*, Oxford University Press, 1984. For the retraction, see "Afterthoughts, 1987", in *Reading Rorty*, ed. A. Malichowski, Blackwell, 1990, pp. 120–38.

[11] For references, and further discussion, see my "The Structure and Content of Truth".

applied to sentences of a language for which that predicate has been defined.

At the same time that we credit Tarski with having shown how to make sense of remarks like "The English sentence Joan uttered about Abbot was true" or "Everything Aristotle said (in Greek) was false" or "The usual truth table for the conditional makes any conditional true that has a false antecedent", we have to recognize that this accomplishment was accompanied by a proof that truth cannot (given various plausible assumptions) be defined in general; there can be no definition of "For all languages L, and all sentences s in L, s is true in L iff $...s...L...$". In other words, Tarski justified the application of a truth predicate to the sentences of a particular language only by restricting its application to the sentences of that language. (It is ironic that in much recent writing on deflationary theories, Tarski has been taken to have lent support to the idea that there is a single, simple, even trivial, concept of truth.)

A deflationary attitude to the concept of truth is not, then, encouraged by reflection on Tarski's work. One can adopt the line advanced by Putnam and Etchemendy, that Tarski was not even doing semantics, despite his insistence that he was; but this construal of Tarski does not support a deflationary theory: it simply denies the relevance of Tarski's results to the ordinary concept of truth. If, on the other hand, one takes Tarski's truth definitions to say something about the relations of specific languages to the world, one cannot at the same time claim that he has told us all there is to know about the concept of truth, since he has not told us what the concept is that his truth definitions for particular languages have in common.

I think that Tarski wasn't trying to define *the* concept of truth—so much is obvious—but that he was *employing* that concept to characterize the semantic structures of specific languages. But Tarski didn't indicate how we can in general reduce the concept of truth to other more basic concepts, nor how to eliminate the English predicate "is true" from all contexts in which it is intelligibly applied to sentences. Convention T isn't a rough substitute for a general definition: it is part of a successful attempt to persuade us that his formal definitions apply our single pre-theoretical concept of truth to certain languages. Deflationists cannot, then, appeal to Tarski simply because he demonstrated how to handle the semantics of quantification for individual languages. Stephen Leeds, Paul Horwich, Michael Williams, and others who have contended that all Tarski did was reveal the usefulness of an otherwise dispensable concept are wrong. They are right that we need a truth predicate for the purposes they, along with Tarski, mention; but they fail to note the obvious fact that at the same time Tarski solved one problem he emphasized another: that he had not, and could not, given the constraints he accepted, define or fully characterize truth.

Over the years, Quine has said a number of things about truth, but there has been, from early days until the most recent, what seems a consistent embrace of a deflationary attitude. Thus Quine has made much of the "disquotational" aspect of the truth predicate, the fact that we can get rid of the predicate "is true" after the quotation of an English sentence simply by removing the quotation marks as we erase the truth predicate. As Quine put it in *From a Logical Point of View*, we have a general paradigm, namely,

(T) "———" is true-in-*L* if and only if———

which, though not a definition of truth, serves to endow "true-in-*L*" with

> every bit as much clarity, in any particular application, as is enjoyed by the particular expressions of *L* to which we apply [it]. Attribution of truth in particular to "Snow is white" ... is every bit as clear to us as attribution of whiteness to snow.[12]

In *Word and Object* Quine remarks that "To say that the statement 'Brutus killed Caesar' is true, or that 'The atomic weight of sodium is 23' is true, is in effect simply to say that Brutus killed Caesar, or that the atomic weight of sodium is 23."[13] The theme is repeated thirty years later in *Pursuit of Truth*:

> ... there is surely no impugning the disquotation account; no disputing that "Snow is white" is true if and only if snow is white. Moreover, it is a full account; it explicates clearly the truth or falsity of every clear sentence.[14]

On this matter, Quine has not changed his mind.

---

[12] *From a Logical Point of View*, rev edn., Harvard University Press, 1961, p. 138.
[13] *Word and Object*, p. 24.
[14] *Pursuit of Truth*, Harvard University Press, 1990, p. 93.

It is the disquotational feature of truth, in Quine's opinion, which makes truth so much clearer a concept than meaning. Comparing theory of meaning and theory of reference, Quine says that they constitute "... two provinces so fundamentally distinct as not to deserve a joint appellation at all".[15] The former deals with such tainted topics as synonymy, significance, and analyticity. The concepts treated by the latter, which include truth, are by contrast "... very much less foggy and mysterious...". For although "true-in-*L*" for variable "*L*" is not definable, "... what we do have suffices to endow 'true-in-*L*', even for variable '*L*', with a high enough degree of intelligibility so that we are not likely to be averse to using the idiom".[16] "What we do have" is, of course, the paradigm (T) and the "expedient general routine" due to Tarski for defining "true-in-*L*" for particular languages.

Quine has made ingenious use of Tarski's "expedient general routine". In a 1952 paper, "On an Application of Tarski's Theory of Truth",[17] he explores the question whether truth for the language *L* of *Mathematical Logic* (1940) can be defined in *L* itself. It is not clear at first what stands in the way, for *L* can be interpreted as containing its own syntax, and much besides. Quine succeeds in giving a recursive definition of satisfaction using only the resources of *L*. If this recursive definition could be turned into a direct definition, *L* would have been proven inconsistent, truth being immediately definable in terms of satisfaction. But an unusual feature of *L* blocks the move from recursive to direct definition: in *L*, the quantifiers range over all entities, and so satisfaction must relate expressions of *L* to all entities. But some entities only, called "elements", are available in *L* as relata of relations. This mismatch prevents Frege's device for converting recursive into direct definitions from capturing the full onto-logical scope needed for the characterization of satisfaction, and hence of truth. Prevents it, that is, provided *L* is consistent.

In *Philosophy of Logic*,[18] Quine makes a connected but more general point: just as a normally equipped language cannot, on pain of contradiction, contain an open sentence "*x* satisfies *y*" true of sequences of objects in the ontology of the language and

---

[15] *From a Logical Point of View*, p. 130.   [16] Ibid., pp. 137–8.
[17] Reprinted in *Selected Logic Papers*, Random House, 1966.
[18] Prentice-Hall, 1970.

sentences (open or closed) of the language, so a consistent set theory cannot tolerate the existence of a set consisting of the ordered pairs of sequences of objects in the ontology of the theory and the sentences (open or closed) of the theory.

These interesting technical applications of Tarski's approach to the concept of truth exploit its disquotational feature, and this encourages the idea that truth and meaning can be kept quite separate. But can they in general? Scattered remarks in Quine's work suggest otherwise. In 1936 Quine published the brilliant and prescient "Truth by Convention". In it he remarks that " ... in point of *meaning* ... a word may be said to be determined to whatever extent the truth or falsehood of its contexts is determined".[19] It is hard to see how truth could have this power of determining meaning if the disquotational account were all there were to say about truth. Other passages in Quine suggest the same idea: "First and last, in learning language, we are learning how to distribute truth values. I am with Davidson here; we are learning truth conditions."[20] Or again, " ... Tarski's theory of truth [is] the very structure of a theory of meaning." *Philosophy of Logic* also stresses, in a way not to be found in earlier works by Quine, the importance of discerning in a language a grammatical structure geared to the workings of a theory of truth; only then will we see how "logic chases truth up the tree of grammar".[21]

Up to a point it may seem easy to keep questions of truth and questions of meaning segregated. Truth we may think of as disquotational (in the extended Tarski sense) and therefore trivial; meaning is then another matter, to be taken care of in terms of warranted assertability, function, or the criteria for translation. This is the line followed, for example, by Paul Horwich in his recent book *Truth*,[22] by Scott Soames,[23] and by David Lewis.[24] It may, at least at one time, have been Quine's view. In *Word and Object*, in a passage that immediately precedes the remark that to say that the sentence "Brutus killed Caesar" is true is in effect

[19] Reprinted in *The Ways of Paradox*, Harvard University Press, 1976, p. 89.

[20] *The Roots of Reference*, Open Court, 1974, p. 65.

[21] *Philosophy of Logic*, Prentice-Hall, 1970, p. 35.   [22] Paul Horwich, *Truth*.

[23] Scott Soames, "What is a Theory of Truth?" *The Journal of Philosophy*, 81 (1984), pp. 411–29.

[24] David Lewis, "Languages and Language", *Minnesota Studies in the Philosophy of Science*, 7, University of Minnesota Press, 1975.

simply to say that Brutus killed Caesar, Quine despairs of a substantive concept of truth, perhaps along the lines of Peirce, and says,

It is rather when we turn back into the midst of an actually present theory...that we can and do speak sensibly of this or that sentence as true. Where it makes sense to apply "true" is to a sentence couched in the terms of a given theory, and seen from within the theory.[25]

This is, I think, what Quine means when he says that truth is "immanent". The point is not merely that the truth of a sentence is relative to a language; it is that there is no transcendent, single concept to be relativized.

But Quine cannot mean that we sensibly speak of the truth of sentences only when those sentences are contained in the language we are using to do the speaking. It may be impossible to give an explicit definition of truth for languages generally, at least following Tarski's method, but of course one can speak sensibly of the truth of sentences in one language using another language. What should we say about the disquotational view of truth in this case?

I'm not sure where Quine comes out. If truth is really "immanent", not only in the sense that the truth of a sentence is relative to the language to which we take it to belong, but in the sense that when we say, in English, for example, " 'Schnee ist weiss' is true in German", we are using a different concept than we use when we say, " 'Snow is white' is true in English". A different concept of *truth*? No: that makes no sense. And much that Quine says belies such a desperate relativism: Tarski's "expedient general routine" endows *the* concept of truth—apparently a single, if indefinable, concept—with a "high enough degree of intelligibility".

I turn now to Paul Horwich's recent book *Truth*, for he seems to me to have accepted the challenge other deflationists have evaded, that of saying something more than we can learn from Tarski's definitions about the content of an unrelativized truth predicate.

Horwich's brave and striking move is to make the primary bearers of truth *propositions*—not exactly a new idea in itself, but new in the context of a serious attempt to defend deflationism.

---

[25] *Word and Object*, p. 24.

He is clear that he cannot provide an explicit definition of a truth predicate applying to propositions, but he urges that we really have said all there is to know about such a predicate (and hence the concept it expresses) when we grasp the fact that the "uncontroversial instances" of the schema:

The proposition that p is true if and only if p

exhaust its content. (The limitation to "uncontroversial instances" is to exclude whatever leads to paradox.) The schema is taken as an axiom schema: the totality of its instances constitute the axioms of his theory.

This theory is, of course, incomplete until the controversial instances are specified in a non-question-begging way; and since the set of axioms is infinite, it does not meet one of Tarski's requirements for a satisfactory theory of truth. But perhaps the first difficulty can be overcome, and the second may be viewed as the price of having an unrelativized concept of truth. There are, further, the doubts many of us have about the existence of propositions, or at least of the principles for individuating them.

All these considerations give me pause, but I plan to ignore them here. I want to give deflationism its best chance, since it seems to me to be the only alternative to a more substantive view of truth, and most substantive views are in my opinion, as in Horwich's, clear failures. But although I enthusiastically endorse his arguments against correspondence, coherence, pragmatic, and epistemic theories, I cannot bring myself to accept Horwich's "minimal" theory.

I have two fundamental problems with Horwich's theory, either of which alone is reason to reject the theory if it cannot be resolved; and I do not think that either can be resolved.

The first problem is easy to state: I do not understand the basic axiom schema or its instances. It will help me formulate my difficulty to compare Horwich's axiom schema with Tarski's informal (and ultimately supplanted) schema:

"———" is true iff———.

Tarski's objection (among others) is that you can't turn this into a definition except by quantifying into a position inside quotation marks. The complaint ends up with a question about the clarity of quotations: how does what they refer to depend on the semantic properties of their constituents? It has sometimes been proposed to appeal to substitutional quantification, and one may wonder why Horwich can't generalize his schema:

(*p*) (the proposition that *p* is true iff *p*)

by employing substitutional quantification. But here Horwich quite rightly explains that he can't appeal to substitutional quantification to explain truth, since substitutional quantification must be explained by appeal to truth.

Why, though, doesn't Horwich try generalizing his schema by quantifying over propositions? The answer should be: because then we would have to view ordinary sentences as singular terms *referring* to propositions, not as *expressing* propositions. This brings me to the crux: how are we to understand phrases like "the proposition that Socrates is wise"? In giving a standard account of the semantics of the sentence "Socrates is wise", we make use of what the name "Socrates" names, and of the entities of which the predicate "is wise" is true. But how can we use these semantic features of the sentence "Socrates is wise" to yield the reference of "the proposition that Socrates is wise"? Horwich does not give us any guidance here. Could we say that expressions like "the proposition that Socrates is wise" are semantically unstructured, or at least that after the words "the proposition that" (taken as a functional expression) a sentence becomes a semantically unstructured name of the proposition it expresses? Taking this course would leave us with an infinite primitive vocabulary, and the appearance of the words "Socrates is wise" in two places in the schema would be of no help in understanding the schema or its instances. A further proposal might be to modify our instance of the schema to read:

> The proposition expressed by the sentence "Socrates is wise" is true iff Socrates is wise.

But following this idea would require relativizing the quoted sentence to a language, a need which Horwich must circumvent.

So let me put my objection briefly as follows: the same sentence appears twice in instances of Horwich's schema, once after the words "the proposition that", in a context that requires the result to be a singular term, the subject of a predicate, and once as an ordinary sentence. We cannot eliminate this iteration of the same sentence without destroying all appearance of a theory. But we can't *understand* the result of the iteration unless we can see how to make use of the same semantic features of the repeated sentence in both of its appearances—make use of them in giving the semantics of the schema instances. I do not see how this can be done.

My second difficulty with Horwich's theory is more dependent on my own further convictions and commitments. Horwich recognizes that to maintain that truth has, as he says, "a certain purity", he must show that we can understand it fully in isolation from other ideas, and we can understand other ideas in isolation from it. He does not say there are no relations between the concept of truth and other concepts; only that we can understand these concepts independently. There are several crucial cases so far as I am concerned, since I do not think we can understand meaning or any of the propositional attitudes without the concept of truth. Let me pick one of these: meaning.

Since Horwich thinks of truth as primarily attributable to propositions, he must explain how we can also predicate it of sentences and utterances, and he sees that to explain this without compromising the independence of truth, we must understand meaning without direct appeal to the concept of truth. On this critical matter, Horwich is brief, even laconic. Understanding a sentence, he says, does not *consist* in knowing its truth conditions, though if we understand a sentence we usually *know* its truth conditions. Understanding a sentence, he maintains, consists in knowing its "assertability conditions" (or "proper use"). He grants that these conditions may include that the sentence (or utterance) be true. I confess I do not see how, if truth is an assertability condition, and knowing the assertability conditions *is* understanding, we can understand a sentence without having the concept of truth.

I realize, however, that this is disputed territory, and that heavy thinkers like Dummett, Putnam, and Soames, following various leads suggested by Wittgenstein and Grice, believe that an account of meaning can be made to depend on a notion of assertability or use which does not in turn appeal to the concept of truth.

My hopes lie in the opposite direction: I think the sort of assertion that is linked to understanding already incorporates the concept of truth: we are *justified* in asserting a sentence in the required sense only if we believe the sentence we use to make the assertion is true; and what ultimately ties language to the world is that the conditions that typically cause us to hold sentences true *constitute* the truth conditions, and hence the meanings, of our sentences. This is not the place to argue this. For now I must simply remark that it would be a shame if we had to develop a theory of meaning for a speaker or a language independently of a theory of truth for that speaker or language, since we have at least *some* idea how to formulate a theory of truth, but no serious idea how to formulate a theory of meaning based on a concept of assertability or use.

I conclude that the prospects for a deflationary theory of truth are dim. Its attractions seem to me entirely negative: it avoids, or at least tries to avoid, well marked dead ends and recognizable pitfalls.

Let me suggest a diagnosis of our aporia about truth. We are still under the spell of the Socratic idea that we must keep asking for the *essence* of an idea, a significant *analysis* in other terms, an answer to the question what *makes* this an act of piety, what *makes* this, or any, utterance, sentence, belief, or proposition true. We still fall for the freshman fallacy that demands that we *define* our terms as a prelude to saying anything further with or about them.

It may seem pointless to make so much of the drive to define truth when it is unclear who is trying to do it: not Tarski, who proves it can't be done; not Horwich, who disclaims the attempt. Who, then, *admits* to wanting to define the concept of truth? Well, that's right. But. But the same ugly urge to define shows up in the guise of trying to provide a brief criterion, schema, partial, but leading hint, in place of a strict definition. Since Tarski, we are leery of the word "definition" when we are thinking of a concept of truth not relativized to a language, but we haven't given up the definitional urge. Thus I see Horwich's schema on a par *in this regard* with Dummett's notion of justified assertability, Putnam's ideally justified assertability, and the various formulations of correspondence and coherence theories. I see all of them as, if not attempts at definitions in the strict sense, attempts at *substitutes* for definitions. In the case of truth, there is no short substitute.

Now I want to describe what I take to be a fairly radical alternative to the theories I have been discussing and (with unseemly haste) dismissing. What I stress here is the *methodology* I think is required rather than the more detailed account I have given elsewhere. The methodology can be characterized on the negative side by saying it offers no definition of the concept of truth, nor any quasi-definitional clause, axiom schema, or other brief substitute for a definition. The positive proposal is to attempt to trace the connections between the concept of truth and the human attitudes and acts that give it body.

My methodological inspiration comes from finitely axiomatized theories of measurement, or of various sciences, theories that put clear constraints on one or more undefined concepts, and then prove that any model of such a theory has intuitively desired properties—that it is adequate to its designed purpose. Since among the models will be all sorts of configurations of abstract entities, and endless unwanted patterns of empirical events and objects, the theory can be applied to, or tested against, such specific phenomena as mass or temperature only by indicating how the theory is to be applied to the appropriate objects or events. We can't demand a precise indication of how to do this; finding a useful method for applying the theory is an enterprise that goes along with tampering with the formal theory, and testing its correctness as interpreted.

We are interested in the concept of truth only because there are actual objects and states of the world to which to apply it: utterances, states of belief, inscriptions. If we did not understand what it was for such entities to be true, we wouldn't be able to characterize the contents of these states, objects, and events. So in addition to the formal theory of truth we must indicate how truth is to be predicated of these empirical phenomena.

Tarski's definitions make no mention of empirical matters, but we are free to ask of such a definition whether it fits the actual practice of some speaker or group of speakers—we may ask whether they speak the language for which truth has been defined. There is nothing about Tarski's definitions that prevents us from treating them in this way except the prejudice that if something is called a definition, the question of its "correctness" is moot. To put this prejudice to rest, I suggest that we omit the final step in Tarski's definitions, the step that turns his axiomatizations into explicit definitions. We can then in good conscience call the emasculated definition a theory, and accept the truth predicate as undefined. This undefined predicate expresses the *general*, intuitive, concept, applicable to any language, the concept against which we have always surreptitiously tested Tarski's definitions (as he invited us to do, of course).

We know a great deal about how this concept applies to the speech and beliefs and actions of human agents. We use it to interpret their utterances and beliefs by assigning truth conditions to them, and we judge those actions and attitudes by evaluating the likelihood of their truth. The empirical question is how to determine, by observation and induction, what the truth conditions of empirical truth vehicles are. It bears emphasizing: absent this empirical connection, the concept of truth has no application to, or interest for, our mundane concerns, nor, so far as I can see, does it have any content at all.

Consider this analogy: I think of truth as Frank Ramsey thought of probability. He convinced himself, not irrationally, that the concept of probability applies in the first instance to propositional attitudes; it is a measure of degree of belief. He went on to ask himself: how can we make sense of the concept of degree of belief (subjective probability). Subjective probability is not observable, either by the agent who entertains some proposition with less than total conviction and more than total disbelief, or by others who see and question him. So Ramsey axiomatized the pattern of preferences of an idealized agent who, more or less like the rest of us, adjusts his preferences for the truth of propositions (or states of affairs or events) to accord with his values and beliefs. He stated the conditions on which a pattern of such preferences would be "rational", and in effect proved that if these conditions were satisfied, one could reconstruct from the agent's preferences the relative strengths of that agent's desires and subjective probabilities. Ramsey did not suppose everyone is perfectly rational in the postulated sense, but he did assume that people are nearly enough so, in the long run, for his theory to give a content to the concept of subjective probability—or probability, as he thought of it.

A brilliant *strategy*! (Whether or not it gives a correct analysis of probability.) The concept of probability—or at least degree of belief—unobservable by the agent who has it and by his watchers, linked to an equally theoretical concept of cardinal utility, or subjective evaluation, and both tied to simple preference by the axiomatic structure. Simple preference in turn provides the crucial empirical basis through its manifestations in actual choice behavior.

We should think of a theory of truth for a speaker in the same way we think of a theory of rational decision: both describe structures we can find, with an allowable degree of fitting and fudging, in the behavior of more or less rational creatures gifted with speech. It is in the fitting and fudging that we give content to the undefined concepts of subjective probability and subjective values—belief and desire, as we briefly call them; and, by way of theories like Tarski's, to the undefined concept of truth.

A final remark. I have deliberately made the problem of giving empirical content to the concept of truth seem simpler than it is. It would be *relatively* simple if we could directly observe—take as basic evidence—what people *mean* by what they say. But meaning not only is a more obscure concept than that of truth; it clearly involves it: if you know what an utterance means, you know its truth conditions. The problem is to give *any* propositional attitude a propositional content: belief, desire, intention, meaning.

I therefore see the problem of connecting truth with observable human behavior as inseparable from the problem of assigning contents to all the attitudes, and this seems to me to require a theory which embeds a theory of truth in a larger theory which includes decision theory itself. The result will incorporate the major norms of rationality whose partial realization in the thought and behavior of agents makes those agents intelligible, more or less, to others. If this normative structure is formidably complex, we should take comfort in the fact that the more complex it is, the better our chance of interpreting its manifestations as thought and meaningful speech and intentional action, given only scattered bits of weakly interpreted evidence.

3 *Method and Metaphysics*

Language is man's metaphysical organ.

—Bruno Schulz

We should like our definition to do justice to the intuitions which adhere to the *classical Aristotelian conception of truth* . . .

I do not have any doubts that our formulation does conform to the intuitive content of that of Aristotle.

—Alfred Tarski[1]

Earlier (Essay 2) I spoke of Aristotle's four kinds of 'basic' sentences: (1) "There does not exist an x such that $x = 4$"; (2) "There exists an x such that $x = 4$ & $x = 5$"; (3) "There exists an x such that $x = 4$"; and, finally, (4) "It is not the case that there exists an x such that $x \ \square \ x$". I have said very little about the semantic structure of these sorts of 'basic' sentences beyond defending the possibility that all of them may be viewed as existential quantifications or their negations. In any case, many sentences are in this form, and those that are apparently say something about ontology. One impressive feature of Tarski's truth definitions is that if the language for which truth is being characterized allows for the indefinitely complex nesting of quantifiers (and this presumably includes all natural languages), there is no way to avoid a semantics of reference, a semantics which systematically relates expressions to objects. The study of

[1] "The Semantic Conception of Truth", *Philosophy and Phenomenological Research*, **4** (1944), pp. 342, 360.

the semantics of a language is necessarily a study of the ontology of the language.[2]

It is one thing to say that the semantics of a language forces us to engage with the ontology of the language; but can we learn anything from this about ontology itself, about what there is? I think we can. If we have the semantics of a language right, the objects we assign to the expressions of the language must exist. The proper semantic method leads to metaphysical conclusions.

Here two problems present themselves. Quine has argued that if one way of assigning objects to expressions will provide a satisfactory semantics for a language, endless other ways of assigning objects to the same expressions will do as well; "doing as well" means that the truth conditions of all sentences will be invariant as we vary the assignments. (This is what Quine calls the inscrutability of reference.) I think Quine is right; but this admission does less damage to the relation between semantics and ontology than we might think. The reason is that if we are to find a language intelligible, we must find it capable of talking about a great many of the same things that we talk about. We would not be able to make sense of a language that could talk about undetached rabbit parts, but could not talk about rabbits. Nor could we understand people who could speak only of numbers. So at worst, the inscrutability of reference may lead to strange assignments of objects to individual words; it cannot affect the overall ontology to which we find the language committed. And since the acceptable assignments are just those which accommodate all the evidence we have for the interpretation of a language, there is no real reason to call any acceptable assignment strange. I have long urged that the inscrutability of reference, like other forms of the so-called indeterminacy of translation, should be viewed as no more threatening to the objectivity of semantic interpretation than the existence of different forms of measurement (Fahrenheit, Centigrade; inches, centimeters; knots, miles per hour) is threatening to the objectivity of measurement.

---

[2] The substitutional interpretation of the quantifiers provides no real escape from this conclusion. For there are good reasons to think there is no avoiding ontic commitment to ordinary objects at the ground level of semantic analysis. See, for example, S. Kripke, "Is there a Problem about Substitutional Quantification?", in *Truth and Meaning*, ed. G. Evans and J. McDowell, Oxford University Press, 1976.

The second problem that arises in trying to draw ontological consequences from semantics is more serious. In describing the semantics, and hence the ontology, of a language we must perforce appeal to the entities *we* think exist. But these are just the entities that belong to the ontology of our own language; there is no way we can progress beyond our own resources by doing semantics. So why pretend that in doing semantics we learn anything more about what exists than we can learn by directly asking (or setting out to discover) what exists?

Part of the answer to this question lies in the systematic character of semantics. The ontological commitments of a sentence like "Whales are mammals" are by no means obvious. The difficulties become apparent when one asks for an account of the truth conditions of this and related sentences that will reveal why certain patterns of inference are valid. It was not until Frege that anything approaching a satisfactory semantics for such sentences was produced. Even Frege did not quite have the concept of a semantic *theory* in the sense in which Tarski's truth definitions can be said to provide such theories. And Tarski's theories are ontological eye openers. Tarski finds no need of entities to correspond to sentences; no facts, states of affairs, no truth values, like Frege's The True and The False. Explaining the semantic role of predicates also requires no entities; no universals or extensions (though the latter are easily constructed). The ontology of a language for someone working with Tarski's methods consists of just the entities over which the variables range; for Tarski, as for Quine, to be is to be the value of a variable.

Much of the work of a systematic semantics consists, then, in locating the positions that can be occupied by variables. This can be difficult and rewarding, as Russell's theory of descriptions demonstrated. When I first came to appreciate the power of systematic semantics, I was convinced that there must be unique solutions to many of the basic problems of ontology. This conviction faded slowly as I discovered that many of the principles I had taken for granted as governing good semantic practice could be challenged. Nevertheless, I remain convinced that the discipline is a productive one. For one thing, it is often easy to demonstrate that one or another semantic proposal is inconsistent with demands one is unwilling to relinquish. Not everyone agrees, for example, that a learnable language must have a finite vocabulary, or that a satisfactory theory of truth for a language must be finitely axiomatizable. Nevertheless, for someone like me who is inclined to accept these conditions, it is instructive to realize that many apparently attractive ways of avoiding ontological commitments are ruled out; and even someone uncertain of the principles may be sobered by the discovery that standard semantic methods may not be available to him. (Examples: if we accept the finitist principles I just mentioned, quotations cannot be regarded as unstructured singular terms; adverbial theories of perception or propositional attitudes are not a way to circumvent positing entities sensed or believed.)

Speaking of adverbs, their semantic analysis is a problem that long vexed me. It is not obvious what semantic category they belong to. They are apparently not names, or predicates, and it is hard to see how they can be functional expressions, since there are no singular terms for them to operate on. In the end, I decided that they were like adjectives, that is, from a semantic point of view, like predicates. But this is possible only if there are entities for them to be true of. This line of reasoning convinced me that there *are* such entities, namely events. This conjecture, though it complicates the seemingly simple structure of sentences like "Joan hit Jack", solves a number of problems about action sentences and sentences of the form "Deborah saw Jonathan wash the dishes". It settles the question of the logical form of singular causal sentences such as "The first shot caused the riot" in a way that is exactly parallel to Frege's solution to the analysis of "before" and "after" in sentences like "The argument came after their wedding". It explains in a natural way the relation between sentences like "Sam collapsed at the door" and "Sam's collapse was at the door". (The semantics of the first is suggested by "There was an event x such that x was a collapse, x was by Sam, and x was at the door"; the second becomes "There was one and only one event x...")

If an ontology of events were the only way to give a satisfactory semantic analysis of these sentences and the relations between such sentences, it would, in my opinion, provide a very strong argument for the claim that there are events. I do not myself think that there is now another satisfactory analysis available, despite the recent efforts of Jonathan Bennett and others to construct a viable alternative. But whether or not I am right about this, the example shows in a clear way how semantic considerations are relevant to questions of ontology.

I claimed just now that if positing events were the only way to provide a satisfactory semantics for a language, this would supply a very strong argument for the existence of events. Why is this? The simplest, though by no means conclusive, argument is this. Speaking from a simple heart, and leaving global forms of skepticism aside, it is hard to accept that *all* sentences about cause and effect, before and after, all sentences like "The earthquake last night was less than 7 on the Richter scale" and "The earthquake last night was at least 7 on the Richter scale," are false. Unless we are massively mistaken about the nature of the world, not just about the objects that exist, but about the things that happen to them, events must belong to the furniture of the world; always provided, of course, we have the semantics right.

It is disappointing, though, not to go further, and show that a correct semantics for any language must hit on the grand outline of the true ontology. I once argued for this idea on the ground that a correct semantic interpretation of a language must be one that makes the speakers of that language intelligible to the interpreter. I urged, correctly it seems to me, that if the meanings of words are due to the sentences in which they occur and which are held true (and the relations of these sentences to other sentences held true), then there are limits to how much of what the interpreter deems to be error the interpreter can attribute to a speaker. Some error, even quite a lot, can be found intelligible, but only if there is an adequate background of agreement. The limits are not clear, since intelligibility is a matter of degree. Nevertheless, it seems plain that intelligible difference cannot go to the point of denying the truth of all the sentences which, if I am right about the semantics, require that there be events.

The argument so far aims only at establishing that a correct interpretation of one person's language by another person must end up with a large degree of basic agreement about ontology— agreement about the sorts of things that exist. But why couldn't it happen that interpreter and interpreted shared massive error? The answer that appealed to me then, and still seems to me essentially correct, is that if we imagine an omniscient and methodologically correct interpreter, we realize that he or she must interpret any speaker as having largely correct beliefs. If an interpreter who is right about the world and correct in his interpretations necessarily finds a speaker largely right, then the speaker must actually be largely right.

This brief argument has, predictably, failed to convince all skeptics, and one sympathizes with the doubters. For one thing it is not obvious exactly what the "omniscient" interpreter is supposed to know. Not everything, for then he would know what the speaker believed without having to go through the process of interpretation the nature of which is supposed to guarantee substantial agreement between interpreter and speaker. And if the precise character of the omniscient interpreter's knowledge can be specified, there remains the vagueness of the claim that a speaker must be "largely" right. How largely? How, in more detail, is the nature of interpretation supposed to insure the right sort of agreement?

If we ask for a somewhat more colorful story about why the correct understanding of a speaker constrains an interpreter to find a speaker mostly right, we find two methodological principles at work. The first concerns the *pattern* of beliefs an interpreter finds it possible intelligibly to attribute to an agent. Thus to return to an earlier point, the interpreter will reject a semantic interpretation of a sentence a speaker holds true if the interpretation makes that sentence an obvious contradiction. The interpreter will look askance at an interpretation that finds contradictory two sentences the speaker holds true. Quite generally he must favor interpretations that make the speaker a subscriber to his own, the interpreter's, standards of consistency and rationality, though of course there are times when inconsistency at some point is the best way to accommodate the data. The point behind this policy should be obvious; propositions are identified by the position they occupy among other propositions. If someone seems to have shifted a proposition too far out of position, the reasons for identifying it as *that* proposition will be lost.

From semantics we have been led to ontology, and now to a closely related truth about people, or, indeed, any creature capable of thought. This is that it is impossible to *believe* a contradiction; in this respect, our beliefs about the world cannot be false. It is possible, however, to believe contradictory propositions: one can believe that some proposition p is true, and also believe that the negation of *p* is true. What one cannot believe is that a proposition of the form [*p* and not *p*] is true. One way to see why this is the case is to realize that nothing could count as an adequate reason for attributing such a belief to a person. Thought and belief belong to the realm of rationality. Considerable deviations from rationality are consistent with an underlying rationality; but the more extreme the deviations, the less clear it is how the deviations are to be described, and so the less clear it becomes that the norms of thought obtain. Flat and obvious contradiction is beyond the limit of deviation; here the concept of thought loses application.

Of course it is possible to *think* you believe a contradiction; Heracleitus thought so. But he was wrong.

The same sort of consideration applies to inductive relations among beliefs, and hence among interpreted sentences held true by an agent. When a word has multiple criteria of application, we can tolerate an interpretation which loosens some of the connections as long as enough are retained. When Tyler Burge asks us to believe that someone means that he has arthritis in his thigh when he says, "I have arthritis in my thigh", Burge is careful to have his speaker use the word "arthritis" in what we would call a correct way in many other situations. (Even then, we have to suppose the speaker has no Greek.)

The second methodological principle deals not with con-sistency but with the causal connections between the agent and the world. These are of two sorts, depending on the direction of the causality: action reveals the effects of an agent's thoughts on the world outside him, while sensation mediates the effects of the world on the agent's beliefs. The principle simply says these causal connections must be respected in interpretation. If someone is regularly prompted by owls attended to in good light to hold the sentence "There's a fowl" true, then, other things being in accord with this interpretation, the best hypothesis is that the speaker uses the word "fowl" to refer to owls. Such direct conditionings of words to objects must lie at the basis of correct interpretation; and if this is so, correct interpretation makes a speaker believe a lot of true things about what exists.

Thus it seems that truth is like the proverbial door which no one can miss; at least it is a door one cannot miss most of the time.

4 *Meaning, Truth, and Evidence*

Our knowledge of the world depends directly or indirectly on elaborate and perilous causal sequences that originate with events like a rabbit scurrying by, or a spasm in the stomach, progress through the nervous system, and terminate in beliefs. Where, in the chain of causes and effects, do we come across the items that give our beliefs their particular contents and our words their meanings? As homespun realists it would be good to be able to point to the rabbit or the muscle as the natural focus of thoughts touched off by the scurrying and the spasm. But simply saying this leaves too much to chance and unexplained invention. How can the mere firing of nerves, so haphazardly correlated with rabbits and muscles, result in states said to be about rabbits and muscles? An intelligible account of the contents of our thoughts must, it seems, start closer to the terminus. What we should look for, perhaps, is the mental raw material of thoughts: sensations, sense data, the unformed stuff of experience. But this too is shaky speculation, an appeal to phenomena more postulated for the sake of the problem than independently open to study and observation.

A clever compromise brilliantly advocated by Quine is to tie meaning and content to the firings of sensory nerves. This comes about as close as science allows to the end product, presumably a brain state or change, and yet remains reassuringly physical and publicly observable, at least in principle. The dependence of meaning and belief on patterns of stimulation is one thing that makes Quine's epistemology naturalistic, and it is what places him in the empiricist tradition. It is also an idea which, for all its attractions, I think Quine should abandon. The abandonment would not entail giving up naturalism, but it would mean relinquishing what remains of empiricism after the first two dogmas have been surrendered.

Empiricism, like other isms, we can define pretty much as we please, but I take it to involve not only the pallid claim that all knowledge of the world comes through the agency of the senses, but also the conviction that this fact is of prime epistemological significance. The pallid idea merely recognizes the obvious causal role of the senses in mediating between objects and events in the world and our thoughts and talk about them; empiricism locates the ultimate evidence for those thoughts at this intermediate step. (This characterization will undergo modification in what follows.)

I once wrote that Quine subscribed to what I called the dualism of scheme and content, and I suggested that accepting this dualism constituted the third dogma of empiricism.[1] What I had in mind as the scheme was language, with its built-in ontology and theory of the world; the content was supplied by the patterned firing of neurons. I argued that something like the notion of uninterpreted content was necessary if we were to make sense of conceptual relativism, and I thought Quine's neurological substitute for sense data provided the needed basis for his conceptual relativism. Quine answered back with 'On the very idea of a third dogma'.[2]

My present concern, however, is not so much with schemes as with the other member of the dyad, content. On this point Quine was, as one might expect, or even hope, unrepentant; he reaffirmed the importance of an essentially private source of evidence. 'Empiricism . . . as a theory of evidence . . . remains with us, minus indeed the two old dogmas. The third purported dogma, understood . . . in relation . . . to warranted belief, remains intact.'[3] I had quoted passages from Quine that appealed to the 'tribunal of experience' and the like, and he pointed out, fairly enough, that such metaphorical talk had been supplanted in *Word and Object* by literal talk of surface irritations and observation sentences.

---

[1]   The reference is to my 'On the very idea of a conceptual scheme', in *Inquiries into Truth and Interpretation*, Oxford University Press, 1984.

[2]   W. V. Quine, 'On the very idea of a third dogma', in *Theories and Things*, Cambridge, Mass., Belknap Press, 1981. In this reply, Quine mistakenly took my picture of his dualism of scheme and content to involve a separation of conceptual scheme and language. I had no such division in mind; what I argued was that something like the notion of uninterpreted content was necessary to make sense of conceptual relativism, and I thought I found more than a hint of such relativism in Quine.   [3]   Ibid., p. 39.

So let's see if the issue can be joined on Quine's chosen territory. I am happy to accept Quine's characterization of empiricism: 'Two cardinal tenets of empiricism remain unassailable... One is that whatever evidence there *is* for science *is* sensory evidence. The other... is that all inculcation of meanings of words must rest ultimately on sensory evidence.'[4] I promise not to misunderstand the word 'sensory' here; it is not intended to refer to something psychological and subjective. The idea is just that 'surface irritations... exhaust our clues to an external world'.[5] Clearest of all, perhaps, is the claim that '... our only source of information about the external world is through the impact of light rays and molecules upon our sensory surfaces'.[6] That Quine had in mind what I call the epistemological dualism of scheme and content is strongly suggested in *Word and Object*, where he writes,

we can investigate the world, and man as a part of it, and thus find out what cues he could have of what goes on around him. Subtracting his cues from his world view, we get man's net contribution as the difference. This difference marks the extent of man's sovereignty the domain within which he can revise theory while saving the data.[7]

The cues or data are what I mean by the content. I think there is no such concept of ultimate evidence, and so the process of subtraction that would legitimate the idea of alternative schemes is not available.

None of these passages really settles the matter, however, since it is not obvious that the concept of evidence is basic in Quine's theory of evidence. Despite the apparent tendency of the remarks I have quoted, it may be that nothing in Quine's official doctrine quite plays the role of evidence or ultimate data.

There is a section of *The Roots of Reference* that helps sharpen the issue.[8] In the course of outlining how a language is acquired Quine turns to the study of the relation between language and

[4] *Ontological Relativity*, New York, Columbia University Press, 1969, p. 75.
[5] *Word and Object*, Cambridge, Mass., MIT Press, 1960, p. 22.
[6] 'The nature of natural knowledge', in *Mind and Language*, ed. S. Guttenplan, Oxford University Press, 1975, p. 68. Also: 'The stimulation of his sensory receptors is all the evidence anybody has had to go on, ultimately, in arriving at his picture of the world': *Ontological Relativity*, p. 75.
[7] *Word and Object*, p. 5. Also: 'Given only the evidence of our senses, how do we arrive at our theory of the world? Bodies are not given in our sensations, but only inferred from them': *The Roots of Reference*, La Salle, Ill., Open Court, 1974, p. 1.
[8] *The Roots of Reference*, p. 10. The quotations that follow are from this section.

observations. This relation has two aspects: an epistemological aspect 'through which the sentences affirmed in the theory gain their support', and a semantical aspect—the relation through which sentences gain their meaning. '... we learn the language by relating its terms to the observations that elicit them... this learning process is a matter of fact, accessible to empirical science. By exploring it, science can in effect explore the evidential relation between science itself and its supporting observations.' Here again the scheme–content idea seems to be operating; but whether there is anything to which to raise a reasonable objection is unclear. No one, surely, can object to the empirical study of how we come to have the views we do.

At first all seems straightforward. 'Ostensive learning', we read, 'is fundamental, and requires observability. The child and the parent must both see red when the child learns "red", and one of them must see also that the other sees red at the time.' This simple triangular arrangement of the two agents and a commonly observed object is indeed fundamental, and I shall return to it presently. But what, in this scenario, counts as the evidence? Is it the seeing of something red—the experienced sensation? Or is it rather the event of seeing that something is red—the coming to have a propositional attitude? Quine wisely chooses neither: he proposes, as he says, to drop the talk of observation and to talk instead of observation sentences like 'This is red' and 'There's a rabbit.' Such sentences do not report observations; in general they are not about sensations or experience but about the objects which are denizens of our theory of the world. Observation sentences are at the 'observational end' of language, and so closest to whatever counts as evidence; but we have not yet discovered what it is that supports the theory and gives sentences their meaning. Quine does not, I think, ever directly answer the question in what the evidence consists on which our theory of the world depends. But the answer is perhaps contained in the definition of observation sentence. Quine defines a sentence as observational 'insofar as its truth value, on any occasion, would be agreed to by just about any member of the speech community witnessing the occasion'. He adds that instead of speaking of the joint witnessing of an occasion it would be more precise to speak of witnesses subject to receptually similar impingements—that is, subject to similar patterns of nerve firings. He allows that there are problems in comparing such patterns from person to person, but contends that the definition is 'good as behavioral concepts go'.[9]

This is not Quine's last word on the subject, for more recently he has introduced an important change in the definition of observation sentence. This is not surprising, since there is a sticky point in the original definition—the dependence on the idea of two speakers belonging to the same speech community. In *The Roots of Reference* and *Ontological Relativity* this idea had been made behavioral by saying 'we can recognize membership in the speech community by mere fluency of dialogue, something we can witness even without knowing the language'.[10] This criterion is threatened on one side by circularity and on the other by contradiction. By circularity, since much of the point of introducing observation sentences is to specify the conditions that must be satisfied by an acceptable translation manual, and a plausible definition of what it is for a speaker to belong to a given speech community is that translation manuals that work for the community work for him. By contradiction, since if fluency of dialogue is an independent criterion, it may not yield the same results as the account of radical translation (there may be fluency of dialogue between speakers for whom the same translation manuals will not work).

In any case, Quine has apparently abandoned the social criterion of the observation sentence in favor of the following: 'If querying the sentence elicits assent from a given speaker on one occasion, it will elicit assent likewise on any other occasion when the same total set of receptors is triggered ... This and this only is what qualifies sentences as observation sentences.'[11] It seems to me that this characterization of observation sentences, while it less clearly distinguishes observation sentences from other occasion sentences, is superior in not assuming that the concept of a speech community is clear in advance of an account of meaning.

---

[9] This characterization of observation sentences is essentially that of *Word and Object*, p. 43, and *Ontological Relativity*, pp. 86–7.

[10] *The Roots of Reference*, p. 39; *Ontological Relativity*, p. 87.

[11] *Theories and Things*, p. 25. A later version: 'An observation sentence in my unproblematic sense of the phrase is just any sentence that we have come to associate with some range of stimulations, and firmly enough to be prepared to accept the occurrence of such stimulation as attesting to the truth of the sentence ... the stimulation decides the truth of the sentence on the occasion of the stimulation.' 'Meaning, truth, and reference', paper delivered to the Institut International de Philosophie in Palermo, 1985.

It is obvious that sensory promptings play a central role in Quine's account of meaning and evidence, but what exactly is that role? One answer is, as we have already noted, that the firing of sensory neurons is an essential intermediate causal link between events in the world and the formation of many beliefs. Another answer is that in learning a language the conditioning of sentences to sensory stimulations is crucial. These remarks—near platitudes as they stand—do not decide what the connection is between sensory stimulations and evidence, and so do not decide the exact nature of Quine's empiricism. What is needed is a description of *how* sensory stimulations determine the meaning—the content— of observation sentences.

We can, then, avoid answering the question about what constitutes evidence and ask instead what determines the meaning of observation sentences. We can't say that sensory stimulations are the evidence, since an agent normally neither observes nor knows about them. Nor can we say sensory stimulations provide the evidence, since the beliefs and the associated verbal dispositions which the stimulations engender are not basic evidence, but based on it. Nothing, it seems, is properly called the evidence. Surprisingly, perhaps, it does not matter; the theory of evidence, as Quine conceives it, can forget about evidence and simply study the relation between sensory stimulations and the meaning of the observation sentences to which the stimulations prompt assent and dissent.

The meaning of an observation sentence is its stimulus meaning. The stimulus meaning of a sentence S for a speaker is, nearly enough, the ordered pair consisting of the set of patterns of stimulation that would prompt assent to S, and the set of stimulations that would prompt dissent from S.[12] Not that Quine has any great interest in finding an entity worth calling a meaning; the concept of stimulus meaning does its work by providing a criterion of sameness of meaning. Two observation sentences have the same meaning for a speaker if the patterns of stimulation that cause assent to one sentence cause assent to the other; similarly for dissent. An observation sentence S of one speaker has the same meaning as the sentence T of another speaker if the prompting patterns are approximately the same. This is the foundation of radical translation.

---

[12] *Word and Object*, pp. 32–3.

If I have labored what is obvious to any student of Quine's work, it is because I want to focus attention on the difference between the account of meaning and evidence that I have been discussing and another account that will also be found in Quine's work, often in the same books and articles from which I have been quoting. The difference between the two accounts may not seem important, but I shall argue that the character of Quine's empiricism depends on which account is accepted.

The alternative theory of meaning and evidence is simply that the events and objects that determine the meaning of observation sentences and yield a theory of evidence are the very events and objects that the sentences are naturally and correctly interpreted as being about. This idea appears frequently in Quine's work, sometimes accompanied by the sensory stimulation story and sometimes not. I have already quoted the bit on ostension in *The Roots of Reference*: 'The child and the parent must both see red when the child learns "red", and one of them must see also that the other sees red at the time.' Perhaps seeing red is just having the right cones irradiated; but then it is not obvious how the parent can see that the child sees red. So I assume that in this passage 'seeing red' must mean 'seeing something (public) that is red'. The same note is struck in a very recent article. Observation sentences, Quine says, '...hinge pretty strictly on the concurrent publicly observable situation'.[13] The idea also comes over strongly in a talk Quine gave in Oxford in 1974:

consider the case where we teach the infant a word by reinforcing his random babbling on some appropriate occasion. His chance utterance bears a chance resemblance to a word appropriate to the occasion, and we reward him. The occasion must be some object or some stimulus source that we as well as the child are in a position to notice. Furthermore, we must be in a position to observe that the child is in a position to notice it...the fixed points are just the shared stimulus and the word...the occasions that make the sentence true are going to have to be intersubjectively recognizable.[14]

Here the stimulus cannot be at or in the nervous system, since it is shared, and one need not be in any particular position to appreciate it.

[13] 'Indeterminacy of translation again', *The Journal of Philosophy*, **84** (1987), p. 6.
[14] 'Mind and verbal dispositions', in *Mind and Language*, pp. 83–4 and 88. The same idea will be found in *Ontological Relativity*, pp. 28 and 81.

The location of a stimulus is, of course, notoriously ambiguous. We can place it almost anywhere in the causal chain that leads from far outside to various parts of the central nervous system. Quine offers us a choice between two of the possible locations: at the sensory receptors, or at the objects and events our observation sentences are typically about. There is no contradiction, needless to say, in acknowledging the role of any and every relevant causal factor in giving an account of learning, language learning included. But it makes a vast difference whether meaning and evidence are tied to the proximal or the distal stimulus. Mindful of a certain tradition, let us call the two resulting theories of meaning and evidence the *proximal theory* and the *distal theory*.

Now to clarify the issue. The analysis of meaning and evidence both depend on meaning, so we may narrow our attention to the question how meaning, particularly at the bottom level ('Lo, a rabbit!', 'That's red') is determined. The point of meaning is synonymy—sameness of meaning, whether of different sentences for the same speaker or different speakers, or of the same sentence from speaker to speaker. Of these cases, interpersonal sameness of meaning is by far the most important and revealing, since it is what is required for communication. Thus whatever difference there is between proximal and distal theories will show up in the answer each theory gives to the question when sentences (the same or different) have the same meaning for two people. In two words: it will show up when we come to do radical translation.

On the proximal theory, which at least until recently seems to have been Quine's official theory, sentences have the same meaning if they have the same stimulus meaning—if the same patterns of stimulation prompt assent and dissent. In such a case we may speak of stimulus synonymy. Stimulus synonymy is not much direct help in translating non-observation sentences, but it does about as well as can be done for observation sentences, and supplies the basis for all translation.

The distal theory, on the other hand, depends primarily on shared causes which are salient for speaker and interpreter, learner and teacher. Meanings are shared when identical events, objects or situations cause or would cause assent and dissent. As a radical interpreter I correlate verbal responses of a speaker with changes in the environment. Inferring a causal relation, I then translate those verbal responses with a sentence of my own that the same changes in the environment cause me to accept or reject. This is the distal theory at its simplest, subject to various fairly obvious caveats.

Do the two theories conflict? If the success, even the truth, of a person's view of the world lies entirely in its ability to organize and predict patterns of sensory stimulation, there would be no difference. It is perhaps thinking along these lines that has encouraged Quine to call ordinary physical objects 'posits' and their existence a 'hypothesis'.[15] Since the stimulations of our sense organs are 'all we have to go on', 'all our evidence', the most we can ask of the posits is that they organize the stimulations in a usefully simple way. 'What', asks Quine, 'does our overall scientific theory really claim regarding the world? Only that it is somehow so structured as to assure the sequences of stimulations that our theory gives us to expect. More concrete demands are indifferent to our scientific theory itself.'[16]

In saying this Quine was replying to Barry Stroud's worry that it might happen that '. . . the world is completely different in general from the way our sensory impacts and our internal makeup lead us to think of it'.[17] Quine replies that this difference would make no difference; since observation sentences are 'conditioned holophrastically to stimulations', all links of sentences to observational evidence will remain unchanged; changes an interpreter might make in the ontology he attributes to the speaker would simply attest to the inscrutability of reference: 'The objects, or values of the variables, serve only as nodes in a verbal network whose *termini a quis et ad quos* are observations, stimulatory occasions.' From the point of view of the subject, nothing detectable would have happened: 'Save the structure and you save all.'[18]

But is this right? Pursuing now my own line rather than Stroud's, let us imagine someone who, when a warthog trots by, has just the patterns of stimulation I have when there's a rabbit in

---

[15] *Word and Object*, p. 22.

[16] 'Reply to Stroud', in *Midwest Studies in Philosophy VI: The Foundations of Analytic Philosophy*, ed. P. A. French, T. E. Uehling, Jr and H. K. Wettstein, Minneapolis, University Of Minnesota Press, 1981, p. 474.

[17] 'The significance of naturalized epistemology', in *Midwest Studies in Philosophy VI*, p. 457.   [18] 'Reply to Stroud', pp. 473–4.

view. Let us suppose the one-word sentence the warthog inspires him to assent to is 'Gavagai!' Going by stimulus meaning, I translate his 'Gavagai!' by my 'Lo, a rabbit' though I see only a warthog and no rabbit when he says and believes (according to the proximal theory) that there is a rabbit. The supposition that leads to this conclusion is not absurd; simply a rearranged sensorium. Mere astigmatism will yield examples, deafness others; little green men and women from Mars who locate objects by sonar, like bats, present a more extreme case, and brains in vats controlled by mad scientists can provide any world you or they please. According to the proximal theory each of these speakers will be wrong to some degree about the world as conceived by a normal interpreter—the brain in the vat can be as wrong as Stroud feared. Yet each has a theory that saves the structure of his sensations. One can see why M. J. Cresswell accused Quine of having a realm of reified experience or appearance set over against an inscrutable reality. Quine replied to Cresswell, 'My naturalistic view is unlike that. I have forces from real external objects impinging on our nerve endings, and I have us acquiring sentences about real external objects.'[19] Quine doesn't settle for a realm of experience or appearance, reified or not, nor is reality for him inscrutable. But there is the realm of sensory stimulations, and a further realm of objects that one can, from another's point of view, have very wrong. The causal connections Quine's naturalism assumes between external situations and stimulations are, if we stick to the proximal theory, no guarantee we have an even roughly correct view of a public world. Although each speaker may be content that his view is the true one, since it squares with all his stimulations, once he notices how globally mistaken others are, and why, it is hard to think why he would not wonder whether *he* had it right. Then he might wonder what it could mean to get it right.

If the difficulty I find in the proximal theory sounds much like old-fashioned skepticism of the senses, this should occasion no surprise. In spite of abjuring sense data and the reduction of theoretical terms to observational, Quine's proximal account of meaning and evidence leads to skepticism in much the same way as older theories did. The reason is that skepticism rests on the

---

[19] 'Replies to eleven essays', in *Theories and Things*, p. 181.

assumption neither of sense data nor of reductionism, but on the much more general idea that empirical knowledge requires an epistemological step between the world as we conceive it and our conception of it, and this idea is at the heart of Quine's proximal theory. An appeal to naturalism will not help, for to appeal to naturalism is to appeal to science as we know it, and if the proximal theory is part of science, then science shows us that we can have no grounds for saying our theory of the world is better than our neighbor's, though we may be in a position to show that if our theory is true, our neighbor's is wildly false.

One possible reaction to this situation is to hold that truth is immanent in the sense that a sentence of yours may be true for you though I correctly translate it into a false sentence of mine. You will, of course, return the compliment. This is relativity of truth not of the familiar and unavoidable kind that relativizes the truth of sentences to a language, but a further and independent relativization to individuals who may (or may not) speak what is, from the proximal point of view, the same language. Our example of the alien who was prompted to assent to 'Gavagai!' by the patterns of stimulation that prompt me to assent to 'Lo, a rabbit' is a case where a sentence true in the alien's language is translated (in accord with the proximal theory) by a sentence false in mine (since he assents to 'Gavagai!' only when I dissent from 'Lo, a rabbit' and vice versa). We can also imagine a case where two people mean the same thing (again according to the proximal theory) by all their sentences and yet the same sentence is true under external circumstances that make that sentence false for the other. It should be noticed that this conclusion is not affected by, nor is a form of, one of the various sorts of indeterminacy of translation Quine has discussed: the relativity of truth that threatens the proximal theory introduces no new indeterminacy.

Quine has at times said some slightly mysterious things about the immanence of truth, but he has come out often and boldly against relativism. This is not inconsistent, since the mysterious remarks were about empirically equivalent but logically incompatible theories, and immanence there concerned not observation sentences but the theoretical part of the language. Such immanence cannot be counted as making truth relative in a pernicious sense, since it is merely a matter of various theories entertained by the same person, a case we may consider on a par with a choice among languages.[20] By contrast, the issue we are considering—the issue of the proximal versus the distal theory of meaning—concerns the meaning and truth conditions of observation sentences; and it arises not for a single agent choosing his theory or language, but for different speakers whose stimulus-synonymous sentences fail to agree in truth value.

The opposition between the proximal and the distal approach to meaning may be viewed as the opposition between a theory of meaning that makes evidence primary and a theory of meaning that makes truth primary. While Quine does not, as we have seen, identify evidence with sensory stimulations, he sees the role of sensory stimulations in defining stimulus meaning as the way to tie meaning to evidence, while a distal theory connects meaning directly to the conditions that make sentences intersubjectively true or false. In a review of a book edited by Gareth Evans and John McDowell Quine allies himself on this point with Michael Dummett and against the truth-conditional approach to meaning.[21] This way of stating the contrast is of course far too simple, since any theory of meaning must relate meaning both to truth and to evidence; and as Dummett and Putnam illustrate, it is possible to give truth itself an epistemic twist. Still, Quine, Putnam, and Dummett have committed themselves in much the same terms on the question as to whether truth or evidence should be considered primary in the theory of meaning, and all three have clearly voted for the latter.[22]

As will have become obvious, I think this is a mistake. I think it is a mistake because to base meaning on evidence necessarily leads to the difficulties of proximal theories: truth relativitized to individuals, and skepticism. Proximal theories, no matter how decked out, are Cartesian in spirit and consequence.

The only perspicuous concept of evidence is the concept of a relation between sentences or beliefs—the concept of evidential support. Unless some beliefs can be chosen on purely subjective

[20] See *Theories and Things*, pp. 21–2 and 29–30; *The Philosophy of W. V. Quine*, ed. L. E. Hahn and P. A. Schilpp, La Salle, Ill., Open Court, pp. 156–7.

[21] W. V. Quine, review of *Truth and Meaning*, ed. G. Evans and J. McDowell, Oxford University Press, 1976, in *The Journal of Philosophy*, 74 (1977), pp. 225–41.

[22] For Quine's vote, see review referred to in n. 21, p. 229; for Putnam's vote, see *Meaning and the Moral Sciences*, London, Routledge & Kegan Paul, 1978, p. 97; for Dummett's vote, 'What is a theory of meaning (II)' in *Truth and Meaning* may be taken as an example.

grounds as somehow basic, a concept of evidence as the foundation of meaning or knowledge is therefore not available. Of course each of us is inclined to trust some beliefs more than others, but this is a fact internal to our theories of the world, and so cannot be used to give them external support. The causal relations between the world and our beliefs are crucial to meaning not because they supply a special sort of evidence for the speaker who holds the beliefs, but because they are often apparent to others and so form the basis for communication.

The distal theory of meaning removes the sense organs and their immediate activities and manifestations, such as sensations and sensory stimulations, from central theoretical importance to meaning and knowledge. As Quine in his distal mood put it, '. . . the fixed points are just the shared stimulus and the world'. The *shared* stimulus is, of course, distal. The unsharable stimulations of the sense organs are not fixed points. In recognizing this we do not deny the causal role of the senses, only a certain epistemological view of that role. A distal theory is as basically causal and in accord with the deliverances of science as a proximal theory. The difference lies in the choice of the appropriate location of the relevant causal factors—and the choice of an epistemological stance. The approaches differ in how we interpret what Quine calls the 'two cardinal tenets of empiricism'. These are, once more, that 'whatever evidence there *is* for science *is* sensory evidence . . . and that all inculcation of meanings of words must rest ultimately on sensory evidence'.[23] The sense in which these tenets are true, I am urging, is one that supports only what I earlier named the pallid version of empiricism; it comes to no more than the factual claim that the sense organs are causally essential to empirical knowledge. It seems to me this is not an epistemological thesis that sets empiricists apart from those who hold other views of the nature of knowledge.

We remember that there are passages in *The Roots of Reference* in which Quine apparently espouses a distal theory: 'a sentence is observational insofar as its truth value, on an occasion, would be agreed to by just about any member of the speech community witnessing the occasion.' But then he corrects himself, maintaining that it would be more precise to speak of witnesses subject to

[23] See n. 4.

receptually similar impingements—that is, subject to similar patterns of nerve firings. Might the two positions, the proximal and the distal, be somehow reconciled, as this passage seems to suggest? One might think to rescue the proximal theory, for example, by counting as stimulus-synonymous sentences to which assent was prompted by different patterns of stimulations— different patterns for different people, according to the way that their nervous systems were variously arranged. The difficulty is that your pattern of stimulations and mine are guaranteed to prompt assent to distally intertranslatable sentences only if those patterns are caused by the same distal events. Such a theory would be a distal theory in transparent disguise, since the basis for translating your sentences into mine (and hence for comparing our sensory stimulations) would depend on the shared external situations that caused both our various stimulations and our verbal responses. All mention of sensory stimulations or other causal intermediaries could be dropped without cost to the theory of meaning, or the account of evidence and knowledge.

On Quine's proximal theory, all that matters to meaning (or the contents of thoughts) occurs within the skin of the speaker, and so this is all with which an interpreter need be concerned. Aside from Quine's physicalism, he here shares the company of Descartes, Frege, and Dummett, to mention a few. On a distal theory, causes external to the speaker matter directly to meaning, and so must be taken into account by an interpreter. But is it sufficiently clear *how* such external causes matter to meaning? The concept of causality is applied according to human interests (as both Quine and Putnam have emphasized in this context). Quine's proximal theory is also causal, but the elements that serve as cause and effect, namely sensory stimulations and verbal responses (or dispositions to such) are explicitly indicated. The distal theory I am urging Quine to accept is stuck with the notion of 'the' common cause of utterances (or dispositions to such). The problem that threatens is that there may be too many candidates for the common cause—for example any large slice of the history of the universe up to a time before the speaker or speakers were born. This slice might be a common cause of two speakers being disposed to assent to 'That's red', but it would be a cause of every other disposition of both speakers; a theory of meaning based on this idea would identify the meanings of all observation sentences.

What narrows down the choice of the relevant cause is what is salient for speakers and their interpreters. Salience is defined in terms of similarity of responses. We respond with the same sentence when presented with various different distal objects and events, or the same objects at different times and in different settings. We respond with 'Mama!' to appearances of mama seen or heard from many angles and distances, with 'Green!' to surfaces seen in many illuminations and reflecting many different wavelengths, with 'Lo, a rabbit!' to rabbits almost no matter what the guise. Mama, things colored green, rabbits are salient, what our verbal responses pick out as 'the' cause from among the many candidates. What makes communication possible is the sharing, inherited and acquired, of similarity responses. The interpreter's verbal responses class together or identify the same objects and events that the speaker's verbal responses class together. If the interpreter also classes together the verbal responses of the speaker, he can correlate items from two of his own classes; verbal responses of the speaker he finds similar and distal objects and events that he finds similar. To the latter he has his own verbal responses; these provide his translation or interpretation of the speaker's words. Thus the common cause becomes the common subject matter of speaker and interpreter.

We need not, then, be worried by the dependence of the concept of cause on our interests; it is our shared interests, our shared similarity responses, which decide what we count as a relevant cause. Science, it is true, strives to overcome the interest relativity of ordinary causality. But science may without prejudice or circularity note the facts about human nature that reflect interests: the facts about salience, attention, and tendencies to generalize in some ways rather than others.

These remarks about salience and its importance to interpretation are not very different from what Quine says in *The Roots of Reference* and elsewhere. He writes ' . . . linguistic inductions tend to be highly successful . . . [owing to] a sharing of similarity standards by the speaker and oneself'.[24] In this paper

---

[24] 'Facts of the matter', in *American Philosophy from Edwards to Quine*, ed. R. W. Shahan and K. R. Merrill, Norman, Okla., University of Oklahoma Press, 1977, p. 180; also *The Roots of Reference*, pp. 23, 44.

I have been arguing that Quine ought to give this insight a more central position in his theory of meaning.

Quine revolutionized our understanding of verbal communication by taking seriously the fact, obvious enough in itself, that there can be no more to meaning than an adequately equipped person can learn and observe; the interpreter's point of view is therefore the revealing one to bring to the subject. By openly espousing a distal rather than a proximal theory of meaning he would also be recognizing, and fully exploiting, the active role of the interpreter. This role, I suggest, requires that the interpreter correlate his own responses and those of the speaker by reference to the mutually salient causes in the world of which they speak.

5 *Pursuit of the Concept of Truth*

The important figures in the history of philosophy have almost always had both a strong negative and a strong positive agendum: they have seen, and made clear to all, what was wrong with ideas importantly current at the time, and they have proposed brilliant and intriguing alternatives. On both scores Quine makes the permanent list.

There is a far shorter roster of those who combine the two agenda in a special and heroic way: they have recognized error in their own work, have explained it far better than anyone else could, and have gone on either to mend what needed mending or to abandon a cherished thesis. I count in this category Hume, who, in an appendix to the first book of the *Treatise*, admitted that, having deconstructed a mind into its atomic parts, he could see no way to put it back together; Frege, who, in the face of Russell's paradox, conceded that his attempt to reduce mathematics to logic had failed; and G. E. Moore, who, when confronted with Charles Stevenson's emotive theory of ethics, allowed that goodness might not be an objective, unanalysable property. Quine belongs in this pantheon.

I cannot resist a parable. There is a retired graffiti artist who calls himself A-One. Reminiscing about his career, he said: A vandal is somebody who throws a brick through a window. An artist is somebody who paints a picture on that window. A great artist is somebody who paints a picture on the window and then throws a brick through it.

Something far more controlled than simple destruction is appropriate in Quine's case: I think of his own favorite image of Neurath's ship being patiently and ingeniously repaired and renewed while at sea.

The shift in Quine's thinking that I want to discuss and praise has been long in preparation, but it has become clearest in his recent book, *Pursuit of Truth* (1990). The shift concerns the relation between meaning and truth.

Early and late, Quine has been a deflationist about truth. A deflationist is one who holds that to say of a sentence in one's own language that it is true is to say no more than one says by uttering that sentence. Truth is disquotational: we can get rid of the predicate "is true" after the quotation of a sentence simply by removing the quotation marks as we erase the truth predicate. As Quine put it in *From a Logical Point of View*, we have a general paradigm, namely,

(T) "——" is true-in-L if and only if ——,

which, though not a definition of truth, serves to endow "true-in-L" with

> every bit as much clarity, in any particular application, as is enjoyed by the particular expressions of L to which we apply [it]. Attribution of truth in particular to "Snow is white" ... is every bit as clear to us as attribution of whiteness to snow.[1]

In *Word and Object* Quine remarks that "To say that the statement 'Brutus killed Caesar' is true, or that 'The atomic weight of sodium is 23' is true, is in effect simply to say that Brutus killed Caesar, or that the atomic weight of sodium is 23."[2] The theme is repeated thirty years later in *Pursuit of Truth*:

> ... there is surely no impugning the disquotation account; no disputing that "Snow is white" is true if and only if snow is white. Moreover, it is a full account; it explicates clearly the truth or falsity of every clear sentence.[3]

On this matter, Quine has not changed his mind.

Of course, Quine realizes that not every use of a truth predicate can be dispensed with so easily. There are times when "semantic ascent", ascent to a metalanguage, or anyway ascent

---

[1] W. V. Quine, *From a Logical Point of View*, rev. edn., Cambridge, Mass.: Harvard University Press, 1980, p. 138.

[2] W. V. Quine, *Word and Object*, Cambridge, Mass.: MIT Press, 1960, p. 24. In a footnote, Quine refers us to Tarski for "the classic development of this theme".

[3] W. V. Quine, *Pursuit of Truth*, Cambridge, Mass.: Harvard University Press, 1990, p. 93.

to talk of sentences rather than talk of what the sentences are about, is forced on us: times when we want to speak of the truth of sentences without having the sentences at hand. Examples: "The premisses of his argument may have been true, but the conclusion certainly wasn't", "What she said to our pursuers can't have been true, for they haven't found us yet". Faced with such uses of the truth predicate, we turn to Tarski, who showed how, by recursively specifying the truth conditions of every sentence in a language, we can avail ourselves of the truth predicate when the sentence or sentences said to be true can be mentioned but for some reason can't be used. Tarski's method still turns on disquotation, but not the disquotation of sentences, there being too many of them, but of the constituent words which, though finite in number, suffice to form all the sentences.

It is the disquotational feature of truth, in Quine's opinion, which makes truth so much clearer a concept than meaning. Comparing theory of meaning and theory of reference, Quine says that they constitute "...two provinces so fundamentally distinct as not to deserve a joint appellation at all".[4] The former deals with such tainted topics as synonymy, significance, and analyticity. The concepts treated by the latter, which include truth, are by contrast "...very much less foggy and mysterious...". For although "true-in-L" for variable "L" is not definable, "...what we do have suffices to endow "true-in-L", even for variable "L", with a high enough degree of intelligibility so that we are not likely to be averse to using the idiom".[5] "What we do have" is, of course, the paradigm (T) and the "expedient general routine" due to Tarski for defining "true-in-L" for particular languages.

Quine has made ingenious use of Tarski's "expedient general routine". In a 1952 paper, "On an Application of Tarski's Theory of Truth", he explores the question whether truth for the language L of *Mathematical Logic* (1940) can be defined in L itself.[6] It is not clear at first what stands in the way, for L can be

---

[4] Quine, *From a Logical Point of View*, p. 130.   [5] Ibid., pp. 137–8.

[6] W. V. Quine, "On an Application of Tarski's Theory of Truth", *Proceedings of the National Academy of Science* **38** (1952): 430–3; repr. in *Selected Logic Papers*, New York: Random House, 1966; *idem, Mathematical Logic*, New York: Norton, 1940.

interpreted as containing its own syntax, and much besides. Quine succeeds in giving a recursive definition of satisfaction using only the resources of L. If this recursive definition could be turned into a direct definition, L would have been proven inconsistent, truth being immediately definable in terms of satisfaction. But an unusual feature of L blocks the move from recursive to direct definition: in L, the quantifiers range over all entities, and so satisfaction must relate expressions of L to all entities. But some entities only, called "elements", are available in L as relata of relations. This mismatch prevents Frege's device for converting recursive into direct definitions from capturing the full ontological scope needed for the characterization of satisfaction, and hence of truth. Prevents it, that is, provided L is consistent.

In *Philosophy of Logic* (1970), Quine makes a connected but more general point: just as a normally equipped language cannot, on pain of contradiction, contain an open sentence "x satisfies y" true of sequences of objects in the ontology of the language and sentences (open or closed) of the language, so a consistent set theory cannot tolerate the existence of a set consisting of the ordered pairs of sequences of objects in the ontology of the theory and the sentences (open or closed) of the theory.

These interesting technical applications of Tarski's approach to the concept of truth exploit its disquotational feature, and this encourages the idea that truth and meaning can be kept quite separate. But can they in general? Scattered remarks in Quine's work suggest otherwise. In 1936 Quine published the brilliant and prescient "Truth by Convention". In it he remarks that " . . . in point of *meaning* . . . a word may be said to be determined to whatever extent the truth or falsehood of its contexts is determined".[7] It is hard to see how truth could have this power of determining meaning if the disquotational account were all there were to say about truth. Other passages in Quine suggest the same idea: "First and last, in learning language, we are learning how to distribute truth values. I am with Davidson here; we are learning truth conditions".[8] Or again, " . . . Tarski's theory of truth [is] the

[7] W. V. Quine, "Truth by Convention", repr. in *The Ways of Paradox and Other Essays*, rev. enlarged edn., Cambridge, Mass.: Harvard University Press, 1976, p. 89.

[8] W. V. Quine, *The Roots of Reference*, La Salle, Ill.: Open Court, 1974, p. 65.

very structure of a theory of meaning."[9] *Philosophy of Logic* also stresses, in a way not to be found in earlier works by Quine, the importance of discerning in a language a grammatical structure geared to the workings of a theory of truth; only then will we see how "logic chases truth up the tree of grammar".[10]

Up to a point it may seem easy to keep questions of truth and questions of meaning segregated. Truth we may think of as disquotational (in the extended Tarski sense) and therefore trivial; meaning is then another matter, to be taken care of in terms of warranted assertability, function, or the criteria for translation. This is the line followed, for example, by Paul Horwich in his recent book *Truth*, by Scott Soames, and by David Lewis.[11] It may, at least at one time, have been Quine's view. In *Word and Object*, in a passage that immediately precedes the remark that to say that the sentence "Brutus killed Caesar" is true is in effect simply to say that Brutus killed Caesar, Quine despairs of a substantive concept of truth, perhaps along the lines of Peirce, and says,

It is rather when we turn back into the midst of an actually present theory . . . that we can and do speak sensibly of this or that sentence as true. Where it makes sense to apply "true" is to a sentence couched in the terms of a given theory, and seen from within the theory.[12]

This is, I think, what Quine means when he says that truth is "immanent". The point is not merely that the truth of a sentence is relative to a language; it is that there is no transcendent, single concept to be relativized.

But Quine cannot mean that we sensibly speak of the truth of sentences only when those sentences are contained in the language we are using to do the speaking. It may be impossible to give an explicit definition of truth for languages generally, at least following Tarski's method, but of course one can speak sensibly

[9] W. V. Quine, *Theories and Things*, Cambridge, Mass.: Harvard University Press, 1981, p. 38. He adds that this insight (which he generously attributes to me) "was a major advance in semantics".

[10] W. V. Quine, *Philosophy of Logic*, Englewood Cliffs, NJ: Prentice-Hall, 1970, p. 35.

[11] Paul Horwich, *Truth*, Oxford: Blackwell, 1990; Scott Soames, "What is a Theory of Truth?", *Journal of Philosophy* **81** (1984): 411–29; David Lewis, "Languages and Language", in *Minnesota Studies in the Philosophy of Science*, vii, Minneapolis: University of Minnesota Press, 1975.   [12] Quine, *Word and Object*, p. 24.

of the truth of sentences in one language using another language. What should we say about the disquotational view of truth in this case?

In "Variables Explained Away",[13] Quine described a language which, like Schönfinkel's combinatorial logic, lacked variables, but unlike it was no stronger than standard quantification theory with identity. This essay left one wondering whether, for such a language, truth could be defined without recourse to something like Tarski's notion of satisfaction, that is, to some systematic way of relating expressions to objects in the ontology of the language. The answer is implicit in "Algebraic Logic and Predicate Functors". There Quine remarks that

When a theory is given the usual quantificational form, the things that the theory accepts as existing are indeed the things that it accepts as the values of its variables of quantification. If a theory is given another form, moreover, there is no sense in asking what the theory accepts as existing except as we are in a position to say how to translate the theory into the usual quantificational form...When we switch to predicate-functor logic, such a mode of translation is available...In the light of it, we find that the things that a theory in predicate-functor form accepts as existing are the things that satisfy its predicates.[14]

Thus "to be is to be the value of a variable" is not quite as general a formula for determining the ontology of a language as "to be is to satisfy the predicates of the language (or their complements)": as Quine puts it, "...the characterization in terms of satisfaction of predicates does have the advantage of applying equally and outright to theories in quantificational form and theories in predicate-functor form, without having to be funneled through a translation".[15]

The question of a truth definition is explicitly answered in "Truth and Disquotation",[16] which explores among other things the question when a theory of truth for a language can evade the

[13] W. V. Quine, "Variables Explained Away", *Proceedings of the American Philosophical Society* **104** (1960): 343–7; repr. in *Selected Logic Papers*.

[14] W. V. Quine, "Algebraic Logic and Predicate Functors", pamphlet, Indianapolis: Bobbs-Merrill, 1976; repr. in *Ways of Paradox*, p. 304.

[15] Ibid. See also W. V. Quine, "Ontology and Ideology Revisited", *Journal of Philosophy* **80** (1983): 499–502.

[16] W. V. Quine, "Truth and Disquotation", in *Proceedings of the 1971 Tarski Symposium*, Providence: American Mathematical Society, pp. 373–84; repr. in *Ways of Paradox*.

Tarskian detour involving a concept like satisfaction with its explicit teaming of expressions in the language to be studied with sequences of entities in the ontology of the theory. In the case of Schönfinkel's combinatory logic, the notion of satisfaction is not required, since a version of designation can be characterized which maps any singular term onto what it designates. This is possible because in Schönfinkel's logic all formulas, including sentences, are singular terms; thus truth turns out to be a special case of designation: a true sentence designates (as in Frege) The True. In some cases, notably elementary number theory, satisfaction and its ontology can be dispensed with because truth for atomic sentences can be specified by direct methods and quantification handled substitutionally. In the interesting case of Quine's predicate-functor language, satisfaction, in its classic form, cannot be directly applied, though it can, of course, be applied to the translation of the predicate-functor language into standard quantificational form.

These experiments in defining truth for various languages are far from proving that only Tarski's methods are sufficiently general to be interestingly applicable to formalized languages that might be viewed as versions of, or substitutes for, natural languages. Nevertheless, Quine has shown that though we can "explain variables away", this in itself does not affect the need, in defining truth, to resort to some analogue of satisfaction. Viewed from the vantage point of truth theory, the ontological burden of a language made explicit by quantificational structure is less "provincial" than it might seem. More important, the immanence of truth is not so restrictive after all: the truth of a sentence may be sensibly spoken of from within what at least appears to be a very different language.

So far we have been assuming, with Tarski, that the metalanguage contains the object language, or that there is a systematic, known way of translating from the object language into the metalanguage. What happens if this assumption is dropped?

A theory of truth for a language in use is an empirical theory: it attempts to specify, for speakers of the language, the conditions under which sentences of their language are true. Of course if "is true" is a truth predicate, and "if and only if" expresses biconditionality, a sentence of the form " 'Snow is white' is true if and only if snow is white" can't be false, whatever "Snow is white" may mean, on the (empirical) assumption that the semantics of the mentioned sentence coincide with the semantics of that sentence as used. But once the question is raised whether the theory, as stated in an interpreter's language, is true of the language of a second person, the empirical and non-trivial character of the theory becomes obvious. What should count as confirming that such a theory is true? To ask this question is to ask a question about the concept of truth that disquotation cannot answer.

We know that if the theory contains a sentence of form (T) for every sentence of the object language, and is otherwise formally correct, the theory uniquely and correctly determines the extension of the truth predicate. So the obvious way to test the truth of the theory is to discover whether each in a reasonable sample of its T-sentences is true, and none false. Since the sample will always be finite, while the theory implies an infinity of T-sentences, the test will be inconclusive; but that is to be expected. The problem is to recognize when a T-sentence is true.

T-sentences were only incompletely characterized by paradigm (T). Truth must be relativized to a language (or, better, to a speaker or group of speakers); if to a language or a group of speakers, then once more to a speaker (because the truth of a sentence containing words like "me" and "here" depends on who utters the sentence); and to a time (to take care of tense, "now", "tomorrow", etc.). We must also allow that what fills the space to the right of the biconditional need not be the very words quoted or otherwise described on the left; if that sentence contains no indexicals, it suffices that the sentence on the right translate the target sentence; when there are indexicals, there will be an open sentence on the right of the biconditional, and its relation to the target sentence will be more complicated still. Translation of a sort will still be relevant, and this is all that will concern us here. Thus the problem of recognizing the truth of a T-sentence boils down to the problem of translation, and the evidence that a theory of truth is empirically correct will be the evidence that a scheme for translating the object language into the metalanguage (a translation manual) is correct.

Quine has famously rejected the traditional goal of translation, that of preserving meaning, as empirically unfounded. In place of translation so conceived, Quine offers an alternative ("radical translation"), characterized by empirical criteria. Radical translation, according to Quine, takes advantage of all empirical evidence relevant to what can be learned and understood by a speaker or interpreter of a language. Quine would then seem to be in a position to answer the question when a theory of truth for another speaker (or group of speakers) is correct. One way is this: first we devise, as far as possible, a theory of truth for our own language. By assuming that the object language is contained in the metalanguage, we avoid raising any obvious empirical problems at this stage. Then we apply the theory to the other speaker or speakers by way of radical translation. It may turn out that they speak "the same language" (the homophonic translation manual works), or it may not; in either case, the discovery is empirical, and supported by the same sort of evidence.

If we were assured of a unique correct way of translating from a foreign tongue into our own, we might fancy that we could somehow disregard the translational step that carried the concept of truth abroad from its disquotational home. But Quine has taught us that there is no reason to believe that if there is one acceptable manual for translating one language into another, then there is only one. Quine has persuasively argued that if there is one acceptable manual for translating the sentences of the object language into the metalanguage, there will be an infinity of equally acceptable alternative translation manuals which differ with respect to the objects that singular terms and predicates are taken to refer to or be true of. (Hence Quine's phrase "the inscrutability of reference".) The simplest examples depend on systematic one-to-one mappings of the objects in the ontology assigned to the object language by a given translation manual onto those same objects; the mapping is used to reinterpret the reference of singular terms and the extension of predicates to yield a new translation manual.

The point transfers directly to theories of truth. Theories of truth in Tarski's tradition depend on specifying the conditions under which an arbitrary sequence of objects satisfies a sentence (open or closed); a true sentence is a closed sentence satisfied by any or all sequences. Quine's thesis of the inscrutability of reference can then be restated: certain global changes in the conditions under which sequences satisfy *open* sentences make no difference to the conditions under which sequences satisfy *closed* sentences: very different ways of connecting terms and predicates to objects may make no difference to the truth of the sentences in which they occur.

Where does this leave the analogues of paradigm (T),

(Ⓡ) the singular term "——" refers to——,

(E) the predicate "——" is true of things that are ——,

for the reference and extension of singular terms and predicates? As with paradigm (T), all instances of these paradigms will be trivially true on the assumption that the object language is contained in the metalanguage. This generates the illusion that the relations of reference and being-true-of are unique. It is easy to see that they are not, however, if the only constraints on these relations are that they yield correct truth predicates—correct, that is, by the standards of Tarski's convention T and Quine's version of translation. For consider a situation in which two speakers, Clara and Dora, speak what is in every empirically determinable respect the same language: for a radical translator with a different language, those and only those translation manuals that work for Clara work for Dora. Clara and Dora can (and presumably do) use the homophonic translation manual in understanding each other. But convenience and custom aside, they could do as well with any of the empirically adequate alternative manuals that systematically reinterpret singular terms and predicates. These alternative manuals will not be consistent with paradigms (Ⓡ) and (E), nor will the theories of truth generated by these manuals yield T-sentences in the format of (T). The truth conditions of sentences will be unchanged, however, in the sense that the various truth predicates will have the same extension; not so for the relations of reference and being-true-of (or the relation of satisfaction).

There is, then, no unique reference of a singular term, nor unique extension of a predicate. The illusion of uniqueness is created by the fact that one can't switch translation manuals in midstream without obliterating relevant distinctions. Thus if Ruth is not identical with Dora, Clara can't substitute "Ruth" for "Dora" in its second appearance in "My word 'Dora' refers to Dora". It would be a mistake to suppose this indicates that her word "Dora" must refer to Dora; the real lesson is merely that the same word can't without ambiguity perform different tasks in a language. Referring to a unique entity is not an intelligible task; distinguishing between entities is.

Relativization cannot fix reference; nothing can. Nevertheless, if not relativization, then something like it is needed to keep talk of reference straight. Since the various ways of relating the words of a speaker to things serve to define the same concept of truth, it is tempting to think of the various corresponding reference- or satisfaction-predicates as variations on a single theme: because all the "satisfaction-predicates" are devised to expedite Tarski's "expedient general routine", they all agree when it comes to the relation between sequences and closed sentences. But the temptation to relativize must be resisted; there is nothing to relativize satisfaction or reference to. (Of course "*x* satisfies *y* in *L*" for variable "*L*" is not available for the same reason its analogue for truth is not.) But although there is no making sense of the question which satisfaction-relation a predicate represents, different relations require different predicates. The need is easily enough satisfied; we can use syntactically distinct predicates for distinct relations.

These reflections should make us wonder how much clarity accrues to the concepts of truth, reference, and satisfaction from the paradigms (T), (®), and (E). The paradigms do require unique extensions for certain predicates, but nothing about the paradigms insures that only predicates with these extensions deserve to be called predicates of truth or reference. And in fact, as Quine has persuasively shown, predicates with very different extensions have equal claim to be called predicates of reference, extension, and satisfaction. So far as the paradigms are concerned, we are free to think the same about truth predicates.

Why don't we think the same? The reason we don't is simple. We assign semantic properties to certain proper parts of sentences only in order to give a finite account of the semantic properties of the infinitude of sentences. It follows that the only constraint on what we say about the parts is that sentences perform as predicted. There is no choosing between ways of relating words to things as long as the truth conditions of sentences come out the same; but this is an interesting fact because there *are* empirical constraints on truth conditions.

These constraints are, as is to be expected from the close relation between translation and truth in Tarski's Convention T, the constraints on acceptable methods of translation. As we have noticed, a single concept of truth, given voice in some language, can be applied to various languages if a systematic way of translating is available, subject to the limitations due to the threat of paradox.

It is not to be expected that the constraints on translation will make no appeal to the concept of truth: good translation preserves truth, truth is what is preserved by good translation, if not sentence by sentence, yet on the whole. The best we can do, by way of breaking out of this circle, is to connect truth or translation with observable reactions of speakers to language and the world. Quine's chosen reaction is prompted assent, assent to a sentence as prompted by events, verbal or otherwise, in the world. What is wanted is honest assent, and here the connection with truth is evident: someone who honestly assents to a sentence holds it true—believes it to be true. The data for translation or a theory of truth for a speaker are thus facts about what causes the speaker to hold various sentences true. In some cases the causes are irrelevant; thus the truth-functional sentential connectives can be translated directly on the basis of patterns of assent and dissent. For the simplest sentences concerning easily observed objects and events, the evidence for translation is the causes of changes in assent. For sentences assent to which is less simply geared to the observable, translation depends on relations among sentences created by patterns of assent.

This, in outline, is Quine's way with translation, and I have nothing but admiration for the aspects of the method that I have outlined. I have remarked that the method carries over directly to truth, since a theory of truth for one's own language (based on paradigm (T)) can be applied to another language by way of translation. One can also skip the detour through translation by using the same data to yield a theory of truth directly; T-sentences will then *display* translations without mentioning this fact, as in Tarski.

I have been stressing the invasion of truth by considerations of meaning, an invasion we cannot ignore as soon as the question of the truth of sentences in languages other than our own arises. The invasion can be direct, if we ask when an alien sentence is true, or indirect if we characterize truth disquotationally for our own language first, and then translate the foreign tongue into our own. The difference, if there is one, is that the first strategy mingles issues of truth and meaning from the start, while the second approach allows for a division of labor. But in either case we have the makings of a transcendent attitude toward, if not definition of, the concept of truth. If we apply truth directly to other languages, we get a multiplicity of truth predicates in our home language, and these are united by our general (transcendental) method of application. If we have just the single truth theory for our own language, what makes it transcendental is our common criteria for translation. Of course, in either case transcendence has its limits; our home language must in part be slighted; no matter how we enlarge it, a part remains beyond the reach of the last truth predicate in the growing hierarchy.

The indeterminacy of translation still raises a problem for truth. The evidence for translation consists of data in which belief and meaning are conflated, since assent to a sentence depends both on what a speaker takes the sentence to mean and what he believes about the world. Quine's method for separating the roles of meaning and belief to the necessary degree depends on assuming that with respect to sentential logic, it makes no sense to suppose that the beliefs of speaker and interpreter differ. He also assumes that in the plainest cases similar stimuli elicit similar beliefs in speaker and interpreter. These methodological assumptions, both of them applications of the "principle of charity", do not dictate a unique best translation or theory of truth; in general the data can be accommodated in more than one way, since it is possible to compensate for a change in the truth conditions assigned to a speaker's sentence by a change in the beliefs attributed to him. This means that on one theory a given sentence may be true for a time and speaker, and on another theory not.

One way to resolve the threatened contradiction is, of course, to introduce separate "truth" predicates; but to do this would seem to amount to forswearing the difference lately claimed between reference and truth. There would, though, remain an important difference of level. Versions of "reference" may be grouped when they serve to define a common truth predicate; truth predicates may be grouped which, when combined with suitable theories of belief, explain the same verbal responses (prompted assents).

We are still left with different concepts of truth, though to the extent that charity enjoins minimizing unexplained disagreement as a way to achieve understanding, it will minimize the differences between accounts of truth for the same sentences. Another, and better, way to view the matter is this: Truth must in any case be relativized to a language. Up to this point we had been thinking of relativization to a language as identical with relativization to a speaker or group of speakers. But there is a point in considering these as separate parameters. Even supposing all the relevant evidence is in for a speaker or group of speakers, we can interpret him or her or them as speaking various languages. This means only that within limits we can assign different truth conditions to a sentence as used by a given speaker or speakers as long as we make appropriate changes elsewhere in the theory. Putting things this way, though it does not point to the possibility of a universal definition or theory of truth, does give color to the idea that we are using the same concept of truth in devising our various theories. What gives unity to the concept is, on the one hand, the formal requirement made explicit by Convention T, and the tie with prompted assent on the other.

There seems no difficulty, then, in applying the concept of truth to speakers of various languages. Of course when we do this we operate with our own language and concepts, but this does not suggest that it makes sense to apply "true" only to our own sentences. Why, then, does Quine say that truth is "immanent"? I quote:

> . . . it is a confusion to suppose that we can stand aloof and recognize all the alternative ontologies as true in their several ways, all the envisaged worlds as real. It is a confusion of truth with evidential support. Truth is immanent, and there is no higher.[17]

Of course, if the "alternative ontologies" or "envisaged worlds" were somehow in conflict, we could not accept them simultaneously. Since the various worlds and ontologies are generated by equally justified, though different, systems of translation from an alien tongue into our home language, the issue is not whether we can describe them all. But do they conflict? At one time Quine thought they might; he claimed that theories " . . . can be logically incompatible and empirically equivalent",[18] and gave this as the

---

[17] Quine, *Theories and Things*, pp. 21–2.
[18] W. V. Quine, "On the Reasons for Indeterminacy of Translation", *Journal of Philosophy* **67** (1970): 178–83.

best reason for supposing translation indeterminate. More recently, though, he has explained away the appearance of incompatibility by recognizing that the apparent contradiction is better seen as ambiguity in one or more key words. In this way

...we can resolve all conflict between the...[empirically equivalent] theory formulations. Both [theories] can be admitted thenceforward as true descriptions of one and the same world in different terms. The threat of relativism of truth is averted.[19]

More recently still, in *Pursuit of Truth*, Quine vacillates on the issue again.[20] But when it comes to contemplating conflicting accounts of truth for the same language, straightforward contradiction threatens. For suppose your language contains a sentence which in one of your theories is true, and in another false. (Unless the two theories are in the same language, there can be no such conflict.) Then my account of truth for you must attribute both truth and falsity to your same sentence. Quine seems to appreciate the point, for elsewhere in *Pursuit of Truth* he considers the case of two different translation manuals for the same language, both of them in accord with all possible evidence, and therefore empirically equivalent. In such a case we should, he says, count both manuals true.[21] Since the divergent manuals gear directly into one's disquotational truth theory for one's own language, we can escape contradiction only by supposing each manual attributes a different (though empirically indistinguishable) language to the speaker.

Applying truth to our own speech, we are prevented, as we saw in the case of reference, from straightforward formulation of the alternatives that would call for relativization. This encourages the illusion that our own speech is not open to alternative interpretations. If we accept this view, we will indeed think of truth as immanent; as having, in fact, no clear application to others, even those who speak, so far as the evidence goes, "our" language. If, on the other hand, we think of truth as a concept that has application only in the context of shared linguistic practice, we will not expect that it can be sheltered from the exigencies of interpretation.

I come now to the development in Quine's views of which I spoke at the start. We have noted the extent to which

---

[19] Quine, *Theories and Things*, p. 30. [20] Quine, *Pursuit of Truth*, p. 100.
[21] Ibid., p. 48.

disquotational truth is enmeshed, through the medium of translation, with untidy matters of meaning. As a result, an interpreter's application of his truth predicate to the sentences of a speaker other than himself will depend on how he understands (i.e., "translates") those sentences, even if they apparently belong to his own language. But translation, as Quine has characterized it in the past, has been in danger of losing track of truth.

A person comes to share observation sentences with someone else when he is caused to be disposed to assent to the same sentences by the same or relevantly similar events or situations. A person comes to understand the speaker of a different language when he can systematically match up his own sentences with those of the alien speaker on the basis of the same or similar causes. The question is, when are events or situations or causes the same or relevantly similar?

Quine's answer in the past has been, when the patterns of sensory stimulation are the same, nearly enough, from speaker to interpreter. We were asked to imagine that we have a way of mapping the nerve endings of one person onto the nerve endings of another: then patterns of stimulation are relevantly similar if all corresponding nerve endings fire. An observation sentence is shared by speakers when the same patterns of stimulation prompt their assent to, or dissent from, the same sentence. We understand an alien observation sentence when we find a sentence of our own to which our assent and dissent is prompted by the same patterns of stimulation that prompt the alien's assent and dissent to his sentence.

This idea is appealing because it takes direct account of the role of the senses in causing us to hold true (or false) sentences like "It's cold in here", "That mouse is mauve", "There's a tiger", "It's raining". It also seems to take account in a natural way of errors due to illusion. As Quine remarks, it is a way of capturing the empiricist principle that all empirical knowledge comes by way of the senses without depending on such suspect entities as sense data, raw feels, or uninterpreted experience. The laudable intent was to make empiricism scientifically respectable by basing both meaning and knowledge on intersubjectively observable states and events.

There are fairly obvious reasons to be dissatisfied with this idea, and they have bothered Quine over the years. One is the difficulty in being clear how to map one person's nerve endings onto another's. A second is that people do not always share operative sense organs. Another is that variations in what one person takes to be evidence for the truth of an observation sentence may not be what another takes to be evidence. It is also a question how similarity of patterns of stimulation could serve as the basis of translation and language learning when such similarities are so evidently unavailable to learner or teacher. In *Roots of Reference* and elsewhere, Quine often slipped into taking shared external circumstances as the key to the correct interpretation of observation sentences rather than shared patterns of stimulation, and in *Pursuit of Truth* a version of this shift becomes official.

The result, in my opinion, is to save the natural relation between meaning and truth. For on the earlier view, there was no reason it might not happen that the correct translation of "Gavagai" was "Lo, a mouse"; then whenever the translating linguist noted a rabbit in plain sight, the alien speaker was interpreted as reporting a mouse. Two things go wrong: the criteria for translation make the alien systematically wrong again and again, as wrong as the most determined skeptic might imagine; and the criteria ignore the obvious clues that any interpreter or linguist or learner would use, clues which would assign truth conditions to the speaker that would make him mostly right.

What is directly available to the learner of a first language or to the jungle linguist is the high correlation between easily observed behavior on the part of the teacher or informant (he says "Gavagai") and easily observed events, situations or occasions in the shared world. We don't need, in order to express this simple idea, an ontology of situations or occasions: what makes the occasions similar is the similarity of the responses of the teacher or informant and the similarity of the learner's or linguist's responses to the world (or, as we can as well say, to the stimulation of his senses). The linguist can put a word to his response: "Rabbit". The learner is coming to class the occasions together, and to put a word to them: "Gavagai", if he belongs to the tribe.

If we want to say in articulate form what it is that makes the occasions similar, the only sure answer we can give is that they are situations in which there is, or appears to be, a rabbit present. The cases of deceptive appearance must, in the nature of things, be explicable and statistically infrequent; otherwise "Rabbit" and "Gavagai" would be true when there was a rabbit appearance unaccompanied by a rabbit.

Quine holds that the stimulus for both learner and teacher is the unshared, and perhaps unlike, stimulations of the nerve endings, not the shared rabbit. I think we can locate the stimulus where we please in the causal chain from the events in the brain that cause a disposition to assent to "Rabbit" or "Gavagai" on out through the sense organs to the rabbit and beyond. But it doesn't matter how we use the word "stimulus"; what matters to meaning and truth is what must be shared for communication to succeed. When we talk of ordinary things like rabbits, what must be shared cannot be, as Quine once held, patterns of stimulation, but the patterns stirred by the same external events, scenes, and objects.

The center of life of meaning has come to coincide with the center of gravity that determines truth. It is meaning that has been shifted, for what fixes meaning is no longer private events designed to echo the role sense data once played, but what is shared in the outside world. No brick has gone through the window, but the repaired ship will sail even better than before.

6 *What is Quine's View of Truth?*

On one important issue concerning his understanding of the concept of truth, Quine has set me straight. I had worried that when he wrote that truth is 'immanent' he was expressing the idea that truth is relative not only to a language, but also is relative in some further way. He assures me that no other relativization is implied beyond the familiar, and unavoidable, relativization to a language. What, then, are we to make of the remark that

It is ... when we turn back into the midst of an actually present theory ... that we can and do speak sensibly of this or that sentence as true. Where it makes sense to apply 'true' is to a sentence couched in the terms of a given theory, and seen from within the theory.[1]

This may seem to say that there is a truth predicate applicable to the sentences of a theory as seen from 'within the theory', but that that predicate is not applicable beyond the theory. This would imply a different concept of truth for each theory, not just an application of the same concept to each new theory. Surely, though, Quine does not mean we cannot intelligibly speak of the truth of a sentence in one language using another language; strictly, this is what Tarski has taught us, we not only can, but must, do. My confusion here may well be traceable to the fact that 'theory' and 'language' are not to be clearly distinguished in Quine's writings. No wonder. Once one repudiates the analytic/synthetic distinction, one has given up the distinction between belief and meaning, overall theory and language. Given a way of translating another's language, one has arbitrarily fastened on a way of seeming to draw the line, but equally good translation

---

[1] W. V. Quine, *Word and Object*, Cambridge, Mass.: MIT Press, 1960, p. 24.

manuals would draw the line in other places, and so dole out truth to the translated sentences in other ways. Hence, perhaps, the apparent relativity of truth to a theory as well as a language.

It may be in somewhat the same vein that Quine has answered those of us who were troubled by the question what ontology is relative to in *Ontological Relativity*.[2] Quine now settles the matter: it is relative to a translation manual.[3] About this I have two questions, neither of them probably more than matters of exposition or terminology. The first question is, is it necessary to relativize ontology both to a language and to a translation manual, or do these come to the same thing? If we start by assuming, with common sense, that a person is normally speaking just one language, then the further relativization is called for. But if we start by relativizing to a translation manual, it would be otiose to suppose we were adding anything by relativizing to a language. So in spite of the somewhat bizarre idea that as interpreters we make a partially arbitrary decision as to the language someone is speaking, it seems to me to clear the air simply to do without the ordinary notion of a language, and say that in choosing a translation manual we are selecting at our convenience one of a set of equally plausible 'languages' we can take someone to be speaking.

The second question goes back to an aspect of the original question about ontological relativity: it is clear that different translation manuals typically treat the singular terms and predicates of the translated language as referring to different objects. But does it decide what those objects are? Clearly not. What a term 'refers' to, or a predicate is true of, is not settled by relativization to a translation manual; it merely relativizes the ontology of one language to that of another without settling the ontology of either, as Quine pointed out in *Ontological Relativity*. So relativizing ontology to a translation manual, though it is the best we can do, is not like relativizing the weight of an object to some weight scale, which is not only as good as is possible, but as good as makes sense. Perhaps 'inscrutability of reference' is, after all, a less misleading phrase than 'ontological relativity'. (In *Pursuit*

---

[2] W. V. Quine, *Ontological Relativity and Other Essays*, New York: Columbia University Press, 1969.

[3] W. V. Quine, *Pursuit of Truth*, rev. edn., Cambridge, Mass.: Harvard University Press, 1992, p. 52.

of Truth, Quine offers an even better tag: 'indeterminacy of reference'.)

Is Quine what is now called a 'deflationist' when it comes to truth? According to Paul Horwich, a deflationist holds that there is no more to the concept of truth than we know when we realize that every instance of the schema

The proposition that *p* is true if and only if *p*

is true. The 'no more than' implies, he says, that we do not need the concept of truth to understand other important concepts like those of meaning or belief, and we do not need those concepts to explain the concept of truth. Horwich counts Quine as an ally, so let us accept something like this account for the sake of examining Quine's position.

It is clear, of course, that Quine would not buy Horwich's formulation, if only because of its dependence on propositions. Quine's deflationism, if that is what it is, treats truth as a predicate of sentences, not propositions. Nevertheless, many philosophers have found Quine's 'disquotational' account of truth deflationary. It is easy to read why. In *From a Logical Point of View*, Quine says 'Attribution of truth . . . to "Snow is white" . . . is every bit as clear to us as attribution of whiteness to snow'.[4] In *Word and Object* he contends that 'To say that the statement "Brutus killed Caesar" is true . . . is in effect simply to say that Brutus killed Caesar . . . '.[5] In *Pursuit of Truth* he remarks:

. . . there is surely no impugning the disquotation account; no disputing that 'Snow is white' is true if and only if snow is white. Moreover, it is a full account; it explicates clearly the truth or falsity of every clear sentence.[6]

Do these remarks assert that there is no more to the concept of truth than is 'explicated' by the disquotational account? No, since the disquotational account does not tell us how to construct a Tarski-style definition, and so does not explicate many legitimate uses of a truth predicate.

This does not complete the list of the limitations of the disquotational account. That account supplies no hint of how

---

[4] W. V. Quine, *From a Logical Point of View*, Cambridge, Mass.: Harvard University Press, 1953, p. 138.   [5] Quine, *Word and Object*, p. 24.

[6] Quine, *Pursuit of Truth*, p. 93.

a truth predicate can be applied to a language not contained in the language of the predicate. The instances of the disquotational schema are guaranteed to be true, in fact, only in the very special case where the quoted sentences are *guaranteed* to have the same truth values as those same sentences shorn of quotation marks on the right of the biconditional. This guarantee is lacking, for example, when I surmise that your sentence 'Snow is white' is true if and only if snow is white. More importantly, the disquotational account gives us no idea how to tell when such a surmise is true. What this makes clear, it seems to me, is that the disquotational account is far from a full account of the concept of truth: in addition to knowing what determines the extension of the concept for the language I speak, I want to know how to determine the extension of my (the) concept of truth for other speakers.

The passages from Quine I quoted in the second paragraph above do not necessarily conflict with these observations. For the first quote, read: 'Attribution *by me* of truth to *my* sentence "Snow is white" ... is every bit as clear to *me* as attribution of whiteness to snow'; similarly for the second quote and the first sentence of the third. For the second sentence of the third quote, take it to say that the disquotational account exactly determines the extension of a truth predicate for an object language contained in the metalanguage. Would these readings satisfy Quine?

My final remark concerns Horwich's second criterion of a deflationist, which requires that the concept of truth be 'independent' of other concepts. It is not easy to be sure one understands this idea, but one testing ground is the relation, or lack of one, between truth and meaning. One connection is made by the necessary mention of translation in Tarski's Convention T, which appeals simultaneously to the intuitive general concepts of truth and translation. Quine substitutes *radical* translation for translation which aims to preserve 'meaning', but although radical translation doesn't always preserve truth value, much less meaning, truth is nevertheless very much in view in the practice of radical translation. Prompted assent is the key to Quine's way of worming one's way into an alien tongue, and one is prompted to assent to what one holds true. The deep connection between truth and meaning comes out also in these quotations: '[I]n point of *meaning* ... a word may be said to be determined to whatever extent the truth or falsehood of its contexts is determined';[7] 'First and last, in learning language, we are learning how to distribute truth values. I am with Davidson here; we are learning truth conditions';[8] 'Tarski's theory of truth [is] the very structure of a theory of meaning'.[9] It seems, then, that we need meaning, as preserved by radical interpretation, if we are to apply our truth predicate to any speech but our own, and we need truth, according to these last two quotations, to understand meaning. Such basic relations between truth and meaning are incompatible with a deflationary attitude toward the concept of truth. Those who have taken the emphasis on the disquotational aspect of the truth predicate as a sign that Quine is a deflationist must, I conclude, be wrong.

[7] W.V. Quine, "Truth by Convention", repr. in *The Ways of Paradox and Other Essays*, rev. enlarged edn., Cambridge, Mass.: Harvard University Press, 1976.

[8] W. V. Quine, *The Roots of Reference*, La Salle, Ill.: Open Court, 1974, p. 65.

[9] W. V. Quine, *Theories and Things*, Cambridge, Mass.: Harvard University Press, 1981, p. 38.

LANGUAGE

7 *A Nice Derangement of Epitaphs*

Goodman Ace wrote radio sitcoms. According to Mark Singer, Ace often talked the way he wrote:

Rather than take for granite that Ace talks straight, a listener must be on guard for an occasional entre nous and me . . . or a long face no see. In a roustabout way, he will maneuver until he selects the ideal phrase for the situation, hitting the nail right on the thumb. The careful conversationalist might try to mix it up with him in a baffle of wits. In quest of this pinochle of success, I have often wrecked my brain for a clowning achievement, but Ace's chickens always come home to roast. From time to time, Ace will, in a jersksome way, monotonise the conversation with witticisms too humorous to mention. It's high noon someone beat him at his own game, but I have never done it; cross my eyes and hope to die, he always wins thumbs down.[1]

I quote at length because philosophers have tended to neglect or play down the sort of language-use this passage illustrates. For example, Jonathan Bennett writes,

I doubt if I have ever been present when a speaker did something like shouting 'Water!' as a warning of fire, knowing what 'Water!' means and knowing that his hearers also knew, but thinking that they would expect him to give to 'Water!' the normal meaning of 'Fire!'[2]

Bennett adds that, 'Although such things could happen, they seldom do.' I think such things happen all the time; in fact, if the conditions are generalised in a natural way, the phenomenon is ubiquitous.

---

[1] *The New Yorker*, 4 April 1977, p. 56. Reprinted by permission, 1977, The New Yorker Magazine, Inc.
[2] Jonathan Bennett, *Linguistic Behavior*, Cambridge, 1976, p. 186. Donald Davidson, 1985.

Singer's examples are special in several ways. A malapropism does not have to be amusing or surprising. It does not have to be based on a cliché, and of course it does not have to be intentional. There need be no play on words, no hint of deliberate pun. We may smile at someone who says 'Lead the way and we'll precede', or, with Archie Bunker, 'We need a few laughs to break up the monogamy', because he has said something that, given the usual meanings of the words, is ridiculous or fun. But the humour is adventitious.

Ace's malaprops generally make some sort of sense when the words are taken in the standard way, as in 'Familiarity breeds attempt', or 'We're all cremated equal', but this is not essential ('the pinochle of success'). What is interesting is the fact that in all these cases the hearer has no trouble understanding the speaker in the way the speaker intends.

It is easy enough to explain this feat on the hearer's part: the hearer realises that the 'standard' interpretation cannot be the intended interpretation; through ignorance, inadvertence, or design the speaker has used a word similar in sound to the word that would have 'correctly' expressed his meaning. The absurdity or inappropriateness of what the speaker would have meant had his words been taken in the 'standard' way alerts the hearer to trickery or error; the similarity in sound tips him off to the right interpretation. Of course there are many other ways the hearer might catch on; similarity of sound is not essential to the malaprop. Nor for that matter does the general case require that the speaker use a real word: most of 'The Jabberwock' is intelligible on first hearing.

It seems unimportant, so far as understanding is concerned, who makes a mistake, or whether there is one. When I first read Singer's piece on Goodman Ace, I thought that the word 'malaprop', though the name of Sheridan's character, was not a common noun that could be used in place of 'malapropism'. It turned out to be my mistake. Not that it mattered: I knew what Singer meant, even though I was in error about the word; I would have taken his meaning in the same way if he had been in error instead of me. We could both have been wrong and things would have gone as smoothly.

This talk of error or mistake is not mysterious nor open to philosophical suspicions. I was wrong about what a good dictionary would say, or what would be found by polling a pod of experts whose taste or training I trust. But error or mistake of this kind, with its associated notion of correct usage, is not philosophically interesting. We want a deeper notion of what words, when spoken in context, mean; and like the shallow notion of correct usage, we want the deep concept to distinguish between what a speaker, on a given occasion, means, and what his words mean. The widespread existence of malapropisms and their kin threatens the distinction, since here the intended meaning seems to take over from the standard meaning.

I take for granted, however, that nothing should be allowed to obliterate or even blur the distinction between speaker's meaning and literal meaning. In order to preserve the distinction we must, I shall argue, modify certain commonly accepted views about what it is to 'know a language', or about what a natural language is. In particular, we must pry apart what is literal in language from what is conventional or established.

Here is a preliminary stab at characterising what I have been calling literal meaning. The term is too incrusted with philosophical and other extras to do much work, so let me call what I am interested in *first meaning*. The concept applies to words and sentences as uttered by a particular speaker on a particular occasion. But if the occasion, the speaker, and the audience are 'normal' or 'standard' (in a sense not to be further explained here), then the first meaning of an utterance will be what should be found by consulting a dictionary based on actual usage (such as *Webster's Third*). Roughly speaking, first meaning comes first in the order of interpretation. We have no chance of explaining the image in the following lines, for example, unless we know what 'foison' meant in Shakespeare's day:

> Speak of the spring and foison of the year,
> The one doth shadow of your beauty show,
> The other as your bounty doth appear . . .[3]

Little here is to be taken literally, but unless we know the literal, or first, meaning of the words we do not grasp and cannot explain the image.

But 'the order of interpretation' is not at all clear. For there are cases where we may first guess at the image and so puzzle out the

---

[3] Shakespeare, Sonnet 53.

first meaning. This might happen with the word 'tires' in the same sonnet:

> On Helen's cheek all art of beauty set,
> And you in Grecian tires are painted new.

And of course it often happens that we can descry the literal meaning of a word or phrase by first appreciating what the speaker was getting at.

A better way to distinguish first meaning is through the intentions of the speaker. The intentions with which an act is performed are usually unambiguously ordered by the relation of means to ends (where this relation may or may not be causal). Thus the poet wants (let us say) to praise the beauty and generosity of his patron. He does this by using images that say the person addressed takes on every good aspect to be found in nature or in man or woman. This he does in turn by using the word 'tire' to mean 'attire' and the word 'foison' to mean 'harvest'. The order established here by 'by' can be reversed by using the phrase 'in order to'. In the 'in order to' sequence, first meaning is the first meaning referred to. ('With the intention of' with 'ing' added to the verb does as well.)

Suppose Diogenes utters the words 'I would have you stand from between me and the sun' (or their Greek equivalent) with the intention of uttering words that will be interpreted by Alexander as true if and only if Diogenes would have him stand from between Diogenes and the sun, and this with the intention of getting Alexander to move from between him and the sun, and this with the intention of leaving a good anecdote to posterity. Of course these are not the only intentions involved; there will also be the Gricean intentions to achieve certain of these ends through Alexander's recognition of some of the intentions involved. Diogenes' intention to be interpreted in a certain way requires such a self-referring intention, as does his intention to ask Alexander to move. In general, the first intention in the sequence to require this feature specifies the first meaning.

Because a speaker necessarily intends first meaning to be grasped by his audience, and it is grasped if communication succeeds, we lose nothing in the investigation of first meaning if we concentrate on the knowledge or ability a hearer must have if he is to interpret a speaker. What the speaker knows must correspond to something the interpreter knows if the speaker is to be understood, since if the speaker is understood he has been interpreted as he intended to be interpreted. The abilities of the speaker that go beyond what is required of an interpreter—invention and motor control—do not concern me here.

Nothing said so far limits first meaning to language; what has been characterised is (roughly) Grice's non-natural meaning, which applies to any sign or signal with an intended interpretation. What should be added if we want to restrict first meaning to linguistic meaning? The usual answer would, I think, be that in the case of language the hearer shares a complex system or theory with the speaker, a system which makes possible the articulation of logical relations between utterances, and explains the ability to interpret novel utterances in an organised way.

This answer has been suggested, in one form or another, by many philosophers and linguists, and I assume it must in some sense be right. The difficulty lies in getting clear about what this sense is. The particular difficulty with which I am concerned in this paper (for there are plenty of others) can be brought out by stating three plausible principles concerning first meaning in language: we may label them by saying they require that first meaning be systematic, shared, and prepared.

(1) *First meaning is systematic.* A competent speaker or interpreter is able to interpret utterances, his own or those of others, on the basis of the semantic properties of the parts, or words, in the utterance, and the structure of the utterance. For this to be possible, there must be systematic relations between the meanings of utterances.

(2) *First meanings are shared.* For speaker and interpreter to communicate successfully and regularly, they must share a method of interpretation of the sort described in (1).

(3) *First meanings are governed by learned conventions or regularities.* The systematic knowledge or competence of the speaker or interpreter is learned in advance of occasions of interpretation and is conventional in character.

Probably no one doubts that there are difficulties with these conditions. Ambiguity is an example: often the 'same' word has more than one semantic role, and so the interpretation of utterances in which it occurs is not uniquely fixed by the features of the interpreter's competence so far mentioned. Yet, though the verbal and other features of the context of utterance often determine a correct interpretation, it is not easy or perhaps even possible to specify clear rules for disambiguation. There are many more questions about what is required of the competent interpreter. It does not seem plausible that there is a strict rule fixing the occasions on which we should attach significance to the order in which conjoined sentences appear in a conjunction: the difference between 'They got married and had a child' and 'They had a child and got married'. Interpreters certainly can make these distinctions. But part of the burden of this paper is that much that they can do ought not to count as part of their basic *linguistic* competence. The contrast in what is meant or implied by the use of 'but' instead of 'and' seems to me another matter, since no amount of common sense unaccompanied by linguistic lore would enable an interpreter to figure it out.

Paul Grice has done more than anyone else to bring these problems to our attention and to help sort them out. In particular, he has shown why it is essential to distinguish between the literal meaning (perhaps what I am calling first meaning) of words and what is often implied (or implicated) by someone who uses those words. He has explored the general principles behind our ability to figure out such implicatures, and these principles must, of course, be known to speakers who expect to be taken up on them. Whether knowledge of these principles ought to be included in the description of linguistic competence may not have to be settled: on the one hand they are things a clever person could often figure out without previous training or exposure and they are things we could get along without. On the other hand they represent a kind of skill we expect of an interpreter and without which communication would be greatly impoverished.

I dip into these matters only to distinguish them from the problem raised by malapropisms and the like. The problems touched on in the last two paragraphs all concern the ability to interpret words and constructions of the kind covered by our conditions (1)–(3); the questions have been what is required for such interpretation, and to what extent various competencies should be considered linguistic. Malapropisms introduce expressions not covered by prior learning, or familiar expressions which cannot be interpreted by any of the abilities so far discussed.

Malapropisms fall into a different category, one that may include such things as our ability to perceive a well-formed sentence when the actual utterance was incomplete or grammatically garbled, our ability to interpret words we have never heard before, to correct slips of the tongue, or to cope with new idiolects. These phenomena threaten standard descriptions of linguistic competence (including descriptions for which I am responsible).

How should we understand or modify (1)–(3) to accommodate malapropisms? Principle (1) requires a competent interpreter to be prepared to interpret utterances of sentences he or she has never heard uttered before. This is possible because the interpreter can learn the semantic role of each of a finite number of words or phrases and can learn the semantic consequences of a finite number of modes of composition. This is enough to account for the ability to interpret utterances of novel sentences. And since the modes of composition can be iterated, there is no clear upper limit to the number of sentences utterances of which can be interpreted. The interpreter thus has a system for interpreting what he hears or says. You might think of this system as a machine which, when fed an arbitrary utterance (and certain parameters provided by the circumstances of the utterance), produces an interpretation. One model for such a machine is a theory of truth, more or less along the lines of a Tarski truth definition. It provides a recursive characterisation of the truth conditions of all possible utterances of the speaker, and it does this through an analysis of utterances in terms of sentences made up from the finite vocabulary and the finite stock of modes of composition. I have frequently argued that command of such a theory would suffice for interpretation.[4] Here however there is no reason to be concerned with the details of the theory that can adequately model the ability of an interpreter. All that matters in the present discussion is that the theory has a finite base and is recursive, and these are features on which most philosophers and linguists agree.

To say that an explicit theory for interpreting a speaker is a model of the interpreter's linguistic competence is not to suggest that the interpreter knows any such theory. It is possible, of

---

[4] See the essays on radical interpretation in my *Inquiries into Truth and Interpretation*, Oxford University Press, 1984.

course, that most interpreters could be brought to acknowledge that they know some of the axioms of a theory of truth; for example, that a conjunction is true if and only if each of the conjuncts is true. And perhaps they also know theorems of the form 'An utterance of the sentence "There is life on Mars" is true if and only if there is life on Mars at the time of the utterance.' On the other hand, no one now has explicit knowledge of a fully satisfactory theory for interpreting the speakers of any natural language.

In any case, claims about what would constitute a satisfactory theory are not, as I said, claims about the propositional knowledge of an interpreter, nor are they claims about the details of the inner workings of some part of the brain. They are rather claims about what must be said to give a satisfactory description of the competence of the interpreter. *We* cannot describe what an interpreter can do except by appeal to a recursive theory of a certain sort. It does not add anything to this thesis to say that if the theory does correctly describe the competence of an interpreter, some mechanism in the interpreter must correspond to the theory.

Principle (2) says that for communication to succeed, a systematic method of interpretation must be shared. (I shall henceforth assume there is no harm in calling such a method a theory, as if the interpreter were using the theory we use to describe his competence.) The sharing comes to this: the interpreter uses his theory to understand the speaker; the speaker uses the same (or an equivalent) theory to guide his speech. For the speaker, it is a theory about how the interpreter will interpret him. Obviously this principle does not demand that speaker and interpreter speak the same language. It is an enormous convenience that many people speak in similar ways, and therefore can be interpreted in more or less the same way. But in principle communication does not demand that any two people speak the same language. What must be shared is the interpreter's and the speaker's understanding of the speaker's words.

For reasons that will emerge, I do not think that principles (1) and (2) are incompatible with the existence of malapropisms; it is only when they are combined with principle (3) that there is trouble. Before discussing principle (3) directly, however, I want to introduce an apparent diversion.

The perplexing issue that I want to discuss can be separated off from some related matters by considering a distinction made by Keith Donnellan, and something he said in its defence. Donnellan famously distinguished between two uses of definite descriptions. The *referential* use is illustrated as follows: Jones says 'Smith's murderer is insane', meaning that a certain man, whom he (Jones) takes to have murdered Smith, is insane. Donnellan says that even if the man that Jones believes to have murdered Smith did not murder Smith, Jones has referred to the man he had in mind; and if that man is insane, Jones has said something true. The same sentence may be used *attributively* by someone who wants to assert that the murderer of Smith, whoever he may be, is insane. In this case, the speaker does not say something true if no one murdered Smith, nor has the speaker referred to anyone.

In reply, Alfred MacKay objected that Donnellan shared Humpty Dumpty's theory of meaning: ' "When *I* use a word", Humpty Dumpty said, … "it means just what I choose it to mean." ' In the conversation that went before, he had used the word 'glory' to mean 'a nice knockdown argument'. Donnellan, in answer, explains that intentions are connected with expectations and that you cannot intend to accomplish something by a certain means unless you believe or expect that the means will, or at least could, lead to the desired outcome. A speaker cannot, therefore, intend to mean something by what he says unless he believes his audience will interpret his words as he intends (the Gricean circle). Donnellan says,

> If I were to end this reply to MacKay with the sentence 'There's glory for you' I would be guilty of arrogance and, no doubt, of overestimating the strength of what I have said, but given the background I do not think I could be accused of saying something unintelligible. I would be understood, and would I not have meant by 'glory' 'a nice knockdown argument'?[5]

I like this reply, and I accept Donnellan's original distinction between two uses of descriptions (there are many more than two). But apparently I disagree with *some* view of Donnellan's, because unlike him I see almost no connection between the answer to

[5] Keith Donnellan, 'Putting Humpty Dumpty Together Again', *The Philosophical Review*, **77** (1968), p. 213. Alfred MacKay's article, 'Mr Donnellan and Humpty Dumpty on Referring', appeared in the same issue of *The Philosophical Review*, pp. 197–202.

MacKay's objection and the remarks on reference. The reason is this. MacKay says you cannot change what words mean (and so their reference if that is relevant) merely by intending to; the answer is that this is true, but you can change the meaning provided you believe (and perhaps are justified in believing) that the interpreter has adequate clues for the new interpretation. You may deliberately provide those clues, as Donnellan did for his final 'There's glory for you'.

The trouble is that Donnellan's original distinction had nothing to do with words changing their meaning or reference. If, in the referential use, Jones refers to someone who did not murder Smith by using the description 'Smith's murderer', the reference is none the less achieved by way of the normal meanings of the words. The words therefore must have their usual reference. All that is needed, if we are to accept this way of describing the situation, is a firm sense of the difference between what *words* mean or refer to and what *speakers* mean or refer to. Jones may have referred to someone else by using words that referred to Smith's murderer; this is something he may have done in ignorance or deliberately. Similarly for Donnellan's claim that Jones has said something true when he says 'Smith's murderer is insane', provided the man he believes (erroneously) to have murdered Smith is insane. Jones has said something true by using a sentence that is false. This is done intentionally all the time, for example in irony or metaphor. A coherent theory could not allow that under the circumstances Jones' sentence was true; nor would Jones think so if he knew the facts. Jones' belief about who murdered Smith cannot change the truth of the sentence he uses (and for the same reason cannot change the reference of the words in the sentence).

Humpty Dumpty is out of it. He cannot mean what he says he means because he knows that 'There's glory for you' cannot be interpreted by Alice as meaning 'There's a nice knockdown argument for you'. We know he knows this because Alice says 'I don't know what you mean by "glory" ', and Humpty Dumpty retorts, 'Of course you don't—til I tell you'. It is Mrs Malaprop and Donnellan who interest me; Mrs Malaprop because she gets away with it without even trying or knowing, and Donnellan because he gets away with it on purpose.

Here is what I mean by 'getting away with it': the interpreter comes to the occasion of utterance armed with a theory that tells him (or so he believes) what an arbitrary utterance of the speaker means. The speaker then says something with the intention that it will be interpreted in a certain way, and the expectation that it will be so interpreted. In fact this way is not provided for by the interpreter's theory. But the speaker is nevertheless understood; the interpreter adjusts his theory so that it yields the speaker's intended interpretation. The speaker has 'gotten away with it'. The speaker may or may not (Donnellan, Mrs Malaprop) know that he has got away with anything; the interpreter may or may not know that the speaker intended to get away with anything. What is common to the cases is that the speaker expects to be, and is, interpreted as the speaker intended although the interpreter did not have a correct theory in advance.

We do not need bizarre anecdotes or wonderlands to make the point. We all get away with it all the time; understanding the speech of others depends on it. Take proper names. In small, isolated groups everyone may know the names everyone else knows, and so have ready in advance of a speech encounter a theory that will, without correction, cope with the names to be employed. But even this semantic paradise will be destroyed by each new nickname, visitor, or birth. If a taboo bans a name, a speaker's theory is wrong until he learns of this fact; similarly if an outrigger canoe is christened.

There is not, so far as I can see, any theory of names that gets around the problem. If some definite description gives the meaning of a name, an interpreter still must somehow add to his theory the fact that the name new to him is to be matched with the appropriate description. If understanding a name is to give some weight to an adequate number of descriptions true of the object named, it is even more evident that adding a name to one's way of interpreting a speaker depends on no rule clearly stated in advance. The various theories that discover an essential demonstrative element in names do provide at least a partial rule for adding new names. But the addition is still an addition to the method of interpretation—what we may think of as the interpreter's view of the current language of the speaker. Finding a demonstrative element in names, or for that matter in mass nouns or words for natural kinds, does not reduce these words to pure demonstratives; that is why a new word in any of these categories requires a change in the interpreter's theory, and therefore a change in our description of his understanding of the speaker.

Mrs Malaprop and Donnellan make the case general. There is no word or construction that cannot be converted to a new use by an ingenious or ignorant speaker. And such conversion, while easier to explain because it involves mere substitution, is not the only kind. Sheer invention is equally possible, and we can be as good at interpreting it (say in Joyce or Lewis Carroll) as we are at interpreting the errors or twists of substitution. From the point of view of an ultimate explanation of how new concepts are acquired, learning to interpret a word that expresses a concept we do not already have is a far deeper and more interesting phenomenon than explaining the ability to use a word new to us for an old concept. But both require a change in one's way of interpreting the speech of another, or in speaking to someone who has the use of the word.

The contrast between acquiring a new concept or meaning along with a new word and merely acquiring a new word for an old concept would be salient if I were concerned with the infinitely difficult problem of how a first language is learned. By comparison, my problem is simple. I want to know how people who already have a language (whatever exactly that means) manage to apply their skill or knowledge to actual cases of interpretation. All the things I assume an interpreter knows or can do depend on his having a mature set of concepts, and being at home with the business of linguistic communication. My problem is to describe what is involved in the idea of 'having a language' or of being at home with the business of linguistic communication.

Here is a highly simplified and idealised proposal about what goes on. An interpreter has, at any moment of a speech transaction, what I persist in calling a theory. (I call it a theory, as remarked before, only because a description of the interpreter's competence requires a recursive account.) I assume that the interpreter's theory has been adjusted to the evidence so far available to him: knowledge of the character, dress, role, sex, of the speaker, and whatever else has been gained by observing the speaker's behaviour, linguistic or otherwise. As the speaker speaks his piece the interpreter alters his theory, entering hypotheses about new names, altering the interpretation of familiar predicates, and revising past interpretations of particular utterances in the light of new evidence.

Some of what goes on may be described as improving the method of interpretation as the evidential base enlarges. But much is not like that. When Donnellan ends his reply to MacKay by saying 'There's glory for you', not only he, but his words, are correctly interpreted as meaning 'There's a nice knockdown argument for you'. That's how he intends us to interpret his words, and we know this, since we have, and he knows we have, and we know he knows we have (etc.), the background needed to provide the interpretation. But up to a certain point (before MacKay came on the scene) this interpretation of an earlier utterance by Donnellan of the same words would have been wrong. To put this differently: the theory we actually use to interpret an utterance is geared to the occasion. We may decide later we could have done better by the occasion, but this does not mean (necessarily) that we now have a better theory for the next occasion. The reason for this is, as we have seen, perfectly obvious: a speaker may provide us with information relevant to interpreting an utterance in the course of making the utterance.

Let us look at the process from the speaker's side. The speaker wants to be understood, so he intends to speak in such a way that he will be interpreted in a certain way. In order to judge how he will be interpreted, he forms, or uses, a picture of the interpreter's readiness to interpret along certain lines. Central to this picture is what the speaker believes is the starting theory of interpretation the interpreter has for him. The speaker does not necessarily speak in such a way as to prompt the interpreter to apply this prior theory; he may deliberately dispose the interpreter to modify his prior theory. But the speaker's view of the interpreter's prior theory is not irrelevant to what he says, nor to what he means by his words; it is an important part of what he has to go on if he wants to be understood.

I have distinguished what I have been calling the *prior theory* from what I shall henceforth call the *passing theory*. For the hearer, the prior theory expresses how he is prepared in advance to interpret an utterance of the speaker, while the passing theory is how he *does* interpret the utterance. For the speaker, the prior theory is what he *believes* the interpreter's prior theory to be, while his passing theory is the theory he *intends* the interpreter to use.

I am now in a position to state a problem that arises if we accept the distinction between the prior and the passing theory and also accept the account of linguistic competence given by principles (1)–(2). According to that account, each interpreter (and this includes speakers, since speakers must be interpreters) comes to a successful linguistic exchange prepared with a 'theory' which constitutes his basic linguistic competence, and which he shares with those with whom he communicates. Because each party has such a shared theory and knows that others share his theory, and knows that others know he knows (etc.), some would say that the knowledge or abilities that constitute the theory may be called conventions.

I think that the distinction between the prior and the passing theory, if taken seriously, undermines this commonly accepted account of linguistic competence and communication. Here is why. What must be shared for communication to succeed is the passing theory. For the passing theory is the one the interpreter actually uses to interpret an utterance, and it is the theory the speaker intends the interpreter to use. Only if these coincide is understanding complete. (Of course, there are degrees of success in communication; much may be right although something is wrong. This matter of degree is irrelevant to my argument.)

The passing theory is where, accident aside, agreement is greatest. As speaker and interpreter talk, their prior theories become more alike; so do their passing theories. The asymptote of agreement and understanding is when passing theories coincide. But the passing theory cannot in general correspond to an interpreter's linguistic competence. Not only does it have its changing list of proper names and gerrymandered vocabulary, but it includes every successful—i.e. correctly interpreted—use of any other word or phrase, no matter how far out of the ordinary. Every deviation from ordinary usage, as long as it is agreed on for the moment (knowingly deviant, or not, on one, or both, sides), is in the passing theory as a feature of what the words mean on that occasion. Such meanings, transient though they may be, are literal; they are what I have called first meanings. A passing theory is not a theory of what anyone (except perhaps a philosopher) would call an actual natural language. 'Mastery' of such a language would be useless, since knowing a passing theory is only knowing how to interpret a particular utterance on a particular occasion. Nor could such a language, if we want to call it that, be said to have been learned, or to be governed by conventions.

Of course things previously learned were essential to arriving at the passing theory, but what was learned could not have been the passing theory.

Why should a passing theory be called a theory at all? For the sort of theory we have in mind is, in its formal structure, suited to be the theory for an entire language, even though its expected field of application is vanishingly small. The answer is that when a word or phrase temporarily or locally takes over the role of some other word or phrase (as treated in a prior theory, perhaps), the entire burden of that role, with all its implications for logical relations to other words, phrases, and sentences, must be carried along by the passing theory. Someone who grasps the fact that Mrs Malaprop means 'epithet' when she says 'epitaph' must give 'epithet' all the powers 'epitaph' has for many other people. Only a full recursive theory can do justice to these powers. These remarks do not depend on supposing Mrs Malaprop will always make this 'mistake'; once is enough to summon up a passing theory assigning a new role to 'epitaph'.

An interpreter's prior theory has a better chance of describing what we might think of as a natural language, particularly a prior theory brought to a first conversation. The less we know about the speaker, assuming we know he belongs to our language community, the more nearly our prior theory will simply be the theory we expect someone who hears our unguarded speech to use. If we ask for a cup of coffee, direct a taxi driver, or order a crate of lemons, we may know so little about our intended interpreter that we can do no better than to assume that he will interpret our speech along what we take to be standard lines. But all this is relative. In fact we always have the interpreter in mind; there is no such thing as how we expect, in the abstract, to be interpreted. We inhibit our higher vocabulary, or encourage it, depending on the most general considerations, and we cannot fail to have premonitions as to which of the proper names we know are apt to be correctly understood.

In any case, my point is this: most of the time prior theories will not be shared, and there is no reason why they should be. Certainly it is not a condition of successful communication that prior theories be shared: consider the malaprop from ignorance. Mrs Malaprop's theory, prior and passing, is that 'A nice derangement of epitaphs' means a nice arrangement of epithets.

An interpreter who, as we say, knows English, but does not know the verbal habits of Mrs Malaprop, has a prior theory according to which 'A nice derangement of epitaphs' means a nice derangement of epitaphs; but his passing theory agrees with that of Mrs Malaprop if he understands her words.

It is quite clear that in general the prior theory is neither shared by speaker and interpreter nor is it what we would normally call a language. For the prior theory has in it all the features special to the idiolect of the speaker that the interpreter is in a position to take into account before the utterance begins. One way to appreciate the difference between the prior theory and our ordinary idea of a person's language is to reflect on the fact that an interpreter must be expected to have quite different prior theories for different speakers—not as different, usually, as his passing theories; but these are matters that depend on how well the interpreter knows his speaker.

Neither the prior theory nor the passing theory describes what we would call the language a person knows, and neither theory characterises a speaker's or interpreter's linguistic competence. Is there any theory that would do better?

Perhaps it will be said that what is essential to the mastery of a language is not knowledge of any particular vocabulary, or even detailed grammar, much less knowledge of what any speaker is apt to succeed in making his words and sentences mean. What is essential is a basic framework of categories and rules, a sense of the way English (or any) grammars may be constructed, plus a skeleton list of interpreted words for fitting into the basic framework. If I put all this vaguely, it is only because I want to consider a large number of actual or possible proposals in one fell swoop; for I think they all fail to resolve our problem. They fail for the same reasons the more complete and specific prior theories fail: none of them satisfies the demand for a description of an ability that speaker and interpreter share and that is adequate to interpretation.

First, any general framework, whether conceived as a grammar for English, or a rule for accepting grammars, or a basic grammar plus rules for modifying or extending it—any such general framework, by virtue of the features that make it general, will by itself be insufficient for interpreting particular utterances. The general framework or theory, whatever it is, may be a key ingredient in what is needed for interpretation, but it can't be all that is needed since it fails to provide the interpretation of particular words and sentences as uttered by a particular speaker. In this respect it is like a prior theory, only worse because it is less complete.

Second, the framework theory must be expected to be different for different speakers. The more general and abstract it is, the more difference there can be without it mattering to communication. The theoretical possibility of such divergence is obvious; but once one tries to imagine a framework rich enough to serve its purpose, it is clear that such differences must also be actual. It is impossible to give examples, of course, until it is decided what to count in the framework: a sufficiently explicit framework could be discredited by a single malapropism. There is some evidence of a more impressive sort that internal grammars do differ among speakers of 'the same language'. James McCawley reports that recent work by Haber shows

> ...that there is appreciable variation as to what rules of plural formation different speakers have, the variation being manifested in such things as the handling of novel words that an investigator has presented his subjects with, in the context of a task that will force them to use the word in the plural...Haber suggests that her subjects, rather than having a uniformly applicable process of plural formation, each have a 'core' system, which covers a wide range of cases, but not necessarily everything, plus strategies...for handling cases that are not covered by the 'core' system...Haber's data suggest that speakers of what are to the minutest details 'the same dialect' often have acquired grammars that differ in far more respects than their speech differs in.[6]

I have been trying to throw doubt on how clear the idea of 'speaking the same dialect' is, but here we may assume that it at least implies the frequent sharing of passing theories.

Bringing in grammars, theories, or frameworks more general than, and prior to, prior theories just emphasises the problem I originally presented in terms of the contrast between prior theories and passing theories. Stated more broadly now, the problem is this: what interpreter and speaker share, to the extent that communication succeeds, is not learned and so is not a

---

[6] James McCawley, 'Some Ideas Not to Live By', *Die Neuern Sprachen*, **75** (1976), p. 157. These results are disputed by those who believe the relevant underlying rules and structures are prewired. My point obviously does not depend on the example, or the level at which deviations are empirically possible.

language governed by rules or conventions known to speaker and interpreter in advance; but what the speaker and interpreter know in advance is not (necessarily) shared, and so is not a language governed by shared rules or conventions. What is shared is, as before, the passing theory; what is given in advance is the prior theory, or anything on which it may in turn be based.

What I have been leaving out of account up to now is what Haber calls a 'strategy', which is a nice word for the mysterious process by which a speaker or hearer uses what he knows in advance plus present data to produce a passing theory. What two people need, if they are to understand one another through speech, is the ability to converge on passing theories from utterance to utterance. Their starting points, however far back we want to take them, will usually be very different—as different as the ways in which they acquired their linguistic skills. So also, then, will the strategies and strategems that bring about convergence differ.

Perhaps we can give content to the idea of two people 'having the same language' by saying that they tend to converge on passing theories; degree or relative frequency of convergence would then be a measure of similarity of language. What use can we find, however, for the concept of a language? We could hold that any theory on which a speaker and interpreter converge is a language; but then there would be a new language for every unexpected turn in the conversation, and languages could not be learned and no one would want to master most of them.

We just made a sort of sense of the idea of two people 'having the same language', though we could not explain what a language is. It is easy to see that the idea of 'knowing' a language will be in the same trouble, as will the project of characterising the abilities or capacities a person must have if he commands a language. But we might try to say in what a person's ability to interpret or speak to another person consists: it is the ability that permits him to construct a correct, that is, convergent, passing theory for speech transactions with that person. Again, the concept allows of degrees of application.

This characterisation of linguistic ability is so nearly circular that it cannot be wrong: it comes to saying that the ability to communicate by speech consists in the ability to make oneself understood, and to understand. It is only when we look at the structure of this ability that we realise how far we have drifted from standard ideas of language mastery. For we have discovered no learnable common core of consistent behaviour, no shared grammar or rules, no portable interpreting machine set to grind out the meaning of an arbitrary utterance. We may say that linguistic ability is the ability to converge on a passing theory from time to time—this is what I have suggested, and I have no better proposal. But if we do say this, then we should realise that we have abandoned not only the ordinary notion of a language, but we have erased the boundary between knowing a language and knowing our way around in the world generally. For there are no rules for arriving at passing theories, no rules in any strict sense, as opposed to rough maxims and methodological generalities. A passing theory really is like a theory at least in this, that it is derived by wit, luck, and wisdom from a private vocabulary and grammar, knowledge of the ways people get their point across, and rules of thumb for figuring out what deviations from the dictionary are most likely. There is no more chance of regularising, or teaching, this process than there is of regularising or teaching the process of creating new theories to cope with new data in any field—for that is what this process involves.

The problem we have been grappling with depends on the assumption that communication by speech requires that speaker and interpreter have learned or somehow acquired a common method or theory of interpretation—as being able to operate on the basis of shared conventions, rules, or regularities. The problem arose when we realised that no method or theory fills this bill. The solution to the problem is clear. In linguistic communication nothing corresponds to a linguistic competence as often described: that is, as summarised by principles (1)–(3). The solution is to give up the principles. Principles (1) and (2) survive when understood in rather unusual ways, but principle (3) cannot stand, and it is unclear what can take its place. I conclude that there is no such thing as a language, not if a language is anything like what many philosophers and linguists have supposed. There is therefore no such thing to be learned, mastered, or born with. We must give up the idea of a clearly defined shared structure which language-users acquire and then apply to cases. And we should try again to say how convention in any important sense is involved in language; or, as I think, we should give up the attempt to illuminate how we communicate by appeal to conventions.

8 *The Social Aspect of Language*

1

Which is conceptually primary, the idiolect or the language? If the former, the apparent absence of a social norm makes it hard to account for success in communication; if the latter, the danger is that the norm has no clear relation to practice. Michael Dummett thinks that by promoting the primacy of the idiolect I run afoul of Wittgenstein's ban on private languages; in my view Dummett, by making language primary, has misplaced the essential social element in linguistic behavior. In this paper I want to try to sort out and clarify the issues involved.

"There is no such a thing as a language", I wrote in a piece called *A Nice Derangement of Epitaphs*.[1] This is the sort of remark for which one can expect to be pilloried, and Michael did not spare me. I must think, he teases, that when Bretons, Catalans, Basques and Kurds declare that language is the soul of their culture, or dictators attempt to suppress minority languages, that Bretons, Catalans, Basques, Kurds and dictators are all suffering from the illusion that there are such things as languages to cherish or suppress. Michael realizes, of course, that what I actually said was, "There is no such a thing as a language, not if a language is anything like what many philosophers and linguists have

---

[1] See Donald Davidson, 'A Nice Derangement of Epitaphs', in R. Grandy and R. Warner (eds.), *Philosophical Grounds of Rationality*, Oxford University Press, 1986. Reprinted in E. Lepore (ed.), *Truth and Interpretation*, Blackwell, 1986. [Also Ch. 7 above.] (Page numbers will be to this reprinting.)

supposed." But he won't let me get away with this, for he contends that I have offered no alternative account of what a language is.[2] This is a little unfair; I did delineate with some care the concept of a language to which I object. If I were right in saying no actual language is like that, it would not invalidate my argument, even if I offered no alternative view. So when Michael says "The occurrence of the phenomena that interest Davidson is incontrovertible: but how can an investigation of them lead to the conclusion that there is no such a thing as a language?" I can only agree; it can't lead to this conclusion. But it does lead to the conclusion that there is no such thing as what some philosophers (including me) have *called* a language.

In fact, I also did offer an alternative; of that, more later. But first, let's look at the concept of a language I opposed. It was this: in learning a language, a person acquires the ability to operate in accord with a precise and specifiable set of syntactic and semantic rules; verbal communication depends on speaker and bearer sharing such an ability, and it requires no more than this. I argued that sharing such a previously mastered ability was neither necessary nor sufficient for successful linguistic communication. I held (and hold) that the linguistic skills people typically bring to conversational occasions can and do differ considerably, but mutual understanding is achieved through the exercise of imagination, appeal to general knowledge of the world, and awareness of human interests and attitudes. Of course I did not deny that in practice people usually depend on a supply of words and syntactic devices which they have learned to employ in similar ways. What I denied was that such sharing is sufficient to explain our actual communicative achievements, and more important, I denied that even such limited sharing is necessary.

It is clear that there are two theses here which must be kept separate. The first thesis is that there is a Platonic concept of a language which is neither instantiated in practice nor (therefore) what we normally mean by the word 'language'. The second is that neither the usual concept nor the philosophical concept is very important in understanding what is essential to verbal communication. The ultimate persuasiveness, if not the correctness,

---

[2] See Michael Dummett, 'A Nice Derangement of Epitaphs: Some Comments on Davidson and Hacking', in Lepore (ed.), *Truth and Interpretation*.

of this second claim depends on presenting an alternative account of what is essential to verbal communication.

Now let me try to clarify, still in a preliminary way, where I think Michael and I agree and where we don't. With respect to the first thesis, that there is no rigid set of rules to which those who share a language must conform, I think we have no serious argument; I have the impression that Michael holds, as I do, that actual linguistic practice is only loosely related to any fully and precisely specified language, with phonetics, semantics, and syntax made explicit. What I say about proper names in this regard, for example, is close to what Michael says;[3] he accepts that there is a good deal of flexibility in what we count as two people speaking the same language and he realizes that in understanding others we must sometimes draw on more than our previously mastered linguistic skills. Our differences here are matters of degree and emphasis. Nor do I think my failure to produce an alternative account of language is really what bothers Michael. I am happy to say speakers share a language if and only if they tend to use the same words to mean the same thing, and once this idea is properly tidied up it is only a short, uninteresting step to defining the predicate 'is a language' in a way that corresponds, as nearly as may be, with ordinary usage. What bothers Michael is not my failure to take this step (somewhere I do take it), but my failure to appreciate that the concept of a speaker meaning something by what he says depends on the notion of a shared language and not the other way around. My mistake, in his eyes, is that I take defining a language as the philosophically rather unimportant task of grouping idiolects, whereas he thinks I have no non-circular way of characterizing idiolects. I shall come to this crux presently; but first I want to try to remove, or defuse, some differences that seem to me to be mainly verbal.

Michael chides me for extending the usual use of the word 'interpret' and its cognates to those ordinary situations in which we understand others without conscious effort or reflection, and he hints that this reveals an underlying error or confusion on my part. I do not think I have ever conflated the (empirical) question how we actually go about understanding a speaker with the

---

[3] See Michael Dummett, *The Interpretation of Frege's Philosophy*, Duckworth, 1981, pp. 189 ff.

(philosophical) question what is necessary and sufficient for such understanding. I have focused on the latter question, not because I think it brings us close to the psychology of language learning and use, but because I think it brings out the philosophically important aspects of communication while the former tempts us to speculate about arcane empirical matters that neither philosophers nor psychologists know much about. So let me say (not for the first time): I do not think we normally understand what others say by consciously reflecting on the question what they mean, by appealing to some theory of interpretation, or by summoning up what we take to be the relevant evidence. We do it, much of the time, effortlessly, even automatically. We can do this because we have learned to talk pretty much as others do, and this explains why we generally understand without effort much that they say.

It is significant, though, that Michael tries to saddle me with the extremely restricted meaning given the word 'interpretation' by the translators of Wittgenstein. According to this meaning, an interpretation of a word or expression is always another word, or expression. This is quite definitely, and I should have thought clearly, not the meaning I have in mind, though confusion is possible. If I ask how someone interpreted an utterance of the sentence 'Snow is white', and am told that she interpreted it as meaning that snow is white (or as being true if and only if snow is white), my question was not, as the answer shows, what other words the hearer might have substituted for the sentence "Snow is white." I am asking how the person understood the utterance of those words. Of course I must use words to say how she understood those words, since I must use words to say anything, but my words are not offered as the interpretation; they merely help describe it. The confusion results from conflating the use of words (to describe, in this case a mental act or state), and the mention of those words (to specify the words that *constitute* an interpretation). I agree with Michael that "one who...understands a sentence need not be able to say how he understands it. He does not have to be able to say it even to himself...."[4]

It would obviously have been absurd of me to have claimed, as Dummett implies I have claimed, that whenever we understand a speaker we translate his words into our own. Translation is no

---

[4] See Dummett, 'A Nice Derangement', p. 464.

part of the transaction between speaker and hearer that I call interpretation. Where translation of a sort may be involved is in the description the philosopher gives in his language of what the hearer makes of the speaker's utterances.

There is, I think, a related confusion about my use of the word 'theory'. I do, in *A Nice Derangement of Epitaphs* and elsewhere, allow myself to speak of the theory a hearer has when he understands a speaker. But like Humpty Dumpty after he has told Alice what he means by "There's glory for you", I explained first that this was a mere *façon de parler*; here is what I said:

To say that an explicit theory for interpreting a speaker is a model of the interpreter's linguistic competence is not to suggest that the interpreter knows any such theory. It is possible, of course, that most interpreters could be brought to acknowledge that they know some of the axioms of a theory of truth; for example, that a conjunction is true if and only if each of the conjuncts is true... In any case, claims about what would constitute a satisfactory theory are not... claims about the propositional knowledge of an interpreter... They are rather claims about what must be said to give a satisfactory description of the competence of the interpreter. *We* cannot describe what an interpreter can do except by appeal to a recursive theory...[5]

So Dummett is agreeing with me when he says, "We shall go astray... if we make a literal equation of the mastery of a practice with the possession of theoretical knowledge of what the practice is".[6] You will notice that I do not speak of implicit knowledge here or elsewhere: the point is not that speaker or hearer has a theory, but that they speak and understand in accord with a theory—a theory that is needed only when we want to describe their abilities and performance.

On a further important issue Michael and I again see eye to eye: we both insist that verbal behavior is necessarily social. In my view, and I think in his, this is not just a matter of how we use the word 'language': there couldn't be anything like a language without more than one person. Perhaps we even agree on the underlying reason, namely Wittgenstein's, that without a social environment nothing could count as misapplying words in speech. Where we part company is in how we think the social environment makes its essential contribution.

---

[5] See Davidson, 'A Nice Derangement', p. 438 [p. 95–6 above].
[6] See Dummett, 'A Nice Derangement', p. 476.

Hilary Putnam has made much of 'the linguistic division of labor', and Michael has made clear that he too thinks the phenomenon is an important example of the way human communication depends on the society in which it is embedded.[7] I do not doubt the existence of the phenomenon, or even its importance. But what does it show? Like Dummett, I don't think it shows, as Putnam insists, that "meanings ain't in the head"; for we can take it to be part of the meaning of an expression that its reference is to be determined by expert opinion. This would demonstrate that a speaker must *believe* there are experts, but not that there must be. So for the words 'elm' and 'beech' to pick out the appropriate trees there would have to be experts, but we cannot conclude that the meaningful use of these words demands a social setting. Dummett makes a similar point against Kripke's causal theory of names. More significantly from my point of view, it is obvious that the linguistic division of labor is a device that can come into play only after the basic linguistic skills that tie words directly to things are already in place. So no matter how universal the linguistic division of labor is in practice, it cannot constitute the essential social element in language. We could get along without it.

Dummett writes "Davidson would like us to believe that our whole understanding of another's speech is effected without our having to know anything" and in support of this attribution he quotes me as saying "there is no such thing as a language to be learned or mastered". Of course even if there were no such thing to be learned it wouldn't follow that we could understand speech without knowing anything; we would have to know much more. And it is in fact a major contention of my paper that we do know, and use, much more, even in grasping just the literal meanings of a speaker's words, than our mastery of any fixed set of rules would allow us to grasp. But this is not the central misunderstanding; it springs once more from the fact that Dummett does not want to notice that what I said was that there is no such thing as what some philosophers have described as a language to be learned. We all do learn languages (in the ordinary, vague sense of language Dummett and I and everyone else have in mind). As a practical matter one can't make too much of this. I did my best to sketch

<hr>

[7] See ibid., p. 475, and Michael Dummett, 'The Social Character of Meaning', in *Truth and other Enigmas*, Harvard University Press, 1980, pp. 424 ff.

how I think this works. However, my interest at this point was not to describe actual practice, but to decide what is necessary to linguistic communication. And here I thought I saw (and see) clear reasons to doubt that language, if language is taken to imply shared ways of speaking, is essential. The same doubts apply to the notion of following a rule, engaging in a practice, or conforming to conventions, *if these are taken to imply such sharing*. (Please note the proviso.)

What is the source of these doubts? Well, starting at the small end, there is the simple fact that almost no two people share all words. Even during a conversation, each is apt to use words the other did not know before the conversation began, and so cannot belong to a practice the speakers shared in detail; here I think particularly of names and of words new to the vocabulary of one or the other speaker. Then there are malapropisms which are nevertheless understood, slips of the tongue, and all the 'errors', as we think of them, that we would not normally commit ourselves (perhaps), but that as hearers we take in our stride: "The plane will be landing momentarily", "The phenomena is...The data is...The octopi are..." These are often part of the practice of one speaker but not of another, but communication does not suffer, though affection or admiration may wither. We have no trouble following the conversation of the child who says "He wented to the store" and who generally forms the past tense according to a rule which is not part of 'the language'. Actual cases grow rarer as they grow more extreme, but more extreme cases certainly exist. People who speak dialects of what we call the same language may not at first be able to make anything of what the other says; after they learn to understand each other, each may continue to speak in his own way, just as I have learned to answer letters in German, Spanish, and French in English. Someone with a unique and serious speech defect may be understood by those around him.

Now to make a leap. There seems to me to be no reason, in theory at least, why speakers who understand each other ever need to speak, or to have spoken, as anyone else speaks, much less as each other speaks. Of course, the concept of 'same' (as in 'speak in the same way', or 'speak the same language') that we are depending on so heavily is already that philosophically teasing notion of similarity. I assume that two speakers couldn't understand each other if each couldn't (pretty well) say in his way what the other says in his. If we employ the translation manual relating the two ways of speaking to define what we mean by speaking in the same way, we can after all salvage something of the claim that communication requires a shared practice. But this is not what anyone would call sharing a language, nor what anyone has meant by a common practice or a shared set of rules or conventions. It is a question how Dummett might specify in a non-circular way how speakers of 'the same language' must resemble one another. As Warren Goldfarb emphasizes (in discussing Kripke's 'sceptical' solution to Wittgenstein's problem), 'any problem we find in rule following will arise even with respect to what counts as the same', and he quotes Wittgenstein,[8]

If you have to have an intuition in order to develop the series 1,2,3,4.... then you must also have one to develop the series 2,2,2,...(*Philosophical Investigations* §214)

I can think of three strategies for dealing with my doubts: one can claim that I have ignored the fact that speakers of a language are responsible to a social norm even if they do not hold to it; one can concede that communication without shared practices may be theoretically possible, but argue that this is pointless speculation given that it never occurs in a pure form and probably couldn't; and, finally, it may be urged that no alternative answer to Wittgenstein's query has been offered, the query being: what is the difference between using words correctly and merely thinking that one is using them correctly? I will take up these three responses in turn.

According to Dummett,[9]

Figures of speech and other deliberately non-standard uses apart, a speaker holds himself responsible to the accepted meanings of words and expressions in the language or dialect he purports to be speaking; his willingness to withdraw or correct what he has said when made aware of a mistake about the meaning of the word in the common language therefore distinguishes erroneous uses from intentionally deviant ones.

Of course it is easy to agree that people speak as they think others do except when they don't. And if dialects can be divided as

---

[8] See Warren Goldfarb, 'Kripke and Wittgenstein on Rules', *The Journal of Philosophy*, 82 (1985), 471–88, p. 485.   [9] See Dummett, 'A Nice Derangement', p. 462.

finely as need be, I can have no objections to much of the spirit of Michael's claim. The blacks in Brooklyn don't want to speak as whites do, and some individuals (James Joyce), though they want to be understood, don't want to talk as anyone else does. But the crux is the idea of obligation to the norm constituted by the 'accepted' meanings of words, for it is in omitting this idea that I have apparently left out something essential to characterizing the kind of meaning involved in verbal communication. I don't see how. Suppose someone learns to talk as others do, but feels no obligation whatever to do so. For this speaker obligation doesn't enter into it. We ask why she talks as others do. "I don't do it because I think I should", she replies, "I just do talk that way. I don't think I have an obligation to walk upright, it just comes naturally." If what she says is true, would she not be speaking a language, or would she cease to be intelligible? In other words, what magic ingredient does holding oneself responsible to the usual way of speaking add to the usual way of speaking?

Perhaps the answer will be that the sense of obligation only reveals itself when one is made aware of a mistake about the meaning of a word in the common language, and one willingly corrects oneself. Of course if one thinks she is wrong about what a word means to others, she will change her mind, just as she would about anything else; will and obligation have nothing to do with it. So it must be the public gesture that counts. And no doubt most of us make such gestures willingly under appropriate circumstances. My wife is embarrassed because I have in my vocabulary the word (non-word?) 'as-cer'tainable'. I'm embarrassed, too, to learn that my word is not part of the English language. I'll try, probably unsuccessfully, to change my ways. But why? Well, I don't want people to think I don't know that others say 'as-cer-tain'able' where I say 'as-cer'tain-able'. Who wants to label himself as ignorant? I'm too old to be embarrassed much by not being able to spell, and it amuses my students; but I'd spell things right if I could. These pressures are social and they are very real. They do not, however, as far as I can divine, have anything to do with meaning or communication. Using a word in a nonstandard way out of ignorance may be a *faux pas* in the same way that using the wrong fork at a dinner party is, and it has as little to do with communication as using the wrong fork has to do with nourishing oneself, given that the word is understood and the fork works.

Of course, I don't mean that there is no reason why we are taught, and why we learn, to speak more or less as others around us do. Nothing could be more obvious: we want to be understood and others have an interest in understanding us; ease of communication is vastly promoted by such sharing. Most of us do not have the time or ability to learn very many different languages. In the case of our children, or certain poets and writers, we must or do make exceptions, but in general our tolerance of strongly deviant idiolects is limited by clear practical considerations. None of this creates a free-standing obligation, however. Any obligation we owe to conformity is contingent on the desire to be understood. If we can make ourselves understood while deviating from the social norm, any further obligation has nothing to do with meaning or successful communication. As Aristotle says, "It would be absurd to wish good for wine; if one wishes it at all, it is that the wine may keep, so that we may have it for ourselves."[10] It is absurd to be obligated to a language; so far as the point of language is concerned, our only *obligation*, if that is the word, is to speak in such a way as to accomplish our purpose by being understood as we expect and intend. It is an accident, though a likely one, if this requires that we speak as others in our community do.

"In employing words of the English language", writes Dummett, "we have to be held responsible to their socially accepted use, on pain of failing to communicate."[11] But if the threat of failure to communicate is the reason for conforming, responsibility is irrelevant: Michael might less tendentiously have written, "If we want to communicate, we should use words in their socially accepted way". The residual problem with this is that it is false in all those cases when we will be better understood if we deviate from the 'socially accepted' use. If we want to be understood, all we need to worry about is how our actual audience will take our words. The correct advice is Lord Chesterfield's: "Speak the language of the company you are in; and speak it purely, and unlarded with any other." What, after all, is the point of speaking in accord with 'accepted usage' to a company that we know will understand us only if we depart from accepted usage? I don't say

[10] See Aristotle, *Nicomachean Ethics*, 1155 B 29–31.
[11] See Dummett, 'Social Character of Meaning', p. 429.

there couldn't be a point in doing this, but what would it have to do with communication?

Now to address the contention that it is pointless to speculate on the remote possibility of there being speakers who, though they express themselves in distinct idiolects, understand one another. I have agreed that the possibility is in practice restricted to special cases, and I have stressed both the obvious utility of the large degrees of overlap in verbal performance we find in groups that live and talk together, and the inevitability that conformity will be learned and encouraged. The theoretical possibility of communication without shared practices remains philosophically important because it shows that such sharing cannot be an essential constituent in meaning and communication. If I am right, then important claims by Tyler Burge, Saul Kripke, and perhaps Wittgenstein and Dummett must be false, for certainly the first two have insisted that speaking in the 'socially accepted' way is essential to verbal communication, and if this is not Dummett's view it is obscure what argument he thinks he has with me. I'd better leave Wittgenstein out of this; I'll just say Kripkenstein. It also seems to me important to emphasize that much successful communing goes on that does not depend on previously learned common practices, for recognizing this helps us appreciate the extent to which understanding, even of the literal meaning of a speaker's utterances, depends on shared general information and familiarity with non-linguistic institutions (a 'way of life').

I now turn to the third challenge the idiolect must face. The challenge is to draw the distinction Wittgenstein has made central to the study of meaning, the distinction between using words correctly and merely thinking one is using them correctly, without appeal to the test of common usage. This is the hardest, and the most important, challenge, and I agree with Michael if he believes the challenge can be met only by appeal to a social setting.[12]

What is needed is a norm, something that provides a speaker with a way of telling (not necessarily always) that he has gone wrong, a norm the failure to satisfy which he or she will count

---

[12] I am not impressed with the self-testing procedures suggested, e.g., by Simon Backburn, nor with David Pears' similar claim.

as having gone wrong. (There is a further condition on a satisfactory description of the norm that I shall come to later.) Speaking in accord with socially accepted usage is such a norm, but one which, I have argued, is irrelevant to communication unless the audience of the speaker happens to speak as he does, in which case the norm is relevant not because it is a shared practice or convention, but because conforming to it results in understanding. My proposal takes off from this observation: what matters, the point of language or speech or whatever you want to call it, is communication, getting across to someone else what you have in mind by means of words that they interpret (understand) as you want them to. Speech has endless other purposes, but none underlies this one: it is not an ultimate or universal purpose of speech to say what one thinks is true, nor to speak as one thinks others do.

The intention to be taken to mean what one wants to be taken to mean is, it seems to me, so clearly the only aim that is common to all verbal behavior that it is hard for me to see how anyone can deny it. But I can easily understand why this observation can seem too true to be interesting, given that it assumes the notion of meaning. Still, if it is true, it is important, for it provides a purpose which any speaker must have in speaking, and thus constitutes a norm against which speakers and others can measure the success of verbal behavior.

Success in communicating propositional contents—not just accidental or sporadic success, but more or less reliable success, achieved by employing devices capable of a wide range of expression—such success is what we need to understand before we ask about the nature of meaning or of language, for the concepts of a language or of meaning, like those of a sentence or a name or of reference or of truth, are concepts we can grasp and employ only when the communication of propositional contents is established. Meaning, in the special sense in which we are interested when we talk of what an utterance literally means, gets its life from those situations in which someone intends (or assumes or expects) that his words will be understood in a certain way, and they are. In such cases we can say without hesitation: how he intended to be understood, and was understood, is what he, and his words, literally meant on that occasion. There are many other interpretations we give to the notion of (literal, verbal) meaning, but the rest are parasitic on this.[13] Thus for me the concept of 'the meaning' of a word or sentence gives way to the concepts of how a speaker intends his words to be understood, and of how a hearer understands them. Where understanding matches intent we can, if we please, speak of 'the' meaning; but it is understanding that gives life to meaning, not the other way around.

This explains why I am not impressed by Michael's or Burge's or Putnam's insistence that words may have a meaning of which both speaker and hearer are ignorant. I don't doubt that we sometimes say this, and it's fairly clear what we have in mind: speaker and hearer are ignorant of what would be found in some dictionary, or of how people with a better or different education or a higher income use the words. This is still meaning based on successful communication, but it imports into the theory of meaning an elitist norm by implying that people not in the right social swim don't really know what they mean.[14]

What should we say of the many cases in which a speaker expects, or hopes, to be understood in a certain way but isn't? I can't see that it matters. If we bear in mind that the notion of meaning is a theoretical concept which can't explain communication but depends on it, we can harmlessly relate it to successful communication in whatever ways we find convenient. So, if a speaker reasonably believes he will be interpreted in a certain way, and speaks with the intention of being so understood, we may choose to say he means what (in the primary sense) he would have meant if he had been understood as he expected and intended. Reasonable belief is itself such a flexible concept that we may want to add that there must be people who would understand the speaker as he intends, and the speaker reasonably believes

---

[13] This formulation of the notion of meaning is not, it should be clear, Gricean, for where the present formulation rests on the (at this point unanalysed) concept of understanding, Grice aimed at defining linguistic meaning, as well as non-natural meaning generally, in terms of intentions that do not involve meaning at all. The Gricean element in my formulation is the dependence of meaning on intention.

[14] In 'the normal' case, Dummett writes, "speaker and hearer treat words as having the meanings they do in the language . . . The view I am urging against Davidson is an adaptation of Alice's picture, according to which words have meanings in themselves, independently of speakers." Not independently of all speakers, he adds, since the meanings do depend on a social practice. So he must mean independently of whether the speaker or his audience happen to know what the social practice is on a particular occasion. See Dummett, 'A Nice Derangement', pp. 472–3.

he is speaking to such a person. Further refinements suggest themselves. But the point remains; the concept of meaning would have no application if there were not endless cases of successful communication, and any further use we give to the notion of meaning depends on the existence of such cases. These remarks should make plain why Dummett's accusation, that I endorse a variety of Humpty Dumpty's theory that meaning depends only on intention, does not find its target.

Michael objects to making understanding depend on the intentions of a speaker, especially intentions that depend on beliefs about how an audience will interpret his utterances. He says that in the 'normal' case speaker and hearer "treat the words as having the meanings they do in the language. Their so treating them does not consist in their having any beliefs about the other person." What they are going on[15]

are their beliefs (if they can be called beliefs) about what the words mean, not about what the other takes or intends them to mean ... No speaker needs to form any express intention, or to hold any particular theory about his audience, or, indeed, about the language, in order to mean by a word what it means in the language.

I agree that the speaker does not usually 'form an express intention', and he does not 'hold a theory', but I do say that even when a speaker is speaking in accord with a socially acceptable theory he speaks with the intention of being understood in a certain way, and this intention depends on his beliefs about his audience, in particular how he believes or assumes they will understand him. It may be that once again Michael and I are using words in somewhat different ways, in this case the words 'intention' and 'belief'. I think someone acts intentionally when there is an answer to the question what his reasons in acting were, and one can often tell what an agent's reasons were by asking whether he would have acted as he did if he had not had those reasons. I don't think of consciously rehearsed beliefs or deliberately reasoned intentions as the only beliefs and intentions we have. Suppose I put one foot in front of the other in the course of walking to the kitchen to get myself a drink. I give the motion of my foot no thought whatever, I don't ask if it is an appropriate means for achieving my purpose.

---

[15] See Ibid., pp. 472 ff.

I am just walking as I habitually do. But if I were to decide I didn't want the drink after all, or that the door I was approaching was locked, I wouldn't take that step. I had reasons for taking the step, and would not take it without the reasons. Similarly, it seems to me obvious that I would not speak the words I do if I thought they would not be understood. In speaking, I intend to accomplish something, perhaps to warn someone of a bear trap he is about to fall into, and I intend to accomplish this through his understanding of my words. I may take for granted how he will understand my words, but taking for granted is a form of belief. If I didn't think he would understand me I would say something else, or warn him in a non-verbal way.

2

When misunderstandings are cleared away, what remains in this apparent dispute? We end up with me claiming that neither the ordinary, nor a certain philosophic, concept of a language is basic to the understanding of verbal communication; Michael thinks at least the former, and probably the latter, is basic. In the papers on which I have been concentrating, Michael avails himself of a notion of meaning that he does not explain, while I avail myself of a concept of understanding I don't explain. Neither here nor elsewhere, so far as I know, has Michael given an argument to show that a shared way of speaking, a practice or convention, is essential to meaning something by what one says. We know there is an argument, however, and it is possible that Michael has it in mind: it is that only a shared practice can supply an answer to Wittgenstein's question what distinguishes following a rule from merely thinking one is following a rule. I accept the fundamental importance of the question: an adequate account of meaning must provide a test of what it is to go on in the same way, that is, to continue to speak as one has previously spoken. At this point a crucial gap opens between my claims and Michael's: he has available an argument that purports to show that a shared practice is required in order to answer Wittgenstein's question, while I have only contended that a common practice isn't necessary for communication if each speaker goes on more or less as before. I have given no answer to the question what it is to go on as before. As a corollary, neither have I given any reason to think meaning is an essentially social phenomenon.

Here I will try briefly to summarize how I have tried to answer these questions. Agreeing with Dummett and Kripke, and perhaps with Wittgenstein, I hold that the answer to the question what it is to go on as before demands reference to social interaction. Where I disagree is on how this demand can be met.

Suppose that each time I point to my nose you say 'nose'. Then you have it right; you have gone on as before. Why do your verbal reactions count as 'the same', i.e., relevantly similar? Well, I count them as relevantly similar; I find the stimulus in each case the same, and the response the same. You must also, in some primitive sense, find my pointings similar; the evidence for this is your similar responses. But there is nothing in the offing to let you tell whether or not your reactions are relevantly similar. No matter what the stimuli, your similar reactions will indicate that you found something similar in the situations; and apparently dissimilar responses to the same stimulus can equally be taken to show that you took the stimulus to be different, or that for you this is a similar response. As Wittgenstein says, by yourself you can't tell the difference between the situations seeming the same and being the same. (Wittgenstein, many commentators hold, thought this point applies only when the stimulus is private; I think it holds for all cases.)[16] If you and I can each correlate the other's responses with the occurrence of a shared stimulus, however, an entirely new element is introduced. Once the correlation is established it provides each of us with a ground for distinguishing the cases in which it fails. Failed natural inductions can now be taken as revealing a difference between getting it right and getting it wrong, going on as before, or deviating, having a grasp of the concepts of truth and falsity. A grasp of the concept of truth, of the distinction between thinking something is so and its being so, depends on the norm that can be provided only by interpersonal communication; and of course interpersonal communication, and, indeed, the possession of any propositional attitude, depends on a grasp of the concept of objective truth.

[16] I have argued this in 'Communication and Convention', in *Inquiries into Truth and Interpretation*, Oxford University Press, 1984, and in a number of subsequent articles.

Those who insist that shared practices are essential to meaning are half right: there must be an interacting group for meaning— even propositional thought, I would say—to emerge. Interaction of the needed sort demands that each individual perceives others as reacting to the shared environment much as he does; only then can teaching take place and appropriate expectations be aroused, It follows that meaning something requires that by and large one follows a practice of one's own, a practice that can be understood by others. But there is no fundamental reason why practices must be shared.

9 *Seeing Through Language*

We see the world through language; but how should we understand this metaphor? Is language a medium that simply reproduces for the mind, or accurately records, what is out there? Or is it so dense there is no telling what the world is really like? Perhaps language is somewhere in between, a translucent material, so that the world bears the tint and focus of the particular language we speak.

All these attitudes have, or have had, their apostles, but none of them seems to me more than half right, and none captures what is most important about language. Language is certainly a convenient human skill which we use in coping with one another in our common terrestrial setting. Without it we would not think of things, as we do. But it does not follow, of course, that we never perceive how the world really is, as Kant thought, nor that every view is necessarily distorted, as Bergson and many others have held. There might be an argument for this view if it were possible, in principle at least, to isolate some unconceptualized given which could be shaped by the mind, for then it might make sense to imagine a multitude of structures within which the given could be shaped. Without the idea of such a given, however, it is hard to divine what it is that wants shaping, and few of us now are taken by the idea of an unprocessed given.

Do we understand what we mean by a real alternative to our conceptual scheme? If a scheme could be decoded by us, then it would not, by this very token, be all that different from ours except, it might be, in ease of description here or there. If we could explain, or describe, in a convincing way, how an alternative scheme deviates from ours, it would again be captured in our system of concepts. This is not to deny that some people have conceptual resources not available to everyone. Biologists, aeronautical engineers, solid state physicists, musicologists, cartographers, molecular biologists, selenographers, and psycho-analysts all command vocabularies and theories many of us do not. In our more restricted way, we common types also have our specialties: our own list of proper names, with their uniquely contextualized references, our private endearments and verbal twists, our own mispronunciations and malapropisms. And there is no denying that some dialects reveal sexist, nationalist or racist features, while all human languages are rife with barely concealed anthropomorphism. These are, if we like to say so, differences or provincialisms in our conceptual schemes. But they are variants or features we can explain to one another, or could, given enough time, adequate attention, and sufficient intelligence on both sides. Not everyone can grasp the concepts of quantum mechanics— I can't—but the language of relativistic quantum physics doesn't constitute a different conceptual scheme. It's just a suburb, though an exclusive one, of the universal scheme which assumes an ontology of ordinary macroscopic objects with their ordinary properties.

The trouble with the idea of genuinely incommensurable languages and conceptual schemes is not that we couldn't understand them, but that the criteria for what would constitute a scheme incommensurable with ours are simply unclear. Perhaps we think we can imagine a culture where creatures communicate in ways we are permanently disabled from penetrating. But speculating on this possibility hardly advances the case until we decide on our criteria for communication. Fluent exchange of information, purposeful interaction? But how are these mani-fested? The only ends we recognize are the same as, or analogous to, our own. Information as we know and conceive it has a pro-positional content geared to situations, objects, and events we can describe in our homespun terms. Of course it happens in exotic settings that we recognize that we are witness to intelligible con-versation, though grasping nothing that is said. It also is possible that the parling parties have agreed (in a language we could learn) to use an apparently unbreakable code. What these folk say has a translation we could understand, but we can't discover it for ourselves. But in such situations we have good grounds for believing that what we do not grasp we could learn to decipher: the parties look to be people like ourselves, and we are justified in thinking we descry known purposes and activities. These cases pose no problem for the anti-conceptual relativist; there is a serious problem only where no translation is possible. It is this supposed case of genuinely incommensurable languages where I sense unintelligibility in the supposition.

Perhaps we don't really understand the concept of radically different ways of thinking and talking. Still, doesn't it make sense to hold that our actual languages mold our perception of the world to such an extent that what we take in is always distorted? What is obvious is that our language is rich in facilities that match our interests, and lacks the means for easily expressing what is orthogonal to those interests. Our basic vocabularies trace out the vectors which point in the directions in which we naturally generalize; apart from discussing why this is so, we have no interest in emeroses and the classes of things that are gred, bleen, or grue. These are concepts at least expressible in terms to be found in our growing dictionaries—in fact, if 'grue' is not already there, I'm sure it soon will be. But there are endless classes for which we have no term, no matter how complex. Is this distortion? If it is, it is not language that is responsible. Of course, language reflects our native interests and our historically accumulated needs and values, our built-in and learned inductive dispositions. But this fact hardly supports the claim that language seriously distorts or shapes our understanding of the world; the influence, such as it is, goes the other way. The most we are entitled to say is that as individuals we happily inherit culturally evolved categories we personally did little to devise. In this case, language does not distort; rather, society gives us a leg up on coping with the environment it partly constitutes.

What we should resist is the claim that it is truth that is bent or distorted by language. My language may (or may not) have something to do with my, or society's, interest in the question whether the clearing of tropical forests is speeding the destruction of the ozone layer, but language has nothing to do with the truth of the matter. Plenty of concepts are vague, but putting grey areas and ambiguity aside, most of our declarative utterances are simply true or false, not true then but false now, not true for me and false for an inhabitant of the Tuamotu Atolls, not partly false and partly true. Our languages do not distort the truth about the world, though of course they allow us to deceive ourselves and others, according to predilection.

I started out by describing three possible poses that have been struck with respect to the role of language in our thinking about the world. One was that language is opaque, hiding the real thing from us. I rejected this view. A second was that language is a translucent medium, leaving its own character written on everything in its domain. This seemed trivially true at best, an exaggeration of the simple and natural fact that language reflects our interests and our needs. There remains the idea that language is transparent, a medium that can accurately represent the facts.

Alas, we know that this too is an idea with no cash value. Nouns, names, and predicates may refer to, or be true of, one or more things, but they cannot, by themselves, represent facts or states of affairs. Only sentences can do this, and no one has discovered a way of individuating facts or states of affairs in a way that would help to explain which fact a given sentence represents. If, in saying that language represents facts, we mean no more than that we can use sentences to describe objects and events, no harm is done. This is, after all, just a fancy version of the platitude that some sentences are true and some false. But we deceive ourselves when we talk of linguistic utterances representing reality (or anything else) unless we can usefully specify the entities represented.

Is anything now left of the metaphor with which we began, the figure that has language as something through which we view the world? No: as a metaphor it is seriously misleading. Language is not a medium through which we see; it does not mediate between us and the world. We should banish the idea that language is epistemically something like sense data, something that embodies what we can take in, but is itself only a token, or representative, of what is out there. Language does not mirror or represent reality, any more than our senses present us with no more than appearances. Presentations and representations as mere proxies or pictures will always leave us one step short of what knowledge seeks; skepticism about the power of language to capture what is real is old-fashioned skepticism of the senses given a linguistic twist.

We do not see the world through language any more than we see the world through our eyes. We don't look *through* our eyes, but *with* them. We don't feel things through our fingers or hear things through our ears. Well, there is a sense in which we *do* see things through—that is, by dint of having—eyes. We do cope through having language. There is a *non*-metaphorical point to my title. There is a valid analogy between having eyes and ears, and having language: all three are organs with which we come into direct contact with our environment. They are not intermediaries, screens, media, or windows.

Perhaps we are influenced by the idea that a language, especially when its name is spelled with a capital, as in 'English', 'Croat', 'Latvian', 'Inuit', or 'Galician', is some sort of public entity to one or more of which each of us subscribes, like the telephone service, and which therefore really is extraneous to us in a way our sense organs are not. We forget there is no such thing as a language apart from the sounds and marks people make, and the habits and expectations that go with them. 'Sharing a language' with someone else consists in understanding what they say, and talking pretty much the way they do. There is no additional entity we possess in common any more than there is an ear we share when I lend you an ear.

Of course there are differences between being able to converse with others, and being able to see. We develop sight early and without social prompting; the conditions for acquiring a language are more complex, and mastery develops later. But it does develop amazingly fast once things get going. The phonemes of our mother's tongue seem to have a start in utero,[1] but sentences emerge only after a year or two. By three years, most children glibly generate sentences, and have the basic grammar of their environment right. The average six-year-old commands about 13,000 words, and a good high school student may know 120,000. The window for learning all this is brief; after eight or so, practically no one can learn to speak a new language (first or second) like a native. There seems little reason to doubt that we are genetically programmed in fairly specific ways to speak as we do; every group and society has a language, and all languages are apparently constrained by the same arbitrary rules. Tribes we consider primitive have languages as complex and complete as those of developed cultures.

We tend to think speech is radically different from the senses partly because there is no external organ devoted just to it, and partly because of the diversity of languages. But these differences

---

[1] John L. Locke, *The Child's Path to Spoken Language* (Cambridge, Mass.: Harvard University Press, 1993).

are superficial. Speech, like the sense organs, has its specialized location in the brain; as a result, brain damage can cause loss of the ability to use language without destroying general intelligence. And, more significantly, all languages apparently share structural rules despite the surface variety. The evidence for this is partly the discovery of universal constraints on grammars. There is also the astonishing fact that children, brought up hearing nothing but pidgin, which is a highly simplified invention of adults who have been thrown together and lack a common language, those children do what adults cannot; they soon elaborate the pidgin into a creole as developed and complicated as French or Turkish.

These bits of information come from various sources, some of them influenced by Noam Chomsky, but particularly from Steven Pinker's recent book, *The Language Instinct*, which brings them persuasively together. Pinker concludes that 'Language is not a cultural artifact that we learn the way we learn to tell time... Instead, it is a distinct piece of the biological makeup of our brains'.[2] My opening metaphor seems to chime with Pinker's remark, 'When we are comprehending sentences, the stream of words is transparent, we see through to the meaning... automatically'.[3] No wonder that, following Chomsky, he calls language a 'mental organ'.[4]

What, though, does all this have to do with the relation between language and thought? According to Pinker, Fodor, and a number of others, the extraordinary ease with which language develops, added to the apparent existence of linguistic universals, shows that what is innate—that is, genetically programmed—is an internal language, the which they call the language of thought, or mentalese. According to the theory, this inner language is not learned, but emerges as part of our genetic heritage, and it is prior to any spoken language. The salient point is that the existence of mentalese does not depend on the development of language, but vice versa. Thus, given the universal grammar that is wired in, 'the connectedness of words... reflects the relatedness of ideas in mentalese'. This solves the 'problem of taking an interconnected web of thoughts in the mind and encoding them as a string of

[2] Steven Pinker, *The Language Instinct* (New York: HarperCollins, 1995), 18.
[3] Ibid. p. 21.
[4] Noam Chomsky, *Rules and Representations* (New York: Columbia University Press, 1980), 138–9; Pinker, *Language Instinct*, p. 307.

words...For the child, the unknown language is English (or Japanese...or Arabic); the known one is mentalese'.[5] In this last quoted passage, Pinker is comparing the child to Quine's radical translator, with the difference that for Pinker the child doesn't need to work things out; the child simply knows right off what idea in mentalese is represented by the words he hears. Pinker has no doubt about the priority of mentalese. Do we think in English or Cherokee or some other language, he asks, '[O]r are our thoughts couched in some silent medium of the brain— a language of thought, or "mentalese"—and merely clothed in words whenever we need to communicate them to a listener?'.[6] He votes for the silent medium. The arguments are various: we often know what we think but can't find the words; we sometimes recognize that what we said was not what we meant; it is a silly myth that conceptual schemes can differ widely; there is the universal grammar; and there is the surprising rapidity with which we master our native tongue.

This general view is now accepted by many linguists and cognitive scientists, but it seems to me the arguments for it are flawed and the conclusions confused. It is no more philosophically significant that major aspects of language ability are wired in than that color and brightness contrasts are carried to the brain by the optic nerve rather than processed by some higher cognitive machinery. It is worth emphasizing that language aptitude is part of our natural equipment, and not a tool we contrived for coping with problems of understanding, calculation, and communication. I like the analogy with the sense organs, and therefore the implication that language is not something that comes between us and reality; it can't come between, since it is part of us. But postulating a language of thought spoils what is attractive about this picture; if the language of thought is what is part of us, then our spoken language *is* an intermediary between thought and what thought is about, and what is genetically engineered *does* threaten to hide or distort the world in much the way Kant thought the architecture of the mind does.

The arguments for the existence of a language of thought prior to, or independent of, a socially engendered language, are feeble. The fact that we sometimes cannot find words for what we want to

---

[5] Pinker, *Language Instinct*, pp. 101, 102, 278.   [6] Ibid. p. 56.

say has simpler explanations than the postulation of a preexisting internal but wordless message striving to find its translation into a spoken idiom. It is enough to suppose we sometimes cannot access words or phrases we already know, or even that, already having a language, we are able to think of new things that need saying. The idea of inborn constraints on syntax, for which Chomsky has argued so vigorously, is, as he has shown, supported by impressive empirical evidence. There may remain, for some of us, a question to what extent these constraints are an artifact of our means of describing alien languages in our own; but the evidence is convincing that this is by no means all there is to it. Not only do we come into the world equipped for language acquisition, but we know something about the constraints on what comes naturally. What conclusions can we draw about real languages, or thought? What is needed in the way of genetically engineered linguistic aptitude to explain the relative ease of language acquisition and the similarities in actual spoken languages has little, if anything, to do with the contents of our thoughts or utterances. What we are born with, or what emerge in the normal course of early childhood, are constraints on syntax, not semantics. There is no reason to suppose that ideas, concepts, or meanings are innate if this is taken to mean anything more than that people have come to have languages and thoughts that reflect the needs and interests of human animals. Nor is it surprising, given our common heritage, that our thoughts and utterances are mutually intelligible—up to a point, of course, since success in interpretation is always a matter of degree. This is not to say that constraints on syntax may not generate structural constraints on semantics; though it is not easy to think how, in detail, the argument would go. In any case, my contention is not that what we think and say is not constrained by our genes; it is the weaker claim that we are not born with anything like a contentful language. Evolution has made us more or less fit for our environment, but evolution could not endow us with concepts. Nature decided what concepts would come naturally, of course; but this is not to say the mind knew in advance what nature would be like.

Something more should be said about the 'argument from the poverty of the stimulus', the argument that much of what we come to know about the language we speak must be inborn because we acquire an accurate (though mostly unconscious) knowledge of the grammar, vocabulary, and even semantics of our mother tongue on the basis of such sparse evidence. I have already expressed my doubts about semantics, at least if semantics has to do with reference and truth. But recent research also throws doubt on the idea that prelinguistic infants lack the general ability to learn very rapidly and accurately from limited and incomplete input. Experiments reveal that eight-month-old children learn to segment speech into words on the basis of nothing but statistical relationships between adjacent sounds, and they do this after only two minutes, 'suggesting that infants have access to a powerful mechanism for the computation of statistical properties of the language input'.[7] In other words, not that much has to be wired in; learning has an important role to play in entry into the realm of speech and thought.

These are important matters of degree. What matters, for present purposes, is that once in place, language is not an ordinary learned skill; it is, or has become, a mode of perception. However, speech is not just one more organ; it is essential to the other senses if they are to yield propositional knowledge. Language is the organ of propositional perception. Seeing sights and hearing sounds does not require thought with propositional content; perceiving how things are does, and this ability develops along with language. Perception, once we have propositional thought, is direct and unmediated in the sense that there are no epistemic intermediaries on which perceptual beliefs are based, nothing that underpins our knowledge of the world.[8] Of course, our sense organs are part of the causal chain from world to perceptual belief. But not all causes are reasons: the activation of our retinas does not constitute evidence that we see a dog, nor do the vibrations of the little hairs in the inner ear provide reasons to think the dog is barking. 'I saw it with my own eyes' is a legitimate reason for believing there was an elephant in the supermarket. But this reports no more than that something I saw caused me to believe there was an elephant in the supermarket. Sometimes we have sensations, and we may, on occasion, refer to them as reasons for

---

[7] Jenny R. Saffran, Richard N. Aslin, and Elissa L. Newport, 'Statistical Learning by 8-Month-Old Infants', *Science*, **274** (13 December 1996): pp. 1926–8.

[8] Donald Davidson, 'A Coherence Theory of Truth and Knowledge', in D. Henrich (ed.), *Kant oder Hegel* (Stuttgart: Klett-Cotta, 1983).

beliefs. But sensations, or their wispy messengers—percepts, sense, data, the like—do not constitute reasons, though the belief that we heard a noise, or witnessed a fiery streak in the sky, may be a reason, when coupled with appropriate subsequent information, for thinking we heard an explosion or a saw a plane crash.

There is a simple explanation for the fact that sensations, percepts, and sense data cannot provide epistemic support for beliefs: reasons have to be geared conceptually to what they are reasons for. The relation of epistemic support requires that both relata have propositional content, and entities like sensations and sense data have no propositional content. Much of modern philosophy has been devoted to trying to arbitrate between an imagined unconceptualized given and what is needed to support belief. We now see that this project has no chance of success. The truth is, nothing can supply a reason for a belief except another (or many another) belief.[9]

Perceptual beliefs are formed at first spontaneously. They are simply caused by what goes on that we can see, hear, touch, taste, and smell. We have no control over the onset of such beliefs, except as we can move our bodies to put ourselves in the way of reception. Control sets in once a belief is caused; another look can correct the first impression, a moment's reflection can cancel the idea that we are seeing a long dead friend. What we see can wipe out what we thought we heard. Comparing observations is what we credit scientists with, but we all do it all the time, though perhaps not as systematically or methodically as scientists do. In the end, it is perceptions we have to go on, but on the basis of perceptions we build theories against which we evaluate further perceptions. I take for granted that the perceptual beliefs we cannot help forming, however tentatively, are themselves heavily conditioned by what we remember, by what we just a moment ago perceived, and by the relevant theories we have come to accept to one degree or another. Beyond the skin there is mindless causality, but what gets bombarded is a thinking animal with a thoroughly conditioned apparatus. There is no simple relation between the stimulus and the resulting thought.

[9] This is a view I argued for in ibid. 50. John McDowell, in his recent John Locke Lectures, accepts the claim that reasons must have propositional content, but rejects the idea that only beliefs can be reasons for beliefs: John McDowell, *Mind and World* (Cambridge, Mass.: Harvard University Press, 1994).

Given the mostly inscrutable complexity of this relation, why should our empirical beliefs, even the perceptual ones, be trustworthy? If the only rational grounds for a belief are other beliefs, what role can nature play in determining the contents of beliefs? The question is akin to the question about language. It is one thing to insist that language, like perception, is unmediated, but this insistence makes it seem impossible to account for the contents of our observation sentences, just as it seems impossible to account for the contents of our perceptual beliefs. The two problems are obviously intertwined, for what accounts for the contents of thoughts must also constitute at least part of the explanation of why observation sentences have the contents they do. What makes these problems pressing is the question how beliefs, if epistemically supported by nothing more than other beliefs, can independently, or as a collection, be connected with the world.

One place to begin is by asking how the sentences directly tied to perception get their content. We may call these *perceptual sentences*. There is no reason to think all perceptual sentences are simple, or that they are the same for everyone. Not necessarily simple, since some of us learn to know directly, just by looking at the glass, that stormy weather is ahead; or we hear certain sounds and know someone has said that the tide is up; or we look in the cloud chamber and remark that we have seen an electron. In these cases we can give reasons for the beliefs we formed so directly; we can explain why what we saw begot the belief it did. And not the same for everyone. Some people don't perceive that stormy weather is ahead because they haven't learned to read a barometer. Each of us has a unique repertoire of people recognized at a glance.

Perceptual sentences have an empirical content given by the situations which stir us to accept or reject them, and the same goes for the beliefs expressed by those sentences. But what reason is there to suppose this content is appropriate? Even someone with a going language into which a new sentence can be fitted can learn to affirm a sentence in situations in which it is true without understanding it. Someone with no understanding of physics could easily come to utter the sentence 'There goes an electron' as the streak appears in the cloud chamber, while having little idea what an electron is. Understanding the sentence depends on prior theory, without which the content would be totally unlike what we think of as the meaning. But isn't theory, in a sense that extends theory to cover tacit understanding, isn't theory always needed for the conditioning of sentence to circumstance to yield the right content? Only someone knowledgeable about sailing ships could recognize on sight that he sees a brig and not a brigantine, though he might use the words in the right situations (a brig is a two-masted ship square-rigged fore and aft, while the latter differs in having a fore-and-aft rigged mainsail). Even a simple sentence like 'That's a spoon' if understood requires knowledge of what spoons are for, that they are persistent physical objects, and so on. So there must be more to content than is conveyed by saying it is given by the situations that stir us to accept or reject sentences appropriate to the situations.

People do not acquire the gift of tongues by themselves; they are tutored intentionally or by accident by parents, playmates, teachers, and Sesame Street. In the process, ostension, or what amounts to it, plays a major role. But how does ostensive teaching differ from the tutoring nature provides in any case? As far as I know, we are not born preferring berries that are blue to berries that are red. But the lone gatherer will be taught by nature to prefer the blue; they are much more apt to be nourishing and sweet. Perhaps an even keener mind will discover that the berries birds eat are almost always human fodder too. Mistakes make their mark: those big, gaudy, but poisonous berries will be avoided next time. What's the difference between this ordinary process of conditioning and the reward-and-punishment conditioning of sentence to situation that makes ostension the successful method it is?

Corrections, whether administered by teacher, parent, playmate, or nature, can in themselves do no more than improve the dispositions we were born with, and dispositions, as Wittgenstein emphasized, have no normative force. A slippery road is disposed to cause cars to skid, but we do not, if we are sensible, hold this against the road, though we may alter its character to suit our purposes by spreading sand or salt. Animals are different in that they are pleased and pained and so their behavior can be altered by means not available with roads. But the point remains: we improve the road, from our point of view, by spreading sand or salt; we improve the child, from our point of view, by causing pleasure or pain. In neither case does this process, by itself, teach road or child the distinction between correct and incorrect behavior. To correct behavior is not, in itself, to teach *that* the behavior is incorrect. Toilet training a child or a dog is like fixing a bathtub so it will not overflow; neither apparatus nor organism masters a concept in the process.

We may be inclined to think that concept formation is more primitive than entering the world of propositional attitudes, the world, in particular, of beliefs. But this is a mistake. Unless we want to attribute concepts to butterflies and olive trees, we should not count mere ability to discriminate between red and green or moist and dry as having a concept, not even if such selective behavior is learned. To have a concept is to *classify* objects or properties or events or situations while understanding that what has been classified may not belong in the assigned class. The infant may never say "Mama" except when its mother is present, but this does not prove conceptualization has taken place, even on a primitive level, unless a mistake would be recognized *as* a mistake. Thus there is in fact no distinction between having a concept and having thoughts with propositional content, since one cannot have the concept of mama unless one can believe someone is (or is not) mama, or wish that mama were present, or feel angry that mama is not satisfying some desire. I stress the connection between concepts and thoughts only to make the point that concept formation is not a way station between mere dispositions, no matter how complex or learned, and judgment.

What must be added to a meaningless sound, uttered at moments appropriate for that same sound, uttered as speech, to transmute the former into the latter? It is not enough that the meaningless sound has been reinforced in the past and is now uttered because of its magical powers; if this were enough, then the fact that cats meow to be fed would count as meaningful speech. What then? I am under no illusion that I can provide anything like an analysis; perhaps there is no answer that does not lead in a circle, for a non-circular answer would tell us how to account for intensionality in non-extensional terms. But I do think it is here that language adds a necessary (though not sufficient) element.

We remarked just now that ostension cannot, by itself, do the job, because of the aid it needs from a prior grasp of how language works. It is worth reflecting, though, on the initial phase of ostensive learning. At the start, there could be no point in the learner questioning the correctness of the teacher's ostensions. The learner may or may not be learning how others in some linguistic community speak, but the learner can discover this only later. In the private lesson, a meaning is being bestowed on words quite apart from any use those words may have at other times and with other people. If we think of ostension only as the teaching of a socially viable meaning we miss the essential lesson, which is that for the learner ostension is not learning something already there. The learner is in at a meaning baptism.

If we ignore the difference between passing on an established meaning and the creation of a new, the difference between teacher and innovator fades, and with it what distinguishes teacher and learner. Paring down the scenario even further, we can imagine a sort of proto-ostension before there is the general grasp of language that allows us to get more out of ostension than goes into it. In this elementary situation we can study some of the necessary conditions for the development of thought and language. These include the fact that all people generalize naturally in much the same ways. They avoid bitter tastes and loud, sudden sounds; they seek the sweet and the quiet. Learning requires three generalizations: the learned association of fire and hurt requires two, and the learning is displayed in the similarity of the responses: we avoid hurt by avoiding fire. Before there can be learning there must be unlearned modes of generalization. Before there can be language there must be shared modes of generalization.

The sharing of responses to stimuli found similar allows an interpersonal element to emerge: creatures that share responses can correlate each other's responses with what they are responses to. Person A responds to person B's responses to situations both A and B find similar. A triangle is thus set up, the three corners being A, B, and the objects, events, or situations to which they mutually respond. This elaborate, but commonplace, triangular interaction between creatures and a shared environment does not require thought or language; it occurs with great frequency among animals that neither think nor talk. Birds and fish do it as well as monkeys, elephants, and whales.

What more is there to linguistic communication and developed thought? The answer is, I think, two things that depend on the basic triangle, and emerge from it. The first is the concept of error, that is, appreciation of the distinction between belief and truth. The interactions of the triangle do not in themselves automatically generate this appreciation, as we see from the example of simple animals, but the triangle does make room for the concept of error (and hence of truth) in situations in which the correlation of reactions that have been repeatedly shared can be seen by the sharers to break down; one creature reacts in a way previously associated by both creatures with a certain sort of situation, but the other does not. This may simply alert the non-reactor to an unnoticed danger or opportunity, but if the anticipated danger or opportunity fails to materialize, a place exists for the notion of a mistake. We, looking on, will judge that the first creature erred. The creatures themselves are also in a position to come to the same conclusion. If they do, they have grasped the concept of objective truth.

With the second, final, step, we move in a circle, for we grasp the concept of truth only when we can communicate the contents—the propositional contents—of the shared experience, and this requires language. The primitive triangle, constituted by two (and typically more than two) creatures reacting in concert to features of the world and to each other's reactions, thus provides the framework in which thought and language can evolve. Neither thought nor language, according to this account, can come first, for each requires the other. This presents no puzzle about priorities: the abilities to speak, perceive, and think develop together, gradually. We perceive the world through language, that is, through having language.[10]

---

[10] I thank Barry Smith and Ernest Lepore for very helpful suggestions and corrections.

10 *James Joyce and Humpty Dumpty*

There is a tension between the thought that what a speaker intends by what he says determines what he means and the thought that what a speaker means depends on the history of the uses to which the language has been put in the past. Relieving this tension, or at least understanding what underlies it, is a leading task of the philosophy of language. To emphasize the role of intention is to acknowledge the power of innovation and creativity in the use of language; seeing history as dominant is to think of language as hedged by—even defined by—rules, conventions, usage. A metaphor, for example, is wholly dependent linguistically on the usual meanings of words, however fresh and astonishing the thought it is used to express; and the interpreter, though he may be hard pressed to decode or appreciate a metaphor, needs know no more about what words mean than can be, or ought to be, found in a good dictionary. A malapropism, on the other hand, is sheer invention. You will not be helped in understanding what Mrs Malaprop means by her words by looking in the dictionary; but you must grasp what she intends. (Sheridan is, of course, another matter; he is a punster, so to get all that *he* is up to you do need to know what "allegory" normally means as well as what Mrs Malaprop intends when she mentions the allegories on the bank of the Nile. The airline pilot or steward who assures passengers that "We will be landing momentarily" is not, alas, uttering a malapropism; we know what is meant because we have heard it so often before.)

Humpty Dumpty features here because he is the pure example of the hopeful innovator: "When *I* use a word it means just what I choose it to mean." Joyce is a somewhat different case, though many people may be inclined to deny the difference. This brings me to my theme: Joyce, his views on the use of language, and his use of language.

A Portrait of the Artist as a Young Man is openly, if not quite accurately, autobiographical, but as Harry Levin remarks, it is more credo than autobiography, and, we might want to add, more manifesto than credo. Nowhere else has Joyce prescribed so plainly the aims and standards of the artist.

"My ancestors," says Stephen Dedalus, Joyce's surrogate in *A Portrait*, "My ancestors threw off their language and took another . . . They allowed a handful of foreigners to subject them. Do you fancy I am going to pay in my own life and person debts they made?" He continues, "When the soul of a man is born in this country there are nets flung at it to hold it back from flight. You talk to me of nationality, language, religion. I shall try to fly by those nets."[1]

How Joyce tried, and the sense in which he succeeded, in flying by the nets of nationality and of religion have been much discussed, and are to some extent understood. He abandoned both his country and his faith, though he never forgot nor forgave either one. Kristian Smidt writes that "Joyce not only feared that Christianity might be true, he felt intimately that behind Christian symbols there 'are massed twenty centuries of authority and veneration'."[2] A similar ambivalence toward Ireland permeated his life and work: in his work he never left it; in his travels he returned seldom and briefly. But how about the other net, the net of language?

Joyce gives this formulation of his *non serviam*: "I will not serve that in which I no longer believe, whether it call itself my home, my fatherland or my church: and I will try to express myself in some mode of life or art as freely as I can and as wholly as I can, using for my defense the only arms I allow myself to use, silence, exile and cunning."[3] Here all reference to language has been dropped, and in a way not surprisingly. Joyce could leave his country and his church, but could not give up language, despite

---

[1] *A Portrait of the Artist as a Young Man*, Random House, New York, 1928, p. 238.

[2] Kristian Smidt, *James Joyce and the Cultic Use of Fiction*, Oslo University Press, Oslo, 1959, p. 25. I wish to thank Professor Smidt for his expert comments; they have influenced my understanding of Joyce, though I know he would not endorse all that I say.   [3] *A Portrait of the Artist*, p. 291.

his weapon of "silence". What then can he have meant by the net of language, and how can he have thought he could fly by it?

In *Stephen Hero*, an earlier and in some ways more revealing autobiographical work than *A Portrait*, Joyce recounts how his friends wanted him, like a patriotic Irishman, to learn Gaelic. He refused. Gaelic is the language Stephen has said his ancestors threw off when they permitted a handful of foreigners to subject them. Stephen will not allow himself to be enlisted by a shallow chauvinism. Should we then, as Harry Levin suggests, conclude that flying by the net of language amounted to no more than— refusing to attend classes in Gaelic?

The subject comes up again in *Ulysses*. Haines, an Englishman visiting Stephen and Buck Mulligan while they are living in the Martello tower at Sandycove, is quizzing Stephen about his religion. "You behold in me, Stephen said with grim displeasure, a horrible example of free thought." While Stephen reflects on the fact that Mulligan will ask him for the key to the tower thus, in Stephen's eye, dispossessing him, Haines goes on, "After all, I should think you are able to free yourself. You are your own master, it seems to me." "I am the servant of two masters, Stephen said, an English and an Italian," and in reply to a question, he rudely explains, "The imperial British state . . . and the holy Roman catholic and apostolic church."[4] It is hard to believe that for Joyce flying by the net of language meant evading the foolish lure of Gaelic in order to accept another foreign master.

In *A Portrait*, Stephen is talking with an English priest. Stephen

. . . felt with a smart of dejection that the man to whom he was speaking was a countryman of Ben Jonson. He thought:

—The language in which we are speaking is his before it is mine. How different are the words *home*, *Christ*, *ale*, *master*, on his lips and on mine! I cannot speak or write these words without unrest of spirit. His language, so familiar and so foreign, will always be for me an acquired speech. I have not made or accepted its words. My voice holds them at bay. My soul frets in the shadow of his language.—[5]

A phrase to notice here is: I have not made . . . its words.

---

[4] *Ulysses*, Vintage Books, New York, 1986, p. 17.
[5] *A Portrait of the Artist*, p. 221.

But of course Joyce valued words of all languages, and especially the words of English.

He drew forth a phrase from his treasure and spoke it softly to himself:

—A day of dappled seaborne clouds.—

The phrase and the day and the scene harmonized in a chord. Words. Was it their colours? He allowed them to glow and fade, hue after hue: sunrise gold, the russet and green of apple orchards, azure of waves, the greyfringed fleece of clouds. No, it was not their colours: it was the poise and balance of the period itself. Did he then love the rhythmic rise and fall of words better than their associates of legend and colour? Or was it that, being as weak of sight as he was shy of mind, he drew less pleasure from the reflection of the glowing sensible world through the prism of a language manycoloured and richly storied than from the contemplation of an inner world of individual emotions mirrored perfectly in a lucid supple periodic prose.[6]

Beauty in language, Stephen maintains, depends on the genre and the form, but in every case "The image . . . must be set between the mind or senses of the artist himself and the mind and senses of others." He then distinguishes the three forms into which art divides. There is first the lyrical form "wherein the artist presents his image in immediate relation to himself . . . he who utters it is more conscious of the instant of emotion than of himself as feeling the emotion." There is then the epical form in which the artist "presents his image in mediate relation to himself and others . . . the centre of emotional gravity is equidistant from the artist himself and from others." Finally, there is the dramatic form. In it, the artist

presents his image in immediate relation to others . . . The dramatic form is reached when the vitality which has flowed and eddied round each person fills every person with such vital force that he or she assumes a proper and intangible esthetic life. The personality of the artist . . . finally refines itself out of existence . . . The mystery of esthetic like that of material creation is accomplished. The artist, like the God of the creation, remains within or behind or beyond or above his handiwork, invisible, refined out of existence, indifferent, paring his fingernails.[7]

These often quoted passages must contain an essential clue to what Joyce had in mind when he spoke of flying by the net of language. The artist, Joyce says, finally "refines himself out of

[6] *A Portrait of the Artist*, p. 194.   [7] Ibid., p. 252.

existence"; Stephen repeats these words, and his listener jokingly repeats them once again. Yet how is it possible for a writer to refine himself out of existence by the use of language?

Joyce's conception of aesthetic freedom required that he not be the slave of settled meanings, hypostatized connotations, rules of grammar, established styles and tastes, "correct" spellings. Winning such freedom was for him a supreme act of creation.

The problem is this. In painting, for example, it is not obvious that the artist needs to depend, in creating his effect, on any particular stock of knowledge he shares with the viewer. It is not even plain that there must be a common culture. The writer, however, cannot ignore what his readers know or assume about the words he uses, and such knowledge and expectations can come only from the reader's exposure to past usage. In Lewis Carroll's *Through the Looking-Glass* Humpty Dumpty, the "perfect" innovator, thinks he can mean what he chooses by his words, at least if he pays them extra. At the end of a speech he says to Alice, "There's glory for you!" Alice says she doesn't know what he means. Humpty Dumpty replies, "Of course you don't— till I tell you. I meant 'There's a nice knock-down argument for you!' "

The absurdity of the position is clear. In speaking or writing we intend to be understood. We cannot intend what we know to be impossible; people can only understand words they are somehow prepared in advance to understand. No one knew this better than Joyce. When he spent sixteen hundred hours writing the Anna Livia Plurabelle section of *Finnegans Wake*, he was searching for existing names of rivers, names he could use, distorted and masked, to tell the story. Joyce draws on every resource his readers command (or that he hopes they command, or thinks they should command), every linguistic resource, knowledge of history, geography, past writers, and styles. He forces us both to look at and to listen to his words to find the puns and fathom the references.

Flying by the net of language could not, then, imply the unconstrained invention of meaning, Humpty Dumpty style. But neither could it be the result of adopting the lyric form, in which emotion is given "the simplest verbal vesture." The epical form would not achieve Joyce's linguistic ambitions, for in it the writer self-consciously invests his story and his characters with his own personality. Somehow it is the dramatic form, at least as Joyce conceived it, that alone was suited to the task, for it is in the dramatic form that the writer "refines himself out of existence."

In the midst of the Circe episode in *Ulysses* Stephen asks abruptly, "What went forth to the ends of the world to traverse not itself. God, the sun, Shakespeare, a commercial traveller, having itself traversed in reality itself becomes that self. Wait a moment. Wait a second. Damn that fellow's noise in the street. Self which it itself was ineluctably preconditioned to become. Ecco!"[8]

We recognize the artist under the guises Joyce gave him: God the father, God the son, the sun, Shakespeare ("who, after God, created most"), Ulysses (or Bloom: both commercial travellers). A shout in the street is Stephen's earlier description of God; a shouting in the street is also, Joyce remarks in *Finnegans Wake*, how many people think of his own writing. Ecco; and, given the theme of return to self as the result of original creation, an echo, a *re*sounding.

An echo, a noise in the street, a ghost, may be much more than it seems. "What is a ghost?" asks Stephen in response to the remark that in his view *Hamlet* is a ghost story. "One who has faded into impalpability through death, through absence, through change of manners. Elizabethan London lay as far from Stratford as corrupt Paris lies from virgin Dublin. Who is the ghost from *limbo patrum*, returning to the world that has forgotten him? Who is king Hamlet?"[9] While Stephen prepares us for the mock-serious theory that Shakespeare identified himself with the ghost in *Hamlet* and that therefore Hamlet is Shakespeare's son, Joyce compares himself, an exile from Dublin living in Paris, with Shakespeare self-exiled from Stratford living in London. It is the father-creator, the "lord of language" as Joyce calls Shakespeare, who is the ghost, one who has faded into impalpability, who has refined himself out of existence. We are asked to remember that Shakespeare not only created the play but is also said to have played the part of the ghost in the first performance of the play. "Is it possible," Stephen asks,

Is it possible that that player Shakespeare, a ghost by absence, and in the vesture of buried Denmark, a ghost by death, speaking his own words to

---

[8]   *Ulysses*, p. 412.   [9]   Ibid., p. 154.

his own son's name (had Hamnet Shakespeare lived he would have been prince Hamlet's twin) is it possible, I want to know, or probable that he did not draw or foresee the logical conclusion of those premises: you are the dispossessed son: I am the murdered father: your mother is the guilty queen, Ann Shakespeare, born Hathaway?[10]

In the Scylla and Charybdis scene in *Ulysses*, from which these quotations come, Stephen is, we realize, not only Joyce's stand-in but also his Hamlet. If Bloom is Stephen's surrogate father, Joyce is Stephen's creator. In *Ulysses*, Bloom is a man *nel mezzo del camin di nostra vita*, as was Dante when he wrote this line, as was Shakespeare when he wrote *Hamlet*, as was Joyce when he wrote *Ulysses*. We cannot read an adulterous wife into Joyce's life, though this was a fantasy he seems to have enjoyed, but the similarity between Stephen's Ann Hathaway and Molly Bloom is clear.

Stephen explains how Shakespeare came to marry: "He was chosen, it seems to me. If others have their will Ann hath a way. By cock, she was to blame. She put the comether on him, sweet and twentysix. The greyeyed goddess who bends over the boy Adonis, stooping to conquer, as prologue to the swelling act, is a boldfaced Stratford wench who tumbles in a cornfield a lover younger than herself."[11] What is the greyeyed goddess doing here? She is, of course, Athena, the most pervasive female presence in Homer's *Odyssey*, Odysseus' guide, mentor, friend, advisor, and above all his admirer and understander. Why does she play so small a part in Joyce's *Ulysses*? She turns up once more as a stuffed owl who regards Bloom at the end of the day "with a clear melancholy wise bright motionless compassionate gaze." Her identification with Ann Hathaway, and later with Molly Bloom, suggests that Athena may, like Cordelia, play a more important role absent than on the stage, like the artist who has refined himself out of existence.

Shakespeare marries and leaves Stratford for London, but his brush with Ann-Athena leaves him altered. "He had no truant memory," Stephen says. "He carried a memory in his wallet as he trudged to Romeville..." The words carry us to another play Joyce had very much in mind as he worked on *Ulysses*, Shakespeare's *Troilus and Cressida*. Written perhaps a year after

---

[10] Ibid., p. 155.   [11] Ibid., p. 157.

Hamlet, it belongs to that same period when Shakespeare dwells on the themes of treachery, adultery, and banishment; and of course its observant hero is Ulysses. In *Troilus and Cressida* Ulysses shames Achilles into returning to battle by reminding him that perseverance alone keeps honor bright, that "to have done, is to hang / Quite out of fashion, like a rusty mail / in monumental mock'ry." The speech begins, "Time hath, my lord, a wallet at his back, / Wherein he puts alms for oblivion . . ."[12] The other theme of *Troilus and Cressida* is also one of a treacherous memory—Cressida's betrayal of Troilus.

If the "note of banishment, banishment from the heart, banishment from the home sounds uninterruptedly" in his middle period, the "plays of Shakespeare's later years . . . breathe another spirit—the spirit of reconciliation." Stephen is not impressed; he drily remarks "There can be no reconciliation . . . if there has not been a sundering." Nevertheless, the concept of the third period as embodying the mature art of the creative writer now begins to embrace another idea besides that of a steady progress from phase to phase. The new idea is that of the *nostos* or return, the bold adventure followed by the dangerous but successful odyssey home, the son who slays and replaces the father to become the father in turn, the writer who flies by the net of inherited or imposed language, but makes or remakes his own. "As we . . . weave and reweave our bodies, Stephen said, from day to day, their molecules shuttled to and fro, so does the artist weave and reweave his image. And as the mole on my right breast is where it was when I was born, though all my body has been woven of new stuff time after time, so through the ghost of the unquiet father the image of the unliving son looks forth."

With Joyce as with Homer's hero we are never quite sure whether exile is voluntary or imposed, whether the lingering in the Calypso's cave of Paris is a delight or a torment. In the same ambiguous vein, it is not clear why a round trip must include a fatal accident, why a return implies a sundering, why a repetition calls for a break. But there seems no question but that in the Joycean-Viconian scheme, creation follows on destruction; the cycle cannot begin again without the vast shattering thunder-clap heard throughout *Finnegans Wake*. It is from the "ruin of

---

[12] *Troilus and Cressida*, III. iii.

all space" that the artist builds his language. "The note of banishment... sounds uninterruptedly from *The Two Gentlemen of Verona* onward till Prospero breaks his staff, buries it certain fathoms in the earth... reflects itself in another, repeats itself, protasis, epistasis, catastasis, catastrophe."[13]

In a brilliant article written a number of years ago, Nathan Halper analyzed one of the most difficult passages in *Finnegans Wake*.[14] It is a passage almost twenty pages long in the eleventh chapter and it concerns an event supposed to have happened during the Crimean War; a man named Buckley shoots a Russian general. Halper convinces us that Buckley, an authentic Irishman who actually did participate in the Crimean War, is the Archetypical Son; the general is the Archetypical Father. There is a horse race shown on the screen. The horses are Emancipator and Immense Pater. The race is a "dawnybreak", a rising of the sun; the time is heliotropical. The Crimean peninsula is where the primeval crime of the paricidical son took place. "Dublin" in Gaelic turns out to mean a black pool, and Siva's black pool becomes Sea vast a pool—Sevastopol. History records that there was a Russian general in the Crimean War named de Todleben.

There is much more of this, all good dirty fun, part of the funferal of *Finnegans Wake*. At the end comes a reference to Joyce himself who is playing a "Cicilian hurdy-gurdy." Cicilian because Cecil was Buckley's first name, but also because "Cecil" is derived from the Latin for blind and thus serves to remind us of Joyce, who was nearly blind by the time he wrote *Finnegans Wake*. In the dark Joyce weaves and reweaves his world; de Todleben is known for the fact that each night at Sevastopol he rebuilt the defenses. There is an explosion, the "abnihilization of the etym". Halper concludes: "Joyce is destroying language. He is annihilating meaning—he is re-creating language. In other words—'in other words'—he is writing *Finnegans Wake*."

Harry Levin, writing on this same passage, but before Halper's useful article, came to much the same conclusion. He says of the lethal explosion, "Pessimists may interpret this ambiguous phenomenon as the annihilation of all meaning, a chain reaction

---

[13] *Ulysses*, p. 174.
[14] Nathan Halper, "James Joyce and the Russian General", *Partisan Review*, vol. 18, 1951, pp. 424–31.

set off by the destruction of the atom. Optimists will emphasize the creation of matter *ex nihilo*, and trust in the Word to create another world."[15]

Joyce's way of resolving the tension between invention and tradition is in a way obvious; like any writer he must depend on the knowledge his readers are able to bring to his writings. Much of this knowledge is verbal of course, knowledge of what words ordinarily mean. But in Joyce's case much of what is required must come from other sources. When he uses the word—if that is what it is—"Dyoublong", there is not much chance of guessing what Joyce means, despite the capitalization of the first letter, unless one has Dublin in mind, something Joyce's readers cannot fail to do. So one needs at least to know the reference of the name "Dublin" and the meaning of the phrase "Do you belong?"; finding them both in "Dyoublong" requires more. The destruction of the ordinary structure of ordinary English is nearly complete, but that it forms a very large part of the foundation of Joyce's structure is obvious. A random paragraph from *Finnegans Wake* begins "He beached the bark of his tale; and set to husband and vine. . . . " Yet in that paragraph fully a third of the "words" belong to no language at all; something like this percentage probably goes for the book as a whole. And of course there is plenty of destruction that goes beyond merely grinding up familiar words and assembling new words from the pieces; there is the destruction of grammar. Yet the destruction is never for its own sake; as Campbell and Robinson say, there are no nonsense syllables in Joyce.[16] This is certainly right. But then one should wonder what philosophers and linguists mean when they say that speaking and writing are "rule-governed" activities.

Many of Joyce's inventions are of the "Dyoublong" kind: "Makefearsome's Ocean", "Persse O'Reilly" (one of Humphrey C. Earwicker's many names; an earwig is called in French a perce-oreille), "the old cupiosity shape" all turn up in his "meandertale". More complex, and more basic to Joyce's methods, are whole sentences (if that is what they are) with systematically related paranomasias. "Nobody aviar soar anywing to eagle it," is a flip

[15] Harry Levin, *The Essential James Joyce*, Penguin Books, Harmondsworth, 1963, p. 15. (First published 1948.)

[16] Joseph Campbell and Henry M. Robinson, *A Skeleton Key to Finnegans Wake*, Harcourt, Brace, New York, 1944, p. 360.

example; "Why do I am alook alike a poss of porter pease?" is another (with suggestions of "like as two peas," a request for a pot of porter, please, and a reference to Piesporter wine). And a last exhibit: "Was he come to hevre with his engiles or gone to hull with the poop." It's clear that when Joyce was flying by the net of language, he did not intend to leave us unentangled.

Joyce achieves many of his effects, it is clear, through a process of accretion: he piles word on top of word, reference on reference, sly hint on crass joke, personal allusion on top of classical quotation. One might expect the result to be a ponderous verbosity, but instead Joyce achieves an extraordinary economy of expression. As he says, "When a part so ptee does duty for the holos we soon grow to use of an allforabit." The child who does his duty soon grows to use the alphabet; so the mature artist learns to let bits of language reverberate on a Viconian scale: at one point Joyce compresses it into "Atom, Adam, etym." "What universal binomial denominations would be his as entity and nonentity?" asks the impersonal catechist of the Ithaca Episode in *Ulysses*. The three word answer glances at *Pilgrim's Progress* and, more significantly, echoes Odysseus' cunning answer to the Cyclops: "Everyman and Noman." That "Noman", Joyce's invisibility act, brings us by a commodious vicus of recirculation back to the point where—well; I began by asking what Joyce may have meant when he declared that he would fly by the net of language, and I connected this youthful boast with two themes in Joyce: the idea, first, that evolution implies revolution, and that revolution entails both destruction and return to the point of origin, and the idea, second, that the mature literary artist refines himself out of existence. Answers that seem relevant to the question, how did Joyce think he was destroying and remaking language, answers of the sort we have just been rehearsing, do not seem pertinent when we face the second issue, how, by making language according to his own taste, Joyce was refining the artist out of existence. I believe there is an answer to this question, but it goes beyond issues of verbal technique.

And so it should, for many of the accomplishments we are crediting to Joyce, which are correctly characterized by Harry Levin as forms of symbolism, though no doubt promoted in novel ways by Joyce's acrobatic stunts with language, might have been achieved in other ways. Symbolism is usually and most easily implemented by the plainest language; plain language by no means entails plain thought or plain effects. Dante, to whom Joyce in effect compares himself (both are exiles writing compendiously and with generalizing intent about the land and society they have left), Dante, writing, as he tells us, on four different levels simultaneously, chose a relatively simple vernacular. The styles of writers who have been truly creative with language, on the other hand—Aristophanes, Rabelaise, Sterne, Céline, for example—have typically not been highly figurative, allegoric or symbolic.

Joyce's use of language is connected to his view that in its most developed form, what he called the dramatic, the artist "remains within or behind or beyond or above his handiwork, invisible." Like Odysseus the artist can make himself invisible, a noman or a ghost, in many ways: by taking another's name, or country, or race, or language; or by changing himself, like Proteus, into another form.

It might seem that the simplest way for the writer to remove himself from the scene is to let his characters speak for themselves, and to refrain from speaking for them or of them. This is more than hinted by calling the third style the dramatic. This hint no doubt contributed to the idea that the truly original element in Joyce's style consists in the use of the interior monologue. Richard Ellman calls the interior monologue "the most famous of the devices of *Ulysses*", and says, "Joyce had been rapidly moving towards a conception of personality new to the novel...His protagonists moved in the world and reacted to it, but their basic anxieties and exaltations seemed to move with slight reference to their environment. They were so islanded, in fact, that Joyce's development of the interior monologue to enable his readers to enter the mind of a character without the chaperonage of the author, seems a discovery he might have been expected to make."[17]

According to Ellman, then, the device of the interior monologue is one way in which Joyce refined himself, if not out of existence, at least out of the picture. This seems to me an oversimplification for at least two reasons. If having his characters speak for themselves were in itself a convincing way for a writer to

[17] Richard Ellman, *James Joyce*, Oxford University Press, New York, 1959, p. 368.

withdraw from his work, there would be no way an author could inject himself into his work. But just as nothing an author says can guarantee that we will take an author as speaking for another, nothing can insure that we will take him as speaking for himself. Sometimes, perhaps, we are sure it is Fielding who is addressing us in his own persona; we are less certain about Sterne; and though the superficial tone is much the same in Defoe, we know he is kidding. Sham prefaces, claims about manuscripts found in bottles, endless declarations of sincerity—none of these suffices to put the man before us, nor, often, is it meant to. Only the total context can do that.

The other side of the story is that the interior monologue seldom so much as pretends to stay entirely inside the appropriate character. Even Molly Bloom's soliloquy conspicuously contains elements we cannot easily suppose were, even unconsciously, in that good woman's head.

Harry Levin thinks that here Joyce errs. Commenting on Joyce's telling of Earwicker's dream, Levin says,

> The darker shadings of consciousness, the gropings of the somnolent mind, the state between sleeping and waking—unless it be by Proust—have never been so acutely rendered. But Joyce's technique always tends to get ahead of his psychology. *Finnegans Wake* respects, though it garbles and parodies, the literary conventions. It brims over with *ad libs*, and misplaced confidences and self-conscious stage-whispers. Now and then it pauses to defend itself, to bait the censorship, or to pull the legs of would-be commentators . . . It includes a brief outline of *Ulysses*, and even a letter from a dissatisfied reader. In reply, frequent telegraphic appeals from the author to his "abcedminded" readers . . . punctuate the torrent of his soliloquy periodically. These *obiter dicta* cannot be traced, with any show of plausibility, to the sodden brain of a snoring publican. No psychoanalyst could account for the encyclopedic sweep of Earwicker's fantasies or the acoustical properties of his dreamwork.[18]

We may not agree with Levin—I don't—that these undoubted features of Joyce's style count as a defect, but we can concur that the interior monologue, as Joyce treats it, is not his way of refining himself out of existence.

If we look back to those pregnant passages on literary form in *A Portrait of the Artist*, an ambiguity now emerges. In the epical form, for example, "the centre of emotional gravity is equidistant

---

[18] Harry Levin, *James Joyce*, p. 175.

from the artist himself and from others." Who are these others, the author's characters or his readers? When, in the dramatic form, the artist refines himself out of existence, is he putting distance between himself and Humphrey C. Earwicker, or between himself and his readers? Perhaps Joyce was mainly thinking of the artist's relation to his characters. But as Levin pointed out in the passage I just quoted, Joyce did not choose to remove himself, stylistically or otherwise, from his characters. The distance his style created, a distance that increased from *Dubliners* through *Ulysses* and reached its extreme in *Finnegans Wake*, was the distance between the text and its readers.

Edmund Wilson, in one of the earliest critical appreciations of Joyce, remarked that both Proust and Joyce express the concept of relativity (which Joyce called parallax in *Ulysses*), in which the world changes "as it is perceived by different observers and by them at different times."[19] Wilson also may have had in mind no more than Joyce's relation to his characters, but it surely would not be wrong to include Joyce's readers as contributing an essential perspective. Shem, "the penman" of *Finnegans Wake*, with whom Joyce clearly identifies, makes clear that this is Joyce's view. "He would not put fire to his cerebrum; he would not throw himself in Liffey; he would not explaud himself with pneumantics." Nevertheless, with "increasing interest in his semantics" you will find him "unconsciously explaining, for inkstands, with a meticulosity bordering on the insane, the various meanings of all the different foreign parts of speech he misused ... "[20] He expects his readers to sympathize when he sings, "Flunkey Footle furloughed foul, writing off his phoney," but for all that he expects his readers to decode the "languish of Tintangle."[21]

All reading is interpretation, and all interpretation demands some degree of invention. It is Joyce's extraordinary idea to raise the price of admission to the point where we are inclined to feel that almost as much is demanded of the reader as of the author. Goading his audience into fairly testing creative activity, Joyce both deepens and removes from immediate view his own part in the proceedings. By fragmenting familiar languages and recycling

[19] Edmund Wilson, *Axel's Castle*, Scribner's, New York, 1948, pp. 221–2.
[20] *Finnegans Wake*, Viking Press, New York, 1939, pp. 172–3.
[21] Ibid., pp. 418, 232.

the raw material Joyce provokes the reader into involuntary collaboration, and enlists him as a member of his private linguistic community. Coopted into Joyce's world of verbal exile, we are forced to share in the annihilation of old meanings and the creation—not really *ex nihilo*, but on the basis of our stock of common lore—of a new language. All communication involves such joint effort to some degree, but Joyce is unusual in first warning us of this, and then making the effort so extreme.

Joyce takes us back to the foundations and origins of communication; he puts us in the situation of the jungle linguist trying to get the hang of a new language and a novel culture, to assume the perspective of someone who is an alien or an exile. As we, his listeners or readers, become familiar with the devices he has made us master, we find ourselves removed a certain distance from our own language, our usual selves, and our society. We join Joyce as outcasts, temporarily freed, or so it seems, from the nets of our language and our culture.

Joyce has not, of course, refined himself out of existence; but by the violent originality of his language he has shifted some of the normal burden of understanding and insight onto his bemused readers. The center of creative energy is thus moved from the artist to a point between the writer and his audience. The engagement of the reader in the process of interpretation, forced on him by Joyce's dense, unknown idiom, bestows on the author himself a kind of invisibility, leaving the interpreter alone with the author's handiwork, absorbed in his own creative task. By creating a hermeneutic space between the reader and the text, Joyce has at the same time doubled his own distance from the reader. This is, I suggest, what Joyce meant by saying the artist refines himself out of existence, and what he implied by his announced intention of flying by the net of language.

11 *The Third Man*

What am I doing here? What is the point of the quotations from my work in these mysteriously explosive pictures by Robert Morris, made with his eyes closed? This is not the first time I have found my writing in unexpected surroundings. Nothing has surprised me more than to discover myself anthologized in books with titles such as *Post-Analytic Philosophy* or *After Philosophy*. That *after* haunts me again from an about-to-be-published book with the title *Literary Theory after Davidson*. Is there something sinister, or at least fin de siècle, in my views that I have failed to recognize, something that portends the dissolution not only of the sort of philosophy I do but of philosophy itself? Why else would I find my name linked with Heidegger and Derrida?[1]

The answer to some of these questions may turn on my rejection of subjectivist theories of epistemology and meaning, and my conviction that thought itself is essentially social; but I have no

---

This essay is a revised version of the catalogue essay for the Robert Morris exhibition held 27 Aug.–8 Oct. 1992, at the Frank Martin Gallery, Muhlenberg College.

[1] "What am I doing here?" I find, not very surprisingly, that I am not the first to ask this question. It's the title of a book by Bruce Chatwin (New York, 1989), and Jean Genet asks himself, "What am I doing here?" when living among the Palestinians. See Jean Genet, *Prisoner of Love*, trans. Barbara Bray (New York, 2003).

For the other books mentioned: *Post-Analytic Philosophy*, ed. John Rajchman and Cornel West (New York, 1985); *After Philosophy: End or Transformation*, ed. Kenneth Baynes, James Bohman, and Thomas McCarthy (Cambridge, Mass., 1987); and *Literary Theory after Davidson*, ed. Reed Way Dasenbrock, University Park, Penn., 1993. For Heidegger, see Dorothea Frede, "Beyond Realism and Anti-realism: Rorty on Heidegger and Davidson," *Review of Metaphysics* 40 (June 1987): 733–57; for Derrida, see Samuel Wheeler, "Indeterminacy of French Interpretation: Derrida and Davidson," in *Truth and Interpretation*, ed. Ernest Lepore (Oxford, 1986), and David Novitz, "Metaphor, Derrida, and Davidson," *Journal of Aesthetics and Art Criticism* 44 (Winter 1985): 101–14.

idea whether it is this that has prompted Morris to use my work. Since I do not know what his reasons were, let me say what strikes me in the result.

Works of art, writings, artifacts of all sorts are among the objects in the world. Our sense organs and brains are organized to pick out objects from their backgrounds, to identify as similar objects seen from different angles and distances and in different lights, even to recognize the same object when glimpsed after absence. These abilities with which nature has endowed us enable us to group together patterns of stimulation, patterns that when registered at nerve ends are often unlike one another. The evidence that these groupings are part of our native apparatus is the similarity of our responses. We respond in similar ways to our mother in dim light and bright, seen or heard from afar or near, and clad in many costumes.

The preverbal child, or other languageless animal, shows such object-oriented behavior; but is this enough to prove it has the concept of an object? No: the power to discriminate does not imply possession of the corresponding concept. Sensory discrimination classifies phenomena as they differ at the periphery of the nervous system; concepts classify in terms of properties that may or may not stir the senses at the moment. With concepts come judgments: this is edible, this poisonous, here is a cube, there a lion. Judgments, unlike mere responses, can be true or false. It is only with concepts and judgments that we can be said to have the idea of an objective world, a world that is independent of our sensations or experience.

What makes the idea of an autonomous object available to us? Its availability requires, above all, the corroboration of others, others who are tuned to the same basic events and objects we are, and who are tuned to our responses to those events and objects. When the second person enters the scene, he or she can correlate my responses with his or her own responses; for the first time it makes sense to speak of responses being "the same," that is, relevantly similar. And for the first time, there is reason to speak of responses being responses to external objects rather than to immediate sensations; when two (or, of course, more) creatures can correlate their responses, those responses *triangulate* the object. It is the common cause of the responses, a cause that must have a location in a shared, interpersonal space. When we can notice, that must have a location in a shared, interpersonal space. When we can notice that we share reactions, the possibility of a check or standard is introduced, the possibility of occasional failures of expected joint reactions and hence of error.

The primal triangle of two observers, each observing a shared world and each observing the other observer, can exist without language, and it does; but the triangle is a necessary condition of language and of a full grasp of the concepts of objectivity and truth. Language fills in and enriches the base of the triangle, and of course language soon reaches far beyond what can be immediately and jointly experienced. But the ability to talk and think about what is too small or distant or abstract to be seen or touched rests on what we have been able to share directly, for the experiences we register as communal tie our words and thoughts to the world.

Art that has been created with the idea of being read or seen or heard by others (or perhaps by its creator at a time subsequent to its creation) enters the conceptual scene at an advanced stage. Artist, writer, and audience are equipped from the start with a vast overlapping set of common assumptions. Nevertheless, one may choose to consider some aspects of art in the light of the foundations of the concept of objectivity.

Writing deviates startlingly from the original triangle. The object directly observed by both reader and writer is the text. It is produced by the writer, but in the case of literature the text is alienated from its creator by the lapse in time between when it is made and when it is read; the interaction between perceiving creatures that is the foundation of communication is lost. Plato marks the gulf between talking to a person and reading his words:

> That's the strange thing about writing, which makes it truly analogous to painting. The painter's products stand before us as though they were alive: but if you question them, they maintain a most majestic silence. It is the same with written words: they seem to talk to you as though they were intelligent, but if you ask them anything about what they say, they go on telling you just the same thing for ever.

It's true that generally neither the text nor its author can respond to the reader. The interaction is of another sort. The text, unlike most objects, has meaning, and its meaning is the product of the interplay between the intentions of the writer to be understood in a certain way and the interpretation put on the writer's words by the reader. For the most part this interplay is, and is meant to be, routine, in the sense that the writer knows pretty well how he or she is apt to be understood, and the typical reader knows pretty well how the writer intended to be understood. This is not always the case. Writers like Shakespeare, Dante, Joyce, Beckett strain our interpretive powers and thus force us into retrospective dialogue with the text, and through the text with the author. Authors may choose from many devices to rouse the reader to wrestle with the text: thought-provoking puzzles, ambiguous authorial attitudes, plays within plays, stylistic references to other writers, autobiographical hints. But however it is done, and to whatever extent the reader's connivance is won, authors have contrived or commandeered an arena of ideas and assumptions large enough to contain both themselves and their audience, a common conceptual space.

Sculpture is similar, except that the space shared by viewer and object is not conceptual but literal. Michael Fried, Annette Michelson, and Maurice Berger have emphasized the ways in which Morris's minimalist sculpture engages the viewer with the object not only by creating a "common dwelling," a "situation" that "includes the beholder' but by making art object."[2] But there is still a vast difference between such sculpture and a written text. Writing depends on meaning, reference to what lies beyond the words. A piece of sculpture may resemble something else, but unless it is a monument (with an inscription) it does not refer to something else. Some of Morris's pieces may have been of a height and bulk to invite a viewer to react as to a person. What this called for, however, was not the thought that the piece resembled a person; rather, the piece provoked an immediate experience in some ways like the experience of encountering a person. The creation of meaning was elicited from the viewer, not something embedded in the work. Wittgenstein said, "Meaning something is like going up to someone."[3]

---

[2] Michael Fried, "Art and Objecthood," *Artforum* 5 (Summer 1967): 15. See also Annette Michelson, "Robert Morris—An Aesthetics of Transgression," in *Robert Morris* (exhibition catalogue, Corcoran Gallery of Art and Detroit Institute of Arts, Washington, D.C., and Detroit, Nov. 1969–Feb. 1970), pp. 7–75, and Maurice Berger, *Labyrinths: Robert Morris, Minimalism, and the 1960s* (New York, 1989).

[3] Ludwig Wittgenstein, *Philosophical Investigations*, 3d ed., trans. G. E. M. Anscombe (New York, 1958), §457.

Robert Morris has remarked that "language is not plastic art but both are forms of human behavior and the structures of one can be compared to the structures of the other."[4] This is the very thought I have been following. But as one notes the parallels one must also be struck by a basic difference between language in its generic use, with speaker and hearer face to face, and exchanging roles, and the creation of the author or artist, which isolates the creator both from the work and from the audience. The "forms of human behavior" to which Morris refers are not the texts or sculptures or paintings that the reader or viewer encounters but the actions that produce these objects. The structures to be compared are not the structures of the works of art but of the actions that produced them.

How can the act of artistic creation, like an ordinary speech act, be presented so that the viewer can react to it along with its product? A writer may simply step out of the work and tell us what he or she is doing, as Trollope repeatedly compared himself as novelist to the shoemaker at his last. The artist may compose a public event or happening in which he or she is seen making or changing or destroying, or altering the work each day. He or she may append to an object a description of how it was manu-factured; he or she may even contrive an object that contains *The Sound of Its Own Making.* I see the pictures in this exhibition as carrying out the project of bringing the act of their making into the works themselves a step further, or at least a step in a new direction. Not only do these pictures graphically display some of the essential features of all intentional actions, but they also engage the collaboration of the viewer in a way that connects with the origins of the concept of an object.

These pictures have four clearly distinguished elements. Taking them in the reverse of their narrative order, they are: (1) The marks and patterns made by Morris with his eyes closed. I will call these the "action." (2) The symmetrical, paired squares and rectangles and other shapes carefully placed on the paper before the action. I call these the "targets." (3) Morris's description of how the action was performed and the rules that guided it. This is both the "description" and the "intention." (4) A fragment of

---

[4] Robert Morris, "Some Notes on the Phenomenology of Making: The Search for the Motivated," *Artforum* 8 (1970), 62–6.

a philosophical discussion of the general nature of action. Taken in the order from (4) to (1) it is easy to notice that there is a progression from the abstract to the concrete, from the very general to the particular. The texts are about actions, and the "action" illustrates and exemplifies what the texts say. The four elements also variously present to the mind and eye the fundamental features of any intentional action. (4) is part of an attempt to make explicit the everyday conceptual apparatus with which we all operate, the part of this apparatus some philosophers like to call "Folk Psychology." All actions are performed within the ambit of these ideas. (3) has two functions; the more important one is to express an intention, the intention to perform a certain action within a given (subjectively estimated) period, and with the eyes closed. (I'll come to the second function in a moment.) (2) establishes some of the parameters of the action; it defines a space in and around which the action is to occur. (1) is not, of course, an action but the result of the action. I call it the "action" not because it moves but because given what we know of the intention with which the action was performed, its defining spatial targets, and the particular and general conceptual background against which it took place, we understand and can vividly picture the act of production.

The reason viewers can understand and interact with these works is not that they know how they were produced but because they know why. They know almost exactly why the "action" looks as it does not because they know what ultimate reasons Morris may have had in making these objects but because they know, for each object, the detailed intention it was meant to realize. What ensures the participation of viewers is the fact that the accomplishment can be measured directly against the intention. There is a fallacy against which we are warned in reading literature. We are told we should not evaluate the work in terms of what we take to have been the author's intentions. Morris is not exactly inviting us to commit the "intentional fallacy," for we do not judge the aesthetic merit of these pictures by how closely he was able to follow his own instructions. But we cannot help being involved, as he must be, in the question of how close he did come. We can see where his patterns fall, and we can see, because he provided us with the "targets," by how much he missed his marks. What we cannot see is how well he estimated the intended times, and so he tells us; this is the second contribution of (3). Why did he make these drawings "blind"? How else could we evaluate so clearly the distance between his intention and the outcome?

Morris has depicted, then, the essential element on which the concept of an autonomous object (and world) depends: an intersubjective measure of error and success, of truth and falsity. He has put his viewers in a position to triangulate with him the location of his creative acts.

This leaves me with the question with which I began: what is my work doing here? I hazard this answer: it expands the background against which we encounter Morris's "actions." Morris's explicit written intentions, and his visual targets, already provide a conceptual and physical space the viewer inhabits with the work and with its maker. But these coordinates are highly particular. Beyond the particular, all our thoughts and actions occur within, and derive their meaning from, a vast system of largely communal assumptions and ideas. Perhaps the quotations from my writings, which are concerned with the nature of thought and of action, hint at this larger canvas.

12 *Locating Literary Language*

Literature poses a problem for philosophy of language, for it directly challenges any theory of meaning that makes the assertorial or truth-seeking uses of language primary and pretends that other linguistic performances are in some sense "etiolated" or "parasitical".[1] The sources of trouble are to be sure far more ubiquitous than the reference to literature suggests: jokes, skits, polite nothings, ironies, all break the mold of sincere, literal, would-be truth-telling. But literature can serve as the focus of the problem if only by dint of its kinship with and employment of such verbal tricks and turns. Literature and these comrade conceits are a prime test of the adequacy of any view of the nature of language, and it is a test I have argued that many theories fail.[2]

But though the literary uses of language have long interested me, I have neglected to indicate, or even to think very hard about, how my account of the origins of intentionality and objectivity (which I see as emerging simultaneously and as mutually dependent) should be adapted to the case of literature. Indeed, it is clear to me now that any gesture in the direction of such adaptation will also reveal the need for a sharper focus on the role of intention in writing, and hence on the relation between writer and reader. I am grateful to the contributors to this volume, and especially to its editor, for prodding me into considering these issues, even if still all too briefly.[3]

---

[1] These words, and the idea behind them, are J. L. Austin's, *How To Do Things with Words*, Harvard University Press, Cambridge, Mass., 1962, p. 22.

[2] See, for example, Essays 8, 17, and 18 in *Inquiries into Truth and Interpretation*.

[3] 'This volume', 'this book', in this chapter refers to R. W. Dasenbrock (ed.), *Literary Theory after Davidson*, Pennsylvania State University Press, University Park, Penn., 1993.

I will concentrate on two related problems: the role of reference in "story-telling", and the changes that occur when we replace the triangle of speaker, hearer, and world with the triangle of writer, reader, and tradition. So far as the geometry of the situation is concerned, I am a commentator on such triangles, as are the writers of the other essays in this book; and like them, I am also inescapably at an apex of various actual and imagined triangles of my own.

First, though, I should say a word about my general theory of action. One commentator labors to make the point that the theme of "Actions, Reasons and Causes" is of little value to the writer or critic of fiction. I certainly agree. If my analysis of the concept of action has any value at all for those who wish to look deep into the springs of action, it is to release them from the conceptual bind imposed on us, first by a series of nineteenth-century German philosophers, and then by Wittgenstein and his followers, who taught that the methods of the poet, the critic, and the social scientist not only are different from, but also opposed to, the methods of the sciences of (the rest of) nature. The latter, materialist, domain they saw as ruled by causality, laws, and the nomological-deductive method, the former, humanistic, domain by insight, empathetic understanding, and teleological explanation. My contribution was to emphasize, somewhat as Spinoza had, that the two domains—of mind and body, intension and extension, law-governed events and thoughtful actions—were parts of radically distinct, but equally legitimate, ways of describing, understanding, and explaining phenomena, but that they applied to a single ontology of events and objects. Causality, I argued, applied to both domains, but by distinguishing causal relations from the descriptions of events under which the events could be viewed as instantiating laws, I removed actions from the realm of deterministic nomological explanation. This view effectively reconciled, I thought, two apparently antagonistic intuitions. One intuition insists that the understanding of the thoughts and actions of people involves the imaginative adjustment of the interpreter's beliefs and values to the attitudes of the interpreted, a process that requires the accommodation of one normative system within another. The other intuition tells us that in the natural sciences such considerations are beside the point: physics strives to find categories from which norms, even causal concepts, are excluded, categories which lend themselves to incorporation in a system of laws with as few ceteris paribus clauses as possible.

It is a serious mistake, if I am right, to suppose that the relatively simple Aristotelian-Thomistic scheme I proposed for analyzing the concept of acting with a reason aims to assimilate this concept to the natural sciences simply because it invokes causality. This gets things backwards: serious science strives to extrude the concept of causality in favor of strict laws. It is teleological explanation that cannot do without the concept of causality, and for that reason, among others, reason-explanations cannot hope to be reduced to, or incorporated in, the natural sciences.

It remains the case that my schematic account of the intention with which an action is performed is no positive help for someone who wants to construct an interesting psychology of action. The imagination might be caught, however, at the point where it becomes appropriate to identify, to give propositional content to, the various beliefs, desires, motives, and attitudes that cause an intentional action, and by causing it, determine in turn its appropriate descriptions.

An ineluctable feature of teleological explanation is its normative character. This does not mean, as one of the contributors to this volume thinks, that I confuse the purported norms of logic or of Bayesian decision theory with descriptive theories.[4] There is no definition of "perfect rationality", whatever we take that to be, according to which people satisfy the definition. My point has rather been that we can explain and understand irrationality only against a background of rationality, a background each of us must, as an interpreter, supply for himself. There is no fixed list of standards, no eternal hierarchy of values, to which we all must subscribe, but some norms are so basic to intelligibility that we cannot avoid shaping thoughts to their patterns. Thus as Quine has pointed out, we can interpret some speaker's device as expressing conjunction only if the speaker generally treats that device in accord with the truth table for conjunction; but then we have attributed a bit of logic to that person. The norms of decision making under uncertainty, of induction, and so on, are far more flexible, and we can understand deviations easily, including differences over what the norms are. But I would

---

[4] I have several times documented my own disillusion with the idea that such theories are experimentally testable. See *Essays on Actions and Events*, pp. 235 f.

argue that we could not understand someone whom we were forced to treat as departing radically and predominantly from all such norms. This would not be an example of irrationality, or of an alien set of standards: it would be an absence of rationality, something that could not be reckoned as thought.

I now revert to the nature of interpretation. It is natural to state the central problem as that of determining the meaning of spoken or written words. This is not wrong, but it can be misleading. Words, Frege emphasized, have a meaning only in the context of a sentence. The basic reason for this is that the work of language, to give information, tell stories, ask questions, issue commands, and so on, is done by sentences; a word which is not being used to convey the content of a sentence cannot do any of these things. It is at the sentential level that language connects with the interests and intentions language serves, and this is also the level at which the evidence for interpretation emerges. But just as words have a meaning only in the context of a sentence, a sentence has a meaning only in a context of use, as part, in some sense, of a particular language. There would be no saying what language a sentence belonged to if there were not actual utterances or writings, not, perhaps of that very sentence, but of other sentences appropriately related to it. So in the end the sole source of linguistic meaning is the intentional production of tokens of sentences. If such acts did not have meanings, nothing would. There is no harm in assigning meanings to sentences, but this must always be a meaning derived from concrete occasions on which sentences are put to work.

The recognition that meaning of whatever sort rests ultimately on intention leads at once into the thickets of densely packed intentions through which philosophers along with psychologists, historians, sociologists, literary critics, and theorists try to pick their way. For we can speak of "the" intention with which an act is performed only by narrowing attention to one among the tangle of intentions involved in any performance. Since most if not all the ambiguities of "meaning" spring from the varieties of intention, I begin by distinguishing some of these varieties.

There are, I think, three distinct sorts of intention which are present in all speech acts. There are ends or intentions which lie as it were beyond the production of words, ends that could at least in principle be achieved by non-linguistic means. Thus one may speak with the intention of being elected mayor, of amusing a child, of warning a pilot of ice on the wings; one may write with the intention of making money, of proving one's cleverness, to celebrate the freedom of the will, or to neutralize a plaguing memory or emotion. Such ends do not involve language, in the sense that their description does not have to mention language. I call these intentions "ulterior". It is a striking fact (if I am right that it is a fact) that all genuine uses of language require an ulterior purpose. Using language is not a game: it is never an end in itself.

Second, every linguistic utterance or inscription is produced with the intention that it should have a certain force: it is intended to be an assertion, or command, a joke or question, a pledge or insult. There can be borderline cases, but only when straddling a border is intended: so it is possible to intend an utterance of "Go to sleep" as somewhere between an order and the expression of a wish, or to intend the remark "See you in July" as part promise and part prediction.

Third, it is a necessary mark of a linguistic action that the speaker or writer intends his words to be interpreted as having a certain meaning. These are the strictly semantic intentions.

Each of these categories may harbor more, in some cases many more, intentions but at least one intention of each sort is always present. A simple case: I shout "Thin ice" as you skate toward disaster. My ulterior motive is to warn you, the force of my utterance is assertory, and I intend you to take my words to mean that the ice towards which you are skating is thin. Even here, though, more intentions are present. I want to warn you, but I want to warn you in order to save you from a chilly plunge. I intend your grasp of the meaning and force of my utterance to be the means of your salvation. In this case, I have no reason to want you to be ignorant of any of my intentions, though it is not necessarily part of my intention that you should grasp all of my ulterior purposes. But here, as always, I use language with the intention that your grasp of my intended meaning and force should function to achieve my ulterior purpose. (This is the Gricean reflex.) A linguistic action is frustrated if its intended audience does not grasp the producer's intended semantic meaning and force. The speaker or writer may have good reasons, however, for wanting ulterior motives to remain undetected. Don Giovanni sings to Zerlina, "Là ci darem la mano". The semantic meaning of the utterance and its force (entreaty) seem clear enough, but of his ulterior aims he wants her to grasp only the most obvious, that she should give him her hand. Like a liar, he cannot afford to have his leading intention known.

It is perhaps obvious that ulterior purposes can be as complex as our thoughts about the relations between means and ends can make them. It is only a little less obvious that semantic intentions can be equally complicated. Thersites, looking at Ajax, says to Achilles, "... whomsoever you take him to be, he is Ajax."[5] To point out only what is obvious: Thersites intends his words to be taken as literally meaning that whatever Achilles may think, the person in front of him is Ajax. Since Achilles of course knows this ("I know that, fool"), Thersites is not *asserting* that this is Ajax, but that Ajax is absurd beyond further description. ("Ay, but that fool knows not himself.") The proposition Thersites asserts is not the proposition his words express. This is a mild case of what Grice calls "implicature"—something which the circumstances make clear the speaker intends to convey. The potential ambiguity which Thersites brings out in Achilles' reply (since the comma in "I know that, fool" can't be spoken) is probably not intended by Achilles, but it does focus attention on the implicature in Thersites' first remark. The playwright wants us to catch what he may want us to think Achilles doesn't.

I have just spoken as if the distinction between the proposition expressed by a sentence and what is asserted by using the sentence were obvious. But sentences express something only as used on particular occasions, and what they express depends, among other things, on the intentions of the speaker or writer. How do the intentions of the author of a linguistic act allow us to distinguish between what her words convey and what she intends to convey by using them? Grice has given us some subtle and convincing principles for making this distinction in the case of certain sorts of implicature, but it is not clear that these principles are designed to handle the gamut of examples we find in literature, nor, surprisingly enough, are the principles based on the intentions of the speaker.[6] Fortunately, however, there is a simple principle which will serve our present purposes.

[5] Shakespeare, *Troilus and Cressida*, Act II, scene I.
[6] Paul Grice, "The Causal Theory of Perception", *Proceedings of the Aristotelian Society*, Supplementary Volume 35 (1961).

The intentions with which an action is done have an order: they constitute a chain built on the relation of means to end as seen by the agent. Thus someone moves his hand in order to move a pen across the paper in order to write his name in order to sign a check in order to pay a bill in order to ... Or, someone moves her mouth and tongue in order to form the sounds "That is an emu," in order to speak words that will be interpreted by a hearer as true if and only if an emu is salient in order to inform the hearer that a salient object is an emu in order to instruct the hearer in how to identify an emu in order to ... In this sequence, the first intention that has to do with what words mean, or are intended to mean, is the intention to speak words that will be assigned a certain meaning by an interpreter. I call this the *first meaning*. It corresponds roughly to what is sometimes called literal meaning, but since this latter phrase has associations I do not want I have coined my own jargon.

The usefulness of the concept of first meaning emerges when we consider cases where what is stated or implied differs from what the words mean. "Sometime too hot the eye of heaven shines" means that the sun sometimes shines too brightly. But the first meaning of "the eye of heaven" purports to refer to the one and only eye of heaven. We can tell this because Shakespeare (we assume) intended to use words that would be recognized by a reader to refer to the one and only eye of heaven (if such a thing existed) in order to prompt the reader to understand that he meant the sun. We may wish to use the word "meaning" for both the first meaning and what the metaphor carries us to, but only the first meaning has a systematic place in the language of the author.[7]

First meaning is first in two related respects: it comes first in the order of the speaker's or the writer's semantic intentions, and it is the necessary basis for all further investigations into what words, as used on an occasion, mean. You do not begin to grasp what Shakespeare meant by "the eye of heaven" if you do not know the ordinary meaning of "eye"; and Shakespeare intended you to understand his metaphor by way of your understanding of the

---

[7] In my essay "What Metaphors Mean", Essay 17 in *Inquiries into Truth and Interpretation*, I was foolishly stubborn about the word meaning when all I cared about was the primacy of first meaning.

ordinary meanings of his words. The dependence of other meanings or implicatures on first meaning should not be taken to suggest that given the first meaning the rest follows. "He was burned up" has (let us say) an unambiguous first meaning, but what it implies depends on the context. When Herrick speaks of the liquefaction of Julia's clothes, how do we know the clothes didn't fall into a vat of acid?

Similarly, first meaning and what it may in specific circumstances implicate are not enough to fix the force of an utterance or writing. Indeed, force and first meaning are entirely independent, a fact which literature makes particularly clear. H. L. A. Hart once suggested that in a sense the use of language in fiction is a "calculated abuse".[8] But what is being abused? We may say that the liar abuses language, but this does not mean it is the language which is badly used, but the victim. The victim of a successful lie understands the liar's words perfectly, both the first meaning and the force (assertion); what he gets wrong is an ulterior motive. Unless the liar may mean the same thing by his words as the honest man, it would be impossible to tell a lie, for to be understood would be to be unmasked.

Of course the fiction writer does not, in general at any rate, aim to deceive his readers. But neither does he pretend to use language: using language in play is not playing at using language. There are a few things I can pretend, for example that I can speak Tagalog, by pretending to use language, but I certainly cannot pretend, by only pretending to use language, that Oedipus killed Laius. But even this is a strained sense of pretense. The storyteller does not, like the liar, normally misrepresent his beliefs. He does not *assert* that Oedipus killed Laius. At most he pretends to assert it.

There are cases where we have trouble telling whether a work is fiction. On the page following the title page of the Modern Library edition of E. E. Cummings' *The Enormous Room* I read, "A note on the author of *The Enormous Room*. During the war Edward Estlin Cummings enlisted in the Norton-Harjes Ambulance Corps. With no charge against him, he was confined in a concentration camp in La Ferté Macé, France. It was there that he gathered material for his first and most successful book." In a Foreword, Cummings' father writes of the trouble he had in locating and finally

---

[8] "A Logician's Fairy Tale", *Philosophical Review*, **60** (1951), p. 204.

freeing his son. The first sentence of the book reads, in part, "We had succeeded, my friend B. and I, in dispensing with almost three of our six months' engagement as *Conducteurs Volontaires,...* had just finished the unlovely job of cleaning and greasing . . . the own private flivver of . . . a gentleman by the convenient name of Mr. A." How much here is true, or intended to be taken as true? Is the Foreword really by Cummings' father, or is that part of the story? Surely no one was named "B." or "Mr. A." The simple point is that nothing that is said in the book can determine the force of these sentences. After all, the Preface of *Moll Flanders* begins, "The world is so taken up of late with novels and romances, that it will be hard for a private history to be taken as genuine, where the names and other circumstances of the person are concealed." Should we say it is not really history if the names are altered? Of course not. But then we must apparently reject the popular view that proper names refer to a person only if their causal history ties them back to something like a christening.

Proper names are a problem whether we come at them from the point of view of sober fact-stating or of fiction. Seen from the former angle it seems natural to claim that if a name fails to refer it simply lacks a sense—a sentence that contains such a name fails to say anything, fails to express a proposition, while when studied in the footlights of fiction we feel compelled to assign as full a meaning to sentences with names of fictional characters as to any sentence. "Was Bloom married?" Yes, to Molly Bloom. "Was Bloom a real person?" No, of course not. Both answers can't be true; but neither questions nor answers would make sense if non-referring names had no meaning.

This is not the place to propose a detailed theory of the semantics of proper names. But I do want to insist on a principle to which any correct theory must conform: a meaning which can be grasped without knowledge of whether it was generated in the context of history or of fiction cannot depend on that context. Of course our response to a work may differ according as we think of it as fact or fiction, and it may differ according as we think of it as intended as fact or fiction (not quite the same question). This difference in response is appropriate, of course: if we are asking directions to the next town, or studying the sexual mores of the natives, we care whether our "informant" is spinning a tale or giving us the real dope. But our concern is pointless if we have not already understood the words. If we apply this simple thought to the case of proper names, I think we should reverse the usual strategy of making the referring use of names primary and the non-referring use a play or pretend use. Using names in fiction is, as I said, a real use of language; so how names function in stories not only can, but must, be how they function elsewhere. (This is not to deny that we might never have come to understand the function of proper names if we had not been exposed to cases in which names had a reference.)

I have been stressing the structured hierarchy of intentions with which sentences are spoken or written in part because it seems to me many debates concerning the relevance of intention to the interpretation of literary texts overlook the differences among these intentions. It is time to turn to the larger picture in which those intentions play their parts.

We would not have a language, or the thoughts that depend on language (which comprise all beliefs, desires, hopes, expectations, intentions, and other attitudes that have propositional content), if there were not others who understood us and whom we understood; and such mutual understanding requires a world shared both causally and conceptually. I have argued for the primacy of this triangular relation at some length elsewhere,[9] and it is well explained by several of the contributors to this book. Intersubjective interaction with the world is a necessary condition of our possession of the concepts of truth and objectivity; this is why I reject as unintelligible most forms of skepticism and of conceptual relativism. The triangle comes directly into play when two (or more) creatures react simultaneously to a common stimulus in the world and to each other's reactions. This is the causal nexus that must exist before there can be answers to the questions, what is the relevant stimulus of the response? and, when are stimuli or responses similar? Much more is required for a complex of such relations to constitute the sort of communication we call language, but no less will do. The triangle models the primitive situation in which we take the first steps into language,

[9] See my "Meaning, Truth and Evidence", in *Perspectives on Quine*, ed. R. Barrett and R. Gibson, Oxford: Basil Blackwell, 1990- [Ch. 4 above]; "Epistemology Externalized", *Dialectica*, **45** (1991), pp. 191–202; and "Three Varieties of Knowledge", in A. J. Ayer: Memorial Essays, Royal Institute of Philosophy Supplement no. 30, ed. A. Phillips Griffiths, Cambridge University Press, 1991.

or begin decoding a totally alien language. It is easiest to think of its operation where there is a teacher (or informant) and a learner (or student), but it must apply also to the origins of language and to the most ordinary conversations.

The objectification of parts and aspects of the world which is made possible by intersubjective triangulation is appropriate to the origins of language and to what I have called radical interpretation. But how does the primordial triangle bear on literature? On the one hand it is clear enough that the elements of the triangle remain; there are the writer, his audience, and a common background. But the distances between the elements have lengthened, the connections have become attenuated and obscure.

Modification of the primal triangle set in almost at the start of language learning. What begins with mutually observed reactions to mutually observed phenomena soon graduates to something more useful: the "speaker" observes the object or event (a snake approaches), and the "hearer", screened in one way or another from the snake, reacts to the speaker's reaction to the snake as he normally would to a snake. The communicative triangle triumphs over the loss of the direct causal relation between hearer and snake. Causal connections further attenuate: the hearer or learner masters words in the absence of the relevant objects, by connecting the words with ones mastered more directly. Thus learn to apply "dog" and "picture of a dog" in the presence of the objects, and you may understand "armadillo" by seeing a picture of an armadillo. More subtle but familiar devices allow us to give content to words and phrases that apply to objects and situations beyond the range of the senses, or remote in space and time. But without direct causal ties of language to the world at some points[10] no words would have a content—there would be no language.

In writing the deictic and demonstrative machinery so readily available in speech cannot in the same way complete the triangle that relates writer, reader, and object or event or time. Ostension, which often serves to relate names and faces, or to help introduce a new color or sound or category, has no immediate analogue in writing. Writing has its ways, however, of establishing ties between writer's intentions, reader, and the world. A personal

---

[10] No *particular* points are essential; different direct connections lead speakers by different routes into the same language.

letter can take advantage of a world of established mutual connections; a set of instructions can make demonstrative use of diagrams or of the apparatus to be assembled. Posted signs ("No dumping", "Dangerous curves", "Grasp the handrail", "Trailhead") simply elide the obvious demonstrative reference to time, place, or direction which is supplied by the location and orientation of the sign. Such props are not in general available to literature, but others are. Almost all connected writing that involves more than a few sentences depends on deictic references to its own text. The linear sequence of words and sentences often indicates the temporal order in which events are represented as occurring. A vast network of anaphoric references connects parts of a text to each other through the use of pronouns, demonstrative adjectives, tense, and parataxis.[11]

Most of the words in a literary work have an ordinary extension in the world. Predicates, adjectives, verbs, common nouns, and adverbs do not lose their normal ties to real objects and events when they are employed in fiction; they could suffer this loss only if their meanings changed, and if their meanings changed we wouldn't understand them.[12] More puzzling, as I noted, is the use of proper names. Some proper names in fiction clearly fail to refer, and though this is a troubling semantic phenomenon, it is no more puzzling in fiction than in other contexts. What should we say, though, of names that have a reference if they appear in a newspaper when they are employed in an historical novel, or of invented names in a roman à clef? In Trollope's *Phineas Phinn*, do "Daubeny" and "Gresham" refer to Disraeli and Gladstone? The *Daily Telegraph* chastised Trollope for putting real politicians in his novels, and particularly criticized his "malignant"

---

[11] In this paragraph I have tried to hold down overt reference in one sentence to an earlier sentence. But the "however" makes sense only in the light of what goes before, as does the "such props". There are many more subtle cross references. If one spells out the reference, the text itself always plays a role: "such props" = "props such as those mentioned in the preceding sentence". Anyone who doubts the overwhelming frequency of such cross-textual demonstrative references should try writing a few paragraphs without them.

[12] Of course a writer, like a speaker, may manage things so that in his work we interpret a familiar word in a novel way. But this can't be the usual situation. We understand the word "cat", whether in fiction or in an advertisement for cat food, if we can tell a cat when we see one; the introduction of a fictional cat in a story does not change the list of objects to which the word applies any more than it changes the meaning of the word.

portrait of John Bright. Trollope claimed he had deliberately avoided any likeness to the real Bright, but another reviewer wrote that Trollope

is cruelly careful that the veriest child shall not fail to recognize his pet aversion under the *alias* he has given him. With historical and needlessly elaborate minuteness [Trollope] describes his robustness, age, hair, height, gait, complexion, eyes, nose, lips, coat, trousers, and waistcoat...[T]he future historian may refer to [this novel] to discover what was the material of which Mr. Bright's waistcoats were made.[13]

Damon Runyon calls a newspaper writer "Waldo Winchester" (Walter Winchell), a restaurant "Mindy's" (Lindy's), and a street "Broadway" in a place he calls "Manhattan". But according to T. J. Binyon, "to imagine that Runyon's stories have anything to do with reality betrays a grotesque misunderstanding of the nature of art".[14]

It depends on what you mean by having "anything to do with reality"; but the issue I raise is, it may seem, more parochial: it is whether the names refer to real people and places. I raise the issue not in order to provide an answer, but to remark that the defense of whatever answer is offered must depend on two matters: the intentions of the author, and the relevance of those intentions to the correct interpretation of the text. The former concern matters of fact, the latter matters for decision, aesthetic and otherwise. It is an empirical question, however difficult or easy it may be to decide, whether Trollope intended his readers to take his "Turnbull" to refer to Bright (in this case it doesn't seem hard to decide). But even this intention isn't completely without its shadows. Which readers? Perhaps the veriest child—but surely only those reasonably in the know. Did Trollope have me in mind? If so, his intention failed until I recently learned more about the politics that interested Trollope. If Homer intended his audience to take his "Troy" to refer to a real place, his intention misfired for many centuries until Schliemann came along.

In any case, the intention by their originator that an utterance or writing be interpreted in a certain way is only a necessary

---

[13] This material is from *Trollope: a Biography*, N. John Hall, Oxford University Press, 1991, pp. 336f.

[14] From Binyon's review of *Damon Runyon: a Life* by Jimmy Breslin, Hodder & Stoughton, London, 1992, in *The Times Literary Supplement*, March 20, 1992.

condition for that being their correct interpretation; it is also necessary that the intention be reasonable. It would have been unreasonable of Trollope, if he gave it a moment's thought, to expect a reader unversed in the history of English politics and more than a hundred years later to have the key to his names. Joyce, annoyed that his readers didn't spot the analogies between his and Homer's Ulysses, spilled the beans to Frank Budgeon in a successful attempt to provide a hint his work had not. Here we come up hard against the questions what intentions an author really has and what it is "reasonable" for him to think his readers will make of his text. The questions are directly related, since one can only intend what one believes he has a chance of bringing off; and the issue ramifies in literature as the proposed or imagined audience fragments in time, place, background, education, politics, and taste. At the same time, matters of fact about an author's intentions begin to depend in part on our judgment as to how reasonable those intentions were.

Joyce's desire to have his work read in the light of a tradition brings out a contrast between much literature and other uses of writing. The writers of proclamations, warnings, declarations of war, writs of habeas corpus, sales catalogues, and political broadsides usually have a pretty good idea of the background knowledge and level of learning of their audiences; by comparison a novelist or poet can take relatively little detailed information about the everyday world for granted. But it is reasonable of the novelist or poet to assume that her reader has read other novels or poems in the same language, just as it is reasonable (usually) to assume that the reader has read the first half of a work of fiction before he reads the second half. Thus literature itself provides an important part of the background an author is apt to assume she shares with her audience. Other books help constitute the world which completes the triangle of author and reader, just as prior conversations provide much of what speaker and hearer depend on for good communication. A related idea is expressed as a constraint on interpretation by T. S. Eliot in "Tradition and Individual Talent":

No poet, no artist of any art, has his complete meaning alone. His significance, his appreciation is the appreciation of his relation to the dead poets and artists. You cannot value him alone; you must set him, for contrast and comparison, among the dead.

I have been concentrating on first meaning and the intentions which most directly affect it, but this should not obscure the fact that there are endless further intentions an author is sure to have. I am not much interested in the question which if any of these intentions are aesthetically relevant. I see little gain in legislation here, or in the kind of rhetoric which can "make" some critic's preferred standards "correct" by persuading others to go along. On the other hand, I see much advantage in admitting the potential contribution to the appreciation of his work of almost anything that can be learned about an author's life and interests. I take Freud to have been right in a sense he may not quite have intended when he wrote in *The Interpretation of Dreams,*

All genuinely creative writings are the product of more than a single motive and more than a single impulse in the poet's mind, and are open to more than a single interpretation.

Should we then agree with Gadamer when he says that what the text means changes as the audience changes: "A text is understood only if it is understood in a different way every time"?[15] I think not. There can be multiple interpretations, as Freud suggests, because there is no reason to say one rules out others. Gadamer has in mind incompatible interpretations. It is true that every person, every age, every culture will make what it can of a text; and persons, periods, and cultures differ. But how can a significant relativism follow from a truism? If you and I try to compare notes on our interpretation of a text we can do this only to the extent that we have or can establish a broad basis of agreement. If what we share provides a common standard of truth and objectivity, difference of opinion makes sense. But relativism about standards requires what there cannot be, a position beyond all standards.

[15] Hans-Georg Gadamer, *Truth and Method*, Crossroad, New York, 1975, pp. 275 f.

ANOMALOUS MONISM

13 *Thinking Causes*

In 1970 I proposed a theory about the relation between the mental and the physical that I called Anomalous Monism (AM).[1] AM holds that mental entities (particular time and space-bound objects and events) are physical entities, but that mental concepts are not reducible by definition or natural law to physical concepts. The position is, in a general way, familiar: it endorses ontological reduction, but eschews conceptual reduction. What was new was the argument, which purported to derive AM from three premises, namely, (1) that mental events are causally related to physical events, (2) that singular causal relations are backed by strict laws, and (3) that there are no strict psychophysical laws.[2] The first premise seemed to me obvious, the second true though contested (I did not present arguments for it), and the third true and worth arguing for. Many readers have found my arguments against the existence of strict psychophysical laws obscure; others have decided the three premises are mutually inconsistent. But the complaints have most often been summed up by saying that AM makes the mental causally inert. The criticisms are connected: if AM makes the mental causally inert, then AM apparently implies the falsity of the first premise and hence the inconsistency of the three premises. The third premise seems to many critics the relevant offender, so they urge that it should be dropped.

In this paper I attempt three things: first, to defend AM against misunderstandings and misrepresentations. This will involve some clarification, and perhaps modification, of the original

---

[1] "Mental Events", 1970, reprinted in *Essays on Actions and Events* (Oxford University Press, 1980).

[2] This summary simplifies the original thesis and argument. Those not familiar with "Mental Events" should consult it for caveats and additional assumptions.

thesis. Second, I want to maintain that the three premises from which I argue to AM are consistent when taken together, and so AM is a tenable thesis (it is weaker than the premises). Third, I shall say why I do not think AM makes the mental causally powerless. I do not plan here to argue for the truth of AM or the premises on which it rests.

In "Mental Events" I endorsed the idea that mental concepts[3] are supervenient, in a sense I explained, on physical concepts. I thought this would make it clear that, contrary to first impressions, AM and its entailing premises were after all consistent. So what I am defending in this paper is in effect not only AM itself, but AM in conjunction with the three premises and the doctrine of supervenience. (In what follows, I shall abbreviate the expression "anomalous monism conjoined with premises (1)–(2)" by "AM + P"; "AM + P + S" will mean supervenience in addition to AM + P.)

When I wrote "Mental Events" I thought I knew that G. E. Moore had used the word "supervenience" to describe the relation between evaluative terms like "good" and descriptive terms like "sharp" or "inexpensive" or "pleasure producing". Moore's idea seemed clear enough: something is good only because it has properties that can be specified in descriptive terms, but goodness can't be reduced to a descriptive property. In fact, Moore apparently never used the word "supervenient". I had probably found the word in R. M. Hare's *The Language of Morals*, and applied it, as he had, to Moore. (Hare has since complained that I got the concept wrong: for him supervenience implies a form of what I call nomological reduction.[4]) In any case, the idea I had in

---

[3] In the present paper I do not distinguish concepts from properties or predicates, except to the extent that I allow that physics may well come to require predicates not now available.

[4] R. M. Hare, "Supervenience", *The Aristotelian Society Supplementary Volume LVIII*, 1984. Hare says,

... supervenience brings with it the claim *that there is* some 'law' which binds what supervenes to what it supervenes upon ... what supervenience requires is that what supervenes is seen as an instance of some universal proposition linking it with what it supervenes upon. (Op. cit., p. 3)

But so far as I can see, Hare's characterization of supervenience, on the page before the one from which the above quotation is taken, does not imply the existence of laws or law-like generalizations linking what supervenes to what it supervenes on. Hare compares his version of supervenience with Kim's "weak" supervenience, but Kim himself (correctly, I think) finds my version of supervenience very close to his "weak" supervenience, and as not entailing connecting laws.

mind is, I think, most economically expressed as follows: a predicate p is supervenient on a set of predicates S if and only if p does not distinguish any entities that cannot be distinguished by S.[5] Supervenience so understood obviously applies in an uninteresting sense to cases where p belongs to S, to cases where p is explicitly definable by means of the predicates in S, and to cases where there is a law to the effect that the extension of p is identical with the extension of a predicate definable in terms of the predicates in S. The interesting cases are those where p resists any of these forms of reduction. I gave as a non-controversial example of an interesting case the supervenience of semantic predicates on syntactical predicates: a truth predicate for a language cannot distinguish any sentences not distinguishable in purely syntactical terms, but for most languages truth is not definable in such terms. The example gives one possible meaning to the idea that truths expressible by the subvenient predicates "determine" the extension of the supervenient predicate, or that the extension of the supervenient predicate "depends" on the extensions of the subvenient predicates.

How can the possibility of a supervenient relation between the mental and the physical help to show that AM (or AM + P) is consistent, since supervenience says nothing about causality? The answer is simple: supervenience in any form implies monism; but it does not imply either definitional or nomological reduction. So if (non-reductive) supervenience is consistent (as the syntax–semantics example proves it is), so is AM. But supervenience is also consistent with premises (1) and (2), which are not implied by AM, since (1) and (2) concern causality, and supervenience says nothing about causality.

It is difficult, then, to see how AM + P together with supervenience can imply a contradiction. So it surprised me to read in

[5] In "Mental Events" I said the supervenience of the mental on the physical "might be taken to mean that there cannot be two events alike in all physical respects but differing in some mental respect". I intended this to be equivalent to the present formulation, but apparently it is easily misunderstood. In answer to a question about "Mental Events", I gave an unambiguous definition of supervenience which is clearly equivalent to the present one: a predicate p is supervenient on a set of predicates S if for every pair of objects such that p is true of one and not of the other there is a predicate in S that is true of one and not of the other. I suggested that it is a common fallacy in philosophy (of which the naturalistic fallacy is an example) to switch the order of the quantifiers in this formula. See "Replies to Essays X–XII", in *Essays on Davidson: Actions and Events*, ed. B. Vermazen and M. B. Hintikka (Oxford University Press, 1985), p. 242.

a recent article by Jaegwon Kim that not only are the premises of AM inconsistent with one another, but "the notion of supervenience Davidson favors" is also inconsistent with the first premise of AM.[6]

Let us look at these supposed inconsistencies. According to Kim,

The fact is that under Davidson's anomalous monism, mentality does no causal work. Remember: on anomalous monism, events are causes only as they instantiate physical laws, and this means that an event's mental properties make no causal difference. And to suppose that altering an event's mental properties would also alter its physical properties and thereby affect its causal relations is to suppose that psychophysical anomalism, a cardinal tenet of anomalous monism, is false.[7]

Of course, if "mentality does no causal work" means that mental events do not enter into causal relations, the first premise of AM is false, for it says mental events cause, and are caused by, physical events. This is not enough to prove AM itself inconsistent, but it certainly would show the three premises of AM inconsistent with one another. And if Kim's last sentence quoted above is correct, then AM is inconsistent with any form of supervenience.

Why does Kim think AM + P + S is inconsistent? At least part of the answer is contained in the sentence in which Kim asks us to "remember" what he thinks is a feature of AM + P; and here I believe Kim speaks for many of the critics of my position. What Kim asks us to "remember" is that "on anomalous monism, events are causes only as they instantiate laws". This is not anything I have claimed. I could not have claimed it, since given my concept of events and of causality, it makes no sense to speak of an event being a cause "as" anything at all. AM + P + S is formulated on the assumption that events are non-abstract particulars, and that causal relations are extensional relations between such events. In his article, Kim does not dispute these two theses. But there is then no room for a concept of "cause as" which would make causality a relation among three or four entities rather than between two. On the view of events and causality assumed here,[8] it makes no more sense to say event c caused event e as instantiating

[6] Jaegwon Kim, "The Myth of Nonreductive Materialism", *Proceedings and Addresses of the American Philosophical Association*, LXIII, 1989, pp. 31–47.

[7] Op. cit., p. 35.

[8] This view is spelled out in detail in the articles in the second part of *Essays on Actions and Events* (Oxford University Press, 1980).

law *l* than it makes to say *a* weighs less than *b* as belonging to sort *s*. If causality is a relation between events, it holds between them no matter how they are described. So there can be descriptions of two events (physical descriptions) which allow us to deduce from a law that if the first event occurred the second would occur, and other descriptions (mental descriptions) of the same events which invite no such inference. We can say, if we please (though I do not think this is a happy way of putting the point), that events instantiate a law only as described in one way rather than another, but we cannot say that an event caused another only as described. Redescribing an event cannot change what it causes, or change the event's causal efficacy. Events, unlike agents, do not care how what they cause is described: an agent may kill a bird because she wanted to perform an action that could be described as "my killing of that bird". But her killing of the bird might have been identical with her killing of the goose that laid the golden egg though "My killing of the goose that laid the golden egg" may have been the last description she wanted to have describe an action of hers.

Kim thinks that AM + P cannot remain consistently anomalous if it holds that altering an event's mental properties would also alter its physical properties. This seems to be a mistake. AM + P + S (which includes supervenience) does hold that altering an event's mental properties would also alter its physical properties. But supervenience does not imply the existence of psychophysical laws. To see this, it is only necessary to recognize that although supervenience entails that any change in a mental property *p* of a particular event *e* will be accompanied by a change in the physical properties of *e*, it does not entail that a change in *p* in *other* events will be accompanied by an identical change in the physical properties of those other events. Only the latter entailment would conflict with AM + P.

The definition of supervenience implies that a change in mental properties is always accompanied by a change in physical properties, but it does not imply that the same physical properties change with the same mental properties. Supervenience implies the first, because if a change in a mental property were not accompanied by a change in physical properties, there would be two events distinguished by their mental properties that were not distinguished by their physical properties, and supervenience, as I defined it, rules this out. Kim says supervenience "is best regarded as independent" of the thesis of AM + P. This is true in the sense that neither supervenience nor AM + P entails the other. But it is not true that the consistency of supervenience is irrelevant to the consistency of AM + P since, as I just argued, supervenience helps not only in showing that AM + P is consistent, but also that there is a version of AM + P that gives a plausible picture of the relation between the mental and the physical. Kim may have made this remark because he mistakenly thinks that my "weak" version of supervenience entails that "the removal of *all* mental properties from events of this world would have no consequence whatever on how physical properties are distributed over them".[9] In fact supervenience entails the reverse. For consider two events with the same physical properties, but one with some mental property and the other with that property removed. These cannot be the same event, since one has a property the other lacks. But then contrary to the definition of supervenience, mental properties would distinguish two events not distinguished by their physical properties.

But the point seems clear enough whatever one wants to say about supervenience: if causal relations and causal powers inhere in particular events and objects, then the way those events and objects are described, and the properties we happen to employ to pick them out or characterize them, cannot affect what they cause. Naming the American invasion of Panama "Operation Just Cause" does not alter the consequences of the event.

So far I have said little about laws because laws are not mentioned in the definition of supervenience, and the logical possibility of supervenience is important in establishing the consistency of AM + P. But of course the thesis that there are no strict psychophysical laws is one of the premises on the basis of which I argued for AM. So even if AM is consistent, there is a question whether the denial of such laws somehow undermines the claim that mental events are causally efficacious. I say "somehow" since it would seem that the efficacy of an event cannot depend on how the event is described, while whether an event can be called mental, or can be said to fall under a law, depends entirely on how the event can be described.

[9] Op. cit., p. 35, note 8.

Let me digress briefly. The second assumption from which I argued to AM was that if two events are related as cause and effect, there must be a law that covers the case. In "Mental Events" I explained in some detail what I meant by a law in this context, and what I meant by "covering". A law (formulated in some language) covers a case if the law, conjoined with a sentence that says the event (described appropriately) occurred, entails a sentence that asserts the existence of the effect (appropriately described). I made clear that what I was calling a law in this context was something that one could at best hope to find in a developed physics: a generalization that not only was "lawlike" and true, but was as deterministic as nature can be found to be, was free from caveats and ceteris paribus clauses; that could, therefore, be viewed as treating the universe as a closed system. I stressed that it was only laws of this kind (which I called "strict" laws) that I was arguing could not cover events when those events were described in the mental vocabulary. I allowed that there are not, and perhaps could not be expected to be, laws of this sort in the special sciences. Most, if not all, of the practical knowledge that we (or engineers, chemists, geneticists, geologists) have that allows us to explain and predict ordinary happenings does not involve strict laws. The best descriptions we are able to give of most events are not descriptions that fall under, or will ever fall under, strict laws.[10]

There are two reasons for reminding those interested in AM (or AM + P or AM + P + S) of these facts. The first is simply that much of the criticism of AM + P has ignored the distinction I painfully spelled out in "Mental Events" between the "strict" laws I think exist covering singular causal relations and the less than strict laws that can be couched in mental terms. Thus Kim, in the article I mentioned, begins by saying correctly that AM + P denies that there are precise or strict laws about mental events, but goes on to criticize AM + P for maintaining that "the mental is

---

[10] "Mental Events", pp. 216–23. There I said, "I suppose most of our practical lore (and science) is heteronomic [i.e., not in the form of strict laws, and not reducible to such]. This is because a law can hope to be precise, explicit, and as exceptionless as possible only if it draws its concepts from a comprehensive closed theory", p. 219. Also see pp. 242–52 in *Essays on Davidson: Actions and Events*, ed. Vermazen and Hintikka, and pp. 41–8 of "Problems in the Explanation of Action", in *Metaphysics and Morality*, ed. P. Pettit, R. Sylvan, and J. Norman, (Oxford: Blackwell, 1987).

anomalous not only in that there are no laws relating mental events to other mental events but none relating them to physical events either".[11] In fact I have repeatedly said that if you want to call certain undeniably important regularities laws—the familiar regularities that link the mental with the mental (as formulated, for example in decision theory) or the mental with the physical—I have no objection; I merely say these are not, and cannot be reduced to, *strict* laws.

Because he ignores the distinction between strict laws and other sorts of regularities, it is by no means clear that Kim really holds views at odds with AM + P. Kim maintains, plausibly it seems to me, that any satisfactory account of the relation between the mental and the physical must permit appeal to "local correlations and dependencies between specific mental and physical properties". But then he adds,

The trouble is that once we begin talking about correlations and dependencies between specific psychological and physical properties, we are in effect talking about psychophysical laws, and these laws raise the specter of unwanted physical reductionism. Where there are psychophysical laws, there is always the threat, or promise, of psychophysical reduction.[12]

But if the laws are not strict, the threat is averted, and the promise false. Kim offers no reason to think the laws can be strict; I have given arguments (which he does not mention or discuss in this article[13]) why I think they cannot. It is not clear that Kim has come to grips with AM + P.

Kim is by no means the only critic of AM + P to fail to notice the crucial importance of the distinction between strict and non-strict laws. Thus J. A. Fodor writes that he is going to defend the view that intentional (mental) properties are "causally responsible" and that there are "intentional causal laws...contrary to the doctrine called 'anomalous monism'". His defense is that in common sense and in many (all?) of the "special" sciences, there are plenty of laws that are far from strict. He cites as an example of a law in geology that mountains are apt to have snow on them;

---

[11] Op. cit., p. 33.   [12] Op. cit., p. 42.
[13] Elsewhere, however, Kim has given a sympathetic account of my arguments. See his article "Psychophysical Laws" in *Actions and Events: Perspectives on the Philosophy of Donald Davidson*, ed. E. Lepore and B. McLaughlin (Oxford: Blackwell, 1985).

it is *because* Mt. Everest is a mountain that it has snow on it.[14] But as I have just pointed out, this defense of the causal efficacy of the mental is consistent with AM + P.

It is a question whether others who have attacked AM + P have taken the distinction between types of regularity fully into account. Fred Dretske has also maintained that AM + P makes the mental causally inert, but he has never claimed that there are strict psychophysical laws. There is thus no clear reason to believe that the sort of account he wants to offer of how the mental causes the physical is itself inconsistent with AM + P. I don't think his account succeeds; but that is another matter. Dagfinn Føllesdal has also thought there must be psychophysical laws; but he gives as an example of such a "law", "Any severely dehydrated person who drinks water will improve".[15] AM + P does not rule out such laws, for such a law is obviously far from strict, and it is not likely that it can be made truly exceptionless.

The second reason for paying attention to the distinction between the laws of an ideal physics and other generalizations (whether or not we call them laws) has to do with the logic of the argument that leads from the premises to AM. The argument does not depend on the claim that there are no psychophysical laws: the argument demands only that there are no laws that (i) contain psychological terms that cannot be eliminated from the laws nor reduced to the vocabulary of physics and (ii) that have the features of lacking ceteris paribus clauses and of belonging to a closed system like the laws of a finished physics. In other words, I argued from the assumptions that mental events are causally

---

[14] J. A. Fodor, "Making Mind Matter More", *Philosophical Studies*, XVII (1989), pp. 59–80. The argument Fodor gives here is, though he does not realize it, a *defense* of AM, since he argues that although there may be no strict laws in geology, this does not show that such properties as being a mountain are not causally efficacious. As he says, to suppose that the lack of such strict laws makes geological properties epiphenominal is absurd: "there are likely to be parallel arguments that *all properties are inert excepting only those expressed by the vocabulary of physics.*" I think this is exactly right if one adds, "expressible in the vocabulary of physics or in a vocabulary definitionally or nomologically reducible to the vocabulary of physics".

The same point is made in Fodor's *Psychosemantics* (Cambridge, Mass.: MIT, 1987). There the example is "A meandering river erodes its outer banks unless, for example, the weather changes and the river dries up", pp. 5, 6.

[15] Dagfinn Føllesdal, "Causation and Explanation: a problem in Davidson's view on action and mind", in *Actions and Events: Perspectives on the Philosophy of Donald Davidson*, ed. E. Lepore and B. McLaughlin (Oxford: Blackwell, 1985), p. 321.

related to physical events, and that all causally related events instantiate the laws of physics, to the conclusion that mental events are identical with physical events: thus monism. The extent to which mental concepts fall short of being reducible to physical concepts measures the degree of anomaly. As far as I can see, the positions of both Kim and Fodor on the relation between the physical and the mental are consistent with AM and AM + P, and it seems to me possible that the same is true of Dretske and Føllesdal.

There remains an issue, however, that separates my views from Kim's and perhaps also from Fodor's. Fodor holds that mental (or intentional) concepts can't be reduced to the concepts of a finished physics, so in this respect his position is that of AM + P. Kim, on the other hand, believes in reduction. But he may simply have different standards for reduction than I do; if this is so, our difference on this point may be mainly verbal. But behind what may be merely a verbal point there lies a substantive issue: both Fodor and Kim seem to think that unless there are psychophysical laws of *some* sort, the mental would have been shown to be powerless. I think the reasoning that leads them (and others) to this conclusion is confused.

Let's be clear about what is at stake. At this point I am not concerned with the question whether or not there are psychophysical laws. In the sense in which Kim and Fodor think there are laws linking mental and physical concepts, I also think there are laws; what I have claimed is that such laws are not strict, and that mental concepts are not reducible by definition or by strict "bridging" laws to physical concepts. But unlike my critics, I do not think it would prove that the mental is causally inert even if there were no psychophysical laws of any kind.

Suppose I create a table in which all the entries are definite descriptions of one sort or another of events. I refer to the events by giving the column and the row where the description is to be found: column 179 row 1044 for example is the event of my writing this sentence. Let us call the events listed in the table "Table Events". The vocabulary needed to describe (needed to provide a definite description of) each event is just the vocabulary needed to pick out the column and row. These events have their causes and effects: for example event 179–1044 caused a certain rearrangement of electric flows in the random access memory of my computer. There are, I imagine, no interesting tablophysical laws whatever, that is, laws linking events described in the table language and events described in the vocabulary of physics. Yet this fact does not show that table events are not causally efficacious.

It will be retorted that it is simply irrelevant to the causal efficacy of table events that they are table events—that they are described in the table vocabulary. This is true. But it is also irrelevant to the causal efficacy of physical events that they can be described in the physical vocabulary. It is *events* that have the power to change things, not our various ways of describing them. Since the fact that an event is a mental event, i.e., that it can be described in a psychological vocabulary, can make no difference to the causes and effects of that event, it makes no sense to suppose that describing it in the psychological vocabulary might deprive the event of its potency. An event, mental or physical, by any other name smells just as strong.

The point seems so simple and so clear that it is hard to see how it can be doubted. Suppose Magellan notices that there are rocks ahead, an event that, through the intervening events of his uttering orders to the helmsman, etc., causes the ship to alter course. Magellan's noticing is a mental event, and it is causally efficacious. That event is also a physical event, a change in Magellan's body, and describable in the vocabulary of physics. As long as the predicates used to describe the mental event are not strictly reducible to the predicates of physics, all this is in accord with AM + P.

Yet according to Kim and others, AM + P implies that the mental is causally inert: Kim asks "What role does mentality play on Davidson's anomalous monism . . . ?", and he answers, "None whatever". Why does he think this? We get a hint when he says " . . . on anomalous monism, events are causes or effects only as they instantiate physical laws". The same idea is expressed by the phrase "in virtue of": mentality is causally effective only if events are causes *in virtue of their mental properties*.[16] "Because of" has been recruited to express the same idea. Kim has even implied that it is my explicit view that " . . . it is only under its physical description that a mental event can be seen to enter into a causal relation with a physical event (or any other event) by being

---

[16] See Kim, op. cit., p. 43.

subsumed under a causal law".[17] Those who are familiar with the literature will recognize other ways of putting the point: on AM + P (so one reads) the mental does not cause anything *qua* mental; the mental is not efficacious *as such*. This is the vein in which Ernest Sosa writes that "The key to [Davidson's] proposed solution . . . is the idea that mental events enter into causal relations *not* as mental but only as physical".[18] Sosa does at least recognize that this is not my way of putting things, but he does not realize that I couldn't put things this way. For me, it is events that have causes and effects. Given this extensionalist view of causal relations, it makes no literal sense, as I remarked above, to speak of an event causing something as mental, or by virtue of its mental properties, or as described in one way or another.

But might it not happen that the mental properties of an event make no difference to its causal relations? Something like this is what critics have in mind when they say that according to AM + P the mental is inert. Of course, the idea that mental properties make no causal difference is consistent with the view that there are no psychophysical laws (strict or not) and with the supposition that every singular causal relation between two events is backed by a strict (physical) law; it is also consistent with the thesis that mental events (i.e., events picked out by mental properties) are causally related to physical events. So AM + P is *consistent* with the (epiphenomenalist) view that the mental properties of events make no difference to causal relations. But this is not enough to discredit AM + P, for it does not follow that AM *implies* the causal inertness of the mental. What they must show is that AM (or AM + P) implies the impotence of mental properties, and this I see no way of establishing.

Another way of putting the point is this: we have the makings of a refutation of AM + P provided it can be shown that AM + P is inconsistent with the supervenience of mental properties on physical properties. The refutation would consist, not in showing AM + P inconsistent, but in showing it inconsistent with supervenience, and so with the supposition that the mental properties of an event make a difference to its causal relations.

[17] Jaegwon Kim, "Epiphenomenal and Supervenient Causation", in *Midwest Studies in Philosophy Volume IX* (Minneapolis: University of Minnesota Press, 1984), p. 267.

[18] Ernest Sosa, "Mind–Body Interaction and Supervenient Causation", in *Midwest Studies in Philosophy Volume IX*, p. 277.

For supervenience as I have defined it does, as we have seen, imply that if two events differ in their psychological properties, they differ in their physical properties (which we assume to be causally efficacious). If supervenience holds, psychological properties make a difference to the causal relations of an event, for they matter to the physical properties, and the physical properties matter to causal relations. It does nothing to undermine this argument to say "But the mental properties make a difference not *as* mental but only because they make a difference to the physical properties". Either they make a difference or they don't; if supervenience is true, they do.

How might one try to show that AM + P is inconsistent with supervenience? Kim, as we noted, thinks my version of supervenience implies that all mental properties could be withdrawn from the world and this would make no difference to causal relations; but this supposition turned out to be incompatible with my understanding of supervenience. He subsequently argues[19] that there is no plausible way to understand my brand of supervenience because there is no plausible way to reconcile the demands that the mental be irreducible to the physical and yet be "dependent" on it. But clearly supervenience gives a sense to the notion of dependence here, enough sense anyway to show that mental properties make a causal difference; so unless it can be shown that even weak supervenience is inconsistent with AM + P, it has not been shown that AM + P makes the mental causally inert.

Kim does have a point. Supervenience as I define it is consistent with the conjunction of AM + P and the assumption that there are no psychophysical laws whatever, strict or not. It is not even slightly plausible that there are no important general causal connections between the mental and physical properties of events. I have always held that there are such connections; indeed much of my writing on action is devoted to spelling out the sort of general causal connections that are essential to our ways of understanding, describing, explaining, and predicting actions, what causes them, and what they cause. But why should the importance and ubiquity of such connections suggest that psychological concepts must be reducible to physical concepts—*strictly*

---

[19] "The Myth of Nonreductive Materialism", pp. 39–41.

reducible? Yet the failure of strict reducibility is all that is required to establish AM.

Why have there been so many confusions and bad arguments in the discussion of AM, AM + P, and supervenience? The main source of confusion, I think, is the fact that when it comes to events people find it hard to keep in mind the distinction between types and particulars. This in turn makes it easy to conflate singular causal connections with causal laws, and invites neglect of the difference between explaining an event and simply stating that a causal relation holds.

Of course those who have commented on AM + P cannot have failed to notice that the argument hangs on the distinction between particular events and types of events. But the distinction has nevertheless proved easy to overlook. Kim, for example, asks whether the identity of mental events with physical events solves the problem of the causal efficacy of the mental. It does not, he says, because what is at issue is "the causal efficacy of *mental properties* of events vis-à-vis their physical properties. Thus the items that need to be identified are properties—that is, we would need to identify mental properties with physical properties."[20] But properties are causally efficacious if they make a difference to what *individual* events cause, and supervenience insures that mental properties do make a difference to what mental events cause. So why is the identity of *properties* required to make mental properties causally efficacious? It isn't; but one might think so if one were confusing individual events with classes of events, i.e., all those that share some property.

I sense a similar slippage in the argument when Kim introduces what he calls "the problem of causal-explanatory exclusion". This is the problem, he says, that "seems to arise from the fact that a cause, or causal explanation, of an event, when it is regarded as a full, sufficient cause or explanation, appears to *exclude* other *independent* purported causes or causal explanations of it".[21] The idea is that if physics does provide such "full, sufficient" explanations, there is no room for mental explanations unless these can be (fully, strictly?) reduced to physical explanations. What can this strange principle mean? If we consider an *event* that is a "full, sufficient" cause of another event, it must, as Mill pointed out

[20] Op. cit., p. 45.   [21] Op. cit., p. 44.

long ago, include everything in the universe preceding the effect that has a causal bearing on it, some cross section of the entire preceding light cone; and even then, if we take "sufficient" seriously, we must assume perfect determinism. How can the existence of such an event "exclude" other causes? It can't, since by definition it includes everything that could be a cause. Given supervenience, such an event would include, as proper parts, all relevant mental events. What has all this to do with explanation? Well, if we ever had the laws of physics right, and we had the appropriate physical description of an event *and* of some cross section of the preceding light cone, we might be able to give a full and sufficient explanation of the second event. How could this exclude any other sort of explanation? It might *preclude* less complete physical explanations, in the sense that we would lose interest in them. But if mental concepts are not reducible to physical concepts, there is no reason to suppose we would lose interest in explanations in mental terms just because we had a complete physical explanation. What is true, of course, is that psychological explanations are never full and sufficient; like most explanations, they are interest sensitive, and simply assume that a vast number of (unspecified and unspecifiable) factors that might have intervened between cause and effect did not. This does not mean they are not causal explanations, nor that physical explanations exclude them. It is only if we confuse causal relations, which hold only between particulars, with causal explanations, which, so far as they are "sufficient" must deal with laws, and so with types of events, that we would be tempted to accept the principle of "causal-explanatory exclusion".[22]

Let me give one more example of what I take to be error brought on by not taking seriously the distinction between particular events and their types. I draw the example from an article by Ernest Sosa; but similar examples can easily be found

---

[22] Kim says a full, sufficient cause or explanation excludes other *independent* causes or explanations; in my discussion, I may seem to have neglected the condition of independence. I have, because dependence means entirely different things in the cases of events and of explanation. Events "depend" on one another causally, and the failure of psychophysical laws has no bearing on the question whether mental and physical events are causally related. Explanation, on the other hand, is an intentional concept; in explanation, dependence is geared to the ways in which things are described. There is no reason why logically independent explanations cannot be given of the same event (as Socrates points out in *Phaedo* 98 ff.).

in the writings of Kim, Dretske, Føllesdal, Honderich, Achenstein, Stoutland, and Mark Johnston.[23] Suppose, Sosa argues, that someone is killed by a loud shot; then the loudness of the shot is irrelevant to its causing the death. "Had the gun been equipped with a silencer, the shot would have killed the victim just the same."[24] In the same way, Sosa thinks, AM + P entails that mental properties are irrelevant to what the events that have the properties cause. Such examples, whether about mental causation or physical, do not establish the conclusion. The crucial counter-factual is fatally (sorry) ambiguous. Had the gun been equipped with a silencer, a quiet shot, if aimed as the fatal shot was, and otherwise relevantly similar, would no doubt have resulted in *a* death. But it would not have been the *same* shot as the fatal shot, nor could the death it caused have been the same death. The ambiguity lies in the definite description "the shot": if "the shot" refers to the shot that would have been fired silently, then it is true that that shot might well have killed the victim. But if "the shot" is supposed to refer to the original loud shot, the argument misfires, for the same shot cannot be both loud and silent. Loudness, like a mental property, is supervenient on basic physical properties,[25] and so makes a difference to what an event that has it causes. Of course, both loud and silent (single) shots can cause a death; but not the same death.

---

[23] For references, see E. Lepore and B. Loewer, "Mind Matters", *The Journal of Philosophy*, LXXXIV (1984), pp. 633–4.

[24] E. Sosa, "Interaction and Supervenient Causation", p. 278.

[25] It is sometimes suggested that if we cannot make sense of the idea of an event losing its psychological properties while remaining the same event, we are stuck with the idea that *all* of an event's properties are "essential". I have no theory about which properties of an event, if any, are essential, but it seems clear that to serve the purposes of my argument, mental properties need supervene on only those physical properties that are required for a complete causal account of the universe (i.e., that suffice for the formulation of a closed system of "strict" laws).

14 *Laws and Cause*

In her inaugural lecture as Professor of Philosophy in the University of Cambridge, G. E. M. Anscombe examined the "often declared or evidently assumed" view that

causality is some kind of necessary connection, or alternatively, that being caused is—non-trivially—instancing some exceptionless generalization saying that such an event always follows such antecedents.[1]

She complained that "the truth of this conception is hardly debated", and surveyed its history from Aristotle to the then present to make her point. I have the honor of bringing up the rear: "even Davidson", she remarks in her last paragraph,

will say, without offering any reason at all for saying it, that a singular causal statement implies *that there is* such a true universal proposition.[2]

In the paper to which Anscombe refers,[3] I offered no reason for saying true singular causal statements (like "The eruption of Vesuvius in 79 A.D. caused the destruction of Pompeii") imply the existence of laws that cover the case, nor did I offer any in my subsequent article "Mental Events".[4] I wrote there that I was treating this relation between the concepts of law and cause as an assumption, observing that even someone who was dubious of the

I wish to thank David Albert and Noa Latham for their help. The central idea in this paper has a Kantian ring, and was used by Gordon Brittan in his *Kant's Theory of Science*, Princeton University Press, 1978. As he generously notes, he first heard the idea in my classes at Stanford University.

[1] *Causality and Determination*, Cambridge University Press, 1971, p. 1.
[2] Ibid., p. 29.
[3] "Causal Relations", *The Journal of Philosophy*, **64** (1967): 691–703. Reprinted in *Essays on Actions and Events*, Oxford University Press, 1980.
[4] First published in *Experience and Theory*, ed. L. Foster and J. W. Swanson, The University of Massachusetts Press, 1970; reprinted in *Essays on Actions and Events*.

assumption might be interested in an argument claiming to show that the assumption, along with other commonly held (though debated) premises, implied a form of monism—what I called "Anomalous Monism".

Various critics have joined me in noting that if the assumed relation between laws and causality (which in "Mental Events" I called, rather windily, "The Principle of the Nomological Character of Causality") is false, the argument for Anomalous Monism fails, and some have enjoined me to produce a reason to accept the assumption. Others, like Anscombe, have expressed doubt that the assumption is true. "I have to doubt Davidson's ... premise, that all pairs of events related by 'cause' are subsumed under laws," writes Jennifer Hornsby.[5] Ernest Sosa asks, "Why must there always be a law to cover any causal relation linking events x and y? What enables us to assume such a general truth?"[6] Tyler Burge is more skeptical still: "I do not think it *a priori* true, or even clearly a heuristic principle of science or reason, that causal relations must be backed by any particular kind of law."[7]

Burge is right that if there is a reason for holding the cause–law thesis, the argument must in some sense be a priori, for the thesis clearly is not a pronouncement of ordinary logic, nor can it be established empirically, a negative point on which Hume and Kant were agreed. To say the cause–law thesis is a priori is not, of course, to say that particular causal laws are a priori. If the thesis is true, what we know in advance of evidence is that if a singular causal claim is true, there is a law that backs it, and we can know this without knowing what the law is.

I

The cause–law thesis needs to be made more definite. By a singular causal statement I mean a statement that contains two singular

[5] "Which Mental Events are Physical Events?", *Proceedings of the Aristotelian Society*, **35** (1980–1), p. 86.
[6] Ernest Sosa, "Mind–Body Interaction and Supervenient Causation", in *Midwest Studies in Philosophy*, IX, 1984, p. 278.
[7] "Philosophy of Language and Mind: 1950–1990", in *The Philosophical Review*, **101** (1992), p. 35.

terms (names or definite descriptions) referring, or purporting to refer, to events, joined by some form of the verb "to cause" (if the statement is expressed in English). Of course other verbs can do the same work, for example "produce", "result in", "have as consequence", etc. Examples of singular causal statements are: "His lighting the match caused the explosion", "The next California earthquake will cause the destruction of the Golden Gate Bridge", "The hurricane is causing the rise in the water level". "The hurricane caused the water level to rise" is not, however, a singular causal statement, since "the water level to rise" is not a singular term; this last sentence says only that the hurricane (a particular event) caused at least one event that was a rising of the water level. "The rise" purports to pick out a particular event; "a rise" marks a general existential claim without implying singularity.

Singular causal statements are extensional: their truth value is invariant under the substitution of one name or description of an event for another name or description of the same event. Thus if Socrates was Xanthippe's husband, and Socrates' drinking the hemlock resulted in Socrates' death, it follows that Socrates' drinking the hemlock resulted in the death of Xanthippe's husband. The point may seem obvious, and indeed it is; yet it has escaped all those who have been tempted to think that if singular causal statements imply the existence of a covering law, they must imply, or somehow indicate, some particular law that covers the case. It is easy to see why this does not follow. Given the endless possibilities for redescribing events (or anything else) in non-equivalent terms, it is clear that there may be no clue to the character of an appropriate law in the concepts used on some occasion to characterize an event. What may be the case is that if a singular causal statement is to be *explanatory* in some desired sense, it must put its hearer in mind of at least the general nature of a relevant law. It also may (or may not) be the case that the only, or best, reason for believing a singular causal statement is evidence for the truth of some law that covers the case. But such epistemological and explanatory issues, however we resolve them, ought not lead us to color singular causal statements intensional.

In formulating the cause–law thesis, what should we count as a law? Laws must be true universally quantified statements. They also must be lawlike: they must support counterfactuals, and be

confirmed by their instances (these conditions are not independent). To qualify as *strictly* lawlike, they should contain no
singular terms referring to particular objects, locations or times
(strictly lawlike statements are symmetric with respect to time and
location). Strictly lawlike statements do not contain open-ended
phrases like "other things being equal", or "under normal conditions". It must be admitted that such phrases are, tacitly or
explicitly, part of the content of many legitimate laws; thus many
laws are not strict, including the laws peculiar to such sciences as
geology, biology, economics, sociology, and psychology.

The distinction between strict and non-strict laws is essential to
the argument for Anomalous Monism. The argument for
Anomalous Monism has three basic premises: (1) there are causal
relations between events described as physical and events
described as mental, (2) there are no strict laws relating events
under physical descriptions with events under mental descriptions, and (3) if two events are related as cause and effect, there is a
strict law covering the case. The first premise I took to be evident:
events in the world we describe in physical terms cause and are
caused by thoughts. The second premise I have defended at some
length, mainly on the grounds of the uneliminably normative or
rational aspect of intentional idioms, and the consequent irreducibility of mental concepts to concepts amenable to inclusion in
a closed system of laws. The argument went this way: It is plausible that there is a set of concepts (perhaps there are many such
sets) which lend themselves to the formulation of a closed causal
system. Let us call these concepts the concepts of physics. In this
case, for any two events related as cause and effect, there will be a
strict law, i.e., a physical law, covering the case. Since mental
concepts are not amenable to inclusion in a closed system, the
strict laws covering singular causal relations expressed in (at least
partly) mental terms must also be expressible in physical terms.
Hence events described in mental terms must also be expressible
in physical terms: in ontic language, mental events are identical
with physical events. It follows that mental concepts are supervenient on physical concepts, in this sense: if two events fail to
share a mental property, they will fail to share at least one physical
property.

Anscombe, as we have seen, attacked the view that causes
"necessitate" their effects, and she explained this as requiring a law

that is an "exceptionless generalization saying such an event always follows such antecedents". The notion of necessity comes in, I suppose, with the idea that one can deduce a statement of the existence of the effect from a statement of the cause and the appropriate law. Anscombe takes this to forbid the indeterministic laws of quantum physics. The constraints I have put on the laws that the cause–law thesis says exist do not, however, disallow probabilistic laws. Such laws are universal and are exceptionless (the probabilities they predict have no exceptions). So it is possible, though unlikely, that Anscombe is not questioning the cause–law thesis as I have stated it. (We do disagree on a consequence of allowing probabilistic laws, since she holds that such indeterminism leaves room for a meaningful concept of human freedom, while I think the indeterminism of quantum physics cannot facilitate, though it might conceivably sometimes frustrate, freedom of action.)

Since it allows probabilistic laws, the cause–law thesis does not (in one fairly standard sense of that messy concept) imply determinism. Neither, then, does it imply complete predictability, even in principle, nor retrodictability.

II

In the *Enquiry Concerning Human Understanding*, Hume defines a cause to be "an object, followed by another, and where all the objects similar to the first are followed by objects similar to the second". If we think of this as a stipulative definition, then one condition for the existence of a law, generality, is built into Hume's definition. But if the definition is intended as an analysis of the common conception of cause we can, with Anscombe, ask if it is correct. It is in any case clear that this definition will not satisfy the cause–law thesis, since it fails to distinguish true but non-lawlike generalizations of the night–day sort from lawlike generalizations. Not that nothing Hume says invites us to observe this distinction; his discussion of induction requires it. Hume's definition of cause just quoted says that the truth of a singular causal statement depends on the existence of a true generalization that covers not only the case at hand, but all other cases, observed and unobserved, past, present, and future. This raises the obvious question what justifies us in believing in the truth of such a generalization, and therefore in the truth of any singular causal statement. Hume's answer, as we know, is that nothing justifies us in either belief; but then we are left to wonder why we have any such beliefs. For this Hume does have an answer, the gist of which is given by his alternative "definition" of cause: a cause is "an object, followed by another, and whose appearance always conveys the thought of that other". Here, as the "always" makes clear, "an object" stands for a class of objects. Although this pronouncement has invited many interpretations, I will take it here to imply at least this: we believe that one event has caused another if every event that seems similar to the first has been followed by an event that seems similar to the second. It adds something to say (as Hume does) that this pairing of sets of events or appearances is a habit of the mind, for this implies a disposition present even when not at work, a disposition to project the pairing beyond what has been given. We *expect* fire to burn and bread to nourish in the future.

Nelson Goodman, in his basic book *Fact, Fiction, and Forecast*,[8] praised Hume for realizing that only human tendencies to classify and associate in one way rather than another could be called on to characterize inductive reasoning, but he criticized Hume on two grounds. The first was for thinking this approach is skeptical; in Goodman's opinion induction does not need justification, only a correct, naturalistic description. The second was that even taken as description, Hume missed the difficulty that lay hidden in the concept of similarity. Goodman brought this out by inventing the predicate "grue". Something is grue if examined before some future time t and found to be green, and otherwise is blue. We have no trouble understanding this predicate; it is defined in a straightforward way in intelligible terms. We can therefore recognize things that are grue as similar: the predicate "grue" is true of all of them; they are alike in being grue. Yet we realize that "All emeralds are green" is, if not true, at least lawlike, while "All emeralds are grue" cannot also be lawlike if induction is to provide any guidance to the future. Even if we abandon the search for an ultimate justification of our inductive practices,

---

[8] First published in 1979. Page numbers here are from the fourth edition, Harvard University Press, 1983.

it is legitimate to ask what those practices, at their reflective best, are. The concept of similarity cannot, by itself, carry the burden of distinguishing the lawlike from the non-lawlike.

Is it quite right, though, to say Hume let matters rest with the unquestioned concept of similarity? According to Goodman,

> The real inadequacy of Hume's account lay not in his descriptive approach but in the imprecision of his description. Regularities in experience, according to him, give rise to habits of expectation; and thus it is predictions conforming to past regularities that are normal or valid. But Hume overlooks the fact that some regularities do and some do not establish such habits; that predictions based on some regularities are valid while predictions based on other regularities are not. . . . Regularity in greenness confirms the prediction of further cases; regularity in grueness does not. . . . Regularities are where you find them, and you can find them anywhere.[9]

If we take Hume's first definition of cause, this criticism is apt. But Hume's reformulation defines cause in terms of the inductions we actually make, not those we might have made had we been differently constituted. When Hume writes that "after a repetition of similar instances, the mind is carried by habit, upon the appearance of one event, to expect its usual attendant, and to believe that it will exist"[10] we notice that "similar" and "usual" are uncritically used. But the second definition of cause doesn't employ these words, and may be viewed instead as defining the relevant concept of similarity. To take one of Hume's examples: if every time we have observed a certain vibration of a string it has been followed by a certain sound, then the next time we observe that vibration, we expect that sound and not another. The phrases "a certain vibration" and "a certain sound" assume the classifications that are appropriate to inductions; but we may take the operative expectations to fix the classifications. Our expectations or "projections" thus distinguish the lawlike from the non-lawlike. It is true that this account differs from Goodman's in several ways, but not, as he suggests, in that Hume provides no answer at all to Goodman's "New Riddle of Induction".

Goodman's analysis is, of course, far more explicit, detailed and precise than Hume's. It also differs in another interesting respect. Goodman's detailed account makes the lawlike status of

---

[9] Ibid., p. 82.
[10] *An Enquiry Concerning Human Understanding*, Sect. VII, Part II.

a statement depend on the projectible status of its individual predicates (which depends in turn on past predictions); Hume's account rather treats whole statements (sentences) as lawlike or not (which depends on present habits as formed by past experience). Thus Hume's analysis allows that a generalization of the form "All F's are G's" may be lawlike and "All F's are H's" not, even though H may occur in other statements that are lawlike. In other words, with respect to things that are F, G may be a projectible predicate, while with respect to things that are F, H may not be projectible. Goodman's analysis does not allow such cases, since for him projectibility is a property of predicates, not of predicates relative to other predicates. In this respect I think Hume's line superior, for reasons I shall presently discuss.[11]

III

Hume says (though not with complete consistency) that we believe in a causal connection between two events only when we have experienced repeated conjunctions and no exceptions (I'm not bothering with the further conditions of succession and contiguity here). It is therefore worth pointing out that the cause–law thesis is not committed to this idea. Nor is it committed to the view that the only way of supporting or confirming a singular causal statement is by reference to relevantly similar cases. I am with those philosophers (for example Anscombe, Ducasse, and McDowell) who think Hume was wrong in supposing we never directly perceive that one event has caused another, even when we have no supporting evidence drawn from similar cases.

John McDowell recognizes that I do not think causal laws are merely true generalizations (though as I say above, neither do I think this is all there is to Hume's view), but he argues that if we give up this reduction, it is hard to see why we should accept the cause–law thesis, which McDowell considers part of the "broadly Humean picture of causation". In other words, McDowell holds that if we give up Hume's epistemic claim that the only evidence we have for causal connections is observed regularities, "it is hard to see what now holds the [broadly Humean] picture of causation in place."

---

[11] I made this point, perhaps too crudely, in "Mental Events".

Hume's own recommendation of it is, in effect, that since singular causal relations are not given in experience, there is nothing for causation to consist in but a suitable kind of generality. And this recommendation seems inextricably bound up with a 'dualism of scheme and content, of organizing system and something waiting to be organized', the untenability of which Davidson has done as much as anyone to bring home to us. Without that dualism, there is no evident attraction left in the thought that singular causal relations are not given in experience.[12]

The connection with scheme–content dualism is obscure to me, but it is in any case irrelevant, since I have never claimed that singular causal relations are not given in experience. The notion of being "given in experience" is not one for which I have felt much need, in this context or any other. But if it means here no more than that the excitation of our senses may sometimes cause us correctly, justifiably and without inference to believe that a particular event has caused another, then I certainly accept that singular causal relations are often given in experience.[13] McDowell apparently holds that once we grant that it is possible to perceive that one particular event has caused another there is no reason to accept the cause–law thesis. But why should we assume this particular connection, or non-connection, between an epistemic and a non-epistemic issue?

C. J. Ducasse believed that a true singular causal statement entails the existence of a general law, and that it is possible to observe that one event has caused another without having any independent reason to accept a generalization. He held that all knowledge of causality depends on observing particular cases, though if we knew that an event *c* caused an event *e* in a situation *S*, we would then know that any event exactly like *c* would cause an event exactly like *e* in a situation exactly like *S*. Unfortunately, his argument for this view seems to rest on two confusions that he elsewhere warns against: the confusion of particular events with events of "the same" type, and the idea that the concept of a sufficient condition can be applied to events as well as to sentences

---

[12] John McDowell, "Functionalism and Anomalous Monism", in *Actions and Events: Perspectives on the Philosophy of Donald Davidson*, ed. E. LePore and B. McLaughlin, Blackwell, Oxford, 1985, p. 398. The inner quote from Davidson is from *Inquiries into Truth and Interpretation*, Oxford University Press, 1984, p. 189.

[13] This has always been my view. See "Actions, Reasons and Causes", in *Essays on Actions and Events*, p. 16.

about, and descriptions of, events.[14] What I find of interest for my present purpose is his definition of cause.

Ducasse tells us that he performed the following "experiment" with his students: He would put a paper-covered cardboard box on his desk, and ask the students to keep their eyes on it. He would then place his hand on the box, and the end of the parcel facing the students would instantly glow. Ducasse next asked them what caused the box to light up when it did, and they would all naturally answer that the glowing was caused by Ducasse's placing his hand on the box.[15] Ducasse notes that the experiment was not repeated, no similar cases were offered for observation. He allows that the students might have the cause wrong; his point was only to establish something about their criteria for judging what had caused the package to glow. On the basis of a single "experiment", they believed there was a causal connection, as, of course, there was. This leads Ducasse to the following definition of cause: if *c* is the only change in a situation *S* which precedes the only subsequent change *e* in *S*, then *c* is the cause of *e*. This formulation is mine, and it does not do full justice to Ducasse's more guarded definition. My formulation does, however, bring out a difficulty Ducasse understandably overlooked. He did not pause to ask what constitutes a change, and therefore what sorts of entities could count as causes and effects.

A natural first stab at saying what a change is goes something like this: some predicate *P* is true of an object or situation at a given time, *t*, and subsequent to *t* *P* is no longer true of that object or situation. If something is green, and then is blue, this is a change, an event. If an emerald before our eyes were to turn blue after being green, we would seek an explanation of such an event, some other change that caused the observed change. Our first stab at defining a change or event would appear to work. But wait: if an emerald were to stay green as time *t* ticked past, it would have changed from grue to bleen (something is bleen if observed before time *t* and is blue, and otherwise is green). The predicate "grue" would not have stayed true of it, for it would have come to instantiate the grue-excluding predicate "bleen". Ducasse did not, as far as I know, suggest my "first stab" at defining a change or

---

[14] Ducasse's most extended discussion of causality is in his *Nature, Mind, and Death*, The Open Court Publishing Co., La Salle, Illinois, 1951.   [15] Ibid., p. 95.

event, but neither did he volunteer any alternative.[16] Without some idea of what constitutes a change, his analysis of cause in terms of "only change" leaves us up in the air. Of course one thing that is green is similar to something else that is green; they are the same color. But this is no help. If grue and bleen aren't colors, let us call them "tolors"—a property is a tolor if it changes color at time t. Then one thing that is grue is similar to something else that is grue; they are the same tolor.

IV

There is an obvious correspondence between Hume's problem and Ducasse's problem. Hume's problem was the problem of relevant generality; he needed to be able to say when one event was relevantly "similar" to another in order to distinguish lawlike generalizations from non-lawlike ones. Ducasse's problem looked at first unrelated, since it apparently concerned particular cases; it arose in the course of trying to define cause in a way Ducasse thought was totally at odds with Hume's approach, a way that makes no appeal to other cases. But in fact Ducasse's definition of the causal relation has no content unless we are able to distinguish changes from non-changes,[17] and this distinction turns out to involve generality in the sense that it is just the predicates which are projectible, the predicates or properties that enter into valid inductions, that determine what counts as a change.

The underlying problem is in both cases the same: neither Hume nor Ducasse has specified when cases are relevantly similar. Hume needs to say when one change is relevantly similar to another ("Same cause, same effect"); Ducasse needs to be able to say when one state is *not* relevantly similar to another, i.e., when a change or event occurs. Thus Hume's and Ducasse's definitions of cause, so apparently at odds, are essentially equivalent. Hume says that c caused e if and only if every event similar to c is

---

[16] Lawrence Lombard does seem to have accepted my "first stab". See his "Events and Their Subjects", *Pacific Philosophical Quarterly* **62** (1981), p. 138.

[17] Ducasse counts "unchanges" as well as changes as events, but this terminological point is unrelated to the problem he faces in distinguishing events that are changes from events that are unchanges. In this essay, I do not follow Ducasse's terminology: I call only changes events.

followed by an event similar to *e*, that is, if and only if every event that is *c*-like is followed by an event that is *e*-like. Ducasse says *c* caused *e* if and only if *e* is the only change that followed *c*, and *c* is the only change preceding *e*. Suppose the *c*-like event is the striking of a particular match and the *e*-like event the lighting of that match. An event is *c*-like if it is a striking of a match and *e*-like if it is the lighting of a struck match. According to Hume, *c* caused *e* if and only if every *c*-like event is followed by an *e*-like event. According to Ducasse, *c* caused *e* if and only if *c* was the only change in a situation in which *e* was the only change that immediately followed. But *c* was the cause of *e* only if *c* and *e* were the relevant changes, and they were this only if *c* was a change from not being struck to being struck, i.e., a *c*-like event, and *e* was a change from not being alight to being alight, i.e., was an *e*-like event. This is the case, Ducasse argues, if and only if every event that is *c*-like is followed by an event that is *e*-like. These formulations are crude, but they serve to bring out the central fact that it is only if "*c*-like" and "*e*-like" are the right sort of predicates, when taken together, that the quoted generalization-schemata are, if true, laws.

It is not surprising, then, that singular causal statements imply the existence of covering laws: events are changes that explain and require such explanations. This is not an empirical fact: nature doesn't care what we call a change, so we decide what counts as a change on the basis of what we want to explain, and what we think available as an explanation. In deciding what counts as a change we also decide what generalizations to count as lawlike.

If the Big Bang left behind a uniformly expanding universe, we should expect that as we expand along with it, the intensity of the background microwave radiation will be the same in all directions. It is not; the radiation is measurably stronger in one direction than in others. This has been explained by assuming that the difference is due to the motion of our galaxy relative to the general expansion. Subsequent observations revealed, however, that over a vast area all neighboring galaxies are moving with us towards a common spot in the sky. This was in turn explained by the hypothesis of some immense but unobserved mass at that spot ("the great attractor"). In December of 1993, careful studies of the motion of galaxies four times further out in space than had previously been studied showed that they too were travelling in company with the rest through the background radiation at about 500 kilometers a second. Nothing has turned up that isn't moving with the crowd. So either the universe is uneven on a far larger scale than had been supposed or explained by present theory, or else the background radiation does not provide a true rest frame. In that case, says Princeton astrophysicist Bohdan Paczynski, there's something wrong with our prior definition of what is at rest and what is moving.[18] Exactly: if you can't explain it using one assumption of what counts as a change, adopt new categories that allow a redefinition of change.

The history of physics is replete with examples of such adjustments in the choice of properties to define change, thus altering what calls for a causal explanation. At a certain level of common-sense physics, nothing is more static than a rock in the desert (unless, of course, someone picks it up, at which point the cause of its change of position is obvious, and a rough law surfaces). Even untutored observation may note a change in the temperature of the rock, but this is geared to an even more noticeable change in the relation of the sun to the rock. More serious science discovers changes in the positions of invisible particles in the rock which take place independent of changes in temperature; recognition of these changes allows for the causal explanation of a far larger range of phenomena.

One way science advances is by recognizing change where none was seen before. It can also work the other way around. Galileo sparked a revolutionary improvement in physics when he proposed that uniform rectilinear motion not be treated as a change requiring an explanation, but as a steady state. The result was to give up the search for a cause of such motion and to treat only deviations from such motion as changes. Further advances made uniform rectilinear velocity only a special case of uniform acceleration; unchanges took over an even larger territory with the idea of not treating gravity as a force, so that the motion of a body along geodesics as defined by a spacial framework determined by the distributions of masses in space became a state not requiring a cause.[19]

---

[18] As related by Faye Flam, "Galaxies Keep Going With the Flow", *Science*, **259** (1993), p. 31.

[19] My discussion here is based in part on Robert Cummins, "States, Causes, and the Law of Inertia", *Philosophical Studies*, **29** (1976), 21–36.

The dispositions to which we advert to explain what happens to objects, or the things they do, encapsulate the relation between causality and laws. We explain why the lump of sugar dissolved when placed in water by mentioning that it was water-soluble; something is water-soluble if placing it in water causes it to dissolve. We gain some understanding of why someone flew into a rage over a trifle if we know he was irascible; some one is irascible if small things cause him to be angry. The causal powers of physical objects are essential to determining what sorts of objects they are by defining what sorts of changes they can undergo while remaining the same object and what sorts of changes constitute their beginnings or ends. Our concept of a physical object is the concept of an object whose changes are governed by laws.

It would, as remarked before, be a large mistake to suppose that every way of referring to a cause or effect tells us how to characterize the change in terms suitable for incorporation in a law. "Hurricane Andrew" is a perfectly good phrase for picking out a particular event, but there is nothing in the concept of a hurricane that allows us to frame precise general laws about the causes or effects of hurricanes. If a hurricane is an event, it is a candidate for causal explanation; to say something caused it (the formation of a certain extreme low pressure area for example) is to claim that the changes involved can be described in terms that would serve to formulate a general causal law.

To revert now to the idea that what makes a statement lawlike is not a matter of the projectible character of its individual predicates, but of the appropriate pairing or matching of predicates. Let us ask how projectible Goodman's favorite projectible predicate "green" is. It picks out a class of objects we project early and easily. "All emeralds are green" is lawlike, until, of course, defeated by counterexamples. But even if not proven false, it is not a strict law; for when is something green? We are inclined to say something is green if and only if it looks green to normal observers under normal conditions. But "looks green" and "normal" are not predicates that can be sharply defined, and they certainly cannot be reduced to the predicates of physics. They cannot feature in the laws of a closed system. If we imagine that a satisfactory definition of "emerald" can be devised in the vocabulary of physics, then "green" is not strictly projectible of emeralds. Of course, "green" is more projectible of emeralds than "grue"; but "green" and "blue" are only as projectible of emeralds and sapphires as "grue" and "bleen" are of emerires and sapphalds. This distinction, between predicates like "green" and "grue" on the one hand, and predicates that together can feature in strict laws, is crucial, as I said, to the argument for Anomalous Monism. It is what distinguishes psychophysical laws from the laws of an advanced physics.

We are born, as Quine has emphasized,[20] treating some pairs of things as more similar than others. We react differentially to sudden loud noises, and since we do not like such sounds, we soon learn to cringe from what has frequently preceded them. Thus long prior to the acquisition of language, or anything that can properly be considered concept formation, we act as if we had learned crude laws. We are inducers from birth; if we were not, infant mortality would be the rule, if there were any infants. Concepts, conceptualized laws, the idea of causal relations between events, build on these foundations. In the course of avoiding and seeking, learning to control our environment, failing and succeeding, we build the lawlike habits that promote survival and enhance life. These laws of action are highly pragmatic not only in their conspicuous ties to action, but in their breezy disregard of the irrelevant or implausible. The generalizations on which not only the untutored infant but also our adult selves mostly depend are geared to the "normal", the "usual". We don't know, and for practical purposes don't care, what would happen if there were no oxygen, temperatures were to fall to absolute zero, or there were a black hole in the closet (I now learn that there may be!). But practical purposes can change, and the conditions at one time happily abandoned to ceteris paribus clauses may become relevant, or come to be recognized as relevant. We then refine our classifications to improve our laws.

Learning laws of greater generality provides no reason for jettisoning our proviso-laden work-a-day causal laws.When I flick on the light switch, I have no reason to reflect on the speed of light, though I may briefly dwell on that magic constant when my telephone calls to Perth are relayed—and perceptibly delayed—by satellite technology. The more precise and general laws are, the less likely it is that we will be in a position to employ

[20] In "Natural Kinds", in *Ontological Relativity and Other Essays*, Columbia University Press, 1969.

them in predicting the outcomes of our ordinary actions or the weather. Our intense interest in the explanation and understanding of intentional behavior commits us irrevocably to such concepts as belief, desire, intention, and action; yet these are concepts that cannot, without losing the explanatory the power they have which binds us to them, be reduced to the concepts of an all-encompassing physics.

We have interests that are not practical. There are things we want to understand whether or not we can control them and whether or not such knowledge will serve our mundane needs. Pursuit of the truth in such cases can in principle proceed without the constraints of practical control and gain. In this mood we can seek laws that have no exceptions.

The same strategy that serves to refine our practical lore, the strategy that leads us to adjust what counts as a change or as requiring a causal explanation, works here too, as is evident in the advances in physics due to Galileo, Newton, and Einstein.

Robert Cummins puts it this way:

A decision about how to characterize [a state]—a choice of state variables—imposes distinctions between states and non-states, and hence determines what is and what is not construed as an effect. Such decisions are not arbitrary, in part *because* they have this consequence. Effects require direct causal explanation; if there is none to be had which satisfies, then we shall alter our taxonomy. This sounds like metaphysics, and indeed it is ... All this presupposes a certain explanatory strategy [which] is easy to state in outline: what requires explanation is change, and changes are to be explained as effects, the trick being to characterize matters in a way which makes this possible, i.e., in a way which distinguishes genuine changes from states.[21]

Cummins notes that physics leading up to and including classical mechanics "and its kin" has followed the strategy he describes and adds, somewhat glumly, "this strategy seems to be breaking down at the quantum level". I am not up to evaluating every implication of this last suggestion, but I do not think quantum physics poses a threat to the cause–law thesis. If what Cummins means is that the ideal of a completely deterministic theory must be given up if quantum physics is the last word, he is of course right. But his strategy would seem to apply to quantum physics if we delete the word "direct" from the requirement that

---

[21] Op. cit., p. 33.

effects require direct causal explanation, and understand the changes that are to be explained as sometimes being changes in probabilities.

This is the view promoted many years ago by Henry Margenau. He formulates what he calls the "Principle of Causality" as follows: "causality is violated when a given state A is not always followed by that same state B".[22] Like Cummins, he notes that without an understanding of what constitutes a state, this tells us nothing; but that, on the other hand, once we decide what constitutes a state, we have decided what counts as a causal law. Why, though, should we count on there being a way of specifying states that allows the formulation of exceptionless laws? Here is Margenau's answer:

[W]henever a physical system does not appear to be closed, that is when the differential equations describing it contain the time explicitly . . . , we conclude that the variables determining the state in question are not completely known. We then look immediately for hidden properties whose variation may have produced the inconsistencies, and whose inclusion in the analysis would eliminate them; moreover if we do not find any we invent them. This procedure is possible because . . . the term "state" is undefined . . . it seems, then, that the causality postulate reduces to a definition of what is meant by "state".[23]

For this reason, Margenau says, "physics can never inform us of a failure of the causality principle". Quantum mechanics, he concludes, poses no threat to the causality principle; it just once again redefines the concept of a state.

Margenau could not, of course, have known about Bell's inequality theorem, nor the experiments that made use of it to prove that there can be no local hidden variable theory. But Margenau did not understand the Principle of Causation to require a deterministic physics: he required only that the notion of a state be formulated in such a way as to insure that the laws be strict. The point comes out clearly in a recent discussion of the philosophical fallout from the experimental proof of the impossibility of a hidden variable theory:

Complete knowledge of the state of a classical system at a given time is synonymous with exact knowledge of all observables at that time.

---

[22] "Meaning and Scientific Status of Causality", *Philosophy of Science*, **1** (1934), p. 140.   [23] Ibid., pp. 144–5.

Complete knowledge of the state of a quantum mechanical system is ensured by the exact knowledge of only a subset of all observables at the same time. . . . Only when one asks for the value of an observable not in the complete set of observables that are knowable simultaneously does one encounter the probabilistic nature of QM. In this sense the probabilistic element enters QM through the measurement process, which is bound to change the observed system. . . . The various possible outcomes of such a measurement occur with probabilities that can be predicted exactly. The outcome of any one such measurement . . . cannot be predicted.[24]

Thus Margenau is borne out: the concept of a state of a quantum mechanical system has been defined to ensure that all that can be known about it at a moment completely determines the state. The identity of a quantum state is sensitive, in a way that states in classical systems are not, to the effect of measurements. In a classical system, it is assumed that the effect of measurements can in principle be reduced to an arbitrarily high degree, while in quantum physics the effect of measurements is integral to the theory: the measuring device becomes part of the same physical system as what is measured, and subject to the same laws. Quantum mechanics sacrifices determinism as the cost of gaining universality. "It states beautifully what is completely ignored in classical physics: through man nature can observe itself."[25] Far from challenging the cause–law thesis, quantum physics exemplifies it.

V

Quantum physics may not, of course, be the last word. It is not only Einstein who dreamed of a theory that would supersede quantum theory, or in effect make quantum theory deterministic. Steven Weinberg, for example, not only dreams of a unified Theory of Everything, but speculates that such a theory might be completely deterministic.[26] But it is hard to think that the question whether such a theory exists is a purely conceptual question, at least a theory human beings could, even in principle, invent and

---

[24] Fritz Rohrlich, "Facing Quantum Mechanical Reality", *Science*, **221** (1983), p. 1254.   [25] Ibid., p. 1253.
[26] In *Dreams of a Final Theory*, Hutchinson, as reported by John Leslie, *The Times Literary Supplement*, Jan. 29, 1993, p. 3.

test. Surely we must allow that the best physics that is possible for us is irreducibly probabilistic. Does this mean the cause–law thesis is not tenable? I think not. Margenau's principle, essentially Hume's "same cause, same effect" principle, put us on the track of the idea that natural and devised standards of similarity play a fundamental role both in the notion of change and the notion of law. This provided a legitimate connection between the concept of causality and the concept of a law. We can imagine this connection being tight enough to support completely deterministic laws. Indeed, this is how classical mechanics assumed things were. But if physics cannot be made deterministic, if the ultimate laws of the universe, so far as we will ever know, are probabilistic, then we must think of causality as probabilistic. Singular causal statements will still entail the existence of strict laws, even at the quantum level, but the laws will not meet Hume's or Kant's or Einstein's standards.

HISTORICAL THOUGHTS

15 *Plato's Philosopher*

It is a fine question how the aim and method of the philosophical enterprise is to be related to the beliefs we bring to that enterprise. It is bootless to pretend we can start by somehow setting aside the equipment with which we approach philosophy, for then there would be nothing with which to work. We can, however, ask whether the main point of philosophizing is to examine, clarify, reconcile, criticize, regroup, or even unearth, the convictions or assumptions with which we began, or whether something more is possible: a search which might lead to knowledge or values that were not in sight at the start, and not necessarily implicit in what we then knew.

Each of these enterprises has its obvious difficulties. No one can object to the attack on confusion, conflict, obscurity, and self-deceit in our everyday beliefs; these defects in our views of ourselves and the world exist in profusion, and if some philosophers can with skill or luck do something about reducing them, those philosophers deserve our respect and support.

But it would be disappointing to suppose this is all philosophy can do, for then philosophy would seem to be relegated to the job of removing inconsistencies while entering no claim to achieve truth. Consistency is, of course, necessary if *all* our beliefs are to be true. But there is not much comfort in mere consistency. Given that it is almost certainly the case that some of our beliefs are false (though we know not which), making our beliefs consistent with one another may as easily reduce as increase our store of knowledge.

On the other hand it is not easy to see how to conduct the search for truths independent of our beliefs. The problem is to recognize such truths when we encounter them, since the only standards we can use are our own. Where the first approach makes no attempt at fixing objective standards, the second can seem to succeed only by illegitimately relabelling some portion of the subjective as objective.

There is an obvious connection between the two pictures of the method and aim of philosophy and two traditional concepts of the nature of truth: one method goes naturally with coherence theories of truth, the other allies itself with correspondence theories. A coherence theory in its boldest and clearest form declares that all beliefs in a consistent set of beliefs are true; coherence is the only possible test of truth, and so coherence must constitute truth. So stated, a coherence theory of truth can be taken as a defence of a philosophical method which claims only to remove inconsistency; for once inconsistencies have been excised, the coherence theory assures us that what remains will be an unadulterated body of truths.

Correspondence theories, on the other hand, maintain that truth can be explained as a relation between a belief and a reality whose existence and character is for the most part independent of our knowledge and beliefs. Truth of this sort is just what the second approach to philosophy seeks. But unfortunately correspondence theories provide no intelligible answer to the question how we can in general recognize that our beliefs correspond in the required way to reality.

No theme in Plato is more persistent than the emphasis on philosophical method, the search for a systematic way of arriving at important truths, and of insuring that they are truths. Yet I think it is safe to say that Plato not only did not find a wholly satisfactory method, but he did not find a method that satisfied him for long. In the early dialogues, in which Socrates takes charge, the elenctic method dominates, and there is nothing in those dialogues to promote the suspicion that Plato, or Socrates, sees the need to add anything to it. Yet it seems clear that it is a method that at best leads to consistency; if it is supposed to yield truth, the ground of this supposition is not supplied. In the middle and some of the late dialogues Plato suggests a number of ways in which the elenchus might be supplemented or replaced by techniques with loftier aims. But what is striking is that Plato does not settle on any one of these methods as a method guaranteed to achieve objective truth; one by one the new methods are discarded, or downgraded to the status of mere useful devices. Plato often makes it clear that he recognizes the inadequacy of his methods for achieving his aims; and the inadequacy is often painfully apparent to the modern reader.

Plato and Aristotle are often held to be paradigms of the contrasting methods. Aristotle insisted, at least in moral philosophy, that views that are widely shared and strongly held within our own community must be taken seriously and treated as generally true. But Plato, we are told,

Throughout the middle dialogues... repeatedly argues against the philosophical adequacy of any method that consists in setting down and adjusting our opinions and sayings. It is Plato who most explicitly opposes *phainomena*, and the cognitive states concerned with them, to truth and genuine understanding. It is also Plato who argues that the *paradeigmata* that we require for understanding of the most important philosophical and scientific subjects are not to be found in the world of human belief and perception at all.[1]

This is, indeed, the standard view, and when, as in this passage, it is restricted to the middle dialogues, it is roughly correct. Even with this restriction, though, it needs to be taken with a grain of salt. Nussbaum gives, as a striking example of the opposition of methods in Plato and Aristotle, their views on *akrasia*, or weakness of the will. Socrates, as we know, paradoxically maintained that *akrasia* was impossible; he argued that if an agent knows what is good, he cannot fail to act in accord with that knowledge. Aristotle, on the other hand, held that the common view must be right: despite Socrates' arguments, there are cases of *akrasia*.

How clear is the contrast here between Plato (really Socrates) and Aristotle? In the early dialogues we meet with the most emphatic cases of conclusions that plainly contradict common conviction; yet nothing is said to show that the elenctic method is capable of more than revealing inconsistencies. In the middle dialogues there are the strong representations just mentioned that philosophy can arrive at truths not dreamed of by ordinary men, and not to be tested by experience; yet in these same dialogues much less is made of the paradoxical character of the doctrines that emerge. In particular, the Socratic denial of the possibility of

---

[1] "Saving Aristotle's Appearances" by Martha Nussbaum: *Language and Logos*, ed. M. Schofield and M. Nussbaum (Cambridge University Press, 1982), p. 270.

akrasia is explicitly dropped. To make our own small paradox, you might say in the early dialogues dogmatic claims are based on a method that cannot support them; in the middle dialogues rather tamer results flow from methods which are advertised as leading to absolute and objective truth.

I think that in the end Plato lost faith in the ability of these methods to produce certified eternal truths that owed nothing to the serious goals and convictions of most people, but came to have a renewed confidence in the elenchus, supplemented and refined in various ways, to arrive at truth by way of consistency; in other words, he returned to something like the Socratic method and its approach to the philosophic enterprise. It is not hard to think of reasons why, in the middle dialogues, Plato decided the elenchus was not enough to prove the sort of theses he wished to establish; nor is it hard to imagine why he became dissatisfied with the alternatives. We can guess why Plato may have become discouraged in his quest for a foolproof, supermundane method, since he himself produced criticisms that must have left him as sceptical as they do us.

It would be foolish to try to demonstrate the historical truth of the idea that at the end of his career Plato returned to something like the Socratic faith in the power of the elenchus; Plato's writings were successfully designed to leave us in doubt about what he believed. I will be more than pleased if my speculations cannot be made to seem wrong.

The line of thought I am pursuing was inspired by a brilliant and provocative paper by Gregory Vlastos called "The Socratic Elenchus"[2]. Viewed logically, the elenchus is simply a method for demonstrating that a set of propositions is inconsistent. In practice, the elenctic method is employed by Socrates, or some other interrogator, to show that an interlocutor has said things which cannot all be true (since they are inconsistent). If this were the whole story, the function of the elenchus would be no more than to reveal inconsistencies; such a revelation should, of course, be interesting to anyone tempted to *believe* all the propositions in the inconsistent set.

There is no obvious reason why a philosopher—or anyone else—should be concerned with inconsistent sets of propositions

[2] *Oxford Studies in Ancient Philosophy* (Oxford University Press, 1983).

only when they happen to be believed; after all, one can prove a proposition true, and hence worthy of belief, by showing its negation inconsistent. This is no help in establishing substantive, or moral, truths as opposed to logical truths. Nevertheless, it is often helpful, when trying to decide where the truth lies, to appreciate the inconsistency of a set of propositions to which one is not yet committed.

It is therefore surprising, and instructive, that in the Socratic dialogues, Socrates usually insists that the interlocutor be seriously committed to the propositions being tested. It is one of the merits of Vlastos' article that he notices this striking feature of Socrates' method, and appreciates how important it is. Vlastos quotes from the dialogues: "By the god of friendship, Callicles! Don't think that you can play games with me and answer whatever comes into your head, contrary to your real opinion" (*Gorgias* 500b); "My good man, don't answer contrary to your real opinion, so we may get somewhere" (*Republic* I. 346a); and when Protagoras says in answer to a question of Socrates, "But what does it matter? Let it be so for us, if you wish," Socrates angrily replies, "I won't have this. For it isn't this 'if you wish' and 'if you think so' that I want to be refuted, but you and me. I say 'you and me' for I think that the thesis is best refuted if you take the 'if' out of it" (*Protagoras* 331c).

This last quotation brings out another feature of the elenchus, and helps answer the question why Socrates is so concerned that the people he questions should express their real opinions. Socrates is interested in *refutation*. The typical elenchus begins by Socrates asking a question, to which the interlocutor gives an answer. Socrates then elicits some further views from the interlocutor (not infrequently by putting them forward himself, and getting the interlocutor to agree), and proceeds to demonstrate that these further views entail the falsity of the original answer. Unless the person being questioned accepts the propositions which refute his original answer, he will have no reason to give up his opening proposal; no *particular* thesis will have been refuted.

As Vlastos points out, all that Socrates has shown is that the interlocutor's beliefs are inconsistent, so at least one of those beliefs must be false. But there is nothing about the elenctic method to indicate which belief or beliefs should be abandoned. In the event, it always turns out to be the original proposal. For pedagogic and dramatic reasons, this is clearly the right strategy. But it is a strategy that will lead to true conclusions only if one is careful to start with a false belief, and then to draw upon additional, but true, beliefs to disprove the starting claim. How can Socrates know in advance of using his method what is true and what false? Is the method after all just a device for persuasion?

What is clear is that Socrates trusts that the elenctic method does lead to moral truths: the negations, in general, of beliefs held by interlocutors at the start of a discussion. Where p is the original claim, Socrates repeatedly sums up the result of an elenctic argument by saying that the negation of p "has become evident to us," or the interlocutor now "sees" or "knows" that not-p.[3] In the *Gorgias*, Socrates says that his thesis (the negation of the interlocutor's p) has been "proved true" (*Gorgias* 479e). (Here not-p is: to suffer injustice is better than to commit it.) Presently he puts it even more strongly: "These things having become evident in the foregoing arguments, I would say, crude though it may seem to say it, that they have been clamped down and bound by arguments of iron and adamant . . . " (*Gorgias* 508e–509a).

According to Vlastos, whose argument I have been following closely up to this point (as well as using his translations), the last two quotations differ substantially in strength from the earlier claims; proving something is more than simply making it evident. Vlastos thinks the claim that the elenchus can "prove" truths is not Socratic; he believes Socrates did assume that the elenchus leads to truth, but it was an assumption on which he did not consciously reflect, and which he therefore felt no need to defend. Vlastos continues,

Throughout the dialogues which precede the *Gorgias* Plato depicts Socrates arguing for his views in much the same way as other philosophers have done before or since when trying to bring others around to their own view: he picks premises which he considers so eminently reasonable in themselves and so well-entrenched in his interlocutor's system of belief, that when he faces them with the fact that these premises entail the negation of their thesis he feels no serious risk that they will renege on the premises to save their thesis. . . . This being the case, the "problem of the elenchus" never bothers Socrates in those earlier dialogues.[4]

---

[3] For references see Vlastos' "Afterthoughts on the Socratic Elenchus," pp. 71–2.

[4] Vlastos, "Afterthoughts", p. 73.

Plato, however (to continue Vlastos' theory), did come to wonder what ensured the choice of true premisses; and well he might have, given how often what seemed common knowledge to almost everyone else was found to be false according to Socrates. Although the words are put in Socrates' mouth, it is Plato who, according to Vlastos, realizes what must be assumed if the elenchus is to produce truths: the assumption is that, *in moral matters, everyone has true beliefs which he cannot abandon and which entail the negations of his false beliefs.* It follows from this assumption that all the beliefs in a consistent set of beliefs are true, so a method like the elenchus which weeds out inconsistencies will in the end leave nothing standing but truths. Therefore Socrates did not need to know in advance which beliefs were true, nor did he have to worry that upon discovering an inconsistency, the inconsistency might be removed by inadvertently throwing out the true. For the retained falsity would itself be found inconsistent with further beliefs.

I shall not consider the textual evidence in the *Gorgias* for this doctrine, since it is clear on the one hand that something very like this assumption is necessary if the elenchus is to be defended as a way of reaching truths, whether or not Plato or Socrates realized it; and on the other hand, it is equally obvious that there is absolutely no argument in the *Gorgias* or any of the earlier dialogues to support the assumption. Vlastos believes that Plato realized this, and that it is for this reason that in the next three dialogues, written just after the *Gorgias*, the *Euthydemus*, *Lysis*, and *Hippias Major*, the elenchus makes no appearance. In these dialogues there is philosophical argument, but Socrates carries on essentially by himself, acting both as proposer and as critic.

In the *Meno* Plato finds a new way of defending the elenchus: the doctrine of recollection. According to this theory everyone is born knowing everything, but the vicissitudes of life have caused him to forget what he knows, and to come to believe falsehoods. Once again, it is clear that a method that claims no more than that it can remove what is inconsistent with what is known is adequate to achieve truth. Vlastos describes the theory of recollection as a "lavish present" by Plato to Socrates. "By the time this has happened," Vlastos concludes, "the moralist of the earlier dialogues has become the metaphysician of the middle ones. The metamorphosis of Plato's teacher into Plato's mouthpiece is complete."[5]

Vlastos sees a vast difference between Plato's two ways of saving the elenchus: the way of the *Gorgias*, which merely assumes the existence of enough ineradicable truths in everyone, and the way of the *Meno*, with the transmigration of the soul and the theory of recollection. Years passed between the writing of these dialogues, years during which Plato lost all confidence in the elenchus. "Then, one day," writes Vlastos, the theory of recollection came to Plato.

This is a fascinating story, and Vlastos makes it plausible with a wealth of references to the texts, and a shrewd consideration of the human and logical probabilities. I have no intention of arguing against it, except on one point which is not explicit in Vlastos' article, but is strongly implied. That implication is that after the *Gorgias*, Plato *permanently* lost faith in the idea that moral truths can be elicited from anyone by something like the elenchus. In any case, I want to put forward the hypothesis that at a certain point late in his career Plato returns to (if he ever departed from) both the Socratic concern with the good life, the right way to live; and that he depends on the assumption that there is enough truth in everyone to give us hope that we can learn in what the good life consists.

First, we ought to notice that though it is certainly true that the doctrine of the transmigration of the soul and of recollection is new in the *Meno*, that doctrine is closely related to the methodological assumption which Plato realizes, in the *Gorgias*, is needed to defend the elenchus. Indeed, the doctrine of recollection doesn't *supplant* the assumption of the *Gorgias*; it *entails* it. Viewed solely as a supplement to the elenchus, the theory of recollection has no need of the doctrine of the transmigration of the soul. Like the methodological assumption of the *Gorgias*, the theory of recollection postulates that there is enough ineradicable truth in each of us to insure that the elimination of inconsistencies ultimately results in the elimination of error; when all inconsistency is removed, what remains will be true. From a strictly methodological point of view, the chief difference between the two doctrines is that while the assumption of the *Gorgias* suggests

---

[5] "Afterthoughts", p. 74.

that the only sure route to knowledge is the elenchus, the theory of recollection places no premium on the elimination of inconsistencies and so invites us to consider methods other than the elenchus in the search for truth.

And of course other methods do come to the fore in the middle and late dialogues: the various methods of "ascent" in the *Republic*, *Symposium*, and *Phaedrus*; the method of "hypothesis", of "collection and division"; and the method or methods of the *Philebus*. There is an obvious transfer of interest from moral problems to epistemological and ontological problems, a new concern (in the *Theaetetus*) about the possibility of perceptual knowledge, and a persistent worry about philosophical method.

Plato did not abandon the elenctic method; what philosopher would? Our concern is with the question what can be expected of that method, and what Plato thought it could deliver. The essential problem is the one with which we began: can philosophy hope to transcend what is inherent in the beliefs and values with which it begins? If not, consistency but not truth is all we can trust it to deliver, and this is what the unaided elenchus promises. But if the theory of recollection is true, the elenchus can do more. The trouble is that the theory of recollection, treated as an essential assumption needed to support knowledge claims, drops out of sight in the dialogues almost as soon as it appears. It is crucial in the *Meno*, and plays an important role in the *Phaedo*. But by the end of the *Phaedo* the doctrine of recollection has been superseded by the method of hypothesis; this is not a method better suited to prove truths, as we shall see in a moment. The important thing is that Plato no longer seems willing to trust the theory of recollection. Recollection is introduced in the *Republic*, but it is obvious that quite different methods are the ones on which Plato relies in that work; there are further mentions of the theory of recollection in the *Phaedrus*, *Philebus*, and *Laws*, but in none of these dialogues does it serve a significant epistemological role.[6]

It seems clear that Plato was not willing for long seriously to embrace the theory of recollection as a source of substantive moral truths. What, then, did he think to put in its place? If, as Vlastos convincingly insists, the "problem of the elenchus"

---

[6] See Kenneth Sayre, *Plato's Late Ontology: A Riddle Resolved* (Princeton University Press, 1983), pp. 188–93.

obsessed the methodologically-minded Plato, how can he have relinquished the substance of his "lavish gift" to his teacher without finding a suitable substitute?

The answer which appeals to most Plato scholars is that Plato did find other methods in which he placed confidence. This may be true: certainly many methods are mentioned, some of them a number of times, and some of these methods come highly recommended by a character named "Socrates" or "The Eleatic Stranger", etc. Nevertheless, there are three good reasons for not accepting this answer as the last word on Plato's last word on the method of philosophy. The first is that we can find arguments in the dialogues that show why these methods are in one way or another inadequate or incomplete. The second is that when, in the *Philebus*, Plato returns once more to the question of the nature of the good life, these methods are not seen to provide the answer; despite several long and difficult discussions of method, it is the elenchus that provides the basic argument. The third reason, which the historically minded may consider irrelevant, is that we can see for ourselves that none of the alternative methods can provide a firm basis for moral truths, while there is, after all, support for the assumption which, in the *Gorgias*, is recognized as sufficient to defend the elenchus, the assumption that (in ethics at least, and perhaps metaphysics more generally) there are enough truths in each of us to make it plausible that once our beliefs in these matters are consistent they will be true. I do not think it ridiculous to suppose that Plato figured this out for himself; but the direct evidence is no more than suggestive.

It is far more than I can attempt here to survey all the philosophical methods Plato discusses, and the arguments he produces against them; and I do not pretend to have made any new discoveries. What I shall do is indicate how, in the *Philebus*, the elenchus, and only the elenchus, can be claimed to have achieved a correct description of the good life.

The *Philebus* is a significant test case. It is a very late dialogue; probably only the *Laws* is later. It is directly concerned with a Socratic question (one might say *the* Socratic question), the nature of the good life. Even the phrasing of the problem reminds us of earlier works: the *Philebus* asks "what is the best possession a man could have" (19c), it enquires after "the proper goal for all living things" (60a). In the *Republic*, Socrates says "our argument is over no chance matter but over what is the way we ought to live" (*Republic* I. 352d; cf. *Gorgias* 500c).

The *Philebus* begins with a double elenchus. Socrates sums up the two starting positions: "Philebus holds that what is good ... is enjoyment, pleasure, delight, and all that sort of thing. I hold, by contrast, that intelligence, thought, memory ... are, for anything capable of them, preferable and superior to pleasure; indeed to all those capable of a share of them, whether now or in the future, they are of the greatest possible benefit" (*Philebus* 11c).[7] As in the early dialogues, it is assumed without question that "everything capable of knowing pursues" the good; this is taken to be an infallible test of what is acceptable as the good life. With the aid of this assumption, Socrates is able to prove that both Philebus' position and his own position are false.

PROTARCHUS: Neither of these lives seems to me worth choosing, ... and I think anyone would agree with me.

SOCRATES: What about a joint life, Protagoras, made up of a mixture of both elements?

PROTARCHUS: One of pleasure, thought, and intelligence, you mean?

SOCRATES: Yes, and things of that sort.

PROTARCHUS: Anyone would choose that in preference to either of the other two, without exception.

SOCRATES: We are clear what follows for our present argument?

PROTARCHUS: Certainly. There are three possible lives before us, and of two of them neither is adequate or desirable for man or beast.

SOCRATES: Then it's surely clear that neither of these at least can be the good ... For if any of us chose anything else he would take it in defiance of the nature of what is truly desirable ... (*Philebus* 21e–22b)

The argument has exactly the pattern Vlastos found problematic in the early dialogues; an interlocutor answers a question; Socrates gets him to agree to further premises; the original answer is shown to be inconsistent with the further premises; it is then agreed by all hands that the negation of the original answer (or answers in the *Philebus*) has been proven true. The correctness of the conclusion depends on the truth of the unexamined further premises; it is just this that made Vlastos decide that Plato could not accept the elenchus as leading to truth. Yet here in the

---

[7] Here and throughout I use J. C. B. Gosling's translation in *Plato: Philebus* (Oxford University Press, 1975). I am also indebted to Gosling's excellent commentary.

Philebus there seems no room for doubt that Plato uses the elenchus, and accepts its results.

Two other features of the early elenchus are also conspicuous in the *Philebus*. There is, first, the feature on which Vlastos laid great stress, the insistence that the interlocutor sincerely express his own beliefs. One may guess that it is just to emphasize this point that has Plato substitute Protarchus for Philebus as the chief interlocutor: Philebus is too stubborn and crude to be counted on to answer honestly. But Socrates repeatedly makes certain that Protarchus is expressing his own views. At one point, Socrates turns to Philebus to ask if he agrees. We get this exchange:

PHILEBUS: My view is, *and always will be*, that pleasure is the undoubted winner,—but it is for you, Protarchus, to decide.

PROTARCHUS: As you have handed the argument over to me it is no longer for you to say whether or not to agree to Socrates' proposal. (*Philebus* 12a)

A second striking point is Socrates' insistence at every point that what he takes to be true, every untested assumption on which further results depend, be agreed upon. As we have just seen, he does not do so well with Philebus. But the agreement on which he depends is the agreement of those engaged in the dialectic. In the passage I quoted a minute ago, Socrates secures Protarchus' agreement no less than three times to "what anyone would choose"; when the question is asked in the right way, what everyone would choose is the good; and when the question is asked in the right way, everyone will agree that the mixed life of pleasure and intellect is better than the life of pure pleasure or the life of pure intellect. Early in the dialogue, Socrates makes clear that his own position is as much at risk as that of Protarchus: he says "I take it that we are not now just vying to prove my candidate or yours the winner, but shall join forces in favour of whatever is nearest the truth" (*Philebus* 14b). And at another point he remarks, "Should we then register our agreement with earlier generations, and instead on just citing other people's opinions without risk to ourselves, stick our necks out too…" (*Philebus* 29a). Towards the end, Socrates asks once more whether everyone would agree with the essential assumption on which the argument rests, and on the conclusion that the mixed life of pleasure and intelligence is best. He even suggests that "If anyone thinks we have overlooked anything…I hope he will now go back and state the matter more accurately" (*Philebus* 60d). At the very end, Protagoras proclaims: "We are now all agreed, Socrates, on the truth of your position" (*Philebus* 67b). This is not, of course, the position with which Socrates began; it is the position reached by following the elenctic argument.

The central argument of one of Plato's last dialogues concerns, then, a major Socratic problem, employs the Socratic elenchus, and unambiguously endorses the outcome of the elenchus. Why, after entertaining such profound doubts about it, does Plato unquestioningly return to Socrates' method?

Those who are familiar with the *Philebus* will, of course, have noticed that I have been discussing a very small proportion of the material in that dialogue: the defeat of the pure lives of pleasure and intellect and the victory of the mixed life is assured in the first fifth of the dialogue, and the actual argument uses up barely more than three Stephanus pages. That is the heart of the dialogue; but there is, after all, a great deal more. And much of the rest is remote from anything we find in the early dialogues, or, for that matter, anywhere else in Plato. There is much confusing discussion of methods, and ontological doctrines are put forward that sound vaguely Pythagorean and perhaps something like the doctrines Aristotle attributes to Plato in the *Metaphysics*. Little of this material can be attributed to Socrates; at one time, scholars were reluctant to attribute it to Plato. We need not be concerned here with how these strange views are to be reconciled with the rest of what we think we know of Plato's late philosophy, nor with how they can be reconciled with one another. For I think it is reasonably clear nothing in the rest of the *Philebus* solves Vlastos' "problem of the elenchus", that is, shows why it yields truths, and if this is so, how the central argument and result of the dialogue can depend on nothing but the unadorned Socratic elenchus.

One important argument is not really elenctic (I have already mentioned it). In proving by the elenchus that neither the life of pleasure nor the pure life of the intellect is the good life, Socrates uses, as we have seen, two unexamined assumptions, which he and everyone concerned agrees are true. These are (1) the good is what everyone ("capable of knowing") prefers or would choose if he could and (2) no one would, on reflection (and aided by Socrates' arguments), choose either the pure life of pleasure or the pure life of the intellect. This completes the elenchus. Socrates then wins agreement to a further claim: (3) everyone would prefer the mixed life of pleasure and intelligence to either of the other two lives. This implies the negative conclusion of the elenchus, and so could have been used in place of (2). It is introduced, however, as an independent conclusion. But nothing here departs from the elenctic method: (3), like (1) and (2), is accepted once agreed to.

The bulk of the dialogue is devoted to a detailed examination of the various kinds of pleasure, with arguments designed to show why most pleasures are unsuited for inclusion in the good life. As a first step, Socrates undertakes to show that although all pleasures are alike in being pleasures, it is possible that they differ in that some are good and some are bad. The demonstration of this elementary point begins with a fairly lengthy, but confusing, description of a method. Protarchus asks Socrates' help in finding a "better way to conduct the argument". Socrates obliges: "There could be no finer way than the one of which I have always been a devotee, though often it has slipped through my fingers and left me empty-handed and bewildered... It is not difficult to expound, but it is very difficult to apply. It has been responsible for bringing to light everything that has been discovered in the domain of any skill... it was a gift from the gods to men..." (*Philebus* 16b, c). The description of the method that follows is open to many interpretations, especially when one tries to square it with the subsequent four-fold division of all things into limits, unlimiteds, mixtures of the two, and the cause or causes of mixtures. But the uses to which Socrates puts this method, or these methods, is easier to understand. The first use is this: if we start with a collection of entities, we must first "posit a single form", then subdivide it into two or three more, until no more organized divisions are called for. This takes skill; it is easy to go wrong. So far the method sounds like the method of collection and division defended and practised in the *Sophist* and *Politicus*. And that is exactly the use to which it is put. Socrates divides up the species of pleasure with the ultimate aim of distinguishing the good from the bad pleasures. But the method of collection and division cannot make these distinctions: at best it shows that there is no contradiction involved in saying pleasures are one in being pleasures, but may differ in other respects.

As the method is elaborated, the importance of limits, measures, proportion, and symmetry is increasingly stressed. Good things, good lives for example, are the result of the imposition of a limit or measure on one or more indefinite continua: such are the mixtures, among which the good life is to be found. Most pleasures, though not all, are argued to be unsuited for inclusion in a properly balanced and stable life; most forms of wisdom and even practical skills are worthy of inclusion. Mind plays a dual role; its functions and objects are admirable and desirable in themselves, and mind, being akin to the cosmic cause which accounts for all that is good in the universe, is itself the cause of the measured life.

I call attention to only two aspects of these somewhat tortured passages in the *Philebus*. The first is that no interpretation of the "god-given method", at least none with which I am familiar, can reasonably be said to provide either a substitute for or a supplement to the elenchus of the kind provided by the assumption of the *Gorgias* or the theory of recollection. The method of collection and division does not itself provide a guide as to which the true "units" are, nor how to tell when a division has been made "at the joints". But even if it did, no substantive moral (or other) truths could emerge; nor does Socrates suggest that they could. The four-fold classification of ontological features of the world does far more work, for it is clear that both the categorization of many pleasures as basically "unlimited" and the principles that guide the construction of the good life draw heavily on the necessity of the presence, in all that is desirable, beautiful, or stable, of a limit. What the method entirely fails to do is to provide criteria for telling when a mixture is a good one. Sometimes Socrates talks as if every true mixture is good, and every limit a principle that produces a mixture. But this is no help, for we then want to know how to tell a limit from some other arrangement of parts; how to tell a mixture from a mere grab-bag of ingredients.

Plato seems aware of the fact that the "god-given" method gives no clear guidance in these matters. Although he stresses the superiority of the pure sciences, like mathematics, to the applied arts such as flute-playing and building, he compares the choice of ingredients for the good life, and their blending, to the work of a craftsman; when it comes to describing the good life, Socrates says: "Well, then, it would be a fair enough image to compare us to builders in this matter of the mixture of intelligence and pleasure, and say we had before us the material from which or with which to build." Protagoras: "That's a good comparison."

Socrates: "Then our next business must be to try to mix them?" (*Philebus* 59e). One is reminded of the detailed examples drawn from music and phonetics earlier in the dialogue, which illustrate that producing a pleasing or acceptable product depends on more than the analytic methods which discriminate the ingredients; it depends as well on the skill and knowledge of the craftsman. The theme is familiar from the early Socratic dialogues.[8]

The second aspect of the methodology of the *Philebus* to which I want to call attention is the role, or lack of it, of the theory of Forms. Critics have argued endlessly over the question whether any of the four elements in the "god-given" method is to be identified with the Forms. From the point of view of the present thesis, it doesn't matter. For as we have already seen, *nothing* in that method could, or is claimed to, yield substantive moral truths. Nor is it likely that at this stage in his development Plato would have relied on the theory of Forms for this purpose. In the late dialogues he found more and more reasons to be dissatisfied with his earlier doctrines about the Forms, and no aspect of this dissatisfaction is more evident than the abandonment of any close connection between the Forms and value. The unity of the Forms which earlier had insured their purity was given up when it became evident that analysis required that the Forms blend with one another (as pleasure does with good and bad; the crucial discovery is made in the *Sophist*). The idea that value depends in some way on being like or resembling a Form was recognized by Plato (in the *Parmenides*) to be incompatible with the epistemo-logical or semantic functions of the Forms. Value in the *Philebus* can no longer be connected with the Forms as such; it may be that limits, or mixtures that have limits, are Forms and are good; but what makes them good is not that they are Forms or limits or mixtures, but that they have symmetry, commensurability, and truth—that they are *proper* limits or *appropriate* mixtures.

My proposal, then, is that when, in almost his last dialogue, Plato returned to the question of the nature of the good life, he also returned to the Socratic elenchus as the clearest and most reliable method for discovering how we ought to live. So it seems no surprise to me that in this dialogue the leader is once again

---

[8] For a revealing treatment of this subject see Terence Irwin, *Plato's Moral Theory* (Oxford University Press, 1977).

Socrates. As we know, Socrates practically disappears from all the other late dialogues. In the *Parmenides* he is portrayed as very young, and it is the great Parmenides who directs the questioning, Socrates who responds. In the *Critias* and *Timaeus* Socrates is present, but makes no serious contribution; he is not present in the *Laws*. In the *Sophist* and *Politicus*, the two dialogues most closely related to the *Philebus*, Socrates turns over the discussion to the Eleatic Stranger. Only in the *Philebus* is he once again Plato's spokesman, and, if I am right, again speaks in his own person so far as basic method is concerned. He is Plato's philosopher.

In the *Sophist* we are apparently promised a trio of dialogues, on the sophist, the politician, and the philosopher. The first two dialogues survive; there is no record of the third. By the most likely dating, the *Philebus* was written soon after the *Politicus*, about when the *Philosopher* should have been written. For a number of reasons we can see why the *Philebus* could not be called the *Philosopher*. But I like to think of it as taking the place of that unwritten dialogue. It is about Plato's philosopher, it comes back to the problem with which that philosopher was most concerned, and it accepts his way of doing philosophy for its most important results.

If, as I have argued, Plato returns in the *Philebus* to the confident use of the elenchus, it must be because he decided in the end that Socrates was right to trust that method. Clearly Plato had found nothing better—nothing that he did not come to criticize himself. What explains Plato's renewed confidence in the elenchus? As Vlastos explains, the elenchus would make for truth simply by insuring coherence in a set of beliefs if one could assume that in each of us there are always unshakable true beliefs inconsistent with the false. It is not necessary that these truths be the same for each of us, nor that we be able to identify them except through the extended use of the elenchus. Thus someone who practises the elenchus can, as Socrates repeatedly did, claim that he does not know what is true; it is enough that he has a method that leads to truth. The only question is whether there is reason to accept the assumption.

I think there is good reason to believe the assumption is true— true enough, anyway, to insure that when our beliefs are consistent they will in most large matters be true. The argument for this is long, and I have spelled it out as well as I can elsewhere.[9] But the argument hinges on a good Socratic intuition: it is only in the context of frank discussion, communication, and mutual exchange that trustworthy truths emerge. The dialectic imposes the constant burden of interpretation on questioner and questioned, and the process of mutual interpretation can go forward only because true agreements which survive the elenchus carry a presumption of truth.

In coming to see that Socrates was right to trust the elenchus to do more than insure consistency, Plato was returning to a point at which he started. James Joyce quotes (or misquotes) Maeterlinck as saying: "If Socrates leave his house today he will find the sage seated on his doorstep." The same, I have urged, can be said about Plato; or even about philosophy.

---

[9] In "A Coherence Theory of Truth and Knowledge": *Kant oder Hegel*, ed. D. Henrich (Klett-Cotta, 1983).

16 *The Socratic Concept of Truth*

Why did Socrates practice the elenctic method? One answer is that he thought that by using it he would be led to moral truths. But then the further question arises, why anyone should think the method would lead to such truths. I shall suggest a reason. Suppose I am right, that there is a good reason to expect the elenchus to lead to moral truths. There remains the puzzle why Socrates thought it worth his while to inflict his persistent questions on anyone who would listen. Why did he go around Athens at all hours of the day and night remorselessly pestering friend and foe, adolescent and graybeard, statesman and general, sophist and slave, wise and obtuse, with questions they could not answer, and that he knew they couldn't answer? Yet he was so determined to persist in bugging those around him that he confesses that his countrymen believe not only that he "pours himself out copiously to anyone and everyone without payment, but that [he] would even pay something if anyone would listen" (*Euthyphro* 3d). In prison he brushes off the warning that if he goes on talking he may have to drink twice or even three times as much hemlock, and goes on talking unperturbed (*Phaedo* 63d–e). He tells the jurors at his trial, that his death will be no loss if he is able to examine and question the dead in Hades (*Apology* 40c–41b). There are, then, two questions. The first is why the elenchus should be believed to lead to truth. The second is: even if it is reasonable to expect or hope that practice of the method may lead to truth, what motive did Socrates have for imposing it on others? Though the answers to these questions need not be the same, I think that in fact they are very closely related; and the answers are in both cases philosophically deep.

It is largely to the inspired scholarship of Gregory Vlastos that we owe the rediscovery of Socrates as a fascinating and original philosopher clearly distinct from Plato. The two questions I have asked grow naturally out of Vlastos' discussion of the Socratic elenchus.[1]

Vlastos characterizes the elenchus as follows: Socrates elicits an answer A to a question he puts to a respondent; Socrates then extracts further admissions from the respondent which turn out to entail the falsity of A. The entailment is accepted by both, and (almost always) both concur that this shows (or even proves) that A is false. Vlastos then raises the question: even granting that the respondent has endorsed contradictory views, why should anyone agree, that it is A that has been shown to be false? All that the elenchus shows (assuming that the logic is sound) is that A is not consistent with the subsequent admissions of the respondent. As Duhem taught us, we can escape from a contradiction by giving up any one of the premises with which we started; there is no principle of logic that prompts us to abandon our original assumption. Giving up one or more of the subsequent admissions would do as well.

As Vlastos emphasizes, the logic of the elenchus can do no more than reveal inconsistencies. Nevertheless, recognizing that one's beliefs are inconsistent is progress. Someone with inconsistent beliefs is guaranteed to have at least one false belief; so if recognizing inconsistency prompts someone to eliminate it, the *certainty* of holding a false belief will be removed. But there is nothing in this process that ensures that any of the remaining beliefs is true.

Since there is clear textual evidence that Socrates is often certain that some of his moral beliefs are true,[2] it is a puzzle why Socrates should think the elenchus alone can certify such truths. Vlastos has a surprising answer: Socrates is not depending on the logic of the elenchus alone. Rather, he relies on an idea that is not

---

[1] The articles on which I particularly depend are "The Socratic Elenchus" [SE], in *Oxford Studies in Ancient Philosophy*, Oxford University Press, 1983, pp. 27–58; "Afterthoughts on the Socratic Elenchus", ibid. 71–4; "Socratic Irony", *Classical Quarterly* **37** (1987), pp. 79–96; "The Paradox of Socrates" [PS], in *The Philosophy of Socrates*, ed. Gregory Vlastos, Doubleday & Co., New York, 1971.

[2] For example, that it is better to suffer injustice than to perpetrate it (*Gorgias* 482a–c).

part of the elenchus but an assumption about the nature of human thought. This assumption is that if a respondent gives a false answer, there will always be further beliefs he has in the light of which his answer is false. These further beliefs may not always be clear or explicit, but they can be made so by elenctic questioning. As Vlastos puts it, "... we may all be said to 'believe' innumerable things that have never entered our heads but are none the less *entailed* by what we believe in the common or garden sense of the word" (SE, p. 51). The elenchus draws out these further beliefs, and demonstrates that they conflict with the original proposal.

The "tremendous" assumption on which Socrates depends is stated this way by Vlastos:

> *A* Anyone who ever has a false moral belief will always have at the same time true beliefs entailing the negation of that false belief.[3]

Even this assumption is not sufficient to insure that the elenchus will lead to truth, however, for no reason has been given for supposing that the beliefs that contradict the original proposal are true. So far as logic is concerned, one can be consistently wrong as easily (*exactly* as easily) as consistently right. What is required in addition is something like this: there are basic truths no one will concede are false. Therefore anyone with a false moral belief is doomed to remain in a contradictory state. There are suggestions that Socrates believed this (*Gorgias* 482a–c), and his practice certainly seems to assume it. Let us then make explicit the assumption Socrates needs in order to justify a claim that the elenchus will force anyone who wants to avoid contradiction to jettison his false beliefs:

> *B* Anyone who ever has a false moral belief will always have at the same time true beliefs which he will not surrender and which entail the negation of that false belief.

I think Vlastos has *B* in mind rather than *A*.[4] In any case, Vlastos notes that Socrates never presents arguments in support

---

[3] SE, p. 52.

[4] Vlastos' discussion leading to the statement of *A* makes it fairly clear that this is what he has in mind.

of his method; it may well rest on assumptions of which he was not aware. According to Vlastos, Socrates was not obsessed with methodology; he believed in his method, but did not reflect on it or defend it. It was Plato who came to question the method, and subsequently invented a number of alternatives, none of which in the end proved superior.[5]

Must we accept *B*, or something like it, on faith? I do not think so. I think there are excellent reasons to accept *B* in a slightly modified form. There is no evidence that Socrates had these reasons, nor that he even asked for reasons for accepting his "tremendous assumption". So let me emphasize that here I depart from scholarship, and ask the unhistorical question: was Socrates right to lodge so much faith in his method, and if so, why?

A is, I have argued, not sufficient to justify the use of the elenchus; now I want to urge that neither it nor *B* is necessary. The elenchus can be justified on the basis of the following, somewhat weaker, assumption:

> *C*   There is a presumption that one's serious (firmly held) moral beliefs are true.

If this is so, it is highly unlikely that a false moral belief can be made to consort with the weight of one's serious moral beliefs.

Elenctic reflection which eliminates contradictions will, then, probably result in true moral beliefs. If we accept *C*, and our moral beliefs are in fact true, we can be said to have moral knowledge, for we would have justified true moral beliefs.

But is *C* correct? I think we can see that it is by asking how it is that we assign contents to the thoughts of others. I begin by making an assumption that is Socratic in character: there is a close connection between thought and language, especially spoken language. At least with respect to our more careful and transparent thoughts—and here I do not distinguish between evaluative judgments and "factual" beliefs—what we say when we honestly speak our minds reveals something we really think. Our thoughts may be confused, and we may think much that we cannot at the

---

[5] This is my conclusion, not Vlastos'. In "Plato's Philosopher", *London Review of Books*, 1 August, 1985 [Ch. 15 above], I suggest that near the end of his writing career, in the *Philebus*, Plato himself despaired of a better method, and returned to the elenchus.

moment articulate, but what we do articulate provides a genuine window on the soul. Language is necessarily public; there can be nothing in the literal meaning of our words that cannot in principle be made out by a sympathetic and persistent interpreter. So what such an interpreter determines our thoughts to be is what, confusion aside, they really are.

The elements of correct interpretation are such as to ensure a large degree of truth. We must find others largely consistent and right in what they believe as a condition of making them intelligible, that is, as having thoughts at all. But since what we find is what is really there, it follows that rational creatures, creatures with thoughts, must be largely consistent and correct in their beliefs.

This is a large and difficult subject about which I have written at length elsewhere.[6] Here I offer an example to give the flavor of the position. Suppose I am trying to interpret a speaker I do not understand. I notice that she is caused to utter the words "Sta korg" when and only when a red object is in plain sight, well illuminated, and she is facing it. If further experiments bear this out, I tentatively translate her sentence "That is red". It is obvious that this is just the sort of evidence on which we depend for learning a language; nor can this fail to be the kind of connection between speaker, interpreter, and world that in fact determines the meanings of the simplest and most basic sentences, and hence also determines the contents of the thoughts expressed by those sentences. But this simple observation has momentous implications; if this is the way the meanings of sentences and the contents of thoughts are determined, there is no way we can be generally mistaken in our overall picture of the world and our place in it. The basis of all social understanding is a background of thoughts on which we are largely in agreement.

Something similar, though more complex, seems to me to hold for evaluative judgments. Just as general concordance makes both communication and thought possible with respect to "factual" matters, so our understanding of the values of others depends on

---

[6] See the essays in *Inquiries into Truth and Interpretation*, Oxford University Press, 1984, and "Rational Animals", *Dialectica* **36** (1982), pp. 317–27. For the application to evaluative judgments, see "Expressing Evaluations", The Lindley Lecture, University of Kansas Press, 1984.

enough that is shared to allow us to make sense of what is not shared, and to provide legitimate grounds for the resolution of moral differences. This holds, of course, only to the extent that we really do understand the thoughts and values of another. To take the very simplest case, and to take it in a way that requires a great deal of elaboration before it can be accepted: in the beginning, there cannot be a complete discontinuity between how we learn the meaning of the word "red", and hence to apply it correctly most of the time, and how we learn the words "good" and "right". There are important differences, but they are not as important as the similarities.

These reflections, adequately developed, can justify Socrates' dependence on the elenchus as a method for achieving moral truth, and to make that dependence something that does not have to be accepted on the basis of unsupported intuition or faith. At the same time, it is clear that beliefs that survive elenctic investigation are not guaranteed to be true. When it is properly practiced, one is justified in accepting the results, and they are probably true. If they are true, they therefore constitute knowledge in the ordinary sense of justified true belief, but the elenchus, as Vlastos says, does not confer certainty. It is when thinking of knowledge as requiring certainty, according to Vlastos, that Socrates says he does not know moral truths.

I come now to my second puzzle: what motive might Socrates have had to employ the elenchus as he did? (What motive might *anyone* have?) This question may seem already to have been answered, since if I am right, it is a method that generally leads to truth. But for whom? If it is Socrates who searches for the truth, what is to prevent him from pursuing his method in seclusion? He seems to accept the oracle's deliverance that no one is wiser than he, even though the reason may simply be that he alone knows that he doesn't have wisdom (in the sense of certainty). And his experience with questioning others seldom if ever suggests that Socrates has learned anything from the exchange.[7] What the dialogues show us, again and again, is that Socrates is able to show

---

[7] The *Philebus*, far too late in Plato's career to count as Socratic for most scholars, may contain an exception: Socrates begins by claiming that a life of pure thought is best, but the elenchus (administered by Socrates to himself) shows that a mixed life of reason and pleasure is better still.

that his respondents are confused, that their claims to know what piety or courage or virtue is are mistaken in the light of other views they themselves hold. The wisdom that is gained is entirely negative: a number of false views are revealed as such, but the elenchus is never shown to lead to a major moral truth. Socrates does claim to know certain moral truths; but these are presented as premises, not conclusions, of elenctic argument, and they are premises with which his respondents agree. There is no reason to think, then, that Socrates practices the elenchus on others in the hope that they know something he doesn't.

Does he do it then for the benefit of others? There are two reasons to doubt this. The first is simply that the Socratic dialogues testify that it doesn't work. Socrates' victims end up confused, irritated, even insulted, but seldom do they claim to be, or seem to be, improved. As Vlastos says, "Plato's Socrates is not persuasive at all. He wins every argument, but never manages to win over an opponent"(PS, p. 2). The unexamined life may not be worth living, but there is no sign that his patient's lives improve after Socrates' examinations.

The second reason for doubting that Socrates examined others primarily for the sake of improving their souls springs from the first. Given that it was overwhelmingly clear that others were annoyed rather than aided by his blunt administrations, it is hard to believe Socrates nevertheless persisted in a hubristic attempt to improve them. Perhaps Socrates did, as Vlastos suggests, lack a kind of human sympathy in not appreciating that it is possible to be virtuous without being able to answer the question "What is virtue?" to Socrates' satisfaction; but he was not stupid or cruel.

There is another reason, or excuse, offered by Socrates himself for his persistent pestering of his fellow citizens (or anyone else in range). This is that he would rather live among good citizens than bad; he must therefore be convinced, whether rightly or wrongly, that his questioning is doing some good, to others as well as to himself (*Apology* 25c ff.). This does perhaps lend some weight to the idea that Socrates believed his ministrations improved others in spite of his apparent failures; but it does not provide a respectable motive unless one supposes he was foolish enough to think he could somehow reform an entire society against its will.

Finally, there is Socrates' daimon who, he tells us, has instructed him to spend his time questioning and examining everyone he meets, especially those who think themselves wise. We can take this seriously as an *additional* reason for pursuing the elenchus only if we suppose Socrates thought he should accept the edicts of an authoritative voice unaccompanied by arguments. I cannot credit this suggestion. Though the urgings and prohibitions of the daimon no doubt accorded with strong Socratic intuitions, intuitions perhaps in some sense religious, Socrates would have heeded them only if he thought them rational.

It may be that I underestimate the power of—and textual evidence for—some of the arguments for the public practice of the elenchus that I have so hastily reviewed. But I would like to suggest that there is a further argument that is more persuasive, and more interesting, than any I have yet mentioned. This is that Socrates was convinced that he himself would gain in wisdom and clarity from elenctic exchanges with others even if they were not as wise as he.

There is doubtless much irony in Socrates' frequently expressed desire to learn from others. There is a serious point, however, behind Socrates' reply to Euthyphro when Euthyphro says Socrates has understood him perfectly: "Yes, my friend (says Socrates), for I am eager for your wisdom, and give my mind to it, so that nothing you say shall fall to the ground" (*Euthyphro* 14d). Socrates may be kidding when he credits Euthyphro with wisdom; but he is serious about wanting to understand him. Socrates frequently remarks that he is as prepared to find that he is wrong as that those he questions are. When Protagoras asks whether he should answer for himself or as "the multitude" would Socrates replies "It makes no difference to me, provided you do the answering. For what I chiefly examine is the proposition. But the consequence may be that I the questioner and you the answerer will also be examined" (*Protagoras* 333b–c). Meno is pleased by the style of Socrates' answers, and he replies "Well then, I will spare no endeavor, both for your sake *and for my own* [my italics], to continue in that style" (*Meno* 77a). A bit later in the same dialogue we find Socrates saying,

It is not from any sureness in myself that I cause others to doubt; it is from being more in doubt than anyone else that I cause doubt in others. So now, for my part, I have no idea what virtue is, while you, though perhaps you may have known before you came in touch with me, are now as good as ignorant of it also. But none the less I am willing to join you in examining it and inquiring into its nature. (*Meno* 80c–d)

When Critias accuses Socrates of trying to refute him rather than pursue the argument, Socrates replies,

And what if I am? How can you think that I have any other motive in refuting you but what I should have in examining into myself? This motive would be just a fear of my unconsciously fancying that I knew something of which I was ignorant. And at this moment, I assure you, I pursue the argument chiefly for my own sake, and perhaps in some degree also for the sake of my other friends. (*Charmides* 166c–d)

Or, again, "Protagoras, do not suppose that I have any other desire in debating with you than to examine the difficulties which occur to me at each point" (*Protagoras* 348c).

What these passages, as well as Socrates' actual practice, strongly suggest is that he believed, to the point of knowingly and willingly risking his life for it, that *verbal exchange*, in the form of the elenchus, provided the main, or sole, access to moral wisdom. I take Socrates seriously when he explains why speech is superior to writing. Writing, he says, is like painting: the figures stand there as if they were alive, but if you ask them a question they are silent. Written words are like that: they seem intelligent, but if you question them they say the same thing over and over (*Phaedrus* 275d).

Why, though, did Socrates believe verbal communication, properly conducted, could lead him to the recognition of truths? He did not say, and I cannot answer for him. But I can give a reason why *I* believe it. The answer lies, as did the answer to our first puzzle, in the way the contents of one person's thought and judgment depend on his relations to other people and to the world. We think of dialogue as a process in which fully formed thoughts are exchanged, and we overlook the fact that dialogue supplies the nexus in which thoughts and concepts are formed and given meaning. Thought and rationality are, as I said before, social phenomena. Without language, thoughts have no clear shape; but the shape language gives them emerges only in the context of active communication. What we think depends on what others can make of us and of our relations to the world we share with them. It follows that we have no clear thoughts except as these are sharpened in the process of being grasped by others. When Socrates insists again and again in the *Meno* that it is bootless to ask whether virtue can be taught until one knows what virtue is, he is not, as is often supposed, bemoaning the failure to come up with a neat and final answer to the question, "What is virtue?" He is inviting his companions to continue in the search for mutual clarity and understanding—the only method he knows for achieving moral truth.

We ought to distinguish between lack of consistency and lack of clarity. In the Socratic dialogues respondents find themselves *saying* things that are contradictory. But what this reveals is not necessarily that they have clear ideas that conflict; the appearance of contradiction more commonly betrays real confusion. There is a genuine sense in which someone who is confused can't be straightforwardly wrong, for he simply doesn't know what he thinks. Dialogue, particularly in the form of the elenchus, provides the forum in which alone words take on meaning and concepts are slowly clarified. The better we understand others the better we know what we think.

It seems puzzling that Socrates is always asking, "What is virtue?", "What is piety?", "What is justice?", and never finding a satisfactory answer. Never. Is he trying to find out what virtue or piety or justice is, or to find out what he and others mean by the words? How can we separate these issues? We cannot hope to learn what these virtues are without learning what the words mean, or to learn what the words mean without learning what people, ourselves and others, mean by them. People mean what others can take them to mean; to learn what we mean *is* to learn what others we talk with mean. Understanding others, agreeing with them on basic concepts, clarity about what we mean, come, to the extent they do, together. The elenchus is a model of our only method for promoting these ends.

17 *Dialectic and Dialogue*

This is the talk I gave when the City of Stuttgart did me the honor of awarding me the Hegel prize. Since I was the first non-European philosopher to receive this award, I interpreted the occasion as marking another step in the remarkable rapprochement that is now taking place between what for a time seemed two distinct, even hostile, philosophical methods, attitudes and traditions. What we are witnessing is, of course, really no more than the re-engagement of traditions that share a common heritage. But this makes it no less surprising, since as we know it is those who are closest in their presuppositions who are most apt to exaggerate and dwell on their differences. To understand is not to forgive, and to half-understand is all too often to reject.

The assumption that there are two radically different traditions is not restricted to continents or countries; the sense that there is a great philosophical divide is perhaps stronger within my country than it is in Europe. I recently read a history of the development of philosophy from Husserl to the present by a fine scholar who was a classmate of mine at Harvard in the late 30s. As far as one can tell, nothing that happened in England, Australia, or the United States, from Russell and Moore to the present day, contributed anything of serious interest to philosophy. His index mentions exactly one English speaking philosopher, and then only to attack him as a shallow commentator on German and French thinkers. (Of course he also ignores the influence of Frege, the Vienna Circle, Wittgenstein, and the Polish logicians.) I am glad to say I do not find this attitude widespread today in Germany. The present volume [*Language, Mind and Epistemology*, ed. G. Preyer *et al.* (Dordrecht: Kluwer, 1994)] is one among a number of evidences of the new openness to the pleasures and advantages of the free exchange of ideas drawn from philosophical cultures that until recently often seemed so disparate as to preclude productive conversation.

When I chose it, I was unaware that the title I had given this talk was nearly identical with the English title of a book of essays on Plato by another recipient of the Hegel prize, Professor Hans-Georg Gadamer.[1] The coincidence of titles was not completely accidental, however. Some half a century ago, when I was writing my doctoral dissertation on Plato's *Philebus,* I discovered that by far the most profound commentary on the *Philebus* was Professor Gadamer's published dissertation.[2] So there is a long history to our shared interest in Plato, the dialectical method, and problems of interpretation. It is natural that Hegel should provide another bridging element.

The *Philebus* was one of Plato's last dialogues, and in it Socrates makes his last appearance as principle interlocutor. It is remarkable that after the didactic splendors of the middle and other late dialogues, Plato here returns to the elenctic method of his early writings, the inconclusive dialectic of conversational give and take, thesis and rebuttal, that we correctly think of as typical of Socrates. What is so special about this method, and why should anyone believe or expect that it would produce valuable results?

In its simplest form, the elenchus involves just two people, one who asks and one who answers. The questioner has some portentous question: what is courage, what is justice, what is virtue? When an answer has been elicited, the questioner then sets about proving to the answerer that his answer is inconsistent with other things he believes. The answerer now tries to amend or replace the original answer in order to bring his answer into line with his other professed beliefs. This process can continue through a number of steps, but it never arrives at a satisfactory conclusion. Those are the bare bones of the method; as fleshed out in the Socratic dialogues, there are additional features that attract our attention. The answerer is usually someone who claims, or should be in a position to claim, that he knows the answer: he is a wealthy landowner who professes to know what piety is, or a general who

---

[1] Hans-Georg Gadamer, *Dialogue and Dialectic*, Yale University Press, 1980.

[2] Hans-Georg Gadamer, *Philebus; Platos dialektische Ethik*, Leipzig, 1931. My dissertation has recently been published: *Plato's* Philebus, Garland Publishing Co., 1990.

should know what courage is. The elenctic treatment discloses his ignorance of what he pretends to know. Given the inconclusive outcome, the method seems designed more to discomfit the victim than to discover the truth.

And how could this procedure discover truth? The original answer proffered by the respondent is shown to be inconsistent with other things he believes, and this is treated as showing that the original answer is false; but logic cannot take us this far. If each proposition in a set of mutually inconsistent propositions is required for inconsistency, then withdrawing any proposition in the set is enough to produce consistency. If consistency is the sole aim, Socrates' respondents could as well cleave to their original answers by abandoning some subsequent admission. Worse still, there is no reason to suppose any proposition in a consistent set is true. The most that can be said for the elenchus is apparently that by eliminating inconsistencies it removes the logical certainty that at least one of a person's beliefs is false; relatively small comfort in return for a considerable investment of time and ego.[3]

It has been suggested that Socrates was convinced that every man is in possession of certain basic truths, so that wisdom can be achieved by weeding out the beliefs that are inconsistent with the basic truths.[4] Whether or not Socrates believed or assumed this I do not know, but I think something like this is a sound idea. There are very good reasons to suppose that it is not possible that most, or even many, of our simplest, and in this sense most basic, beliefs are false; we cannot be wrong in thinking there is a world outside our minds, a world that contains other people, plants and animals, pastures and mountains, buildings and stars. To argue for this view is a large task that I cannot undertake now;[5] and it would be to no avail, for though the assumption of a general endowment of truths may improve the odds that the elenchus will clear out the deadwood of error and leave the trees of truth standing, this cannot explain Socrates' faith in his method. The

---

[3] The importance of this feature of the elenchus is stressed in Gregory Vlastos' brilliant book, *Socrates: Ironist and Moral Philosopher*, Cambridge University Press, 1991.

[4] Vlastos has suggested something close to this in "The Socratic Elenchus", in *Oxford Studies in Ancient Philosophy*, Oxford University Press, 1983, pp. 27–58.

[5] Arguments in support of this thesis can be found in my "A Coherence Theory of Truth and Knowledge", in *Kant oder Hegel*, ed. Dieter Henrich, Klett-Cotta, 1983, pp. 423–38.

reason is that it cannot explain why the elenchus is the sole, or even an efficient, route to the truth.

If Socrates knew the way to the truth, why didn't he follow it on his own and announce the result to those who would listen? Instead, he insisted that he did not know the truth. Many scholars have taken this disclaimer as Socratic irony, a form of open pretense. But I think we must take him at his word, for he also stoutly maintains, with no touch of irony that one can detect, that he himself expects to profit from the elenctic exchange, even though the elenchus seems to do no more than reveal the ignorance of his respondents. Socrates says,

It is not from any sureness in myself that I cause others to doubt; it is from being more in doubt than anyone else that I cause doubt in others. So now, for my part, I have no idea what virtue is, while you, though perhaps you may have known before you came in touch with me, are now as good as ignorant of it also. But none the less I am willing to join you in examining it and inquiring into its nature. (*Meno* 80C–D)[6]

Finally, we should bear in mind the famous passage in the *Phaedrus* where Socrates explains why a living discussion is altogether superior to a written record of that discussion. Written words, he says, seem alive, but when you question them they always give the same answer. A word, once written, is tossed about both by those who understand it and by those with no interest.[7]

So there are two vital aspects of the Socratic dialectic which transcend the mere attempt to convict a pretender to knowledge of inconsistency. One is that both participants can hope to profit; the other is that unlike a written treatise, it represents a process which engenders change. If it attains its purpose, an elenctic discussion is an event in which the meanings of words, the concepts entertained by the speakers, evolve and are clarified. In this respect it is a model of every successful attempt at communication.

[6] Here are two more examples: When Protagoras asks whether he should answer for himself or as "the multitude" would, Socrates replies "It makes no difference to me, provided you do the answering. For what I chiefly examine is the proposition. But the consequence may be that I the questioner and you the answerer will also be examined" (*Protagoras* 333B–C). Meno is pleased by the style of Socrates' answers, and Socrates replies "Well then, I will spare no endeavor, both for your sake *and for my own* [my italics], to continue in that style" (*Meno* 77A).   [7] *Phaedrus* 275E.

There can be a great difference between a dispute involving people who understand each other well, and an exchange in which achieving mutual understanding is a large part of the problem. But there is an even greater chasm between an exchange viewed as a situation in which the participants have clear concepts whether or not they use the same words to express those concepts, and an exchange seen as a process in which the concepts themselves come into focus. A written discussion veils this distinction almost completely. Writing reduces the number of active interpreters to one, the reader, thus eliminating the interaction of minds in which words can be bent to new uses and ideas progressively shaped. Writing may portray, but cannot constitute, the intersubjective exchanges in which meanings are created and firmed. Socrates was right: reading is not enough. If we want to approach the harder wisdom we must talk, and, of course, listen.

I have just alluded to the passage in which Plato explains the superiority of the spoken word over the written. We should interpret this passage in the light of another passage in which Socrates persuades his respondent, Euthyphro, that he cannot mean what he has said about the nature of piety. Euthyphro complains that Socrates makes his words move about; they won't stay put. Socrates agrees that he does this, though not intentionally; just as Daedalus made his statues move, Socrates makes the words of others move, though he would rather that they stood still.[8] This is just the sort of movement that is at its best in an oral exchange. As they try to understand each other, people in open discussion use the same words, but whether they mean the same things by those words, or mean anything clear at all, only the process of question and answer can reveal.

It is easy to confuse what goes on in a live conversation with what we find in a written dialogue. If we read that someone, under questioning, says "Justice is doing good to one's friends and evil to one's enemies", and subsequently is honestly persuaded that it is not just to do evil to anyone, using the same word, "justice", we are almost certain to conclude that the speaker has radically changed his mind. The original statement and the later admission, we say to ourselves, contradict each other. And so they do if the word "justice" means the same thing in both occurrences. We are

---

[8] *Euthyphro* 11B–E.

almost certain to take fixity of meaning for granted because as passive readers we attach the same meaning to the word each time we read it—or at least we assume the word has the same meaning from start to finish, for otherwise what are the discussants discussing? Yet in truth it often happens that what is being discussed is exactly the issue.

We have a strong tendency to believe that thoughts almost always have a definite content. Like Euthyphro we may have trouble finding the right words; a clever questioner like Socrates may be able to trip us up; we may fall into confusion on occasion. But for the most part, we think we know what we think and mean. Language is just the sometimes awkward tool we use to express our thoughts. I suggest that this picture, which seems so natural, misrepresents the actual situation; until we abandon the assumption that our important ideas are clear, we will not appreciate the power and purpose of the elenctic method. Let me give an admittedly contentious example. Many people are convinced that if they are sometimes free to act as they please, then their actions cannot be caused, or, if caused, then caused by a will that is not itself caused. Such a person may also believe he is in fact sometimes free to act as he pleases, and yet that determinism is true. This looks like outright inconsistency, and it may be. But more likely it is a matter of confused or unclear concepts: both the idea of a free action and the idea of determinism are difficult concepts, for most of us they are concepts clouded with confusion. A discussion cannot be expected to solve the "problem of free will" if the concepts used to state "the problem" are murky, for no clear problem will have been formulated. What a discussion can do, with luck, is dispel some of the fog; it can at least reveal that our aporia is due to the fact, not that we are grappling with a deep metaphysical puzzle, but that we need better or different concepts.

It may seem that all that is needed to improve matters is to insist that the key terms be defined at the start. This strategy supposes, however, that we already have at hand a supply of clear concepts, and words to express them. But if the word on which we are trying to bestow a clear meaning is not yet clear, it is unlikely that we will have an appropriate reservoir of precise words and concepts available to employ in the definition. There is also the question, given that the word we wish to define stands for no clear idea, how we will recognize that a definition is correct. There is another, even more basic difficulty with the definitional strategy: there may not be a satisfactory definition. The Socratic dialogues typically have the form of a search for a definition; what is it, Socrates will ask, that all cases of virtue, or beauty, have in common, and the proposed answers have the form of definitions. Why is the search always a failure? The reason, I think, is simple. We have no interest in a definition that does not employ concepts or words that are simpler and more basic than the definiendum. But the words and ideas we seek to define in philosophy, words like "justice", "beauty", "truth", "virtue", "knowledge", are as basic as you can get. Unless you are going to go in circles, everything can't be defined. These words and the work they do, confused and murky as they may be, are part of the foundations of our thinking. It is a mistake to try to dig deeper. Definition is not the way to make the foundations firm.

It often happens that we use words we do not fully understand, but this is possible only if there is something there to be understood. I may use the word "quark", for example. I have a vague idea what it means, and I know where to go to find out more. (To find out much more I would have to learn a lot of physics and mathematics that I don't now begin to command: a full understanding of the word "quark" would require knowing how it features in certain theories.) In such a case there is more to know about the word because there are others who use it for communication and calculations in ways I cannot; there is something for me to learn. The advances we can hope for in philosophical dialogue are not like this; as Socrates insists, he cannot teach people what virtue or justice are, for he does not know himself. I take this to mean, not that there is a clear concept available, but that the elenchus may, if properly conducted, help the participants create a clearer idea.

Discussion that revolves around the word "freedom", to choose another example, may bog down because there may be an unnoticed ambiguity in the way the word is being used. Heeding the existence of ambiguity and resolving it is an obviously useful exercise. It is frequently necessary if a conversation is to make progress. But again, important as disambiguation is to clarity and understanding, it requires that there already be available the two or more concepts into which the various meanings of the ambiguous word are resolved. This process therefore cannot be the same process in which a new concept is forged, perhaps by giving an old word a clearer or a more productive role.

Definition and disambiguation are powerful tools in the service of better thinking and improved communication. It is a mistake, though, to suppose we understand what a perfect language would be like. It is possible to imagine, or even invent, languages with a simpler and less misleading grammar than English or French or Croatian, a language in which the logical relations among sentences are easy to discern, and the rules of deductive reasoning made perspicuous. We might even learn to speak such a language, as our computers in a sense already do. But there would remain the task of assigning meanings to the elements, the basic vocabulary of nouns and verbs and the rest, and this we could do only by using our familiar resources.

We are apt to think of a natural language as a definite monolithic structure. As each of us learns his or her first language, it seems like a given, something each person absorbs as best he or she can, something which, if completely mastered, would insure flawless mutual understanding. It is hard to shake this conception of language, but of course it must be wrong. Languages were not bestowed on mankind; until people talked there were no languages. The ultimate goal in speaking cannot be to get the language right, but to be understood, for there is no point to language beyond successful communication. Speakers create the language; meaning is what we can abstract from accomplished verbal exchanges. It follows that a language cannot have a life of its own, a life apart from its users.

I see the Socratic elenchus as a crucible in which some of our most important words, and the concepts they express, are tested, melted down, reshaped, and given a new edge. It is a microcosm of the ongoing process of language formation itself, though a sophisticated and self-conscious microcosm which takes advantage of rich and complex linguistic and cultural institutions already in existence. To illustrate the point, let me compare a feature of elementary language learning with the cooperative reworking of verbal usage that occurs in dialectical exchange.

In learning a first language, many words must be learned by ostension, which involves pointing or otherwise indicating objects, surfaces, or events to which the word applies: we all first learned how to use words like "green", "horse", "hammer" and "rain" in this way. Of course some of these words might be learned instead by looking in a dictionary; but only if other words had first been learned by ostension. Ostension has an obvious limitation: in our whole lives we can be exposed to no more than some finite number of examples. There is always the chance that when a new case arises the learner will deviate from the norm. As the new word is gradually surrounded by a growing ocean of other words, some of them closely connected to the new, the chances of deviation shrink, but never vanish. At some point, the difference between learning a new word and sharpening the use of a familiar word in the process of discussion disappears. After all, even in the learning situation the deviant learner deviates not from some abstract rule or norm but from what the teacher, and perhaps the rest of the community, agree on. The ordinary learner is simply someone who, perhaps wisely, has been persuaded for the moment to suit his practice to that of one or more others. A stubbornly deviant learner, on the other hand, may have an insight into a deep similarity of cases that others have missed, and she may carry the community with her. This is exactly what Socrates does, or attempts to do, when he tries to persuade his companions to stop using the word "just" to apply to acts in which someone returns harm for harm, and to apply it instead to acts that return benefit for harm.

Our words are at their best when applied to familiar examples. They become increasingly vague or undefined as we approach the borderlines or the unusual. When does green become blue? Is disagreement here disagreement over the word, or the color? It hardly matters, for the outcome is the same: what we come to agree on shapes our language and our thinking, and it shapes how we come to view the world. Color words are a trivial example. When the words concern our fundamental values and beliefs, words like "knowledge" and "virtue", "honesty" and "person", the changes effected in our language by searching, sympathetic discussion can make a profound difference to how we live together. As Gregory Vlastos splendidly says, someone who, like Socrates, practices the dialectic method accepts "the burden of freedom which is inherent in all significant communication".[9]

---

[9] *Socrates: Ironist and Moral Philosopher*, p. 44.

18 *Gadamer and Plato's* Philebus

In 1931 Gadamer published his first book, *Platos dialektische Ethik*; a second edition, with additions, came out in 1968; the first edition was reprinted in 1982; and an English translation (*Plato's Dialectical Ethics*) appeared in 1991.[1] The book was Gadamer's *Habilitationsschrift,* written under the supervision of Martin Heidegger. It would be strange to make this early work, written more than sixty years ago, the launching platform for a discussion of, or reaction to, certain lasting themes in Gadamer's writings if it were not for two things: despite the enormous enlargement in the areas and problems on which Gadamer has worked, the direction in which his ideas were to develop was already quite clear. The second thing is personal: where Gadamer sensed from the start the goal he would pursue, and pursued it with brilliant success, I by chance started in somewhat the same place (but without the clear goal) and have, by what seems to me a largely accidental but commodius vicus of recirculation, arrived in Gadamer's intellectual neighborhood.

Plato's Dialectical Ethics is, as its author points out in the Preface to the first edition, really two extended essays. The first of these essays is a general discussion of Plato's dialectic, and its basis in dialogue. It is clear that though the ostensible purpose is to allow us to approach the Platonic texts with a fresh eye, Gadamer is also illustrating not only his idea of how the interpretation of any text is to proceed, but the foundation of the possibility of objective thought. Gadamer makes no excuses for

[1] First edition, F. Meiner, Leipzig; German reprinting of the first edition, F. Meiner Verlag GmbH, Hamburg; English edition (translated and with an introduction by Robert M. Wallace), Yale University Press, New Haven.

the "distance" between the issues he raises and the actual texts of Plato; on the contrary, he advertises this distance: "The closer these interpretations adhere to Plato's text, the more distant they are from their task of clearing the way toward that text. The more distant they are from the world of Plato's language and thought, on the other hand, the closer I believe they come to performing their task."[2]

The second essay is on the text for which the first essay clears the way: Plato's *Philebus*. At first this dialogue seems a curious choice. It is in many ways an awkward piece. The construction lacks the easy grace of many of the early and middle dialogues: highly general and abstract passages are seemingly patched together with the most practical consideration of what makes various pleasures worthwhile; details expand to pages while vital issues are passed over. It is unclear what role the Forms play if any; yet this is a treatise on the highest good for man. Most unsettling of all is the fact that Socrates practices the elenctic method in ways that are highly reminiscent of the early dialogues, while at the same time promoting doctrines with which he is not explicitly associated in any other dialogue—indeed, doctrines it is not easy to identify elsewhere in the Platonic corpus. Perhaps it is not surprising that the text is apparently corrupt in some of the most troublesome passages, almost as if copiers could not believe what they were reading, and attempted crude improvements. One has only to glance at Jowett's translation of the *Philebus* to appreciate how strongly he was tempted to warp what is plainly in the text in the effort to make it fit with what Jowett felt was the true Platonic line.

None of this fazes Gadamer. While he is a superb Classicist, and discusses textual problems when they seem important, his interest in the *Philebus* is entirely centered on its philosophical content. This makes Gadamer's book unique. There is not, as far as I know, anything like it; not in English, not in German, not in French is there another book about the *Philebus,* or an edition or translation, which concentrates on the ethical, methodological, and ontological thought in the dialogue. Gadamer's book is, as he plainly intended, not only an eye-opening account of what is to be found in Plato, not only a stunning essay on the origins of

---

[2] *Plato's Dialectical Ethics*, p. xxv.

objectivity in communal discussion; it is a demonstration of what the interpretation of a text can be.

It was about the year 1938 that I became interested in the *Philebus*; I was an undergraduate at Harvard, studying Greek and philosophy. My concern with the dialogue was more literary than philosophical; to be more accurate, I was interested in the history of ideas. Under the influence of the writings of Cherniss and of my tutors, particularly John Finley, Harry Levin, and Theodore Spencer, I became fascinated with the hints of Pythagoreanism in the *Philebus,* and the suggestion that in this dialogue one finds apparent confirmation of some of Aristotle's reports of Plato's late views. I also proposed that the *Philebus,* if not actually the promised dialogue on the Philosopher which was to follow the *Sophist* and the *Politicus,* could be viewed as a sort of substitute for it. When the time came, a few years later, to write a doctoral dissertation, I naturally turned to the *Philebus*. It was then that I came across Gadamer's book. Being a product of American education, neither my German nor my Greek was very good (they still aren't), and so I unfortunately learned very little from Gadamer; for one thing, the Heideggerian background of his ideas was completely unfamiliar to me. What I did notice, however, was the concentration on the philosophical content for its own sake, and this impressed me.

My progress toward the Ph.D. was interrupted by the war; after the war I took on heavy teaching duties, and it was not until 1949 that I completed my degree. Meanwhile my interests had largely shifted from the history of philosophy to the analytic problems of the period. As a result my dissertation on the *Philebus* was a rather plodding attempt to see Plato as much as possible in the light of the contemporary methods and issues with which I was involved.[3] Plato slowly receded into the background of my thoughts, though from time to time I taught a course or a seminar on the later dialogues until, in 1985, I was invited to give the S. J. Keeling Memorial Lecture in Greek Philosophy at University College London. This led to a renewed interest in Plato and the *Philebus*; I read some of the more recent literature, and was particularly struck by the treatment of the elenchus by my

---

[3] This curious product of my philosophical youth has now been published: *Plato's* Philebus, Garland Publishing Co., New York, 1990.

friend and ex-colleague from Princeton, Gregory Vlastos. Vlastos was engaged in writing his magisterial book on Socrates.[4] He was mainly concerned to distinguish, even contrast, the views of Socrates and Plato, and so his treatment of the elenchus, which he considered to be characteristically Socratic, was restricted to the early dialogues; already in the *Meno,* he thought, Plato had taken over from his mentor. I was impressed, however, with the extent to which the *Philebus* seemed to mark a return to the earlier methodology, with the extent to which its concern with human virtue looked back to the early dialogues, and with the fact that Socrates again guided the discussion without assuming he knew all the answers in advance. In writing my Keeling Lecture, "Plato's Philosopher", I found it natural to connect my present philosophical interests with what I now found in the *Philebus.*[5] Thus there is a certain parallel between my experience and Gadamer's with one of Plato's oddest dialogues; and a vast difference. The dialogue touched both of us near the beginnings of our professional careers, and it connects with our present interests. The difference is that Gadamer appreciated from the start what was in the dialogue for him, and though his views developed, and his interpretation of Plato underwent some change, he never backed away from the thesis that free discussion is the source of human understanding, nor from his recognition that Plato had revealed and exploited this truth; I, on the other hand, lost my fascination with Plato over a period of decades, and only recently, and by a very different path from Gadamer's, have come to grasp some of what I dimly, if at all, understood the first time around.

The *Philebus* opens with a discussion led by Socrates that is more reminiscent of the early elenctic dialogues in mood and method than anything else in Plato's middle or late dialogues. The question to be decided is what is most excellent and advantageous in a human life; or, as the issue is sharpened, what is the character of the best life. Socrates and Philebus each have a candidate answer: Philebus says the good is pleasure, Socrates that it is wisdom. As in the early dialogues, Socrates does not claim to know the answer; he insists that only a free discussion can hope

---

[4] The book was not published until 1991: *Socrates: Ironist and Moral Philosopher,* Cambridge University Press.

[5] "Plato's Philosopher", *London Review of Books,* vol. 7, no. 14, 1985, pp. 15–17; [Ch. 15 above].

to illuminate the subject. He is determined that his interlocutor shall say what he really thinks, and not merely strive for a verbal victory. It may well be, as Gadamer suggests, that Protarchus takes over the "defense" of Philebus' position because Philebus seems uninterested in an honest communal attempt to find the truth. Here, as elsewhere, Gadamer shows delicate insight into the human relations that shape the course of the discussion, arguing that it is only by appreciating all aspects of the context that we can hope to understand the philosophical issues. It is a kind of insight for which he gives Plato enormous credit. When Gadamer calls his book *Plato's Dialectical Ethics,* what he mainly has in mind, he tells us, is the moral element in serious philosophical conversation, not the subject matter of the conversation in the *Philebus,* though that too is moral. As recently as 1989, Gadamer remarked, "The formula 'dialectical ethics' indicates an intention that remains throughout all of my later work."[6]

Gadamer is equally interested in how Plato illustrates the creative aspects of discussion, and what he has to say about the dialectical method; this is at least one reason for his fascination with the *Philebus.* Given his (laudable) view that a satisfactory interpretation of a text may be "distant" from it, Gadamer is more than justified in not remarking on several unusual features of the elenctic discussion of the *Philebus.* But there may be a gain in pointing some of these features out. One I have already mentioned: there is no comparable example among the other late dialogues. In fact, there is only one other dialogue now considered late in which Socrates plays a leading part in the discussion, and that is the *Theaetetus.* The reemergence of Socrates thus coincides with the return to the early Socratic method. This is plausibly explained by the return to a typically Socratic subject, the good life; and there may be a further reason, which I shall mention presently.

The method is that of the elenctic, but the pattern is not standard. In the early dialogues, though Socrates claims ignorance of the truth, he is never shown to be wrong; it is always the proposals of the interlocutor that are found wanting. In the

---

[6] From an interview published in the *Frankfurter Allgemeine* (October 1989). Translated in *Gadamer and Hermeneutics*, ed. Hugh J. Silverman, Routledge, New York, 1991.

Philebus, both Socrates' and Philebus' original proposals are rejected in favor of a third position, which is then accepted by the main discussants. This is perhaps the most strikingly original feature of the dialogue's method: where the early dialogues end without a clear answer to their various questions, and the answers to important questions to be found in the middle and other late dialogues are put forward not in the course of dialogue but as "found" objects, in the *Philebus* the answer emerges directly from the conversational exchange. While Gadamer titles the first part of *Plato's Dialectical Ethics* "Conversation and the Way We Come to Shared Understanding", he does not emphasize how seldom conversation is seen to result in shared understanding in Plato's writings.

Another, and related, feature of the *Philebus* is the discussion of the "method of collection and division", and the use to which that method is put. The method had been introduced in the *Sophist,* and further employed in the *Politicus* (I assume here that the *Philebus* was composed after those two dialogues). The method could not have been made explicit before the *Sophist,* since it depends on the "blending" of ideas which is shown for the first time in that dialogue to be consistent with the essential unity of the ideas. Collection is the process, for which there is no fixed method, of discovering, intuiting or hunting out, and then defining, the genus to which the subject at hand belongs. Since collection includes definition (or the provision of a "criterion"), the result of collection, and the testing of its adequacy, can include the employment of the elenctic. But collection may differ from the method of the early dialogues in at least two ways: where the early dialogues typically revolve around the search for just one idea, an idea which defines some virtue or ultimate value, collection often arrives at the genus by surveying subordinate universals, and the genus may not define a value or goal, but merely help to place the topic under study. Division is the process of discerning the species and subspecies on down to the infima species which fall under the genus. As in the case of collection, Plato stresses the fact that neither of these aspects of the dialectic can be mechanized; art is required at each stage, both in perceiving the right head idea under which to gather the rest, and in "dividing at the joints".

Collection and division are put to quite a different use in the *Philebus* than they were in the *Sophist* and the *Politicus*. The genus which is subdivided in the *Sophist* is art, and the Sophist is defined by naming the species to which he belongs, and describing how it differs from other species of art. The statesman is found in a species of science. In theory, the sole function of the method of collection and division in these dialogues is to make clear the essential nature of one of the subdivisions. Contrast this with its role in the *Philebus*. The opening question was: which is the good life, the life of pleasure or the life of the intellect? An elenctic investigation ends with agreement that neither of these lives is as good as a life that combines pleasure with intellectual abilities and activities. The discussion that provides the criteria by which the excellence of a life is to be judged may be thought of as a collection, but this is certainly not a genus that is subsequently divided. Division is rather practiced twice over, once to uncover the differences among the sorts of pleasure, and once to distinguish the various mental aptitudes. These two divisions form much of the bulk of the dialogue, and they serve not only to make clear the "ingredients" that are available for inclusion in the good life, but also to emphasize the aspects of the potential choices that suit them for inclusion or exclusion.

At this point it is obvious that collection and division have done what they can to delineate the good life; it is equally obvious that the good life has not yet been described, for that requires the exercise of judgment in selecting the best blend of pleasures and intellectual elements. Plato's method, at least in the *Philebus,* comprises three parts: collection, division, and combination. Only the third part shows how the purely theoretical exercise that precedes it can be applied to the world, to a life. I am inclined to include the third part in the overall description of the developed Platonic dialectic. This inclusion is not, I confess, directly confirmed by the text: Plato mentions only collection and division in the section on the dialectic (15D–17A). This section is, however, directly followed by two familiar examples of the application of the dialectical method, and reflection on these examples reinforces the idea that combination was part of Plato's method. One example is phonetics, or the "art of letters". What is presented to the senses is undifferentiated sound as it issues from human mouths; this is the subject matter of the art. But collection requires that we discover the "seal of unity" that unites this subject matter. Plato credits an Egyptian, Theuth, with having collected sound into three species, vowels, mutes, and sonants, and these in turn into the generic concept "letter". Collection in this case partly depends on what then becomes the division of the letters into the three sorts; this process is then followed by the division of each of the species into the individual letters. Is this all there is to the art of letters? Of course not: the art must include the ability to assemble letters into words and words into sentences and sentences into narrative or poetry or a lecture. Plato's second example proves the same point. The art of music requires more than that we discover the genus (which may variously be interpreted as note, scale, or interval) and the various subdivisions of the genus; it requires in addition the ability to blend or combine these elements in a pleasing way.

The combining of elements in view here should not be confused with the blending of the ideas of which so much is made in the *Sophist*. That blending traces out the analytic relations among concepts: it tells us such truths as that, while biped and quadruped each blend with animal, they do not blend with each other. These are the truths with which division is concerned, truths of logic in a broad sense. The combining of elements that have been revealed by division is an entirely different matter, and requires a skill of higher order. Plato explains the methodological and ontological considerations that lie behind this skill as involving a fourfold classification of entities: the unlimited, the limit, the mixture, and the cause of the mixture. We can, very roughly, think of these four sorts of entity as follows. An unlimited is any entity viewed merely as determinable; a limit is a defining shape, proportion, or number; a mixture is any definite object—metaphorically, it is a mixture of an unlimited and a limit. Somewhat less metaphorically, it is an entity whose parts or aspects are fixed in relation to one another, as the good life is a mixture of pleasures and intellectual elements. The fourth entity, the cause of the mixture, is the rational agency which creates the mixture.

When this new apparatus is employed to answer the question, which is the more significant part of the good life, pleasure or mind, the answer is overdetermined. Many varieties of pleasure, but none of mind, are not limited; they depend on alteration, as in the relief of pain. Mind shares with the purer pleasures a part in the final mixture that makes up the good life; but far more important is the fact that mind is the cause of the very mixture of which it is part.

I have reviewed this much of the structure of the *Philebus* for a purpose. I mentioned the fact that this dialogue is in some ways a return to a theme and a method of Plato's earlier works: the theme is a human aspect of the good; the method is elenctic. The return is symbolized by the fact that Socrates here makes a last appearance as the leader of the discussion. Now I want to stress the extent to which the *Philebus* diverges from what might have been expected from the author of the *Phaedrus* or the *Republic* on the same subject.

The essential use of division is justified only by the discussion in the *Sophist* which makes clear the sense in which the ideas can be "divided"; this in turn answers a difficulty raised in the *Parmenides*. The real significance of this discovery is not, however, the discovery of a sense in which the unity of each idea is compatible with its being many. The real significance is the recognition that the ideas cannot serve this necessary analytic or epistemic purpose and at the same time serve as norms, as patterns of positive value. Thus when art is divided in the search for the sophist, a number of the species are of unattractive types: one is the hired hunter of rich young men, another is the maker of false conceits of wisdom. The ideas which represent or constitute these species are not norms that set positive values. Similarly in the *Philebus,* among the classifications are the many impure, or "mixed", types of pleasure; these are all to be rejected in the most desirable life. We also remember Parmenides' teasing question to the young Socrates, whether there are ideas of hair or mud or dirt "or any other trivial and undignified objects". Socrates denies that there are such ideas; Parmenides gently suggests that this is because he is still young; when philosophy has taken hold of him more firmly, he will not despise such objects. Plato took the point to heart: he preserved the epistemological and semantic features of the earlier ideas, but divorced them from their normative role. This also solved another problem: if, by participating in them, particulars came to share some of the value of the ideas, there was the embarrassing question whether this resemblance of particular to idea did not require yet another idea.

Having given up the ideas as the source and explanation of value, Plato needed a new account, and this was provided by the concept of a well-proportioned, rationally generated mixture. Commentators on the *Philebus* have tried to locate the ideas somewhere in the fourfold ontology of unlimited, limit, mixture, and cause, but no consensus has emerged. This is not surprising; the ideas, as employed in the *Philebus,* did their work in implementing collection and division. The remaining task, of combining in the right way the elements revealed by division, was a task for which the ideas could no longer consistently be used. The fourfold ontology has a further purpose, that of providing a framework in which the powers of the mind, of judging, selecting, and combining the parts or aspects of a balanced, functioning mixture, can be understood. It is an error to expect to find the ideas in this practice-oriented classification.

In the *Republic* we are led to think of the ideas, particularly the idea of the good, as the source of all that is real. The ideas are therefore generative, a source of existence. In the *Philebus,* the ideas no longer have this power or function: they are neutral classifiers, known, of course, only to the mind, but powerless in themselves to bring anything into existence. Mind has become the sole mover, as well as the source of value. Here, as in the case of the elenctic method, there is a return to the early dialogues: the ideas in dialogues like the *Euthyphro* and *Laches* are what "makes" each case of piety a pious act, or an act of courage courageous. But there is no suggestion that this "makes" is generative in character. Though for the most part only ideas of virtues are discussed, the ideas themselves are not put forward as a source of value, nor is there a claim that they exist separately from particulars. I think it is no accident that the return, in the *Philebus,* to the early, purely epistemic, use of the ideas, is accompanied by a return to the elenctic method. There is a trajectory in Plato's thinking about how to discover what is good or has value. In the early dialogues, there is little discussion of method; it is simply assumed that the elenchus can lead to truths about what is good and virtuous. Presently Plato appears to have become dissatisfied with this reliance on the elenctic method; the theory of ideas is made explicit, and it is elaborated by adding the doctrine of anamnesis, and the whole metaphysical apparatus of the *Republic.* During this period, as Vlastos emphasizes, the use of the elenchus gives way to an openly didactic style: we are urged to view the realm of ideas as the repository not only of truth but of all value and reality. With the *Parmenides,* various difficulties with the metaphysical doctrine of ideas are aired, but not answered. In the *Theaetetus,* the ideas apparently drop out of sight, and there is a brilliant study of the concept of ordinary empirical knowledge. The *Sophist* and *Politicus,* by stressing the concept of division, reinforce the doubts of the *Parmenides.* I would place the *Philebus* just here, as if, as I suggested in my dissertation, this dialogue were some sort of substitute for the promised dialogue on the Philosopher, following the studies of the Sophist and the Politician. Now deprived of the normative and generative theory of ideas, Plato makes explicit an addition to his methodological tools, an addition which can take their place—the theory of the mixture and its cause.

The renewed and refreshed use of the conversational, interpersonal method of the elenchus makes the *Philebus* particularly relevant to Gadamer's discussion of the dialectic in the first chapter of *Plato's Dialectical Ethics.* This discussion makes little mention of the *Philebus*; its function is to prepare the way for the interpretation of that dialogue (in the second chapter) by drawing its examples from various other dialogues. Thus the organization of the book inadvertently leaves in shadow the extent to which the dialectic of the *Philebus* differs from the dialectic of the earlier dialogues, and, in a quite different way, from the dialectic of the middle dialogues.

Gadamer is, of course, fully aware of the features which make the *Philebus* unique. In the introduction to *Plato's Dialectical Ethics* he writes,

The fact that the *Philebus*'s position in regard to ontology is identical with the general Platonic position that we call the doctrine of the Forms cannot conceal the distinctive concentration of the *Philebus*'s inquiry on the ethical problem—that is, on the good in *human* life. The goal, after all, is to argue from the general ontological idea of the good precisely to the good of actual human existence. In the context of this substantive intention we are given a thorough dialectical analysis of *hēdonē* (pleasure) and *epistēmē* (knowledge), an analysis whose positive content and methodological attitude both make the *Philebus* the proper basis for an interpretation of the specifically Aristotelian problem of a science of ethics.[7]

A few pages later, Gadamer speaks of "the derivation and philosophical coherence of the unity of dialogue and dialectic which *only* the *Philebus,* out of all Plato's literary works, presents in this way."[8]

---

[7]   *Plato's Dialectical Ethics*, pp. 1–2.   [8]   Ibid., p. 15.

The treatment of pleasure as a necessary ingredient in the good life for a person is particularly emphasized by Gadamer; this shows a human orientation not so clearly marked elsewhere. This corresponds to the quite different role played earlier by the idea of the good:

> One should note that unlike the *Republic,* the *Philebus* does not inquire about the idea of the Good and its function as a paradigm for human life; rather its questioning is the opposite of that. It asks how the concrete life of human beings with all its contingency and impurity, and determined as it is by impulse and pleasure just as much as by knowledge and insight, can nevertheless be "good," i.e., can participate in the Good.[9]

In the recent interview mentioned above, Gadamer discusses his view of the *Philebus* as it developed over the years. He sees it as the connecting link between the Socrates of the early dialogues and Aristotle's ethics; in each case there is the concern with "the question of the good for human existence".

The differences between the early dialogues, the middle dialogues, and the *Philebus* are thus not ignored, but at the same time they are muted. These differences, even the differences between Plato and Aristotle, are seen more as a matter of emphasis, of "highlighting", of adjustment of method to subject, than as actual inconsistencies. The picture is not one of stasis, but of a fixed center about which there is movement; for example, "the *Philebus*'s position in regard to ontology is identical with the general Platonic position that we call the doctrine of the Forms". I suppose it is a question how far a "general position" can be stretched before it tears. But it seems to me that it is difficult to bring the Socratic dialogues, which make no mention of a realm of separate ideas which are the only reality, and the source of all value and existence, into line with the middle dialogues which do so treat the ideas. Nor do I see how to reconcile the ideas of the *Philebus* (which are in a clear sense divisible) with either the "ones" which Socrates seeks to define, or the ideas of the *Phaedrus* and *Republic*.

It is a matter of delicate judgment how far to emphasize the continuities among Socrates, the periods of Plato's thought, and the periods of Aristotle's thought on the one hand, and the differences that separate them on the other. If I have been emphasizing

---

[9] *Dialogue and Dialectic; Eight Hermeneutical Studies on Plato*, Yale University Press, New Haven, 1980, pp. 190–1.

the latter, it is not for the sake of airing my particular vision, but because there seems to me some discrepancy between Gadamer's own idea of understanding, and his resistance to finding real development in Plato's attitudes and methods. To put this positively: I think a Platonic dialectic seen as more open to serious revision would cohabit more happily with Gadamer's own conception of dialogue and conversation.

I accept Gadamer's demonstration that the *Philebus,* more than any other of Plato's works, both illustrates and describes "the way we come to shared understanding", "the motives of a concern for the facts of the matter in a shared world". The early elenctic dialogues contained many models of determined and devoted search for the essential nature of one virtue or another, or of virtue itself. There was Socrates' repeated insistence that his interlocutors say only what they really think, his concern that they follow with him every step of the way; and along with the ironic pretense that he could learn the truth from his interlocutors, there was Socrates' genuine modesty in confessing his own ignorance. But it seems to me these dialogues nevertheless fall short of the ideal of a communal search for understanding in at least two ways. First, there is the vast asymmetry, taken for granted by Socrates and his friends, that however ignorant Socrates was of the final truth, he was right in what he did claim; and he made some astonishing claims. It was always the interlocutor who turned out to have inconsistent opinions, never Socrates. So even though Socrates sometimes seems genuinely to think he may learn something from the discussion, we are shown no real cases where this happens.

The second way in which these dialogues fail, at least to my mind, to embody the ideal of fruitful communication is that the discussants assume from the start that there is a fixed, definite answer to the deep moral questions asked. There is no suggestion that the goal as well as the search owes something to the human minds at work. Along with this assumption goes the unexpressed conviction that the words that enable the discussion have settled meanings; at the most, the parties to the dialogue may need to determine whether they mean the same thing by the same words; but this is something to find out, not something that may evolve. This attitude makes words the tools of discussion rather than a central aspect of what is to be made intelligible.

In these two matters, the *Philebus* differs from the early dialogues both in spirit and in theory. As I mentioned above, Socrates astonishingly turns out to have held at the start a thesis which must be abandoned. The study of the good life develops from a manifest exchange of originally opposed opinions. The goal is not fixed in advance, for the goal is not represented as a matter of finding the nature of some single idea, but rather as knowing the art of discriminating, judging, selecting, and mixing the appropriate elements of a life in a way that exhibits measure, proportion, and stability. The cause of this mixture is not some abstract, eternal principle, but the mind of the person who lives the life. The goal is in every sense a human goal: an end set by a human being for that human being. This humane conclusion, reached in the course of a collaborative dialogue, seems to me what must, in large part, have attracted Gadamer to the *Philebus* in the first place, and it exudes an attitude we find expressed throughout Gadamer's work.

"Language has its true being only in conversation, in the exercise of understanding between people."[10] This saying of Gadamer's goes far beyond the linguist's insistence on the primacy of spoken over written words, for it implies that it is only in the context of discussion that language comes to have a content, to be language. (This is a view often attributed to Wittgenstein.) But Gadamer has a much more basic claim, that thought itself depends on language: "All understanding is interpretation, and all interpretation takes place in the medium of language which would allow the object to come into words."[11] "Language is not just one of man's possessions in the world, but on it depends the fact that man has a world at all."[12] Putting these themes together, we must conclude that it is only in interpersonal communication that there can be thought, a grasping of the fact of an objective, that is, a shared, world. Not only is it the case that the aim of conversation is "shared understanding"; we must also acknowledge that without sharing there is no understanding.

The reason for this is, in my opinion, that there is no other way to answer Wittgenstein's question, in what consists the difference between thinking one is following a rule, and actually following it. I interpret this as asking how words can have an objective

---

[10] *Truth and Method*, p. 404.　　[11] Ibid., p. 350.　　[12] Ibid., p. 401.

reference, how sentences can have a truth value independent of the individual. Our thoughts and words carry us out into the world; this is why we can have true and false beliefs and say what is false as well as what is true. This connection with the world can be established only by shared reactions to a shared environment. "Speech, in its primordial form, is part of a shared having to do with something," as Gadamer puts it.[13] He goes on:

Language, in which something comes to be language, is not a possession of one or the other of the interlocutors. Every conversation presupposes a common language, or, it creates a common language. Something is placed in the center, as the Greeks said, which the partners to the dialogue both share, and concerning which they can exchange ideas with one another. Hence agreement concerning the object, which it is the purpose of the conversation to bring about, necessarily means that a common language must first be worked out in the conversation. This is not an external matter of simply adjusting our tools, nor is it even right to say that the partners adapt themselves to one another but, rather, in the successful conversation they both come under the influence of the truth of the object and are thus bound to one another in a new community. To reach an understanding with one's partner in a dialogue is... a transformation into a communion, in which we do not remain what we were.[14]

I am in agreement with almost all of this. Where I differ (and this may merely show I have not fully understood Gadamer) is that I would not say a conversation presupposes a common language, nor even that it requires one. Understanding, to my mind, is always a matter not only of interpretation but of translation, since we can never assume we mean the same thing by our words that our partners in discussion mean. What is created in dialogue is not a common language but understanding; each partner comes to understand the other. And it also seems wrong to me to say agreement concerning an object demands that a common language first be worked out. I would say: it is only in the presence of shared objects that understanding can come about. Coming to an agreement about an object and coming to understand each other's speech are not independent moments but part of the same interpersonal process of triangulating the world.

[13] *Plato's Dialectical Ethics*, p. 29.   [14] *Truth and Method*, p. 341.

19 *Aristotle's Action*

Aristotle's *Organon* covers several of the areas into which we sometimes divide philosophy. Philosophy of language and hermeneutics may roughly be said to be the subject of the *De Interpretatione*, logic of the *Prior Analytics*, and epistemology of the *Posterior Analytics*. Yet when we look at the ten categories, only the ninth can comfortably be identified with a contemporary field of study, and that is action.

Aristotle pretty much invented the subject as we now think of it; he was fascinated by it, and returned to it again and again. No wonder. Action is the philosophical sibling of perception, and hence of epistemology. Both compel us to face the problem of the relation between the mind and the body, thought and the world. The physical world assails our senses, and the outcome is a sophisticated conceptual picture of that world; by appealing to that picture we reason how to achieve our purposes through action. In perception the physical world causes thought; in action thought brings about changes in our physical environment. The notion that our will is free from physical determination has prompted many to hold that the mental and the physical must be discrete realms, but if they are somehow decoupled, it is a question how knowledge is possible. Skepticism and the problem of free will are symmetrical problems.

Since it is clear that the concept of action is central to many of the perennial concerns of philosophy, what is surprising is not Aristotle's interest, or ours, but rather the relative neglect of the subject during the intervening millennia. The reason may be that the connection of action with ethics has been so strong as to overshadow the interest in action for its own sake. But whatever the reason, the consequence is that the subject has progressed, or changed, relatively little since Aristotle. Aristotle thought that by surveying what has been said by our forebears we can avoid previous errors and benefit from accumulated wisdom. But in the case of action, such a survey would not include a great deal besides Aristotle, at least before the twentieth century. Our topic has flourished, then, mainly in two periods: Aristotle's and our own. As we begin a new era, it is appropriate to try to predict what will, or perhaps should, become of the subject in the twenty-first century. So my talk naturally divides into three main divisions: Aristotle, the century we are leaving, and the next century.

I. Aristotle on Action

Although Aristotle was interested in the connection of action with ethics, he treated it independently. Here he departs from Plato, for though both philosophers were deeply concerned with the question how a person should live his life, Plato's interest in action was almost exclusively focused on the normative claims on behavior. Aristotle's analysis of voluntary, or as we might say intentional, action had the following main features.

Aristotle distinguished voluntary actions mainly in terms of the cause: the cause of voluntary actions is internal and mental, whereas involuntary actions are caused by external forces. In the *Categories* he gives as examples of actions cutting and burning; his examples of involuntary actions (also called affects, sufferings, and passions) are being cut and being burned. The cause of voluntary actions is the conjunction of appetite and thought (*De Anima* 433a). Appetite, which has as its object something valued or desired, initiates the causal chain; thought then determines the means by which the desired end can be achieved. At this point, action ensues. Aristotle stresses that thought alone would never result in action. Thought, he says, is always good, by which he does not mean that we cannot reason badly, or harbor false beliefs, but that thought is not to be evaluated morally. Appetite, on the other hand, may be good or bad depending on whether what it takes to be valuable really is valuable or not. Appetites may run counter to one another, and are easily fooled by distance in space or in time.

Interested as always in the logic of reasoning, Aristotle compares the nature of reasoning about what to do with pure syllogistic reasoning. "How does it happen", he asks, "that thinking is sometimes followed by action and sometimes not, sometimes by motion, and sometimes not?" (*De Motu Animalum* 701a.) The difference is not, Aristotle implies, in the formal features of the logic, but in the subject matter. In theoretical reasoning the conclusion is coming to believe what is entailed by the premises, as when someone who accepts that all men are mortal and that Socrates is a man comes to believe that Socrates is mortal. In practical reasoning, on the other hand, the conclusion is an action, as when someone who wants shelter and believes he can provide shelter by building a house forthwith builds a house.

Aristotle holds that reason, what he calls the "faculty of knowledge", is passive, it never moves us to act; only an appetite or desire can prompt an action. This idea was echoed by David Hume when he said "Reason is, and only ought to be the slave of the passions." A difficulty would seem to lurk here, for how can reason be passive if it is a cause of action, and as essential to action as desire? Perhaps Aristotle is only emphasizing his disagreement with Plato, who held that knowledge of the good is in itself sufficient for action, or the point may be that in the temporal order, appetite or desire comes first.

Plato (or Plato's Socrates) had also denied that it is possible to recognize a good and not act to promote it. Here again Aristotle disagreed. It seemed to him clear that someone could voluntarily act contrary to her own best judgment: this is akrasia, what is sometimes called weakness of the will. Here Aristotle faced another problem, for he had said that given an apparent good, one desired it, and if one saw a way to attain it, straightway one acted. He decided that this sequence could fail when appetite distorts one's perception of the wrongness of the action. No doubt there are many cases like this, but Aristotle's solution does not solve the general problem for reasons to which I shall come.

One feature of Aristotle's theory of action is particularly striking, for it goes against the general subsequent tradition: he left no role for the concept of a will. Deliberation plays a role, but no separate act of decision enters the causal chain. When reason discovers a means to a desired end, one does not then decide to act or even reason to the conclusion that action is appropriate and desirable. One simply, "straightway", as Aristotle repeatedly puts it, acts. There is no mental act parallel to drawing the conclusion of a theoretical syllogism; in the case of practical reasoning, drawing the conclusion *is* acting. It is just this contrast that distinguishes practical reasoning from theoretical.

Aristotle discusses the mind–body problem at length in the *De Anima*, and concludes that the mental and the physical are in effect two aspects of the same phenomena. "It is obvious", he writes, "that the affections of the soul (e.g. anger, courage, appetite, sensation) are enmattered." Thus definitions of these affections should define movements of the body (or a part or faculty of the body). The physicist will define anger as a boiling of the blood; the dialectician will define it as an appetite for returning pain for pain. Given this (enlightened) view, no problem can arise concerning the causal relations between thought and the physical world.

II. Transition to the Present

Philosophers have not been silent about action between the time of Aristotle and the twentieth century. Of course not. But for the most part, their interest has been in the role of action in ethics: the question has generally been not, what is the nature of action? but what ought we to do? Nevertheless, important issues have been raised. Aquinas, for example, realized that there are cases of akrasia that do not satisfy Aristotle's description. It often happens, Aquinas thought, that a person is faced with a choice between two legitimate values, let's say whether to vote for the best candidate thus probably wasting one's vote, or to vote for a less attractive candidate who has a good chance of winning over an even less savory candidate. In such a case, one reasons from various principles, some of which support one course of action and some of which support a contrary action. The akratic agent may yield to the temptation of what that agent judges to be the less valuable outcome. This cannot be explained as a failure of reason, but of judgment. Aquinas puts it this way:

He that has knowledge of the universal [that is, the major premise which expresses a value] is hindered, because of a passion [another value], from reasoning in the light of that universal, so as to draw the conclusion [i.e., to do the right thing]; but he reasons in the light of another universal proposition suggested by the inclination of the passion, and draws his conclusion [acts] accordingly. . . . Hence passion fetters the reason, and hinders it from thinking and concluding under the first proposition; so that while the passion lasts, the reason argues and concludes under the second. [*Summa Theologica*, Part II, Q. 77, Art. 2]

This seems to me a real improvement on Aristotle, for it explicitly recognizes that motives may conflict. It need not be a matter of being carried away by passion; one may be aware that one is not doing the best thing and do it cooly.

Hobbes is in agreement with Aquinas that there are many situations in which we must weigh competing values, and he combines this point with the Aristotelian theme that there are no volitions or acts of the will in addition to the reasoning process. Hobbes says that when we deliberate we consider the pros and cons of various actions, and one desire will win out. What we call a volition is simply the last appetite, the one on which we act. "In deliberation", Hobbes remarks, "the last appetite or aversion, immediately adhering to the action, or to the omission thereof, is what we call will."[1]

Developments in other aspects of philosophy and in science had repercussions for the study of action. The materialist La Mettrie, drawing on Descartes's view of animals, held that a mechanistic explanation of human thought, desire, and action was possible, thus assimilating psychology to a general theory of nature (*L'Homme machine*, 1745). But it was the success of Newtonian physics that inspired David Hume to attempt a scientific account of the mind, of ethics, and of action. While his simple associationist psychology now seems absurdly inadequate for explaining thought generally, much that he said about action in relation to ethics echoes Aristotle's views, and is appealing to many philosophers today. Hume's account of practical reasoning is essentially that of Aristotle, with appetite (which Hume calls passion) determining the ends and reason the means. Ask a man, says Hume, why he takes exercise, and he will tell you it is to preserve his health; ask him why he wishes to preserve his health, and he will tell you it is to avoid pain. At some point he

---

[1] Thomas Hobbes, *Leviathan*, ed. C. B. MacPherson, Harmondsworth: Penguin Books, 1968, p. 127.

will run out of reasons, for some desires are, at the moment at least, final.

The apparent success of science in explaining many physical phenomena raises the question whether the same methodology is applicable to human actions and the mental states and events to which we appeal in order to explain those actions. The work of R. G. Collingwood made the issue central to the study of history insofar as it delves into the explanation and understanding of action. According to Collingwood, the methodology of history (or, for that matter, any of the social sciences that treat individual human behavior) differs markedly from the methodology of the natural sciences. The natural sciences seek laws that enable us to predict and explain particular events in terms of their causes. We cannot expect to find strict laws that govern intentional behavior. In the case of human action, what we seek is understanding: we want to know why someone acted in terms of that person's beliefs, desires, and other attitudes. Empathy and imagination and general knowledge of why people act as they do under various pressures and in various circumstances are our main resources in arriving at such understanding, though of course we sometimes also know what people said in explanation of their actions, or what they confided to their diaries. Collingwood has had many followers in this matter, but there are others who think that psychology should strive to emulate the natural sciences, or be absorbed by them.

Modern epistemology, both in its Cartesian and its empiricist forms, made skepticism a basic issue over a period of four centuries or so, and general skepticism of the senses seemed to apply to knowledge of other minds, and so raise the question how we can ever know why someone else has acted. It is already a problem how we can infer, as we surely must, a person's motives from his observable behavior, but this problem becomes totally intractable if we cannot even tell what we observe. Rather surprisingly, however, a number of philosophers, even those who, like Hume, are general skeptics, have been willing to speculate on how, supposing the general problem solved, we might arrive at justified opinions about other people's thoughts, motives, and intentions. Here behaviorism in one form or another has played an active role in the philosophy of mind, and so of action. But behaviorism in what form? The question can't be whether observed behavior (including, of course, verbal behavior) yields all the evidence we have as to what others think, mean, and intend. There is no alternative; to this extent we are all practicing behaviorists. More serious behaviorists have thought that we could do away with mention of such publicly unobservable states as beliefs, intentions, and desires. Gilbert Ryle, in *The Concept of Mind*, sometimes tends this way (1949); so does Wittgenstein. But neither of these two philosophers would have called himself a behaviorist, for both were scornful of the idea that everyday psychology, what we now call folk psychology, could ever be made into a serious science, and serious science was, after all, what behaviorism was about. Nevertheless, the question how we do in fact learn so much about why people act from just noticing their outward behavior remains one of the most fascinating, and contested, areas in philosophy.

Economists are naturally interested in voluntary behavior, and along with psychologists, statisticians, logicians, and philosophers have developed sophisticated formal models for patterns of decision making when the outcome of action is uncertain (which, strictly speaking, is always). Such models typically assume an idealized degree of rationality on the part of individuals, but this assumption has sometimes been modified in various ways. Since models of rational decision theory must be interpreted before they can be tested, the question how realistic they are has been hotly debated during recent decades.

III. The Present

This concludes my summary of some of the post-Aristotelian developments in philosophy and other subjects that have influenced how philosophers now think about action. Until relatively recently, little has happened to change Aristotle's account of how thought eventuates in reasoned behavior. The work of the later Wittgenstein, of Ryle, Austin, Hampshire, and others stirred up interest and discussion, but perhaps the crucial event in stimulating a new look at the concept of action was the publication of Elizabeth Anscombe's *Intention* in 1957. In this short book she raised the question how various actions are related to one another. If a man pays a bill by writing a check, how are his acts of writing a check and paying the bill related? Her answer was that they are identical: the writing of the check and the paying of the bill are one and the same act. This claim immediately raises a number of questions, the first of which is, what are the entities that are identical or different? Actions, we answer; but then, what sort of entities are actions? They would seem to be events. But modern logic had assigned no role to events as serious members of the ontology of the world, nor is it clear how events, particularly actions, are named or referred to in sentences like "Arthur wrote a check." This is an issue of a kind Aristotle was not in a position to discuss with the relative clarity with which it can be raised in the context of today's logic and semantics. I'll come back to this issue in a moment.

A second question Anscombe emphasized concerns a deep question about the commonly accepted account of practical reasoning—the Aristotelian practical syllogism. The problem, Anscombe pointed out, is how we are to think of the major premise, the "universal" premise concerned with the contents of an appetite or desire or other motivational apprehension of a perceived value. This premise is universal because at the start it points to no particular action; it simply expresses a wish for any action which will satisfy it. If the practical syllogism is to yield its conclusion with necessity, as Aristotle had insisted, then the major premise had to be such that, combined with appropriate minor premises, the unconditional value of a particular action would follow. Otherwise there would be no excuse for Aristotle's claim that, given the premises, the agent would "straightway" act. But then, what is the form of the major premise? It had always been assumed that it was a universal conditional like "One must always keep a promise", "I must do what I can to avoid an accident". Anscombe pointed out, however, that it is sometimes wrong to keep a promise, and that it is logically impossible to do everything one can to avoid an accident, since one might avoid a head-on collision by turning either to the right or to the left, but one cannot do both. It is implausible that in every situation in which action is called for there is a single duty, obligation, or value which bears on the case. But of course there are moral philosophers who deny this.

If to these two problems raised by Anscombe we add the already familiar problem of the nature of psychological explanation, we have a fairly complete list of the areas in which contemporary philosophy of action has moved to positions different from, if not beyond, Aristotle. Since here we come to a time that includes me, I cannot pretend that my account will be neutral or disinterested. I will concentrate on what I take to be movements in the right direction, and will not give equal time (or in some cases any time at all) to alternatives.[2]

1. I turn first to the **ontology** of action. Because I was much interested in the semantics (or logical form) of the sentences of natural languages, I asked how events, and particularly actions, are referred to in ordinary sentences. Anscombe had repeatedly spoken of actions "under a description", thus reminding us of, say, Frege on such alternative descriptions of Venus as "the Morning star" and "the Evening star", or Russell on "Scott" and "the author of *Waverley*". I realized that if there were names or phrases that named or described events, adverbs would be what, in effect, modified them. But modern logic had no apparatus for referring to events, and therefore no way of treating adverbs. There were suggestions afloat in the work of Reichenbach and others, but none of them yielded a systematic account of how talk of events fitted with the rest of our talk. It was easy enough to say that expressions like "Arthur's writing of a check" or "Arthur's paying of the bill" referred to actions—the very same action in some cases, according to Anscombe. The problem was to relate such expressions to simple sentences like "Arthur wrote a check". If "Arthur's writing of a check" referred to an action, so also, I thought, must "Arthur wrote a check". But the latter seems to refer to only Arthur and the check.

The solution I have proposed to these problems may at first seem ontologically excessive, but I believe it is now fairly widely accepted by logicians, philosophers, and those linguists who are interested in the semantics of natural languages. The idea is that we must take events seriously as part of the furniture of the world, and in particular accept actions as a species of event. As it turns out, the sentence "Arthur wrote a check" *doesn't* refer to a particular event in the way a name or description might: rather the

---

[2] My early work on action is collected in *Essays on Actions and Events*, Oxford University Press, 1980. French edition, translated by Pascal Engel: *Actions et Événements*, Presses Universitaires de France, 1994.

sentence says there was at least one event of which Arthur was the agent, it was a writing, and it was of a check. It is an existentially quantified claim. This makes sense: if we say Arthur wrote a check, we don't imply that he wrote only one check, but that he wrote at least one. We can now say that there was at least one such check-writing event which was identical with some event that was a paying of a bill by Arthur. Still no reference to any particular action, just quantification over types of events. But we do refer to a singular event when we speak of Arthur's writing of the check. Adverbs and adverbial modification also fall into line. A sentence like "Arthur wrote a check on Saturday in his study" has many modifiers, properties which we here attribute to some event: we claim there was at least one event with all these properties: it was a writing, it was of a check, the agent was Arthur, it was on Saturday, and it was in Arthur's study. (I suppress the further indexical element which identifies the relevant Saturday as an event prior to the event of the utterance of the sentence.) Adverbial modification becomes identical to adjectival modification once we accept events along with objects as part of our everyday ontology.

Making sense of talk of "actions under a description" and therefore of claims of identity does not solve the problem of whether any particular descriptions *do* describe the same event. If I accomplish one thing by doing something else, let's say I play an e^b with the intention of completing a C minor chord, is my action of playing e^b identical with my completing a C minor chord? In this case the answer would seem to be yes. But suppose I accidentally make a friend sick by giving him a drink. Is my giving him the drink identical with my making him sick? Here we tend to balk at identifying the acts for a simple reason: events are surely not identical if there is a property one has that the other does not. Yet here one action is intentional and the other not. Worse still, the action of giving him a drink was finished before my unintended victim even began to get sick.

Here there are two things to set straight. The first concerns intention. Strictly speaking, all actions are intentional provided there is at least one description which reveals a feature of the action which prompted the agent to perform it. But of course all actions have unintended or non-intended features such as unwanted or unexpected consequences. The concept of intention does not directly modify acts, but rather whole propositions. Thus if Arthur signed the check, what was intended by Arthur was that he sign the check. This explains why an action can be intentional under some descriptions and not under other descriptions. We also see that talk of voluntary actions has the same semantic character as talk of beliefs, desires, expectations, and hopes.

The second problem—the time of the action—does not depend on anything as subtle as intensionality. It concerns, rather, the relation of any event to its causes and effects. We constantly identify or describe things partly in terms of their causal relations. A substance is soluble if it is caused to dissolve when placed in liquid. A rock is igneous if its present condition was caused by volcanic activity. Someone has the disease of favism only if his condition is caused by contact with fava beans. A male is a grandfather if he has helped cause a child come into existence who has helped cause another child come into existence. Many verbs incorporate this idea: if John breaks a window, something he did caused a window to break. This obvious analysis explains what would otherwise be a mystery: the relation between the transitive and the intransitive forms of many verbs; here, for example, the transitive "break" means "cause to break". Causality is a relation between events. So to grasp what it means to say that John broke the window, we need to invoke the existence of two events: we are saying, "There were two events: one was something that John did, one was a breaking of the window, and the first event caused the second." Once we see how easily the description of an object or event can surreptitiously involve a cause or effect, it is obvious how to explain, and explain away, our aporia about the time of an action. If there are two events, their times may be different, and if one caused the other, the time of the first must be before the time of the other. So "John threw a stone" and "John broke the window" can involve just one *action*, but two events, because "John broke the window" just means John did something (in this case threw a stone) which caused the window to break. If I make someone sick by giving him a drink I don't do two things (give him a drink and make him sick); all I do is give my friend a drink. But that event caused him to get sick later, so it becomes true of my action that it has an unwanted consequence. The time of my action is not affected by the time of its consequences, just as the life span of a person is not affected by his becoming a grandfather. Of course we neither say I made my friend sick when I have just given him a drink but before he is sick, just as we don't call someone a grandfather if no offspring of his has yet had a child.[3]

I praised Aristotle, Hobbes, and Spinoza for assigning no independent ontological or psychological reality to something called the will, or to acts of willing. But how about intentions? At one time I thought they too could be dispensed with in favor of the relation between ends and means expressed by the claim that someone threw a stone with the intention of breaking a window. But this will not do for two reasons. One is that we often form intentions for the future, and these are surely states of mind, just as forming an intention is a mental event. The other reason is closely related: any action which takes time to perform, like building a house or writing a novel, requires a more or less constant plan or intention in terms of which we monitor the action as things develop. Such intentions exist whether or not they are completed, or even begun. (Think of the intention of writing a novel.) As states of mind such settled plans or intentions are much like pro-attitudes of any sort, fairly narrowly focused, and always based on more fundamental ends and relevant beliefs about how those ends can be realized.

2. Anscombe's attack on a common theory of **practical reasoning** led to the need for a radical modification of the Aristotelian model. The need should have been clear once one shifted from trying to say how one ought to act to trying to describe how and why we do act. For it is obvious that the principles and values, the perceived duties and obligations, which motivate our actions can, and very often do, compete. Unless there are ultimate principles which brook no exceptions (as Kant is often thought to have held, and Richard Hare certainly does hold, as do many utilitarians), the major premises in practical reasoning cannot be universally quantified conditionals (e.g., "Tell no lies," "Maximize pleasure"). Many moralists, including G. E. Moore, Henry Sidgwick, H. A. Pritchard, W. D. Ross, and Bernard Williams are pluralists, as I am myself, and pluralists in moral philosophy

---

[3] Given the causal relations built into the descriptions of many actions, it is not surprising that Arthur Danto some time ago suggested that actions like moving one's arm (which he called "basic actions") are causes of such actions as breaking a window. As my discussion shows, this cannot be correct since only one action is involved.

believe there may be irreconcilable, but valid, moral principles. When principles conflict with each other, we don't give up one of the principles. When we decide, in a particular case, that it is better to lie, we continue to consider the principle which is outweighed—the principle on which we fail to act—as valid, and as relevant to the case in hand. We simply judge that other considerations are, under the circumstances, more pressing, even though we regret the road not taken.

W. D. Ross tried to resolve this difficulty by saying all duties (and, he might have added, other values) are *prima facie*. This can't mean such duties merely seem, at first glance, to be valid, but that they may conceivably be overruled. "Defeasible" would have been a better term than *prima facie*. Still, what is the logical status of the principles we bring to bear on our judgments of what to do? It would be no help to put them in this form: "It is always defeasibly wrong to lie," for then there would simply be endless valid principles from which we could conclude that almost any action we contemplate is both defeasibly right and defeasibly wrong. The idea is rather that an act is wrong or bad *in so far as* it is a lie; in other words, it is a good reason, as far as it goes, against an action that it would be a lie.

The solution I have proposed is to model such principles on premises that state that something constitutes evidence for or against an empirical hypothesis. (This sort of principle has been discussed at length by Carl Hempel.) I will skip the details. I was led to think of this solution by the special case of conflict that eventuates in akrasia. For even in this case, Aquinas pointed out, the akratic agent reasons from what may all be valid values and beliefs which he recognizes to be for and against what he ends up doing. If the agent's will is weak, he fails to act on his considered judgment, but he does have a reason for what he does, just not a good enough reason. A problem remains. If all that practical reasoning can deliver is that there are reasons for and against an action, practical reasoning can never tell us what to do. There is a missing step. When the reasons have been weighed, we must decide where the weight of the considerations lies. Weakness of the will—akrasia—occurs when an agent judges that on the whole one action is best, and yet he acts on a reason his judgment tells him is inadequate to justify the action. In other words, he acts against his own best judgment. But even the akratic agent has taken the extra step that Aristotle left out: he has decided on which reason or reasons to act. This process, that of weighing the considerations on both sides, cannot be reduced to a piece of deductive reasoning.

Akrasia is only one of the many forms of irrationality. Others include wishful thinking and self-deception. All irrationality is a challenge to the philosopher as well as to the psychologist. The central dilemma that must be faced when we try to comprehend almost any kind of crooked thinking and acting arises from the need to find an agent sufficiently rational to enable us to make sense of his behavior on the one hand, and the fact that most irrationality involves inconsistent or incompatible thoughts and desires on the other. We are caught attempting to rationalize the irrational. Different forms of irrationality require different analyses, but none is simple to understand or explain, either for the psychologist, psychoanalyst, or philosopher.[4]

3. I turn to the third area of perennial philosophical interest raised by the study of action, an area still being actively debated, the **mind–body problem**. Aristotle is to be admired for having rejected the Platonic dualism of two realms; his position is equally at odds with Descartes's ontological dualism. As we saw, Aristotle insisted that mental states are embodied, and he claimed that the mental and the physical are just two ways of describing the same phenomena. Spinoza elaborated this idea, and was perhaps more explicit in his insistence both that there is only one substance and that the mental and the physical are irreducibly different modes of apprehending, describing, and explaining what happens in nature. I applaud Aristotle and Spinoza; I think their ontological monism accompanied by an uneliminable dualism of conceptual apparatus is exactly right. Most, though of course not all, philosophers today are monists, but for various reasons many reject the conceptual irreducibility of the mental to the physical. Those who belong to this latter camp differ: some think that to hold the mental to be conceptually irreducible implies that we can never unify science; some think it means that we would have to give up the attempt to make psychology a serious science; some argue that anomalous monism (which is what I call my version of

---

[4] Several of my essays on irrationality are collected and translated by Pascal Engel in *Paradoxes de l'irrationalité*, Combas: L'Éditions de L'Éclat, 1991.

Spinoza) implies that the mental is causally ineffectual. This is not the place to try to refute these views, so I shall merely state what I take to be the truth.

The main reason for holding that concepts like belief, desire, intention, and intentional action cannot be incorporated into physics or any of the natural sciences is that these psychological concepts deal with states of mind and mental events that have propositional contents—they are *about* a subject matter. Whatever is identified in terms of a propositional content has logical relations to other such entities, and so the application of these concepts is subject to the demands of consistency and rationality. These demands are normative. We use our own rationality in pursuing any science, but only in the sciences that deal with thought do we treat the phenomena to be studied as themselves conscious and potentially rational. The irreducibly normative character of the mental and what is understood in relation to it, like voluntary action, does not prevent us from studying thought and action systematically, but any resulting science will be, in part, a science of rationality.

IV. The Future

I haven't left much space for the future, but then, we haven't seen much of it yet. I will hazard some predictions concerning the directions in which we may expect philosophy of action to develop, and express some hopes.

The study of action, along with other contemporary seismic shifts, will continue to contribute to the breakdown of the administratively ordained boundaries between the various fields of philosophy. Plato, Aristotle, Descartes, Spinoza, Leibniz, Hume, and Kant, to pick a few winners, recognized no lines between metaphysics, epistemology, moral philosophy, psychology, philosophy of language, and the history of philosophy, and neither would we if our universities and colleges didn't often compel us to think of ourselves and our colleagues as belonging in one or another field. Most of us in fact ignore distinctions between the sub-disciplines of philosophy as well as the lines between philosophy and linguistics, classics, musicology, psychology, physics, and so on. The philosophy of action is well-suited to promote the breakdown of these tribal divisions.[5]

Decision theory—that is, the theory of choice when the outcome is uncertain—will, I believe, come to be studied and modified by those interested in action far more than it has been. For it is a theory of measurement in areas where measurement often seems irrelevant: it purports to show how, on the basis of expressed preferences for one action over another, we can construct numerical measures of strength of belief (often called subjective probability) and relative degrees of preference for various possible outcomes of actions (a subjective scale of utilities). A model of this kind does not attempt to reduce psychological concepts to physical concepts. What it does do is show how a well-understood pattern can lead from simple to sophisticated distinctions. As such, it is a philosophical tool of great power, and one that is particularly appropriate to the study of action. Philosophers and psychologists alike amuse themselves by pointing out the apparent shortcomings of such idealized theories of rationality, but I predict that as time goes on they will come to appreciate the value this discipline.[6]

These are days when empirical knowledge of the workings of the brain, and the relation of those workings to perception and action, are increasing by leaps and bounds. For example, I am impressed by the recent demonstration that perception of the cause of a pain and perception of the pain itself are carried out by discrete parts of the brain. Judging that something is painful, and judging that something is the painful stimulus may seem similar, but the fact that these attitudes are processed by different parts of

---

[5] I do not want to suggest that it is only philosophy of action that is involved in a continuing interdisciplinary movement. Since the sixties there have been productive relations among philosophers, linguists, logicians, neurologists, psychologists, and workers in artificial intelligence. Today there is an increasing effort to bring together (among others) molecular biologists and geneticists who study the patterns of gene activation in neurons, cell biologists investigating synapses between neurons, researchers who study networks of nerves and patterns of neural firing, and psychologists studying behavior. Philosophers interested in thought and action can find a role in this movement.

[6] Some have long appreciated the philosophical importance of decision theory. Frank Plumpton Ramsey invented a form of decision theory ("Truth and Probability", 1926), and Richard Jeffrey another (*The Logic of Decision*, University of Chicago Press, 1965). Isaac Levi has discussed its uses and shortcomings in several books.

the neural apparatus is philosophically suggestive.[7] More recently still it has been confirmed that short- and long-term memory are stored in distant areas of the brain, thus explaining why one can lose the ability to remember what one is now doing while remembering the past vividly.[8] We can anticipate many more such discoveries. We are just beginning to learn in any real detail how the brain controls the muscles that actualize actions, or how we process the enormous amount of potential information provided by the senses. Such understanding of correlations between events described psychologically and described in neurological terms will, and should, influence the philosophy of action. But I do not predict extensive elimination of our mental terms, nor reduction of psychological understanding and explanation to the resources of the natural sciences. Interaction is one thing, reduction another.

Science is just beginning to learn how human development takes place. An area of very special interest to philosophers of action is the development of thought and language and the relation between the two. Here philosophical problems and empirical discovery interact. At one time W. V. Quine speculated (on purely logical and *a priori* grounds) on the order in which various grammatical features of language are mastered.[9] But according to the psycholinguist George Miller, subsequent studies by psycholinguists have shown that the actual sequence is quite different. On the other hand we have Elizabeth Anscombe's answer to the question how we know where our limbs are. She said it was not, in general, due to proprioception, and therefore not a matter of something like perception; we know where our limbs are because we put them there. Years later I learned that experiment had proven her right: we typically know where our limbs are sooner (by microseconds) than we could have learned it from proprioception. This is philosophically important, for it provides an example of empirical knowledge that is not based on empirical evidence.

The early stages in the development of thought and language are a challenge for the philosopher because it is difficult to think

[7] See A. Bechara *et al.*, "Double Dissociation of Conditioning and Declarative Knowledge Relative to the Amygdala and Hippocampus in Humans", *Science*, **269** (1995), pp. 1115–18.

[8] G. Fernández, *et al.*, "Real-Time Tracking of Memory Formation in the Human Rhinal Cortex and Hippocampus", *Science*, **285** (1999), pp. 1582–85.

[9] In particular, in *The Roots of Reference*, La Salle, Ill.: Open Court, 1974.

how they can be accurately described. We have our behavioral, neurological, physical, chemical, and genetic modes of description on the one hand, and our full-fledged manner of attributing beliefs, desires, and intentions on the other. But we have no dedicated vocabulary for what goes on in the mind of the infant before there is a full grasp of a language or the concepts that come with it. We are therefore constantly tempted to over-describe the behavior of neonates and other animals, or, a related mistake, to think of the early stages as learning first one concept and then another, forgetting that concepts as we know them cannot stand alone, but are shaped by a sophisticated pattern of knowledge and know-how. Having little idea how to satisfy the need for a way to describe the transition from the pre-propositional workings of the mind to a formed intellect, we fumble our way through this fascinating territory attributing thoughts to simple animals and infants as if they were normal human adults. In this area psychologists and educators are no better off than philosophers.

Another stretch of psychological country shared by psychologists (including psychoanalysts) and philosophers is irrationality. Freud, like Plato, Aristotle, Hume, and John Dewey, was as much a philosopher of mind and action as he was an empirical theorist and practitioner. It seems to me inevitable that during the years ahead interaction between philosophers and psychologists in this field will increase.

I mention last a central interest of my own: the empirical and theoretical understanding of how one person comes to understand another—not just how it is done in practice, but also what it is about the structure of thought, emotion, and desire that makes understandings and communication possible. Our understandings of the world, of other minds, and of ourselves are mutually dependent, so that coming to know what others think is not just a sophisticated addition to our knowledge of the world we share, but is an essential part of it. Epistemology cannot be the work of a solitary mind as Descartes and many empiricists have assumed. I do not predict so much as hope that the study of interpretation—the process of learning what others believe, want, fear, and intend, and so coming to grasp the aspects of a person that explain that person's actions—I hope this study will flourish. If it does, it may even do us all some good.

20 *Spinoza's Causal Theory of the Affects*

Our bodies constitute the essential link between our minds and the rest of nature, and the character of this linkage poses some of the most difficult problems in philosophy. Understanding the relations between mind and body, the mental and the physical, the domains of psychology and the natural sciences, is necessary if we are to give an adequate account of action, perception, memory, or empirical knowledge generally.

It is natural to think of actions as events whose causal histories begin with the thoughts, desires, and intentions of an agent and whose effects ripple outward through the motions of the body to the outside world. Perceptions and emotions, on the other hand, we view as caused by events in the world outside our bodies which terminate, after the mediation of the senses, in beliefs and specific fears, desires, loves, and hates. "Our mind," says Spinoza, "does certain things [acts] and undergoes other things, viz. insofar as it has adequate ideas, it necessarily does certain things, and insofar as it has inadequate ideas, it necessarily undergoes other things."[1] This sounds at first like the familiar opposition of acting and being acted on. But the repeated "insofar as" suggests instead that it is a matter of degree how far an event can be regarded as an action or as a passion, a matter of the extent to which the causes of certain events are in us, and the extent to which they are not.

Whatever we may think of the idea that acting and being acted on are just directions, like left and right, on what is really a

---

[1] *Ethics* IIIP1. All translations are from *The Collected Works of Spinoza*, vol. 1, edited and translated by Edwin Curley, Princeton University Press, 1988. Further references to the *Ethics* will be in the text.

continuum, it is striking how similar the problems are that arise in the course of the attempt to analyze perception and action. In the case of perception we start by noting that if someone sees that the moon is rising, then it must be true that the moon is rising, the perceiver must have come to believe that the moon is rising, and the rising of the moon must have caused the belief that the moon is rising. The difficulties concern the last clause. It is clear that it states a necessary condition, since someone could not be said to have perceived that the moon is rising simply because she came to believe truly that the moon is rising: she might have come to believe it because she was told so, or because she had read an almanac that predicted the movements of the moon and the tides. But the three conditions together are not sufficient conditions for perception, since the actual rising of the moon might cause the belief that the moon is rising in ways that would not count as perceiving that the moon is rising. For example, the rising of the moon might have caused a coyote to howl, and one might believe, falsely, that coyotes always and only howl when the moon is rising. Then the rising of the moon would have caused the agent to believe the moon was rising, but the agent would not have perceived that this was the case. At this point in the analysis, the philosopher tries adding conditions to the way the event believed to have occurred caused the belief. One could, for example, plausibly supplement the account by requiring that the sense organs play a specific role in the causality. But it is very hard—impossible, in my opinion—to state the conditions with such precision that no counter-examples can be produced.

A suspiciously similar problem arises in the analysis of intentional action. An intentional action is one performed for a reason: the agent has an answer, however absurd or trivial it may be, to the question "Why did you do that?" Reasons rationalize an action in the following sense: in the light of those reasons, the action is intelligible to others. The reasons reveal what the agent saw in the action, his end or purpose. Reasons fall into two main categories: cognitive and conative. The latter are the values, aims or goals of the agent—the ends, distant or immediate, that made the action seem to the agent worth performing; the former are the beliefs that prompted the agent to transfer the value he put on the end to the means, ultimately the action, which he thought would achieve the end. We cannot, however, simply define acting on a particular reason as acting in a way that is rationalized by one's beliefs and values, for one may act in a way that is rational in view of certain of one's beliefs and values, but do it for quite other reasons. Thus I might want to help an old man and believe I could help him by paying him to mend my umbrella. Yet these reasons might have nothing to do with my paying him to mend my umbrella—I might simply have wanted my umbrella fixed. Clearly we must add something more to the analysis of acting on a reason: we must insure that the reasons that a person has for performing an action are the reasons that *explain* his performing the action. One suggestion, which I believe is right as far as it goes, is to say that a person's reasons explain his acting only if they *cause* the action. Yet this is still not sufficient, since causality can work in devious ways; the reasons must cause the action in just the right way if they are to be the reasons the agent had in acting. I do not know how to make the conditions immune to counter-example, nor do I think it can be done. The problem, which relates the mental and the physical through causality, is the mirror image of the problem of perception.

Those familiar with the difficulties that arise in analyzing empirical knowledge will recognize the pattern of which I have just given two examples. Memory supplies a closely related puzzle. If I remember that I left my glasses in my office, then I must have left my glasses in my office, I must believe I left my glasses in my office, and my leaving my glasses in my office must be the cause of my belief that I left my glasses in my office. But once more, these conditions, though all necessary, are not sufficient: the causality must be of the right, but apparently unspecifiable, sort.

Not all such problems involve, or at least clearly involve, both mental and physical factors. For consider what it is to *reason*—a process we may think of as entirely mental. In reasoning, propositions do not occur in the mind at random: if the sequence of entertained propositions is to constitute a course of reasoning, the propositions must be logically related to each other. The mere occurrence of logically related propositions in the mind does not in itself suffice for reasoning, however; the consideration or affirmation of certain thoughts must beget, i.e. cause, other thoughts. But once more, not any causal relation will do: we affirm the conclusion not only because we affirm the premises, but also because we appreciate that the premises entail the conclusion.

This is still not sufficient: believing that *c* follows from *a* and *b*, and believing that *a* and that *b* is not enough to ensure that we believe that *c* for the right reason unless we connect the logical entailment with the case at hand; this is the psychological analogue of Lewis Carroll's "What the Tortoise Said to Achilles". What we need is a correct account of *how*, in reasoning, the belief in the premises causes the belief in the conclusion.

These puzzles all concern the causal relations of thoughts, of thoughts as the causes of actions, as the effects of perception, and of thoughts as the causes of other thoughts. The fact that these relations are so deeply puzzling suggests some sort of misfit between the concept of causality and the concept of a thought.

No philosopher was more obsessed with these problems than Spinoza, and few philosophers have made such dramatic proposals for their solution. I sketched at the start the problems as they might be described by a contemporary philosopher. To appreciate how Spinoza may have viewed the ancestors of these problems (which may not be all that different from their modern versions), let me state some of the assumptions from which Spinoza started, and which he sought to reconcile.

(1) In the sequence of events in the material world—the world of extended objects—everything happens according to the laws of nature. There is no event that is not fully determined by what goes before, and no state of the universe that does not fully determine what follows. The system is comprehensive, deterministic, and closed. If nothing can interfere with the working of this system, we, as human agents, cannot interfere. Our actions, so far as they belong to this system, cannot be free in the sense of undetermined; our actions are caused by what goes before, and what we effect by our actions is likewise just part of the ineluctable course of nature. God can neither interfere in the natural course of events, nor can he be prior to it as an independent creator. Since everything that can affect the system is included in it, every natural event can be fully explained by the laws of nature and any total prior state of the universe.

(2) Both thoughts and extended bodies are real. Yet our conception of thoughts, of desire, of memories, and of reasoning is a conception that does not include the defining properties of physical objects such as precise location in space, a shape, physical texture, and chemical composition. For this reason our

physical system, which explains causal interactions in terms of such properties, leaves no room for mental events. It would seem to follow that if there are mental events (which Spinoza takes as evident) then they can neither be caused by events in the physical world (as perception apparently requires) nor can they cause events in the physical world (as action apparently requires).

(3) Aside from the fact that action and perception seem to demand some close relation between thought and the world of extended objects, we have other reasons to believe in a close relation. We are constantly aware, for example, of what goes on in our bodies. We are not aware, in the same way, of what goes on in the bodies of other people. (The close connection between our bodies and our sensations Edwin Curley rightly sees as a major consideration for Spinoza.[2]) Our thoughts are directly expressed in the physical motions of our bodies in a way that our thoughts are not expressed in the bodies of others.

There is a further, and global, respect in which the order of thoughts precisely parallels the order of extended things and events. If the physical world is fully determined by laws and the distribution of bodies and their motions at some one moment, then we know that there exists an infinite set of propositions about the distribution of bodies and their motions at some moment which, in conjunction with the laws, would enable an infinite mind to calculate the entire history of the universe. If we think of the world of thought as consisting of all these truths, then there is a clear sense in which "the order and connection of ideas is the same as the order and connection of things" (IIP7). The connection of ideas is that of deduction: a proposition describing one state of the universe may be deduced from a description of an earlier state of the universe by appeal to the laws of nature. The order in which one state of the universe may be inferred from a prior state is the same as the temporal sequence of events it predicts and explains.

These three assumptions, of a closed deterministic system of physical nature, of a world of thought which does not interact with the physical, and of a very close connection between the

---

[2] Edwin Curley, *Behind the Geometrical Method: A Reading of Spinoza's Ethics*, Princeton University Press, 1988, p. 82.

mental and the physical world, set the problem. The problem is, what can the connection between the mental and the physical be if it is to satisfy these conditions? Spinoza's answer, as we know, is that the mental and the physical are just two ways of viewing and understanding one and the same world.

It is clear that this proposal brilliantly reconciles the existence of the mental with the existence of a deterministic closed system of the physical which leaves nothing out, but makes no reference to the mental. An ontology that comprises just material objects and events may yet be complete if the mental objects and events are identical with the material, and so a purely physical science can, in one clear sense, be complete. Spinoza's monism is also consistent with the failure to conceive how interaction between the mental and the physical takes place, though this point is much harder to grasp.

One reason it is hard to grasp is that there is, or seems to be, a way in which we do conceive causal relations between the physical and the mental, and this is a manner of conception at which Spinoza constantly hints. Thus he defines love as "Joy with the accompanying idea of an external cause". Joy is an affect of the mind, but what is the idea of an external cause? It may be that Spinoza means only that there is an association of two items in the mind, one the affect of joy, the other the mind's (inadequate) idea of an event in the body. This would not imply interaction. But it seems more reasonable to view the second item as the *belief* that the cause of one's joy is a certain external object, and this does imply the *conception* of causal interaction between the mental and the physical. Or again, "If someone has done something which he imagines affects others with joy, he will be affected with Joy accompanied by the idea of himself as cause" (IIIP30). If you can imagine that something you have done affects others with joy, it is hard to see how you are not at least imagining a case where a physical event causes a mental affect.

The most obvious objection to Spinoza's apparent denial of interaction is, however, far more direct. Spinoza insists on causal relations among physical events, and each of these physical events is identical with some thought. Suppose, then, that the ringing of a bell causes some complex event in my brain, and this event is identical to my awareness of the sound. If the ringing of the bell caused the event in my brain, and this event *is* (in the sense of identity) a thought, how can Spinoza consistently deny that the physical sound caused the thought? How can he plausibly deny that we believe in such causal relations, and so conceive them?

Marx Wartofsky suggests a solution. He writes, apropos Spinoza's identity theory:

The radical consequence of this view is a rejection both of a mechanistic determinism of psychic states by bodily states...and of a psychic determination of bodily states...For if one takes the identity seriously...every change in a psychic state is a change in a bodily state, necessarily; but not causally. A change in the psychic character, or intensity, or quality of an emotion does not *lead* to a change in a bodily state; it *is* one. Thus, the mistaken notion that Spinoza proposes a parallelism as against Cartesian interactionism simply has the model wrong. There is conceptual parallelism, insofar as we think of bodies and minds. But what we think, under these two attributes, is not parallel, but identical.[3]

The idea here, as in much of Spinoza's Appendix to *Ethics* i, is: the relation between mind and body is not causal *because* it is the relation of identity. But clearly this response does not answer a criticism *based* on the claimed identity. If *a* causes *b* under the attribute of extension, and *b* is identical with *c*, where *c* is conceived under the attribute of thought, how can we deny that *a* caused *c*, where *a* is conceived as extended, and *c* as a modification of mind?

The difficulty, put this way, is so apparent that one must assume that we have misinterpreted Spinoza on some essential point, or have failed to make a distinction that was crucial to his position. What are the possibilities?

One interpretation would deny the apparent element of dualism in Spinoza. If there is no distinction to be made between the mental and the physical, then it makes no sense to speak of interaction. Thus Curley argues that "the fundamental thrust of Spinoza's system is anti-dualistic, ... it is a form of materialistic monism".[4] If we take Spinoza as denying the reality of the mental, of course there can be no problem about interaction. But before we could accept this solution, we would have to explain away Spinoza's denial of interaction and his apparent insistence on the

[3] Marx Wartofsky, "Action and Passion", in *Spinoza: A Collection of Critical Essays*, ed. Marjorie Grene, Anchor Books, Garden City, NY, 1973, p. 349.
[4] Curley, *Behind the Geometrical Method*, p. 82.

reality of the mental. In fact, Curley does not try to explain away Spinoza's very evident commitment to an attribute of mind in every way parallel to the attribute of extension.[5] His arguments for Spinoza's materialism are rather arguments for a complete parallel between the mental and the physical: he points out how Spinoza emphasizes the complexity of the body, which makes it plausible that it can echo the complexity of thought, and he stresses the doctrine that all human knowledge is in the first instance knowledge of one's own body. These are considerations which, in another philosopher, might be employed in defense of a reduction of the mental to the physical, but there is no evidence that Spinoza contemplated such a reduction.

Alan Donagan takes almost the opposite tack; he comes close to denying that Spinoza is a monist. "Since each attribute is really distinct", he writes, "Spinoza allows no possibility of reducing even human thought to processes in human bodies, which used to be the programme of materialism when philosophers were serious about it. From no point of view is he a materialist."[6] Donagan allows that, though there is a "sense" in which "a given human individual's mind and body are...the same thing, constituted respectively by the really distinct attributes of thought and extension, they cannot be causally related to one another, because those attributes are really distinct".[7] Curley can be excused for saying that Donagan "seems to think that Spinoza's monism about substance is spurious".[8] If Spinoza is not a genuine monist, mind and body are not really identical, and the apparent contradiction I pointed to disappears. But then, so would the apparent contrast between Spinoza's metaphysics and Descartes's also disappear, and Spinoza would need some substitute for the pineal gland.

There remains, as far as I can see, only one other avenue of escape from the problem we have set, and it involves the concept of causation and the interpretation of Spinoza's denial of interaction. What did Spinoza mean when he wrote, "The Body

---

[5] In an important respect, Spinoza's attribute of mind is infinitely greater than that of extension, for since mind has an idea of everything that exists, it not only has an idea of every mode of extension, but also of every mode of mind, which implies an infinite regress of ideas for every extended object.

[6] Alan Donagan, *Spinoza*, University of Chicago Press, 1988, p. 119.

[7] Ibid., p. 124.   [8] Curley, *Behind the Geometrical Method*, p. 158, n. 38.

cannot determine the Mind to thinking, and the Mind cannot determine the Body to motion..." (IIIP2)? Did he mean by "determine" what we mean by "cause"?

Hampshire warns us that although both we and Spinoza mean by a cause "anything which *explains* the existence or qualities of the effect," Spinoza has a different standard of explanation than that of modern science:

To Spinoza... to "explain" means to show that one true proposition is the logically necessary consequence of some other; explanation essentially involves exhibiting necessary connections... The ideal of scientific explanation is here purely deductive and mathematical...[9]

The idea that the occurrence of a particular event can be explained entirely by appeal to logic seems to require both that the laws of nature be regarded as laws or truths of logic, and that there is a logical truth from which to reason, by way of the laws, to the logical necessity of the effect. This view, that all the truths of nature are ultimately truths of logic, or at least of reason, is not my concern here. I am interested in an ideal of explanation which modern science may be said to share with Spinoza: the ideal of discovering a system of laws from which the occurrence of the event to be explained can be deduced from a description of the relevant causal conditions. Achieving this ideal implies, first, that nothing that can affect the operation of nature lies outside the system of explanation, and, second, that there is a preferred vocabulary in terms of which the laws are stated and in which the events to be explained and the relevant causal conditions can be described. This is the vocabulary of the ultimate science of nature.

No doubt it is true, as Hampshire says, that Spinoza wanted the laws and ultimate starting point to be truths of reason; but setting aside this essential point of difference from modern science, the concept of explanation is the same: given the laws and the prior conditions, the rest is logic and mathematics.

The distinction I wish to emphasize is not, then, Hampshire's distinction between science viewed as dealing only with truths of reason and science as experimental and empirical; it is rather a distinction available *within* the concept of explanation shared by Spinoza and modern science. Within that common concept it is

---

[9] Stuart Hampshire, *Spinoza*, Penguin Books, 1951, p. 35.

easy to grasp the possibility of *degrees* of explanatory adequacy. A completely adequate explanation is one that deduces the occurrence (or probability of occurrence) of the event to be explained from the laws of nature and a statement of the prior conditions. We fall away from such complete adequacy as our knowledge of the laws of nature or the relevant causal conditions diminishes. Take an example. The cause of some particular event, say the San Francisco earthquake of 1906, is some other particular event, perhaps the sudden release of energy as the Pacific plate slid northwards along the San Andreas fault. Of course we could not predict the earthquake from this description of either cause or effect, even given correct laws: before we could predict the earthquake we would need descriptions of cause and effect that would bring them under the laws: the descriptions would have to instantiate the laws. It is clear that such descriptions would have to be far more detailed and complete than any we are prepared to give. Because our descriptions of the events involved are incomplete, our explanation of the earthquake is inadequate.

The inadequacy of our knowledge of the cause and the effect does not throw in doubt the causal connection; we may have correctly identified the cause of the earthquake, even though our knowledge of that cause, and hence our understanding of the earthquake, are partial. So there are at least two ways in which our ability to explain an event may fall short: we may be ignorant of some of the causal factors (and so take advantage of a phrase like "other things being equal"), or we may lack the appropriate descriptive vocabulary for specifying the cause or the effect in a way that would allow us to see them as instantiating a law. These two sources of failure, or partial failure, converge in the case where we command the appropriate vocabulary, but do not know how to describe the cause or the effect, or both, in that vocabulary.

The ideal of a comprehensive vocabulary in which complete explanations could in theory be given of any event does not rule out the possibility of another, irreducibly different, vocabulary in which alternative explanations of the very same events could be produced. There might be many such possible systems. So nothing precludes as unintelligible the idea that the vocabularies of the mental and the physical belong to two different, but equally complete, systems of explanation for the same world. The

possibility just bruited describes Spinoza's metaphysics: ontological monism and a multiplicity of conceptual systems.

In what sense can such a metaphysics maintain the irreducibility of one system to another? Clearly Spinoza's metaphysics
depends on ontological reduction: each material entity is identified with a mental entity.[10] The failure of other forms of reduction
is consistent with such monism. Definitional reduction, for
example, whatever its standards, is not implied by ontological
monism. There is no reason to suppose that mental concepts like
loving, intending, fearing, and deciding can be defined in purely
physical terms, and the failures of definitional behaviorism suggest that there are principled reasons why this cannot be done.

We should not be seduced by the fact that each particular
which can be identified in the physical vocabulary can also be
identified in the mental vocabulary into thinking that therefore
one vocabulary is superfluous. The purpose of a vocabulary is to
classify particulars, to gather them into classes, and from the fact
that each individual in a set can be described in a given vocabulary
it does not follow that the set, if it is infinite, or a property that
applies to all and only the items in that set, can be defined in that
same vocabulary.

If it is the case that there is no class of particulars picked out by
the mental vocabulary which corresponds to (is identical with) a
class picked out by the physical vocabulary, then there cannot be
any strict laws connecting particulars characterized in mental
terms with particulars characterized in physical terms. So monism
is also compatible with the failure of *nomological* reduction, with
the absence of strict psychophysical laws. Monism, coupled with
the failure of nomological connections, implies that a complete
or adequate explanation of a mental event cannot be given in
physical terms, and a complete and adequate explanation of a
physical event cannot be given in mental terms.

Given nomological irreducibility, it is correct to insist, as
Spinoza does in IIIP2, that "the Body cannot determine the Mind
to thinking, and the Mind cannot determine the Body to motion".
We should take this to mean that we cannot infer from a cause
described in physical terms that a specific mental event will ensue

---

[10] The reduction is not symmetrical, since there are ideas of ideas and of the modes
of other attributes in addition to the ideas of material objects.

as effect, for this would require either psychophysical causal laws or psychophysical bridging laws, and nomological and definitional irreducibility prohibit such laws; mental and physical concepts belong to independent explanatory systems. This comes out clearly in the demonstration of IIIP2: "All modes of thinking have God for a cause, insofar as he is a thinking thing, and not insofar as he is explained by another attribute (by IIP6). So what determines the Mind to thinking is a mode of thinking and not of Extension, i.e., it is not the body." The demonstration of the converse is parallel. This demonstration takes us back to IIP6, which states: "The modes of each attribute have God for their cause only insofar as he is considered under the attribute of which they are modes, and not insofar as he is considered under any other attribute," and the demonstration goes on, "For each attribute is conceived through itself without any other." If we accept the emphasis on how things are "conceived" or "considered" and remember that a cause for Spinoza is primarily something that explains, even fully explains, its effect, then we can understand IIIP2 as denying only that a full and adequate explanation of an event described under one attribute can be given by appeal to a cause described under another attribute. Spinoza holds that it makes no sense to speak of explaining or understanding the existence or modification of anything except under one or another system of description, that is, as viewed under one attribute or another.

The point of IIIP2 is not, then, to deny that mental events can *cause* physical events, but to deny that they can *explain* them (and conversely, of course). Nothing in this picture of the relations between mind and body, the mental and the physical, rules out what we would call the causal interaction of particular physical events with particular mental events. We therefore do not have to saddle Spinoza with the logical absurdity that would result from holding that the physical event of a bell ringing cannot cause a mental awareness of the ringing even though that mental awareness is identical with a physical event in the brain caused by the ringing. In my view, Spinoza does not deny that the ringing of the bell may cause us to be aware of the ringing; what he denies is that it is possible to give a fully adequate explanation of the occurrence of the belief by appeal to the laws of nature and to the cause described in physical terms. I do not even see why he should deny that it is useful to know that a certain sort of physical event is likely to cause a certain sort of mental event; Spinoza would not call this an explanation because the description of the cause and the description of the effect did not belong to the same system of explanation, and so the effect could not, in Spinoza's phrase, be "clearly and distinctly perceived through" the cause—through the cause as conceived or described in a certain way, of course. Those whose standards of explanation are less Euclidean are free to say that describing the cause of a mentally described event in physical terms may still be a form of explanation, and, of course, to say the same of the describing of the cause of a physically described event in mental terms. To stay within the bounds of Spinoza's metaphysics, however, they would have to hold that such explanations could not be made fully adequate: adequate explanations are necessarily intra-attribute. Curley speaks of Spinoza's "tendency to identify *causa* and *ratio*".[11] Clearly this notion of cause, which is closely tied to explanation, and is therefore sensitive to how cause and effect are described, differs radically from the notion of cause we employ when we are describing a relation in nature between events. Causal relations in nature are indifferent to how we describe them.

At the start of this paper I outlined a number of basic problems that arise when we attempt to give a complete analysis or definition of such concepts as those of perception, memory, and action. In each case there seemed a point at which the transition from the physical to the mental (as with perception and memory), or the transition from the mental to the physical (as in the case of action) could not be fully explained. Exactly *how,* we asked, must the beliefs and desires that rationalize and so explain an action cause the action? We can specify the *logical* relations between the propositional *contents* of the appropriate beliefs and desires and the description of the action under which they rationalize it. What we apparently can't do is say in clear detail how the mental attitudes cause the action. A similar aporia afflicted us when we inquired into the question how, exactly, an event causes the belief that it

---

[11] *The Collected Works of Spinoza*, p. 628. Curley instances IP11D2: "For each thing must be assigned a cause, *or* reason, as much for its existence as for its nonexistence."

occurred when the event is correctly said to be remembered. The analysis of perception led to an analogous impasse.

The interpretation of Spinoza's view of the relation between the mental and the physical modes of explanation, and of causation, which I have proposed is not only consistent with the existence of these failures of complete analysis or explanation; it makes them inevitable, and offers an account of why they are inevitable. If the attempt to analyze action or memory or perception in terms of the causal relations between the mental and the physical were to succeed, nothing would stand in the way of complete inter-attribute explanations. In particular there would have to be psychophysical laws as precise as the laws of physics. But if Spinoza (on my interpretation) is right, there are no such precise laws. The systems of explanation to which the mental and the physical belong are irreducibly different, despite the fact that the mental and the physical are just two different ways of conceiving—and hence of classifying—the same particulars.

I suppose it is inevitable that when we try to understand a philosopher whom we find altogether admirable, yet difficult and obscure, we are drawn to an interpretation which we find as consistent and congenial as charity prompts and honesty permits. Thus I do not feel abashed to admit that the reading I find plausible of Spinoza's ontological monism coupled with a dualistic (or multiple) explanatory apparatus is close to my own view of the relation between the mental and the physical. I call this position *anomalous monism*, and I have from the start recognized its kinship with Spinoza's views.[12] The similarities are these: (1) Ontological monism: there are no particulars (and here I included both objects and events) that cannot be uniquely identified by definite descriptions which are couched exclusively in the language of physics, and by definite descriptions which are "mental" (I allowed the mental descriptions to include physical concepts as long as a mental term occurred "essentially"—that is, the mental term could not be removed from the description while leaving its reference unchanged). (2) Conceptual dualism: the mental and the physical vocabularies are neither definitionally nor nomologically reducible in either direction. (3) Explanatory

---

[12] In "Mental Events" (1970), reprinted in *Essays on Actions and Events*, Oxford University Press, 1980, p. 212.

dualism: although the natural sciences may arrive at the point where they can fully explain, and hence in theory predict, any event, they cannot, even in principle, predict or fully explain any event under a mental description. Nor (even more obviously) could a perfected science of psychology ever fully explain or predict any event under a physical description. (4) It follows that there are no strict, deterministic laws connecting the mental and the physical. (5) Finally, these points do not contradict the recognition that there are causal relations between the mental and the physical: causal *relations*, as I conceive them, are between events however described; causal *explanations*, on the other hand, depend on the vocabulary or concepts used to describe events and to formulate laws.

I have now described Spinoza's theory of the relation between the mental and the physical in a way that makes it consistent, and, except for a remaining doubt, makes it correct in my view. The doubt concerns the nature of the parallelism between the mental and the physical. It is one thing to postulate two irreducibly different systems for explaining the same world; it goes beyond this to insist that "the order and connection of ideas is the same as the order and connection of things". What does this additional claim come to? I proposed above one possibility: there is a sequence of propositions arranged in a natural deductive order which corresponds to the temporal order of cause and effect in the world of extended things. Then the order of deduction is the same as the temporal order: the connection of ideas is the same as the causal connection of things. However, this sequence of ideas cannot be in any finite human mind, it can only exist in God's mind. Individual items from the sequence can exist in human minds, but they are scattered and confused, constituting a woefully gerrymandered selection.

Human psychology is the study not of God's mind, but of what goes on in human minds. There can be no doubt that Spinoza was interested in human psychology, and that he took serious steps towards demonstrating its possibilities. As he famously announces in the Preface to Part III,

The affects . . . of hate, anger, envy, etc., considered in themselves, follow from the same necessity and force of nature as the other singular things. And therefore they acknowledge certain causes, through which they are understood, and hence have certain properties, as worthy of our knowledge as the properties of any other thing.

He then promises to inaugurate the scientific study of these matters by treating the "nature and powers of the Affects, . . . human actions and appetites" as if they were "lines, planes, and bodies". He has two strategies in behalf of this project.

One is to remove seeming obstacles. He explains the illusion of an autonomous will by maintaining that, though we are aware of our volitions and appetites, we generally have no idea of their causes, and so assume they have no causes. He explains the human tendency to suppose that God has arranged things to serve human ends, or any other ends, by plausibly claiming that through failure to imagine volitions different from our own, we invent God in our own image. He seeks to remove the objection to the view that the complexity of thoughts corresponds to something in the body by pointing out the enormous complexity of our bodies, and our almost total ignorance of the details of the body's structure and operations.

On the positive side, Spinoza gives analyses of volition, perception, and the emotions consistent with his thoroughgoing naturalism and determinism. Perhaps the most striking feature of his concept of action is his view that it differs from being acted on just to the extent that its causes and effects lie within rather than outside us, and that this in turn is a matter of the extent and character of our knowledge. The idea that acting and being acted on differ only in degree does, we realize, follow directly from an objective view of human beings as integral parts of the causal chain of natural events, but even to us to whom this attitude comes perhaps more easily than to Spinoza's contemporaries, it is a sobering perspective.

Spinoza's treatment of particular emotions is also interesting for its method. The "causes" of joy and sadness, pleasure and pain, of an increase or decrease in the mind's power of thinking, or in the body's power of acting, are sometimes referred to by Spinoza as "things", but as often are called "imaginings". Thus what is translated as "pride" ("superbia") is defined as joy born of the fact that a man thinks more highly of himself than is just (IIIP26S). Here it seems clear that it is a propositional thought, such as, "I am swifter than my neighbor," which causes the joy. What Spinoza calls "self-esteem" provides a better characterization of pride, since pride can, after all, be born of a correct estimate of one's worth. Self-esteem, Spinoza says, is joy arising from thinking of our power of acting or of our actions (IIIP55S). Here Spinoza seems unexpectedly close to Hume, who has a very similar analysis of pride. Neither Hume nor Spinoza allows a separate judgment that having a certain strength is estimable; rather, to be caused pleasure (approbation) by the belief that one has a certain ability or strength *is* to value that ability or strength.

I believe these causal analyses of action and the emotions are correct in one very important respect: such psychological concepts are irreducibly causal in character. An action is necessarily a movement caused by thoughts and desires; pride is necessarily a positive attitude caused by a belief that one has some esteemed property; a desire is necessarily something that causes action under appropriate circumstances.

This fact suggests a difficulty in accepting Spinoza's theory of the affects. It is true that many of our most important psychological concepts are causal, but this very feature unsuits them to the most complete sort of explanation. We are forced to appeal to causal powers in natural objects such as brittleness (easily caused to shatter), elasticity (caused by some internal feature to return to its original shape when deformed), or afterglow (a glow in the sky caused by the sun after setting) just when we are ignorant of the actual causal mechanism. But a fully adequate science does not employ causal concepts: it relies on knowledge of the structure that explains why the brittle object shatters when it does, or allows us to predict when, and to what degree, an object will return to its original shape after being subjected to precisely specified forces. A science which could not get along without causal concepts could not provide the sort of total and detailed explanation to which physics aspires and which constitutes Spinoza's ideal of an adequate explanation.

Even if we put aside the thought that causal concepts are out of place in an advanced science as anachronistic when applied to Spinoza,[13] there remains a puzzle about how a scientific psychology can hope to parallel physics in precision and comprehensiveness. As we have seen, if God is omniscient, then his knowledge of the world as extended may reasonably be

---

[13] Though Molière recognized the explanatory inadequacy of causal concepts. It is a shallow explanation of why a substance put someone to sleep to note that it was a soporific, since "*x* is a soporific" means "*x* tends to induce sleep".

considered to consist of ideas "ordered and connected" as are the modes of extension. God's knowledge of psychology, his knowledge of the totality of what we may call first-order ideas, is presumably another, or second-order level, of ideas. These are three levels of entities: extended objects, and first- and second-order ideas. Within each level the "order and connection" must be the same. The first- and second-order ideas constitute two total world schemes: one scheme treats the world under the attribute of extension, the other under the attribute of thought.

Does it follow, though, that human beings can reasonably aspire to construct a psychology as comprehensive as the physics they reasonably aspire to construct? It seems to me no such human science of psychology is possible. Though the human mind cannot hope to know all the details of the natural universe, it can conceive this totality and hope to learn its laws. This does not require that the human mind begin to harbor ideas corresponding to all physical phenomena. But then a human science of psychology must be radically incomplete: the entities it studies, namely human thoughts, correspond to so little of the material world that no self-contained science can be based exclusively on them. Too many of the causes and effects of human thoughts are unknown to human thought.

So I confess that I do not see how even the most complete understanding of human psychology can avoid essential reference to the material forces that impinge on us. Nor do I see how psychology, as long as it deals with such concepts as those of action, intention, belief, and desire, can either be reduced to the natural sciences or made as exact and self-contained as physics. As I suggested, we may even take Spinoza as having shown why such a psychology is impossible; the nomological irreducibility of the mental to the physical can be taken to point in this direction.

Spinoza did not follow this pointer. To have followed it would, after all, have been to abandon his idea of a symmetrical relation between first-order ideas and the physical, the idea that both of these two aspects of reality can be fully systematized, and that any event, conceived under either attribute, can be completely explained within a science of that attribute. It is an inspired vision; perhaps we should not be too easily persuaded that it is illusory. The problems I rehearsed at the beginning of this paper: the problem of how beliefs and desires cause an action when they give the reason it was performed; the problem of how external events cause sensations and beliefs in perception and memory; the problem of how one belief causes another when we reason—could it be the case that there exist "solutions" to these problems, even if for some reason we cannot arrive at them?

Appendix: Replies to Rorty, Stroud, McDowell, and Pereda

These essays give me much pleasure.[1] They are written by friends with my welfare in mind, showing the measured attention and understanding one always secretly hopes for, and full of avuncular advice gently administered. They are friends of each other, of mine, and of philosophy, and when it comes to a choice, they prove they would not be such good friends loved they not philosophy more. This practically ensures that they do not always agree with each other, or with me, and where one agrees with me, another differs. It will not harm this happy state of affairs if I try to bring about agreement, for the more agreement there is (or so I have always argued), the more intelligible and rewarding further discussion will be.

Richard Rorty sees some of my views as serving his Wittgensteinian agenda, which is flattering if deserved. He is less pleased by my persistent interest in Tarskian semantics. Like many others, he views these tendencies as opposed, and urges me to forgo the second. But I can't, because what Rorty holds to be antithetical modes of philosophizing I see as interdependent aspects of the same enterprise. Insofar as I have arrived at, or remembered, Wittgensteinian thoughts, it is largely through having taken a third person approach to the problems of intentionality, and this is an approach which has always seemed to me to require (along with much more) the framework provided by the structures of formal semantics and decision theory. Rorty suggests that you can grasp my arguments for saying that interpreting a speaker involves knowing one's way around in the world even if you have

---

[1] The reference is to essays in *Crítica* 28 (1998).

no interest in a systematic theory of language. But I did not say that knowing one's way around in the world didn't include skills that can only be described by appeal to a formal theory. I'll revisit these matters presently. But now I turn to Rorty's first suggestion, that I give up subscribing to Quine's thesis of the indeterminacy of translation, or, as I translate it, the indeterminacy of interpretation.

What he fears is that this thesis implies that there is something mysterious, second rate, or even not quite real, about the mental, that there are no "facts of the matter" about meaning or the propositional attitudes. Let me put his mind at rest on this score. In my view, the mental is no more mysterious than molecular biology or cosmology. Our mental concepts are as essential to our understanding of the world as any others; we could not do without them. The propositional attitudes, such as intentions, desires, beliefs, hopes, and fears, are every bit as real as atoms and baseball bats, and the facts about them as real as the facts about anything else. How could there be a question about the *ontology* of mental entities for me if, as I hold, they are identical with entities we also describe and explain, in different terms, in the natural sciences?

Rorty's fears are partly based on an early mistake of mine. In "Mental Events" I did maintain that the irreducibility of mental concepts was due, among other things, to the indeterminacy of interpretation. This was wrong, as I have since admitted. The error is obvious: indeterminacy as I understand it is endemic in all disciplines. Indeterminacy is nothing more than the flip side of invariance. Indeterminacy occurs whenever a vocabulary is rich enough to describe a phenomenon in more than one way. It doesn't matter whether you say Sam is to the left of Susan, or that Susan is to the right of Sam. If you have the axioms that define some system of measurement, whether it is of weight, temperature, or subjective probability, you can represent the structure so defined in numbers in endless ways. What matters is what is *invariant*. With weight, an arbitrarily chosen positive number is assigned to some particular object; relative to that assignment, the numbers that measure the weights of all other objects are fixed. So you can get an equally good way of keeping track of weights by multiplying the original figures by any positive constant; it's the *ratios* that are invariant. Only invariances are "facts of the matter".

This is how I understand the indeterminacy of translation and interpretation. Given the richness of all natural languages, it would be surprising if it were not always possible to describe the facts of any discipline in many ways. Such indeterminacy does not threaten the reality of what is described. Of course, confusion results if we do not take into account the relativity of some way of describing things to the appropriate scale or mode of description: it matters whether your numbers are Fahrenheit or Centigrade, your weights pounds or kilos, your distances miles or kilometers. The analogy with the case of sentences or the contents of propositional attitudes is this: Each of us can think of his own sentences (or their contents) as like the numbers; they have multiple relations to one another and to the world. Keeping these relations the same, we can match up our sentences with those of a speaker, and with the attitudes of that speaker, in different ways without changing our minds about what the speaker thinks and means. Just as endless sets of numbers allow us to keep track of the same complex structures in the world, so our sentences can be used in endless different ways to keep track of the attitudes of others, and of the meanings of their sentences. Quine made this point in order to emphasize that there is no more to the identification of meanings than is involved in capturing these complex empirical relations. This can sound like a negative thesis, and it is; it is an attack on the idea that meanings can be captured in exactly one way, by pinning Platonic meanings on expressions. But this negative point does not entail that there are no facts of the matter; the facts are the empirical relations between a speaker, her sentences, and her environment. This pattern is invariant.

If we actually employed more of the possible ways of reporting what someone means and thinks, we would want to be explicit about the system we were using. In practice, we pretty much stick to one way; it's as if everyone spoke Centigrade or Miles or Kilograms. But for theoretical purposes, it is good to know what our assignments are relative to; they are relative to a language. Not our own language, of course, but the language of the speaker or agent. When in our ordinary dealings with others we make small adjustments in our reporting of what someone meant or thought, we silently change the language we take that person to be speaking. Quine calls this changing the translation manual, but this makes it seem that there is something in addition to the usual relativity of a theory of meaning to a language, while in fact only one relativization is required, and it is familiar.

Rorty says he discerns no distinction between the under-determination of a theory and indeterminacy. I do. Theories are interesting and valuable mainly because they entail what hasn't been observed, particularly, though not only, in the future. It is an empirical question whether such a theory holds for the unobserved cases—a question to which we shall never know the answer. As Hume and Nelson Goodman have told us, there are endless things that may happen next, many of which would confirm theories at odds with our present theories. This is underdetermination. Indeterminacy is not like this; no amount of evidence, finite or infinite, would decide whether to measure areas in acres or hectares.

John McDowell is clear that nothing I say makes the mental mysterious or any less real than the subject matter of the natural sciences. He also agrees with me that there is a reason to emphasize the irreducibility of the mental, but only because the irreducibility springs from something more interesting than the indeterminacy of translation and interpretation. He rightly stresses the constitutive role of normativity in all mental or psychological concepts. This was what I had made central in "Mental Concepts" (1970), and again in "Three Varieties of Knowledge" (1991), where I took back the claim that the irreducibility of mental concepts followed from the indeterminacy of interpretation. The mental vocabulary isn't "privileged" *because* it is irreducible (as Rorty thinks I think), it is irreducible because it is normative.

Normativity is constitutive of the mental because the mental is built on a framework of attitudes which have a propositional content, and propositions have logical relations to one another. Reasoning, no matter how simple and unstudied, is a matter of putting thoughts together in ways that are assessable as reasonable both by the agent and by others. Every action is describable in terms of intentions, and intentions are based on reasons that are, again, judged as rational or not by the agent and others. All genuine speech is intentional, and can be understood only by interpreters equipped to grasp key intentions of speakers. The norms I am mainly concerned with are not the norms of responsibility, trustworthiness, morality. The basic "virtue" that sets mental concepts off from those of the natural sciences is the special sort of charity required for understanding the thoughts, speech, and other actions of agents, and such charity is not a virtue, but simply a condition of understanding others at all (and so, of course, it is a necessary preliminary to treating others as moral agents).[2]

Charity is a matter of finding enough rationality in those we would understand to make sense of what they say and do, for unless we succeed in this, we cannot identify the contents of their words and thoughts. Seeing rationality in others is a matter of recognizing our own norms of rationality in their speech and behavior. These norms include the norms of logical consistency, of action in reasonable accord with essential or basic interests, and the acceptance of views that are sensible in the light of evidence. These various norms can suggest conflicting ways of interpreting an agent (for example, there are different things an agent may mean by what she says), and there may be no clear grounds for preferring one of these ways to others. Balancing the claims of competing norms in interpretation thus introduces a form of indeterminacy not found in the indeterminacy that abounds in physical measurement. This is the connection between indeterminacy and the irreducibility of the mental I had in mind in "Mental Events"; it is badly expressed in the passage from that essay which McDowell quotes at the start of his paper. It is a special twist the norms of rationality impart to interpretation.

Such indeterminacy does not make the mental mysterious or unreal, nor does it suggest that there is no fact of the matter about what people think and mean; it is a harmless consequence of the fact that there is more than one way of describing what is invariant. But whether or not one accepts the thesis of indeterminacy, here we come to something that puts an end to a certain regress. For when we ask where the norms come from that each of us applies in understanding others, the answer is that they cannot be derived from a source outside ourselves, for any attempt to check with others drives us back to the process of interpretation in

[2] I am happy to have McDowell remind me of Wilfred Sellars's "Empiricism and the Philosophy of Mind" in this connection. I read it many years ago and was permanently influenced, though what I remembered learning there was the attack on the Myth of the Given.

which we necessarily employ our own norms. This is the step Rorty says he has come to understand, having been persuaded by Bjørn Ramberg's perceptive paper. As Rorty puts it, "the inescapability of norms is the inescapability, for both describers and agents, of triangulating".

McDowell and I seem to have in mind the same distinction between mental concepts and those of the natural sciences, and we agree that it is the rationality of propositional thought that sets the mental apart.[3] There also seems to be a shade of difference in how we want to describe the distinction. He writes:

> The separation of logical spaces or constitutive ideals that underwrites the irreducibility thesis reflects a distinction between two ways of finding things intelligible. Both involve placing things in a pattern. But in one case the pattern is constituted by regularities according to which phenomena of the relevant kind unfold; in the other it is the pattern of a life led by an agent who can shape her action and thought in the light of an ideal of rationality.

It is only the last sentence that gives me pause. I agree that the norms of rationality do define a "pattern of life led by an agent who can shape her action and thought in the light of an ideal of rationality". But this is only one feature of "the space of reasons". Whether or not an agent "shapes" her action and thought in the light of an ideal, and whether she acts or thinks well or badly, when we represent her thoughts and actions to ourselves as thoughts and actions, we have placed her in the space of reasons. Perhaps McDowell would agree. My more serious misgiving concerns the implication that mental concepts, unlike those of the natural sciences, are not concerned with "regularities" (elsewhere he calls them laws). The point of concepts is to classify things, and concepts survive only if they are found useful. "Useful" here means leading to valuable generalizations. I have myself urged that the generalizations mental concepts lend themselves to are less strict than those physics aims for, but they are ones we could

---

[3] I am surprised to find Rorty, who is so opposed to distinguishing the mental vocabulary from the vocabulary of natural science, buying the old positivist distinction between the "descriptive vocabulary of intentionality" and the "prescriptive vocabulary of normativity". Maybe there is some respectable way to set apart the concepts sometimes conveyed by words like "obligation", "duty", "right", and "good" from mental concepts, but I would say both sorts of concepts are based on norms, and both are descriptive.

not live without. Many mental traits are, or at least involve, dispositions, and dispositions are, of course, lawlike. If we know what someone wants, we know a lot about the circumstances under which she is apt to act; similarly for beliefs, conditional intentions, and a host of features of personalities like pride, generosity, ambition, courage, lasciviousness, and so on.

I cannot go along with McDowell when he says that what I call the myth of the subjective cuts against the idea that "mental acts are intrinsically characterized by being semantically related . . . to elements in the extra-mental order." I like McDowell's defense, as against Sellars and Rorty, of the "relational" conception of semantics, and the importance he attaches to it. But what I called the Myth is the view that there are mysterious entities "before the mind" which come between our thoughts about the world and the world itself, what I have called "epistemological inter-mediaries". I do not deny that we often perceive how the world is, or that perceiving is an "experience" (though the scare quotes register my distrust of accounts that assume the meaning of the word is clear enough to explain the nature of perception).

McDowell has an agenda that is not fully expressed in this paper. Rorty brings it out when he says I hold that "empirical content can be intelligibly in the picture even though we carefully stipulate that the world's impacts on our senses have nothing to do with justification". He is right that sense data, uninterpreted experience, sensations, do not justify our beliefs, and in this the three of us agree. Our difference is this: Rorty and I think the interface between our bodies and the world is causal and nothing more, while McDowell holds that the world directly presents us with propositional contents. McDowell sees no trouble in accounting for the contents of perception, since nature provides these. I have the problem, which I think a form of externalism at least partly solves, of explaining how external features of the world cause us, through the medium of the senses, to form largely correct beliefs. This is a debate I look forward to pursuing on future occasions.

Rorty thinks I make too much of the concept of truth. I have come to agree with Rorty that there is no point in calling truth a norm or a goal. No doubt it is often desirable to believe or say what is true, because we are then more apt to get what we want. But there is no guarantee that the true and the good will coincide; the goal, after all, is the desired outcome, not the truth. In searching for the truth we check our sources, ask the experts, repeat our experiments with more controls, and so forth. There isn't some further activity we can undertake which will prove that we have arrived at the truth. So it would be better to say that our goal (and a legitimate norm) is to be justified; but of course we can be justified and wrong.

The importance of the concept of truth is rather its role in understanding, describing, and explaining the thought and talk of rational creatures. The best way of characterizing an important part of what someone knows who understands and speaks a language is to give a systematic account of the truth conditions of the sentences of that language. We do not grasp the concept of belief if we do not know that a belief may be true or false, nor do we know what it is that someone believes if we do not know under what conditions it would be true. We do not have a concept unless we know what it would be for it to apply to (be true of) some things and not to others. Rorty is willing, I think, to allow that the concept of truth has these uses, but he reminds us that it has many other uses, and that there are other concepts that play as central a role in our mental equipment. I am happy to grant both points, with the proviso that many of the uses of "true" that Rorty mentions would be hard to understand if we did not grasp what I take to be the basic use.

I am sure that a philosopher may be interested in many things while not giving a hoot about formal, or semi-formal, semantics as applied to natural languages. But why does Rorty mind if I, Barry Stroud, John McDowell, and Carlos Pereda happen to find formal semantics useful, interesting, and capable of throwing light on a number of concepts such as truth, the validity of logical inferences, the learnability of natural languages, and relations between a speaker and the world as mediated by language? He does not say, but I suspect that his distaste springs in part from the fear that by formulating this relation, normal semantics is in danger of encouraging the dread idea that language and thought *represent* or mirror the world. But there is no danger. Tarskian semantics introduces no entities to correspond to sentences, and it is only by introducing such entities that one can make serious sense of language mirroring or corresponding to or representing features of the world. As McDowell says, the simple thesis that names and descriptions often refer to things, and that predicates often have an extension in the world of things, is obvious, and essential to the most elementary appreciation of the nature both of language and of the thoughts we express using language. Sellars was wrong to deny the thesis, and so is Rorty in holding it suspect.

Stroud and Rorty both like "A Nice Derangement of Epitaphs", but for different reasons. Rorty likes it because it seems to break down the distinction between the sort of meaning that formal semantics deals with and the rest of what we know about the world. Stroud likes it because, while recognizing the role of formal semantics in understanding language, it denies that knowledge of such a theory is either necessary or, more importantly, sufficient for understanding a speaker. Since what Stroud emphasizes in my essay is a Wittgensteinian point, Stroud's position suggests how Rorty might be persuaded to accept my perverse interest in Tarskian semantics.

Before taking up this theme, I want to correct two misleading features of "A Nice Derangement of Epitaphs". The first is this: I failed to distinguish sufficiently clearly between two points I wanted to make: that people don't need to speak the same language in order to understand each other, and that the same person needn't continue to speak as he has in the past in order to be intelligible. Some examples illustrate both of these theses, but the issues are separable. An example of the first kind would be a fluent speaker of Spanish and a fluent speaker of Portuguese, each speaking his own language, but being perfectly understood by the other. These two languages have much in common, but obviously a similar situation could involve speakers of very different languages. I gave several examples of the second kind in my essay; such examples show that the interpreting hearer frequently has no trouble comprehending words she has never heard before, even words that have never been spoken before. Cases of these two kinds are enough to show that there is more to understanding (and therefore speaking intelligibly) than is involved in speakers' and interpreters' being supplied with identical kits of rules.

The second way I have misled readers is by sometimes writing as if I thought speakers and interpreters have, and form, theories of meaning on the basis of which they speak and interpret. Stroud asks why I would want to speak of a theory in the case of

Mrs. Malaprop, and Rorty dumps on the idea that people ever operate with theories of meaning. He has a proposal:

Why not treat the work of grammarians and lexicographers (or their ideal counterparts, the devisers of Tarskian truth-definitions...) as bearing the same relation to the speaker in the street as the physical scientists bear to the bicycle-rider on the road?

I took this advice long before it was given. Almost from the start I held that those who use language do not normally have a theory; all I asked of a satisfactory theory in this respect was that *if* someone had such a theory for a speaker, at a time, that theory would suffice for understanding an arbitrary utterance of that speaker, at that time (see, for example, the first paragraph of "Radical Interpretation", 1973). Somewhat more recently I have taken to emphasizing that it is the philosopher, trying to understand understanding, who needs the theory in order to say what it is that the interpreter knows if he understands a speaker. A flawless interpreter is prepared, I thought, to interpret anything a speaker says—a potential infinity of utterances. So the interpreter knows what is conveyed by every T-sentence entailed by a theory of truth for the speaker's language, and only a theory can specify this totality in finite terms. I have always been clear that this does not suggest that the flawless interpreter knows such a theory.

A number of readers sense a conflict between the importance I assign to formal semantical theories and the "there is no such thing as a language" attitude of "A Nice Derangement of Epitaphs". Among such readers are Pereda and Rorty. Pereda has the sensible idea of trying to reconcile the Wittgensteinian and Tarskian modes by emphasizing the importance of a general institutionalized linguistic background against which deviant verbal behavior is understood, while Rorty just wants me to abandon the theorizing. I see nothing wrong with Pereda's view, as long as it is taken as saying that members of a "speech community" share a host of overlapping, non-identical, habits of speech, and have corresponding expectations about what others in the community will mean by what they say (such a set of expectations is what is characterized by what I called a "prior theory"). It would be possible for each speaker to have a radically different language; then each hearer would have to extemporize a mode of interpretation. In practice this would be intolerable, perhaps humanly impossible: hence the survival value of conforming.

But does it make sense to speak of a theory in the case of Mrs. Malaprop? The idea I had in mind was simple. An interpreter in a particular conversational situation is prepared with a general set of expectations (which the "prior theory" describes). When expectation is thwarted, what is novel is (usually automatically) accommodated (read "arrangement" for "derangement", "epithets" for "epitaphs"). If the speaker goes on like this, these substitutions in all possible contexts yield a new language, which can be delineated by a "passing theory". Slots in the "prior theory" have been filled in new ways. The apparatus of a "prior theory" and "passing theory" was an unnecessarily cumbersome way of expressing this thought.

Knowing a language is, in some respects, like knowing how to ride a bicycle. In both cases, as Rorty points out, we talk of knowing how, and in neither case is it necessary or common to know a theory that explains what we do. But there are also striking differences. There are endless things a speaker or interpreter must know: the truth conditions a hearer will probably take her utterances to have, the truth conditions that most of the sentences she hears will have, relations of entailment, contradiction, and evidential support among sentences. And this is just a start, as I argued in "A Nice Derangement of Epitaphs". Bicycle riding requires no propositional knowledge at all. Speechless animals can be taught to ride bicycles.

Barry Stroud correctly catches my attitude towards many of these issues. He is right that I don't deny that people learn to speak one or more languages, which equips them "in advance" to understand much of what they hear. This is because, as he says, there are a lot of regularities in how people talk; "there is nothing else for a theory of meaning of a particular language to capture". And Stroud is certainly right when he says that I am against the idea that we understand speakers by appealing to, or applying, rules, conventions, or a theory. Unlike Stroud, however, I balk at using words like "rule" or "convention" to describe what speakers of what is called the same language share. My reason is that it seems to me we have said it all when we say that some speakers speak in much the same way, and that therefore speakers and hearers have natural expectations about how their words will be understood, and what other speakers will mean by what they say. My objection to assimilating regularities to rules or conventions is that the latter sound like norms, and I do not believe there are norms inherent in language itself. Of course there are plenty of norms that bear on what we say when. I don't deny that it is virtuous to try to preserve valuable distinctions, that we are wise to speak in a way that will be understood by others, or that efforts should be made to keep Basque from dying out. But these are norms entirely contingent on further values, not intrinsic values of language. It is wrong, normally, to act counter to a convention; there is nothing inherently wrong in twisting language any way we want.

There are many ways in which we may fail in our intentions in speaking, and these are sometimes confused with one another. We may think we are saying something true when we are not. In this case the error is not linguistic; our error is in saying and believing what is false. (Of course, in learning a new word, there is no point in this distinction: error, linguistic or otherwise, is not yet in the picture.) Or we may think a word or expression we are using usually (or in the best company, or in a good dictionary) means something it does not; this is an error in what we believe about the speech habits of others, or of lexicographers, but it would not be a communicative error unless we fail in our intention to be understood. I don't think of T-sentences as normative in themselves: they don't, for example, tell us what truth conditions we ought to assign to a sentence, nor do they tell us when we would be "correct" to assert it, unless "correct" here just means "true". T-sentences are descriptive: I think of them as describing a practice. Using a T-sentence to interpret a speaker whose practice at the moment it correctly describes will yield a correct interpretation, or at least so I have long held, and still do.

Why, then, does Stroud say, as if he agreed with me, "A theory of meaning alone does not suffice for interpreting speech, even in the normal case in which a single, widely-shared language is being used correctly"? He says it because he *does* agree with me, and has correctly understood the principle theme of "A Nice Derangement of Epitaphs". The point is, as Stroud says, that even if one has a "prior theory" which not only correctly describes a widely shared linguistic practice, but also correctly applies to the case in hand, one still must apply that theory to the case in hand (or simply interpret the present utterance in accord with the theory), and no theory tells us to do that. Stroud reminds us that according to Wittgenstein there must be a way of interpreting or understanding something which is not a matter of following instructions or being guided in one's interpretation. The reason is simple. The kind of knowledge a theory of meaning describes is not irrelevant. But it never can instruct us when to apply it. The knowledge on which we rely, however intuitively, is just about everything we know. This is why I wrote that there are no rules for arriving at passing theories, no rules in any strict sense, as opposed to rough maxims and methodological generalities. A passing theory really is like a theory at least in this, that it is derived by wit, luck, and wisdom from a private vocabulary and grammar, knowledge of the ways people get their point across, and rules of thumb for figuring out what deviations from the dictionary are most likely. There is no more chance of regularizing, or teaching, this process than there is of regularizing or teaching the process of creating new theories to cope with new data in any field.

Contents List of Volumes of Essays

by Donald Davidson

Volume 1
Essays on Actions and Events

Intention and Action
   1. Actions, Reasons, and Causes (1963)
   2. How is Weakness of the Will Possible? (1969)
   3. Agency (1971)
   4. Freedom to Act (1973)
   5. Intending (1978)

Event and Cause
   6. The Logical Form of Action Sentences (1967)
   7. Causal Relations (1967)
   8. The Individuation of Events (1969)
   9. Events as Particulars (1970)
  10. Eternal *vs.* Ephemeral Events (1971)

Philosophy of Psychology
  11. Mental Events (1970)
  12. Psychology as Philosophy (1974)
  13. The Material Mind (1973)
  14. Hempel on Explaining Action (1976)
  15. Hume's Cognitive Theory of Pride (1976)

Appendices
  A. Adverbs of Action (1985)
  B. Reply to Quine on Events (1985)

Volume 2
Inquiries into Truth and Interpretation

Truth and Meaning
  1. Theories of Meaning and Learnable Languages (1965)
  2. Truth and Meaning (1967)
  3. True to the Facts (1969)
  4. Semantics for Natural Languages (1970)
  5. In Defence of Convention T (1973)

Applications
  6. Quotation (1979)
  7. On Saying That (1968)
  8. Moods and Performances (1979)

Radical Interpretation
  9. Radical Interpretation (1973)
  10. Belief and the Basis of Meaning (1974)
  11. Thought and Talk (1975)
  12. Reply to Foster (1976)

Language and Reality
  13. On the Very Idea of a Conceptual Scheme (1974)
  14. The Method of Truth in Metaphysics (1977)
  15. Reality Without Reference (1977)
  16. The Inscrutability of Reference (1979)

Limits of the Literal
  17. What Metaphors Mean (1978)
  18. Communication and Convention (1982)

Appendix to Essay 10
  Replies to Quine and Lewis (1974)

Volume 3
Subjective, Intersubjective, Objective

Subjective
  1. First Person Authority (1984)
  2. Knowing One's Own Mind (1987)
  3. The Myth of the Subjective (1988)
  4. What is Present to the Mind? (1989)
  5. Indeterminism and Antirealism (1997)
  6. The Irreducibility of the Concept of the Self (1998)

Intersubjective
  7. Rational Animals (1982)
  8. The Second Person (1992)
  9. The Emergence of Thought (1997)

Objective
  10. A Coherence Theory of Truth and Knowledge (1983)
       Afterthoughts (1987)
  11. Empirical Content (1982)
  12. Epistemology and Truth (1988)
  13. Epistemology Externalized (1990)
  14. Three Varieties of Knowledge (1991)

Volume 4
Problems of Rationality

Rationality
1. The Problem of Objectivity (1995)
2. Expressing Evaluations (1984)
3. The Objectivity of Values (1995)
   Appendix: Objectivity and Practical Reason (1999)
4. The Interpersonal Comparison of Values (1996)

Problems and Proposals
5. Turing's Test (1990)
6. Representation and Interpretation (1990)
7. Problems in the Explanation of Action (1987)
8. Could There be a Science of Rationality? (1995)
9. What Thought Requires (2001)
10. A Unified Theory of Thought, Meaning, and Action (1980)

Irrationality
11. Paradoxes of Irrationality (1974)
12. Incoherence and Irrationality (1985)
13. Deception and Division (1986)
14. Who is Fooled? (1997)

Volume 5
Truth, Language, and History

Truth
1. Truth Rehabilitated (1997)
2. The Folly of Trying to Define Truth (1996)
3. Method and Metaphysics (1993)
4. Meaning, Truth, and Evidence (1990)
5. Pursuit of the Concept of Truth (1995)
6. What is Quine's View of Truth? (1994)

Language
7. A Nice Derangement of Epitaphs (1986)
8. The Social Aspect of Language (1994)
9. Seeing Through Language (1997)
10. Joyce and Humpty Dumpty (1989)
11. The Third Man (1992)
12. Locating Literary Language (1993)

Anomalous Monism
13. Thinking Causes (1993)
14. Laws and Cause (1995)

Historical Thoughts
15. Plato's Philosopher (1985)
16. The Socratic Concept of Truth (1992)
17. Dialectic and Dialogue (1994)
18. Gadamer and Plato's *Philebus* (1997)
19. Aristotle's Action (2001)
20. Spinoza's Causal Theory of the Affects (1993)

Appendix
Replies to Rorty, Stroud, McDowell, and Pereda (1998)

Bibliographical References

ANSCOMBE, G. E. M., *Causality and Determination* (Cambridge University Press, 1971).

AUSTIN, J. L., *How to Do Things with Words* (Cambridge, Mass.: Harvard University Press, 1962).

BAYNES, KENNETH, JAMES BOHMAN, and THOMAS MCCARTHY (eds.), *After Philosophy: End or Transformation* (Cambridge, Mass.: MIT Press, 1987).

BECHARA, A., *et al.*, 'Double Dissociation of Conditioning and Declarative Knowledge Relative to the Amygdala and Hippocampus in Humans', *Science*, 269 (1995).

BENNETT, JONATHAN, *Linguistic Behavior* (Cambridge University Press, 1976).

BERGER, MAURICE, *Labyrinths: Robert Morris, Minimalism, and the 1960s* (New York, Harper & Row, 1989).

BINYON, T. J., review of *Damon Runyon: A Life* by Jimmy Breslin, *Times Literary Supplement*, 20 Mar. 1992.

BURGE, TYLER, 'Philosophy of Language and Mind: 1950–1990', *Philosophical Review*, 101 (1992).

CAMPBELL, JOSEPH, and HENRY M. ROBINSON, *A Skeleton Key to Finnegans Wake* (New York: Harcourt, Brace, 1944).

CHATWIN, BRUCE, *What am I Doing Here?* (New York: Viking, 1989).

CHOMSKY, NOAM, *Rules and Representation* (New York: Columbia University Press, 1980).

CUMMINS, ROBERT, 'States, Causes, and the Law of Inertia', *Philosophical Studies*, 29 (1976).

CURLEY, EDWIN, *Behind the Geometrical Method: A Reading of Spinoza's Ethics* (Princeton University Press, 1988).

DASENBROCK, REED WAY (ed.), *Literary Theory after Davidson* (University Park, Penn.: Pennsylvania State University Press, 1993).

DAVIDSON, DONALD, 'Causal Relations', *Journal of Philosophy*, 64 (1967).

—— 'Mental Events', in L. Foster and J. W. Swanson (eds.), *Experience and Theory* (University of Massachusetts Press, 1970).

—— *Essays on Actions and Events* (Oxford University Press, 1980).

DAVIDSON, DONALD, 'Actions, Reasons, and Causes', in *Essays on Actions and Events* (Oxford University Press, 1980).
—— 'Rational Animals', *Dialectica*, 36 (1982).
—— 'A Coherence Theory of Truth and Knowledge', in D. Henrich (ed.), *Kant oder Hegel?* (Stuttgart: Klett-Cotta, 1983).
—— 'Expressing Evaluations', The Lindley Lecture (University of Kansas Press, 1984).
—— *Inquiries into Truth and Interpretation* (Oxford University Press, 1984).
—— 'Communication and Convention', in *Inquiries into Truth and Interpretation* (Oxford University Press, 1984).
—— 'What Metaphors Mean', in *Inquiries into Truth and Interpretation* (Oxford University Press, 1984).
—— 'True to the Facts', in *Inquiries into Truth and Interpretation* (Oxford University Press, 1984).
—— 'Plato's Philosopher', *London Review of Books*, 7/5, 1 Aug. 1985.
—— 'Replies to Essays X–XII', in B. Vermazen and M. B. Hintikka (eds.), *Essays on Davidson: Actions and Events* (Oxford University Press, 1985).
—— 'A Nice Derangement of Epitaphs', in R. Grandy and R. Warner (eds.), *Philosophical Grounds of Rationality* (Oxford University Press, 1986).
—— 'Problems in the Explanation of Action', in P. Pettit, R. Sylvan, and J. Norman (eds.), *Metaphysics and Morality* (Oxford: Blackwell, 1987).
—— 'Afterthoughts, 1987', in A. Malichowski (ed.), *Reading Rorty* (Oxford: Blackwell, 1990).
—— 'Meaning, Truth, and Evidence', in R. Barrett and R. Gibson (eds.), *Perspectives on Quine* (Oxford: Blackwell, 1990).
—— *Plato's* Philebus (New York: Garland Publishing Co., 1990).
—— 'The Structure and Content of Truth', *Journal of Philosophy*, 87 (1990).
—— 'Epistemology Externalized', *Dialectica*, 45 (1991).
—— 'Three Varieties of Knowledge', in A. P. Griffiths (ed.), *A. J. Ayer Memorial Essays* (Cambridge University Press, 1991).
—— 'Method and Metaphysics', *Deukalion*, 11 (1993).
DONAGAN, ALAN, *Spinoza* (University of Chicago Press, 1988).
DONNELLAN, KEITH, 'Putting Humpty Dumpty Together Again', *Philosophical Review*, 77 (1968).
DUCASSE, C. J., *Nature, Mind, and Death* (La Salle, Ill.: Open Court, 1951).
DUMMETT, MICHAEL, 'What is a Theory of Meaning (II)', in G. Evans and J. McDowell (eds.), *Truth and Meaning* (Oxford University Press, 1976).
—— *Truth and Other Enigmas* (London: Duckworth, 1978; Cambridge, Mass.: Harvard University Press, 1980).
—— 'The Social Character of Meaning', in *Truth and Other Enigmas* (London: Duckworth, 1978; Cambridge, Mass.: Harvard University Press, 1980).

——*The Interpretation of Frege's Philosophy* (London: Duckworth, 1981).

——'A Nice Derangement of Epitaphs: Some Comments on Davidson and Hacking', in E. Lepore and B. McLaughlin (eds.), *Truth and Interpretation* (Oxford: Blackwell, 1986).

ELLMAN, RICHARD, *James Joyce* (New York: Oxford University Press, 1959).

ENGEL, PASCAL (ed.), *Paradoxes de l'irrationalité* (Combas: L'Éditions de L'Éclat, 1991).

FERNÁNDEZ, G., *et al.*, 'Real-Time Tracking of Memory Formation in the Human Rhinal Cortex and Hippocampus', *Science*, 285 (1999).

FLAM, FAYE, 'Galaxies Keep Going with the Flow', *Science*, 259 (1993).

FODOR, J. A., *Psychosemantics* (Cambridge, Mass.: MIT Press, 1987).

——'Making Mind Matter More', *Philosophical Studies*, 17 (1989).

FØLLESDAL, DAGFINN, 'Causation and Explanation: A Problem in Davidson's View on Action and Mind', in E. Lepore and B. McLaughlin (eds.), *Actions and Events: Perspectives on the Philosophy of Donald Davidson* (Oxford: Blackwell, 1986).

FREDE, DOROTHEA, 'Beyond Realism and Anti-realism: Rorty on Heidegger and Davidson', *Review of Metaphysics*, 40 (1987).

FRIED, MICHAEL, 'Art and Objecthood', *Artforum*, 5 (Summer 1967).

GADAMER, HANS-GEORG, *Platos dialektische Ethik* (Leipzig: F. Meiner, 1931).

——*Truth and Method* (New York: Crossroad, 1975).

——*Dialogue and Dialectic: Eight Hermeneutical Studies on Plato* (New Haven: Yale University Press, 1980).

——*Plato's Dialectical Ethics*, trans. Robert M. Wallace (New Haven: Yale University Press, 1991).

GENET, JEAN, *Prisoner of Love*, trans. Barbara Bray (New York: New York Review of Books, 2003).

GOLDFARB, WARREN, 'Kripke and Wittgenstein on Rules', *Journal of Philosophy*, 82 (1985).

GOODMAN, NELSON, *Fact, Fiction, and Forecast*, 4th edn. (Cambridge, Mass.: Harvard University Press, 1983).

GOSLING, J. C. B., *Plato: Philebus* (Oxford University Press, 1975).

GRICE, PAUL, 'The Causal Theory of Perception', *Proceedings of the Aristotelian Society*, suppl. vol. 35 (1961).

HAHN, LEWIS E., and P. A. SCHILPP (eds.), *The Philosophy of W. V. Quine*, Library of Living Philosophers (La Salle, Ill.: Open Court, 1986).

HALL, N. JOHN, *Trollope: A Biography* (Oxford University Press, 1991).

HALPER, NATHAN, 'James Joyce and the Russian General', *Partisan Review*, 18 (1951).

HAMPSHIRE, STUART, *Spinoza* (Harmondsworth: Penguin Books, 1951).

HARE, R. M., 'Supervenience', *Proceedings of the Aristotelian Society*, suppl. vol. 58 (1984).

HART, H. L. A., 'A Logician's Fairy Tale', *Philosophical Review*, 60 (1951).

HENRICH, DIETER (ed.), *Kant oder Hegel?* (Stuttgart: Klett-Cotta, 1983).

HOBBES, THOMAS, *Leviathan*, ed. C. B. MacPherson (Harmondsworth: Penguin Books, 1968).

HORNSBY, JENNIFER, 'Which Mental Events are Physical Events?', *Proceedings of the Aristotelian Society*, 35 (1980–1).

HORWICH, PAUL, *Truth* (Oxford: Blackwell, 1990; Cambridge, Mass.: MIT Press, 1991).

IRWIN, TERENCE, *Plato's Moral Theory* (Oxford University Press, 1977).

JEFFREY, RICHARD, *The Logic of Decision* (University of Chicago Press, 1965).

JOYCE, JAMES, *A Portrait of the Artist as a Young Man* (New York: Random House, 1928).

—— *Finnegans Wake* (New York: Viking Press, 1939).

—— *Ulysses* (New York: Vintage Books, 1986).

KIM, JAEGWON, 'Epiphenomenal and Supervenient Causation', in *Midwest Studies in Philosophy*, 9 (Minneapolis: University of Minnesota Press, 1984).

—— 'Psychophysical Laws', in E. Lepore and B. McLaughlin (eds.), *Actions and Events: Perspectives on the Philosophy of Donald Davidson* (Oxford: Blackwell, 1985).

—— 'The Myth of Nonreductive Materialism', *Proceedings and Addresses of the American Philosophical Association*, 63 (1989).

KRIPKE, SAUL, 'Is there a Problem about Substitutional Quantification?', in G. Evans and J. McDowell (eds.), *Truth and Meaning* (Oxford University Press, 1976).

LEPORE, E. (ed.), *Truth and Interpretation* (Oxford: Blackwell, 1986).

—— and B. McLAUGHLIN (eds.), *Actions and Events: Perspectives on the Philosophy of Donald Davidson* (Oxford: Blackwell, 1985).

—— and B. LOEWER, 'Mind Matters', *Journal of Philosophy*, 84 (1984).

LEVIN, HARRY, *The Essential James Joyce* (Harmondsworth: Penguin Books, 1963).

LEWIS, DAVID, 'Languages and Language', in K. Gunderson (ed.), *Language, Mind and Knowledge*, Minnesota Studies in the Philosophy of Science, 7 (Minneapolis: University of Minnesota Press, 1975).

LOCKE, JOHN L., *The Child's Path to Spoken Language* (Cambridge, Mass.: Harvard University Press, 1993).

LOMBARD, LAWRENCE, 'Events and their Subjects', *Pacific Philosophical Quarterly*, 62 (1981).

MacKAY, ALFRED, 'Mr Donnellan and Humpty Dumpty on Referring', *Philosophical Review*, 77 (1968).

MARGENAU, HENRY, 'Meaning and Scientific Status of Causality', *Philosophy of Science*, 1 (1934).

McCAWLEY, JAMES, 'Some Ideas Not to Live By', *Die neuern Sprachen*, 75 (1976).

McDOWELL, JOHN, 'Functionalism and Anomalous Monism', in E. Lepore and B. McLaughlin (eds.), *Actions and Events: Perspectives on the Philosophy of Donald Davdison* (Oxford: Blackwell, 1985).

—— *Mind and World* (Cambridge, Mass.: Harvard University Press, 1994).

MICHELSON, ANNETTE, 'Robert Morris—An Aesthetics of Transgression', in *Robert Morris*, exhibition catalogue, Corcoran Gallery of Art and Detroit Institute of Arts, Washington DC and Detroit, Nov. 1969–Feb. 1970.

MORRIS, ROBERT, 'Some Notes on the Phenomenology of Making: The Search for the Motivation', *Artforum*, 8 (1970).

NEALE, STEPHEN, 'The Philosophical Significance of Godel's Slingshot', *Mind*, 104 (1995).

NOVITZ, DAVID, 'Metaphor, Derrida, and Davidson', *Journal of Aesthetics and Art Criticism*, 44 (Winter 1985).

NUSSBAUM, MARTHA, 'Saving Aristotle's Appearances', in M. Schofield and M. Nussbaum (eds.), *Language and Logos* (Cambridge University Press, 1982).

PINKER, STEVEN, *The Language Instinct* (New York: Harper Collins, 1995).

PUTNAM, HILARY, *Meaning and the Moral Sciences* (London: Routledge & Kegan Paul, 1978).

QUINE, W. V., *Mathematical Logic* (New York: Norton, 1940).

—— 'On an Application of Tarski's Theory of Truth', *Proceedings of the National Academy of Science*, 38 (1952).

—— *From a Logical Point of View* (Cambridge, Mass.: Harvard University Press, 1953, 1961, 1980).

—— 'Variables Explained Away', *Proceedings of the American Philosophical Society*, 104 (1960).

—— *Word and Object* (Cambridge, Mass.: MIT Press, 1960).

—— *Selected Logic Papers* (New York: Random House, 1966).

—— *Ontological Relativity and Other Essays* (New York: Columbia University Press, 1969).

—— 'Natural Kinds', in *Ontological Relativity and Other Essays* (New York: Columbia University Press, 1969).

—— 'On the Reasons for Indeterminacy of Translation', *Journal of Philosophy*, 67 (1970).

—— *Philosophy of Logic* (Englewood Cliffs, NJ: Prentice-Hall, 1970).

—— *The Roots of Reference* (La Salle, Ill.: Open Court, 1974).

—— 'Truth and Disquotation', in *Proceedings of the 1971 Tarski Symposium* (Providence, RI: American Mathematical Society, 1974).

—— 'Mind and Verbal Dispositions', in S. Guttenplan (ed.), *Mind and Language* (Oxford University Press, 1975).

—— 'The Nature of Natural Knowledge', in S. Guttenplan (ed.), *Mind and Language* (Oxford University Press, 1975).

—— 'Algebraic Logic and Predicate Functors' (pamphlet, Indianapolis: Bobbs-Merrill, 1976).

—— *The Ways of Paradox and Other Essays*, rev. enlarged edn. (Cambridge, Mass.: Harvard University Press, 1976).

—— 'Truth by Convention', repr. in *The Ways of Paradox and Other Essays*, rev. enlarged edn. (Cambridge, Mass.: Harvard University Press, 1976).

QUINE, W. V., 'Facts of the Matter', in R. W. Shahan and K. R. Merrill (eds.), *American Philosophy from Edwards to Quine* (Norman, Okla.: University of Oklahoma Press, 1977).
—— review of *Truth and Meaning*, ed. G. Evans and J. McDowell, *Journal of Philosophy*, 74 (1977).
—— *Theories and Things* (Cambridge, Mass.: Harvard University Press, 1981).
—— 'On the Very Idea of a Third Dogma', in *Theories and Things* (Cambridge, Mass.: Harvard University Press, 1981).
—— 'Replies to Eleven Essays', in *Theories and Things* (Cambridge, Mass.: Harvard University Press, 1981).
—— 'Reply to Stroud', in P. A. French, T. E. Uehling, and H. K. Wettstein (eds.), *The Foundations of Analytic Philosophy*, Midwest Studies in Philosophy, 6 (Minneapolis: University of Minnesota Press, 1981).
—— 'The Significance of Naturalized Epistemology', in P. A. French, T. E. Uehling, and H. K. Wettstein (eds.), *The Foundations of Analytic Philosophy*, Midwest Studies in Philosophy, 6 (Minneapolis: University of Minnesota Press, 1981).
—— 'Ontology and Ideology Revisited', *Journal of Philosophy*, 80 (1983).
—— 'Meaning, Truth, and Reference', paper delivered to the Institut International de Philosophie in Palermo, 1985.
—— 'Indeterminacy of Translation Again', *Journal of Philosophy*, 84 (1987).
—— *Pursuit of Truth* (Cambridge, Mass.: Harvard University Press, 1990; rev. edn. 1992).
RAJCHMAN, JOHN, and CORNEL WEST (eds.), *Post-Analytic Philosophy* (New York: Columbia University Press, 1985).
RAMSEY, FRANK PLUMPTON, 'Truth and Probability' in R.B. Braithwaite (ed.) *The Foundations of Mathematics and Other Logical Essays* (Harcourt, Brace & Co., 1926).
—— 'Facts and Propositions', in *Philosophical Papers*, ed. D. H. Mellor (Cambridge University Press, 1990).
ROHRLICH, FRITZ, 'Facing Quantum Mechanical Reality', *Science*, 221 (1983).
RORTY, RICHARD, 'Is Truth a Goal of Inquiry? Davidson *vs.* Wright', *Philosophical Quarterly*, 45 (1980).
—— 'Something to Steer by', *London Review of Books*, 20 June 1996.
RYAN, ALAN, *John Dewey and the High Tide of American Liberalism* (New York: Norton, 1996).
SAFFRAN, JENNY R., RICHARD N. ASLIN, and ELISSA L. NEWPORT, 'Statistical Learning by 8-Month-Old Infants', *Science*, 274 (13 Dec. 1996).
SAYRE, KENNETH, *Plato's Late Ontology: A Riddle Resolved* (Princeton University Press, 1983).

SELLARS, WILFRED, 'Empiricism and the Philosophy of Mind', in H. Feigl and M. Scriven (eds.), *Minnesota Studies in the Philosophy of Science* (Minneapolis: University of Minnesota Press, 1956).

SMIDT, KRISTIAN, *James Joyce and the Cultic Use of Fiction* (Oslo: Oslo University Press, 1959).

SOAMES, SCOTT, 'What is a Theory of Truth?', *Journal of Philosophy*, 81 (1984).

SOSA, ERNEST, 'Mind–Body Interaction and Supervenient Causation', in *Midwest Studies in Philosophy*, 9 (Minneapolis: University of Minnesota Press, 1984).

SPINOZA, BENEDICT DE, *Ethics*, in *The Collected Works of Spinoza*, i, ed. and trans. Edwin Curley (Princeton University Press, 1988).

TARSKI, ALFRED, 'The Semantic Conception of Truth', *Philosophy and Phenomenological Research*, 4 (1944).

—— 'The Concept of Truth in Formalized Languages', in J. H. Woodger (ed.), *Logic, Semantics, Metamathematics* (Oxford University Press, 1956).

—— 'The Establishment of Scientific Semantics', in J. H. Woodger (ed.), *Logic, Semantics, Metamathematics* (Oxford University Press, 1956).

—— 'On the Concept of Logical Consequence', in J. H. Woodger (ed.), *Logic, Semantics, Metamathematics* (Oxford University Press, 1956).

—— 'Truth and Proof', *Scientific American*, 220 (1969).

VLASTOS, GREGORY, 'The Paradox of Socrates', in G. Vlastos (ed.), *The Philosophy of Socrates* (New York: Doubleday, 1971).

—— 'Afterthoughts on the Socratic Elenchus', in *Oxford Studies in Ancient Philosophy* (Oxford University Press, 1983).

—— 'The Socratic Elenchus', in *Oxford Studies in Ancient Philosophy* (Oxford University Press, 1983).

—— 'Socratic Irony', *Classical Quarterly*, 37 (1987).

—— *Socrates: Ironist and Moral Philosopher* (Cambridge University Press, 1991).

WARTOFSKY, MARX, 'Action and Passion', in Marjorie Grene (ed.), *Spinoza: A Collection of Critical Essays* (Garden City, NY: Anchor Books, 1973).

WHEELER, SAMUEL, 'Indeterminacy of French Interpretation: Derrida and Davidson', in E. Lepore (ed.), *Truth and Interpretation* (Oxford: Blackwell, 1986).

WILSON, EDMUND, *Axel's Castle* (New York: Scribner's, 1948).

WITTGENSTEIN, LUDWIG, *Philosophical Investigations*, trans. G. E. M. Anscombe (New York: Macmillan, 1953; 3rd edn. 1958).

Index

Ace, Goodman 89
action 283, 307, 308, 311
  and appetite 278, 279–80
  Aristotle on 277–80
  and causality 287, 296–8
  concept of 168–9, 310
  Hume on 281–2
  and intentions 286–7, 288
  ontology of 285–8
  reasoning and 279–80
  reasons and 296–7
adverbs 42
affects, theory of 300, 309–11
akrasia 225–6, 279, 280–1, 289–90
ambiguity 10, 93–4
Anomalous Monism (AM) 185–200,
    201–2, 215, 308
  and causal relations 185, 188,
    193–4, 196–7, 198, 204
  and extensional relations 188
  laws and 189, 190–1, 204
Anscombe, G. E. M. 201, 202, 204–5,
    283, 284, 285, 293
appetite, action and 278, 279–80, 281
Aquinas, St Thomas 280–1, 289
Aristotle 39, 118, 225, 290
  on action 277–80
  practical syllogism 284
  truth, concept of 21–5
assertability 8, 29, 33–4, 67
atomic sentences 69
autonomous will 310

basic sentences 39
behaviorism 36–7, 138–9, 282–3

beliefs 16, 19, 45
  perceptual 136–7
  and truth 17, 224
Bennett, Jonathan 42–3, 89
Berger, Maurice 162
Big Bang theory 212–13
Binyon, T. J. 179
Burge, Tyler 45, 119, 202

Campbell, Joseph 152
Carroll, Lewis 147
causal explanations 198–9, 309
causal relations 309
  AM and 185, 188, 193–4, 196–7,
    198, 204
causality 45, 168–9
  and action 287, 296–8
  definition of 210–11
  and events, relation between 185,
    188–9
  laws and 201–2, 204, 209
  Margenau's principle of 217, 219
cause-law thesis 202–5, 208–9, 216
  and quantum physics 218
changes 214
  definition of 213, 216–17
Chesterfield, Philip Dormer Stanhope,
    4th Earl of 118
Chomsky, Noam 132, 134
Church, Alonzo 5
closed sentences 25, 28–9, 71
Collingwood, R. G. 282
communication 62, 91–3, 127–30
  disambiguation and 93–4
  and intention 121–3

communication (*cont.*):
  interpretation and 105
  Joyce and 157
  and language 258
  linguistic skills and 102, 110–12
  and meaning 54, 59, 93, 94–6,
    97–101, 120–2
  norms and 116–17, 119–20, 121
  obligation 117–18
  and salience 61
  shared practices and 115–18, 123–4
  without shared practices 119,
    124–5
  society and 114–16
  translation and 112–13
concepts 20, 129, 139, 311
  mental 316, 318–19, 320–1
  objects and 160–1, 205–6
conceptual relativism 176
conjunction 169
consistency 44–5, 224, 253: *see also*
  inconsistency
contradictions 44–5, 77
conversation 15, 255, 266, 273, 275
Cresswell, M. J. 56
Cummings, Edward Estlin 174–5
Cummins, Robert 216
Curley, Edwin 299, 301, 302, 307

Dante Alighieri 154
Danto, Arthur 288 n. 3
decision theory 292, 315
definitions 19–20, 35–6, 256–8
deflationism 7, 8–9, 11, 12, 21
  Horwich on 9, 30–2, 83
  Quine's 64, 83
  Tarski and 25–7
  truth theories and 25–6
Defoe, Daniel 175
descriptions 5–6, 95, 97, 286–7, 304
determinism 205, 218, 256
Dewey, John 4, 5
dialects 115, 116–17
Diogenes 92
disambiguation 93–4, 257–8
disquotation 65
  truth and 10–11, 27–9, 64, 66,
    67–70, 77–8, 83–4

Donagan, Alan 302
Donnellan, Keith 97–8
Dretske, Fred 193, 194
dualism 49, 209, 308–9
Ducasse, C. J. 209, 210–12
Duhem, P. 242
Dummett, Michael 8, 34, 58
  and Davidson's account of
    language 109–22

elenchus 224, 225, 226–8, 233–4, 252–4,
    258
  defence of 229–30
  and definitions 257
  in *Philebus* 233–6, 239, 265–6, 270
  problem of 231–2
  and recollection, theory of 231
  and refutation 227
  and truth 241–4, 246–7, 250,
    253–4
  Vlastos on 235, 242–4, 246,
    263–4
Eliot, T. S. 180
Ellman, Richard 154
emotions 310–11
empiricism 47–9, 52–3, 55, 59, 78
error 43, 141, 161, 326
Etchemendy, J. 25, 26
events:
  evidential support for 58–9
  existence of 42–3
Everything, Theory of 218–19
explanation 307–8
  causal 309
  ideal of 303–4
extension-thought interaction 298–301,
    306

Fodor, J. A. 192, 194
folk psychology 164, 283
Føllesdal, Dagfinn 193, 194
Forms, theory of 3, 238, 272
free will 256, 277
Frege, Gottlob 63, 170
  Slingshot argument 5–6, 11
Freud, Sigmund 181
Fried, Michael 162
function, meaning and 29, 67

Gadamer, Hans-Georg 181, 252
  Plato's Dialectical Ethics 261–3,
    265, 271
Galileo Galilei 213
generalization, learning and 140
God 306
  and autonomous will 310
  and psychology 309, 311–12
Gödel, Kurt 5
Goldfarb, Warren 116
good life 232–7, 264–5, 267, 268, 271,
    272, 274
Goodman, Nelson 206–8, 318
grammar 29, 104, 105
  universal 132
Grice, Paul 93, 94, 172

Haber 105, 106
Halper, Nathan 151
Hampshire, Stuart 303
Hare, R. M. 186
Hart, H. L. A. 174
Heidegger, Martin 261
Heracleitus 45
hidden variable theory 217–18
Hobbes, Thomas 281
Homer 149, 150, 179
Hornsby, Jennifer 202
Horwich, Paul 25, 27, 29, 67
  and deflationism 9, 30–2, 83
  truth theory, objections to 32–3
Hume, David 63, 279, 318
  action 281–2
  cause, definition of 205–6, 208,
    211–12
  on objects 205–6
  similarity, concept of 206–7,
    211–12

ideas, theory of 269–71
identity theory 301
idiolects 109, 111, 118, 119
immanence 30, 57, 67, 69, 76, 77, 81
imperatives 16
implicature 172, 174
inconsistency 223, 229, 230, 242:
    see also consistency; elenchus
indeterminacy 316

of interpretation 318, 319
thesis of 319
of translation 57, 75, 76–7, 316,
    317–18
and underdetermination 318
indeterminism 205
intensionality 287, 296, 315
intention 17
  action and 286–7, 288
  and communication 121–3
  implicature 172
  and interpretation 143
  and meaning 92–3, 170
  order of 173
  in speech acts 170–2
interior monologues 154–5
interpretation 6, 245
  and ambiguity 93–4
  communication and 105
  framework theory 104–5
  indeterminacy of 318, 319
  and intention 143
  language and 274
  and linguistic competence 95–6
  of literary texts 178–80
  and meaning 98–101, 112
  nature of 170
  and ontology 43–4
  passing theory 101–3, 104, 105–6,
    107, 327
  prior theory 101–2, 103–4, 105–6,
    326–7
  and reading 156
  translation and 112–13
  and understanding 274, 275, 294
interrogatives 15–16
intersubjective interaction 176–7
invariance 316–17
irrationality 290, 294: *see also*
    rationality

Joyce, James 144–7, 180, 240
  and communication 157
  Finnegans Wake 147, 148, 150, 151,
    152, 155, 156
  interior monologues 154, 155
  and language use 144–5, 147–8, 151,
    152–5, 156–7

Joyce, James (*cont.*):
　*A Portrait of the Artist as a Young
　　Man* 144, 145–6, 155–6
　and Shakespeare 148–51
　Stephen Hero 145
　symbolism 153–4
　Ulysses 145, 148–50, 153
judgements 160, 245–6
justified assertability 34

Kim, Jaegwon:
　on AM 187–8, 191–2, 194, 195–6,
　　198
　and causal explanations 198–9
　on supervenience 190, 197
knowledge 19–20
Kripke, Saul 119

La Mettrie, Julien Offroy de 281
language:
　acquisition of 13–15, 49–50, 53–4,
　　131–2, 134, 135, 258–9, 293–4
　and communication 258
　and conversation 275
　innate 134–5
　and interpretation 274
　Morris on 163
　non-standard usage 116, 117
　and perception 127–30, 135
　Platonic concept of 110
　predicate-functor 69
　primacy of 109–10
　and shared experience 140–1, 161,
　　176–7
　and thought 132–3, 244–5, 249,
　　256
　and translation criteria 75
　and truth 68–70, 75–6, 129, 274–5
　and understanding 274–5, 324–6
　see also malapropisms
laws:
　AM and 189, 190–1, 204
　and causality 201–2, 204, 209, 215–16
　definition of 203–4, 214–15
　Hume on 208
　probabilistic 205
　psychophysical 192, 193, 194, 196,
　　197

　and similarity 206–7
Leeds, Stephen 25, 27
Levin, Harry 144, 145, 151–2, 153, 155, 156
Lewis, David 29, 67
linguistic ability 106–7
linguistic competence 95–6
　and communication 102
　principles of 93, 95–6, 107
literary texts:
　interpretation of 172, 173–5,
　　178–80, 181
　proper names in 175–6, 178–80

MacKay, Alfred 97–8
McCawley, James 105
McDowell, John 208–9, 318, 320–1, 322–3
malapropisms 89–91, 94–5, 103–4, 105,
　　143
Margenau, Henry 217, 219
meaning 37, 52, 143
　communication and 54, 59, 120–2
　and deflationism 12
　first 91–3, 102, 173–4
　and function 29, 67
　Grice's non-natural 93
　and implicature 174
　and intention 92–3, 170
　and interpretation 98–101, 112
　literal 91, 173
　Quine on 29, 59, 64, 65, 66
　theories of 28, 58, 65, 323–7
　and translation 12, 29, 67, 84
　and truth 12–13, 29, 33–4, 64,
　　67, 84–5
　and warranted assertability 29, 67
　and writing 161–2
meaning and evidence:
　distal theory 54–5, 58, 59, 60
　proximal theory 53, 54, 55, 56–8, 60
memory 20, 293, 297, 307–8
mental, normativity of 316, 318
mental events 299
　AM and 185, 188, 190, 191–2,
　　193–4, 195–6, 204
mentalese 132–3
mentality, causal inertia of 185, 195–6,
　　197
metaphors 15, 143

in Shakespeare 173–4
metaphysics, semantics and 39–40
Michelson, Annette 162
Miller, George 293
mind–body interaction 277, 279–80,
    290–1, 299–302, 309
  Spinoza on 295, 300, 302–3, 306–7,
    309
monism 193–4
  anomalous 185–201, 204, 215,
    290–1, 308
  ontological 290, 305, 308
  Spinoza's 300, 302, 305
  and supervenience 187
Moore, G. E. 63, 186
Morris, Robert 159–65

names, theory of 99
natural sciences 168–9
naturalism 47–8, 56, 57
nomological reduction 186, 187
normativity, of the mental 316, 318
number theory, elementary 69
Nussbaum, Martha 225

objectivity 7, 176
objects 160–1, 205–6
observation sentences 50–2, 53,
    78–9, 137
  Quine on 50–1, 55, 59–60
  and stimulus synonymy 54, 60
ontological relativity 82
ontology:
  and interpretation 43–4
  and semantics 39–43
open sentences 28–8, 66, 71
ostension 53, 138–40, 258–9
  and writing 177
ostensive learning 13–15, 50, 53, 140

Paczynski, Bohdan 213
painting 147
perception 160, 277, 292–3,
    307–8, 321
  causality and 296
  language and 127–30, 135
perceptual sentences 137–8
Pereda, Carlos 322, 324

phonetics 238, 267–8
physics 168–9
  and change, definition of 213
  quantum 205, 216–17, 218
Pinker, Steven 132–3
Plato:
  Charmides 249
  collection and division
    method 236–7, 266–7
  collection, division and
    combination 267–8, 269–70
  division 269
  elenctic method 229–30, 231–2,
    233–6, 239, 265–6, 270
  entities, fourfold classification of
    236, 268, 269–70
  Forms, theory of 3, 238, 272
  on good life 264–5, 267, 268, 271,
    274, 332–7
  Gorgias 227, 228, 229, 230–1, 232, 243
  ideas, theory of 269–71
  Jowett's translation of 262
  on knowledge 19–20
  Meno 229, 230, 231, 248, 249, 254,
    264
  Phaedo 231, 241
  Phaedrus 249, 254
  Philebus 231, 232–8, 239, 252,
    262–3, 264, 265–6, 270
  on philosophical methods 224–5, 226,
    231–2, 244
  phonetics 267–8
  Protagoras 227, 248, 249
  recollection, theory of 229, 230–1
  Republic 227, 231, 232–3
  Theaetetus 6, 19, 231
  on writing 161
pleasure 233, 234, 235–7, 264, 267, 268,
    272
predictability 205
probability 36–7
propositions:
  and truth 30–2
  and truth values 9–10
proprioception 293
psychology 281, 290–1
  God and 311–12
  Spinoza on 309–10, 312

psychophysical anomalism 188
Putnam, Hilary 8, 25, 26, 34, 58, 114

quantum mechanics 217–18
quantum physics 205, 216–17, 218
Quine, W. V. 24, 25, 293
  conceptual relativism 48
  on conjunction 169
  deflationism of 64, 83
  dualism of scheme and content 48, 49
  and empiricism 47–8, 52–3, 55, 59, 78
  evidence, theory of 52
  immanence 30, 76, 81
  on language acquisition 49–50, 53–4
  on meaning 29, 59, 64, 65, 66
  meaning and evidence, proximal
    theory of 53, 56, 60
  on observation sentences 50–1, 55,
    59–60
  on reference 65, 71
  satisfaction, recursive definition
    of 28, 66
  on semantics 40
  on translation 70–1, 76–7, 78, 317–18
  on truth 10, 27–30, 65–6, 76, 81, 83–4

radical interpretation 176, 177
radical translation 52, 54–5, 70–2, 84
Ramsey, Frank 8–9, 36–7
rationality 169–70, 319
reading, interpretation and 156
reality 5–6, 130, 133
reasoning 297–8, 318
  and action 279–80
  practical 281, 288–90
reasons 296–8
recollection, theory of 229, 230–1
reduction 194, 305
  definitional 187, 305–6
  nomological 186, 187, 305–6
reference 39, 73, 75, 97–8
  indeterminacy of 82
  inscrutability of 40, 55, 71, 82
  theory of 28, 65
refutation 227
relations, singular causal 209
relativism 57, 76–7, 156
relativization 73, 76, 81–2

retrodictability 205
Robinson, Henry M. 152
Rorty, Richard 315, 320, 323, 324
  and indeterminacy 318
  on truth 4, 5, 6, 7 n. 5, 17, 321
Ross, W. D. 289
Runyon, Damon 179
Russell, Bertrand 5–6
Ryle, Gilbert 283

salience 61
satisfaction 11, 25, 28, 66, 68–9, 70
Schönfinckel 68–9
Schulz, Bruno 39
sculpture 162
Sellars, Wilfred 323
semantics 315, 322–3
  formal 322, 323
  metaphysics and 39–40
  and ontology, relationship with
    39–43
  of reference 39
  systematic 41–2
  and truth 21–3
sensations 135–6
sentences 15–16, 33–4, 39, 69, 70
  closed 25, 28–9, 71
  observation 50–2, 53, 54, 55,
    59–60, 78–9, 137
  open 28–9, 66, 71
  perceptual 137–8
  true 21–6, 29–30, 69, 71
  T-sentences 70, 72, 74
Shakespeare, William:
  and Joyce 148–51
  metaphors in 173–4
  Sonnet 53: 91–2
similarity 206–7, 211–12, 215
Singer, Mark 89, 90
skepticism 20, 56–7, 176, 277, 282
Slingshot argument 5–6, 11
Smidt, Kristian 144
Soames, Scott 25, 29, 67
Socrates 239
  on *akrasia* 225–6
  elenchus 224, 225, 226–8, 240, 241,
    242–4, 246–50, 252–4
  in *Euthyphro* 19, 241, 248, 255

in *Philebus* 233, 234–5, 239
  on writing 249, 254
Sosa, Ernest 196, 199–200, 202
soul, transmigration of 230
speech 120, 131–2, 133, 135, 139, 275
  intention in 170–2
Spinoza, Benedict de 290
  on action 298, 310
  affects, theory of 309–11
  on autonomous will 310
  on emotions 310–11
  identity theory 301
  on mind–body interaction 295, 300,
    302–3, 306–7, 309
  monism of 300, 302, 305
  on psychology 309–10, 312
statements, singular causal 55, 202–3,
  205–6, 208, 209, 212, 219
stimulus synonymy 52, 54, 60, 78–80
Stroud, Barry 322, 323–4, 325, 326–7
subjective, myth of 321
subjective probability 36–7
substitutional quantification 32
supervenience 186–8, 189–90, 196–7,
  200, 204
symbolism 153–4

Tarski, Alfred 39
  Convention T 23, 26, 73, 84
  and deflationism 25–7
  and disquotation 65
  satisfaction 11, 25
  and semantics 41, 322, 323
  on truth 10, 11–12, 22–6
thoughts 17, 298
  and language 132–3, 244–5, 249, 256
  propositional 135
  and truth, concept of 16
translation 81–2
  communication and 112–13
  criteria 29, 67, 75, 79
  indeterminacy of 57, 75, 76–7, 316,
    317–18
  interpretation and 112–13
  and meaning 12, 29, 67
  Quine on 70, 78
  radical 52, 54–5, 84
  and stimulus synonymy 54

and truth 12, 70, 73–4
  understanding and 275
Trollope, Anthony 178–9, 180
true sentences 21–6, 29–30, 69, 71
truth 4, 7
  and beliefs 17, 224
  definitions 11–12, 22–6, 35–6
  and deflationism 25–34
  and disquotation 10–11, 27–30, 64,
    66, 67–70, 77–8, 83–4
  elenchus and 241–4, 246–7, 250,
    253–4
  and immanence 30, 57, 67, 69, 76,
    77, 81
  and language 14–15, 68–70, 75–6,
    129, 274–5
  and meaning 29, 33–4, 64, 67,
    84–5
  predicates 9, 10, 12
  and propositions 30–2
  Ramsey on 8–9
  and reality, correspondence
    with 5–6
  relativism of 57, 76–7
  search for 223–4
  and semantics 21–3
  and translation 70, 73–4
  see also truth, concept of; truth
    theories
truth, concept of 3–5, 6–8, 9, 321–2
  Aristotelian 21–5
  deflationism and 26–7
  disquotation and 10–11
  and intersubjective interaction 176
  and language 75–6
  and language acquisition 14–15
  and thought 16
  and translation 12
truth theories 2, 4, 29
  coherence 8, 224
  correspondence 5–6, 8, 224
  and deflationism 25–34
  epistemic 8, 16–17
  for language 68–70
  objections to 32–3
  pragmatic 4, 7, 16–17
  Quine on 29–30, 65–6
T-sentences 70, 72, 74

underdetermination 318
understanding 318–19, 324
  conversation and 266, 273, 323
  interpretation and 274, 275, 294
  and language 274–5, 324–6
  and translation 275
uniqueness 72
University College London 263

Vlastos, Gregory 226, 227, 228, 229,
    239, 259
  on elenchus 235, 242–4, 246, 263–4
  on recollection, theory of 229,
    230–1

on Socrates 247
vocabulary, mental/physical 304, 305

warranted assertability 8, 29, 67
Wartofsky, Marx 301
Weinberg, Steve 218
Williams, Michael 25, 27
Wilson, Edmund 156
Wittgenstein, Ludwig 116, 124, 162, 283
writing 147, 161, 177–8, 254–6
  and meaning 161–2
  and ostension 177
  Plato on 161
  Socrates on 249, 254